CliffsNotes®

Verbal Review
for
Standardized Tests

CliffsNotes®

Verbal Review
for
Standardized Tests

2ND EDITION

by
Deborah Covino, Ph.D.

Contributing Authors
William A. Covino, Ph.D.
Peter Z Orton, Ph.D.

WILEY

John Wiley & Sons, Inc.

About the Author

A university instructor and English professor for more than twenty years, Deborah Covino, Ph.D., is an expert on the verbal skills and strategies that are crucial to success on standardized tests. Her scholarship and creative writing have been published in nationally recognized journals and magazines.

Author's Acknowledgments

My sincere thanks to Joy Gilmore at BTPS Testing for her extraordinary expertise and support, to Project Editor Christy Scannell for her scrupulous attention to detail, and to my husband Bill—who co-authored an earlier edition of this book—for his generous advice along the way.

Editorial

Acquisition Editor: Greg Tubach
Project Editor: Christy Scannell
Copy Editor: Christy Scannell
Technical Editor: Jane Burstein

Composition

Proofreader: Mildred Rosenzweig
John Wiley & Sons, Inc., Composition Services

CliffsNotes® Verbal Review for Standardized Tests, 2nd Edition

Published by:
John Wiley & Sons, Inc.
111 River Street
Hoboken, NJ 07030-5774
www.wiley.com

Copyright © 2013 John Wiley & Sons, Inc., Hoboken, NJ

Published by John Wiley & Sons, Inc., Hoboken, NJ

Published simultaneously in Canada

Library of Congress Control Number: 2012947690
ISBN: 978-1-118-33425-6 (pbk)
ISBN: 978-1-118-37926-4; 978-1-118-37929-5; 978-1-118-37927-1 (ebk)

Printed in the United States of America

10 9 8 7 6 5 4 3 2 1

Table of Contents

PART II: READING COMPREHENSION

Chapter 5: Reading Comprehension Review............................293

PART III: WRITING TIMED ESSAYS

Preface

CliffsNotes Verbal Review for Standardized Tests, 2nd Edition is designed specifically to review, refresh, and reintroduce essential grammar and verbal abilities skills. It focuses directly on test-oriented question types. If you are planning to take one of the following tests, then this guide will be invaluable to you:

- GRE – Graduate Record Exam
- GMAT – Graduate Management Admissions Test
- SAT – Scholastic Aptitude Test
- ACT – American College Testing exam
- LSAT – Law School Admissions Test
- CBEST – California Basic Educational Skills Test
- PPST – Pre-Professional Skills Test
- PSAT/NMSQT – Preliminary Scholastic Aptitude Test/National Merit Scholarship Qualifying Test
- State Teacher Competency and Credentialing Exams
- Education Program Entry Exams
- College Entrance or Advanced Placement Exams

In keeping with the fine tradition of CliffsNotes, this guide was developed by leading experts in the field of test preparation, and graduate school and college entrance preparation. The material, strategies, and techniques presented in this guide have been researched, tested, and evaluated in preparation classes at leading state university programs.

Introduction

This study guide is the most distinctive verbal guide available today. It is much more than simply a grammar or verbal review book. It is clear, concise, easy to use, and full of insights into the types of questions you'll face on your exam. It demonstrates how to avoid the common and costly errors that will trap those unprepared for the kinds of questions the test-makers ask. Our unique approach not only reviews essential basic skills but also shows you how to apply them *effectively and specifically on standardized tests*. Throughout the guide, the language is nontechnical yet consistent with the terminology and conventions you need to know for standardized verbal skills tests.

What This Guide Contains

Verbal Review for Standardized Tests provides an excellent and extensive overview of important information and the tools necessary for comprehensive verbal skills preparation. As you work through this book, focus on the specific types of questions that will appear on your exam. Each chapter presents material in a structured format to focus on areas of concern for most test-takers:

- Review of grammar and usage question types
- Strategies for each question type
- Sentence correction
- Sentence completion
- Sentence equivalence
- Improving paragraphs
- Grammar and usage review
- Reading comprehension questions
- Timed essay writing
- Practice exercises with hundreds of questions and complete explanations

If you're taking the GRE, GMAT, SAT, ACT, CBEST, LSAT, PPST, PSAT/NMSQT, or any other exam with a grammar or verbal section, this book was designed for YOU!

How This Book Is Organized

- **Introduction.** A general description of what this guide contains, including general guidelines to review this material and an introduction to the question types.

- **Chapter 1 – Grammar and Usage Question Types** will acquaint you with standardized test question types.

- **Chapter 2 – Grammar and Usage Diagnostic Test.** The short diagnostic test will evaluate your areas of weakness and provide you with a baseline starting point.

- **Chapter 3 – Grammar and Usage Review** focuses on verbal abilities for standardized exams. Review this chapter for *all* exams that test grammar and usage. You will also find this material very helpful for all essay-writing assignments. This chapter provides you with the skills and concepts tested, directions, suggested strategies with samples, and review practice exercises.

- **Chapter 4 – English Grammar and Usage Practice Test**

- **Chapter 5 – Reading Comprehension Review** is an intensive review in the basics of analyzing and drawing conclusions from written material. Read this chapter if you are taking the GRE, GMAT, SAT, ACT, LSAT, CBEST, PPST, PSAT/MNSQT, and other reading comprehension exams.

- **Chapter 6 – Approaches to Writing Timed Essays** presents strategies and practice to help you effectively communicate your written ideas for GRE, GMAT, SAT, ACT, LSAT, CBEST, PPST and other essay exams.

Note: As mentioned above, candidates for *all* grammar and usage exam sections should thoroughly study the Grammar and Usage Review. Regardless of the specific question type in your exam, practice in all question types is very beneficial because many question types test for precisely the same knowledge, but in varying formats.

How to Use This Guide

Start your preparation by identifying question types, assessing your skills, reviewing content material, understanding strategies, and practicing what you have learned. For optimal results, take detailed notes on the pages of this book to highlight important information.

1. **Identify question types.** Review the materials the testing organization provided for your test. This information is usually available online for free and will detail the areas and question types for your particular exam. Based on the information the testing organization provides and on the list of question types on page 4 of this book, determine which sections pertain to your specific exam. Here are the websites for the major testing organizations:

GMAT	http://www.gmac.com/gmac/thegmat/
GRE	http://www.ets.org/gre
SAT	http://sat.collegeboard.org/home
ACT	http://www.actstudent.org/
LSAT	http://www.lsac.org/JD/LSAT/test-dates-deadlines.asp
CBEST	http://www.cbest.nesinc.com/
PPST	http://www.ets.org/praxis
PSAT/MNSQT	http://www.collegeboard.com/student/testing/psat/about.html

2. **Assess your skills.** Take the Grammar and Usage Diagnostic Test in Chapter 2, and note any area of particular difficulty. The diagnostic test will help you pinpoint any areas that may require more preparation time. Focus on specific topic areas as you assess your strengths and weaknesses.

3. **Review.** Study Chapter 3, Grammar and Usage Review, in its entirety. Concentrate particularly on those areas you found challenging on the diagnostic test. Complete each of the exercises in this section to be sure you've thoroughly understood each concept.

   It is also very important to work through the strategy and practice sections that are *not* specific to your exam. Because all question types draw from the same set of verbal skills, this additional practice will contribute a great deal to your success.

4. **Understand strategies.** Thoroughly study the strategy sections in this book for each of the question types.

5. **Practice.** Work all the practice sections for all question types, breaking the work into shorter timed study sessions. The web pages for each testing organization will tell you how many questions you will be expected to answer in a given time period. Base the length of your work sessions on these requirements. You will find it helpful to allow yourself slightly *less* time than you will have on the actual exam.

Types of Questions

All of the tests listed contain questions that test your reading comprehension; all except the LSAT and CBEST contain questions that test your knowledge of grammar and usage; and all except the PSAT/NMSQT require you to write essays.

Before you start your preparation, use the following chart to note the chapters containing material specific to certain exams.

Verbal Question Types							
Test	**Question Type**						
	Sentence Correction			Improving Paragraphs	Sentence/ Text Completion	Sentence Equivalence	Reading Comprehension	Essay Writing
	Type I p. 8	Type 2 p. 10	Type 3 p. 11	p. 14	p. 18	p. 22	p. 293	p. 397
GRE					X	X	X	X
GMAT			X				X	X
SAT	X		X	X	X		X	X
ACT		X					X	X
LSAT							X	X
CBEST							X	X
PPST	X		X				X	X
PSAT/ NMSQT	X		X	X	X		X	

Range of Difficulty and Scope

The difficulty range of question types varies significantly for each of the grammar and usage, reading comprehension, and essay-writing areas of the various tests. Typically, all questions on the GRE, GMAT, and LSAT will be more difficult than the similar questions on the SAT, ACT, CBEST, and PPST teacher exams.

PART I

GRAMMAR AND USAGE

Chapter 1
Grammar and Usage Question Types

This section deals with questions of grammar and usage that appear on most standardized exams. A brief description of the major English grammar and usage question types you will encounter in these tests follows. Even if a specific question type does not appear on your exam, you should review all of this chapter thoroughly, because it deals with material that is used in virtually every standardized test containing grammar and usage sections, though a question's form may vary.

After reading this chapter, be sure to take the diagnostic test in Chapter 2 to find areas that are difficult for you. The results of the diagnostic test will guide you in choosing areas on which to concentrate. To be sure of the best test preparation possible, read the entire Grammar and Usage Review in Chapter 3, and do all of the exercises. This review focuses on areas that are most commonly tested. Finish your review by completing the practice sections and reading the answers carefully.

Quick Reference Guide

Sentence Correction – Type 1 (p. 8): SAT, PPST, PSAT/NMSQT

Sentence Correction – Type 2 (p. 10): ACT

Sentence Correction – Type 3 (p. 11): GMAT, SAT, PPST, PSAT/NMSQT

Improving Paragraphs (p. 14): SAT, PSAT/NMSQT

Sentence/Text Completion (p. 18): GRE, SAT, PSAT/NMSQT

Sentence Equivalence (p. 22): GRE

General Strategies for Sentence/Text Completion and Sentence Equivalence (Vocabulary Skills) Questions

1. Look up unfamiliar words whenever you encounter them.
2. Review and practice with common roots, prefixes, and suffixes (p. 149).
3. Look for the *best* answer choice, rather than the *perfect* answer choice.

4. Use logic and context clues to judge the relationship between the words you are considering. For instance, remember that fill-in words for sentence/text completion must fit the relationship suggested by the sentence's structure and content. After you select an answer, be sure there is a logical relationship between the answer you have chosen and the sentence.

5. When taking the actual exam, use the process of elimination whenever possible to exclude one or more answer choices. Be sure to read all the answer choices carefully, eliminating obvious wrong answers as soon as you recognize them.

6. Always read the entire sentence and review all of the answer choices. Do not make a hasty assumption that you know the correct answer without reading the whole question and all its possible answers. If the sentence contains two blanks, remember that both words in a two-word answer choice must fit for that answer choice to be correct!

7. In Chapter 3, Grammar and Usage Review, you will find other kinds of errors of grammar, sentence structure, usage, or diction that appear in the verbal ability sections of many tests.

Sentence Correction – Type 1

This type of question appears on exams such as the PPST and the SAT, which calls this question type "Identifying Sentence Errors." Sentence Correction questions test your ability to identify errors of standard written English as they appear in sentences.

Directions

Each sentence may contain one error in grammar, usage, or word choice. You are to mark the letter—A, B, C, or D—labeling the part of the sentence that is incorrect. If no part of the sentence is incorrect, mark letter E.

It is important to remember that you are looking for errors in standard *written* English, not *conversational* English, and that the parts not underlined in the sentence are correct. Thus you must use the non-underlined parts to help you determine which underlined part may be wrong.

Examples:

1. Each boy in the third and <u>fourth</u> sections <u>of the class</u> gave <u>their</u>
    A B C
    reasons <u>for liking</u> sports. <u>No error.</u>
    D E

Note that *Each boy* is not underlined, so the subject of the sentence is singular. Therefore, *their* is incorrect. It should be *his* to agree with the singular subject. The incorrect part of the sentence is choice **C**.

Other agreement errors in standard written English may include subject-verb errors such as:

2. The <u>wandering</u> pack of dogs, first <u>seen</u> by the citizens many years
    A B
    ago, <u>were</u> feared by all <u>who</u> lived in the town. <u>No error.</u>
    C D E

Here, since the subject of the sentence is *pack*, which is singular, the verb must also be singular: *was.* The incorrect part of this sentence is choice **C**.

Other errors may include faulty parallelism:

3. Ernie's diligence in <u>studying every night</u> allowed him to score
    A
    <u>high grades</u>, to gain the respect <u>of his peers</u>, and <u>admission</u> to
    B C D
    college. <u>No error.</u>
    E

The final part of the series is not in the same form as the first two parts. It should be something such as *to earn admission or to win admission* so that it parallels the form of the other items—*to score* and *to gain.* Choice **D** is the incorrect part of the sentence.

You may also find an error in idiom (nonstandard usage):

4. <u>Compromising over</u> a number of delicate issues, the members
　　　 A
of the school board <u>successfully</u> resolved <u>their</u> problems. <u>No error</u>.
　　　 B 　　　　　　　　 C 　　　　　　 D 　　　　　　 E

The expression *compromising over* is nonstandard usage. It should be *compromising on*. Choice **A** is the error in this sentence, and therefore is the correct answer.

Many other types of usage errors will appear in this question type. You will find them explained in the Grammar and Usage Review that follows the diagnostic test.

Sentence Correction – Type 2

This type of question appears on the GMAT, PPST, PSAT/NMSQT, and SAT, where it is called "Improving Sentences."

Directions

In this question type, you must choose the best of five different versions of a sentence. If the original sentence most fully meets the requirements of correct and effective English, choice A, which repeats the underlined portion exactly, is correct. If the underlined part is incorrect, awkward, or ambiguous, you must pick the version that best corrects it and retains the meaning of the originally underlined phrase. Again, you must assume that any part of the sentence not underlined is correct and cannot be changed.

Examples:

1. The rigors of high office often demand <u>stamina, persistence, and having great patience</u>.

　　A.　stamina, persistence, and having great patience
　　B.　stamina, persistence, and great patience
　　C.　that a person has stamina, persistence, and patience
　　D.　having stamina, persistence, and having great patience
　　E.　having stamina, being persistent, and having patience

B. The underlined part contains faulty parallelism. The last item in the series should not be preceded by *having* but should be in the same form as *stamina* and *persistence.* By omitting the word *great,* choices C and E slightly change the meaning of the original; in addition, choice C contains an error in verb form, and choice E is needlessly wordy.

2. Rushing to avoid being late, <u>Bill's head collided with the cabinet door, which was open</u>.

   A. Bill's head collided with the cabinet door, which was open
   B. Bill's head hit the open cabinet door
   C. Bill's head collided with the open cabinet door
   D. Bill hit his head on the open cabinet door
   E. Bill hit the cabinet door, having been opened

D. The sentence begins with an *-ing* phrase that modifies what immediately follows the comma. In the original, *Bill's head* follows the modifying phrase. Was Bill's head doing the rushing? Certainly not. The sentence should read, *Rushing to avoid being late, Bill hit his head.* So *Bill* should follow the modifying phrase because he, not his head, was doing the rushing.

Sentence Correction – Type 3

Another kind of English usage question appears on the ACT. This type offers complete paragraphs and requires you to determine if part of a sentence is incorrect.

Directions

In the left-hand column, you will find passages with various words and phrases underlined. In the right-hand column, you will find a set of responses corresponding to each underlined portion. If the underlined portion is correct as it stands, mark the letter indicating *NO CHANGE*. If the underlined portion is incorrect, decide which of the choices best corrects it. Consider only underlined portions; assume that the rest of the passage is correct as written.

Examples:

"The <u>best laid</u> plans of mice and
¹
men often go astray" is a well-
known saying from a poem by the

<u>well-known</u> eighteenth century
²
Scottish writer Robert Burns. The

poem was inspired when Burns

disrupted a nest of mice <u>after</u> he was
³
plowing a field, leading him to reflect

on how the <u>mouses'</u> plans for an
⁴
uninterrupted winter had been ruined.

Although the best English translation

of Burns' Scottish dialect is "askew"

rather than "astray," the latter term is

1. A.   NO CHANGE
    B.   best laden
    C.   best lied
    D.   best known

A. Each of the other choices includes phrases that are either incorrect in meaning or ungrammatical.

2. By changing *well-known* to "famous" in this passage, the writer would avoid which of the following:

    F.   misinterpretation
    G.   repetition
    H.   inaccuracy
    J.   anachronism

G. *Well-known* repeats the same phrase that is used on the previous line.

3. A.   NO CHANGE
    B.   like
    C.   for
    D.   as

D. This choice fits the overall meaning of the sentence better than any of the others.

4. F.   NO CHANGE
    G.   mice's
    H.   mices'
    J.   mouses's

G. The plural of mouse is mice, and the possessive of *mice* is *mice's*.

used <u>these days</u>. For modern readers,

5

the saying documents something all

5. If this phrase is removed from the sentence, what meaning is lost?

- A. that *askew* is an older translation than *astray*
- B. that the use of *askew* is incorrect
- C. that *astray* would not be understood by modern readers
- D. that *askew* is a latter-day form of *astray*

A. Since we are told that *astray* is used *these days,* it is implied that *askew* was used in earlier days. We are not told that *askew* is an incorrect term, just an older one.

of us have experienced: <u>making</u>

6

our careful plans ruined by some

unexpected or accidental event,

6. F. NO CHANGE
  G. hoping
  H. having
  J. leaving

H. This choice is consistent with the experience of the mice that had their carefully planned nest ruined.

<u>as if when a thunderstorm ruins</u> a

7

family picnic that has been planned

for days.

7. The best wording for this phrase is

- A. as it is now
- B. whenever a thunderstorm ruins
- C. such as when a thunderstorm ruins
- D. in the case of a thunderstorm ruining

C. Each of the other choices is either ungrammatical or inconsistent with the intended meaning of the sentence.

13

Many other kinds of usage errors will appear in this question type, and they are included in Chapter 3, Grammar and Usage Review.

Improving Paragraphs

This question type, which appears on the SAT, asks you to correct or improve sentences from a student-level writing sample.

Directions

Carefully read the excerpts below, which represent writing one might find in drafts of student papers. Here, you will find questions that ask you to address not only grammar and usage within individual sentences, but also questions that deal with the excerpt more globally, asking you to address features such as organization and the development of ideas.

Each item is generally made up of two or three paragraphs, and is about two hundred to three hundred words long.

For these questions, you should first read the essay through, and then answer the questions that follow. Answers should conform to the requirements of standard written English as well as reflect the intended meaning.

Examples:

(1) Romantic poet William Wordsworth (1770–1850) wrote endlessly about getting back to childhood when we are more in touch with nature and beauty. (2) He was fully aware, though, that this is not really possible. (3) We cannot return to an earlier state of being and feeling, however appealing that might be. (4) This fact is expressed in the title of Thomas Wolfe's famous novel, *You Can't Go Home Again.*

(5) However, nostalgia for bygone days when everything was perfect and pleasurable is characteristic of many adults. (6) Disney's "Remember the Magic" advertising campaign was created for Walt Disney World's 25th Anniversary celebration. (7) It calls upon Baby Boomers to bring back something from the past that's been lost, namely childhood joy and wonder activated by the Disney experience. (8) The campaign targets adults who are

invited to bring their children and grandchildren back to the Disney parks in order to relive, through the children, an experience they once enjoyed. (9) The folks at Disney figure that adults who experienced Disneyland or Disney World as children have a strong attraction to a past associated with their experiences going there, and a strong desire to recreate those experiences. (10) There's nothing necessarily wrong with nostalgia, and sometimes good can even come from it (suppose you become an environmental activist in order to return air quality to a more pristine state, motivated by nostalgia for a childhood when the air was cleaner). (11) However, we should all sit up and take notice whenever we hear or see ads that invoke a more ideal past. (12) As Billy Joel reminds us in his song "Keeping the Faith," our memories of the past are sometimes more positive than what we actually experienced.

1. In context, what is the best version of sentence 1 (reproduced below)?

Romantic poet William Wordsworth (1770–1850) wrote endlessly about getting back to childhood when we are more in touch with nature and beauty.

A. (as it is now)

B. Poet William Wordsworth wrote endlessly about getting back to childhood, when we were more in touch with nature and beauty.

C. The famous Romantic poet William Wordsworth (1770–1850) wrote endlessly about getting back to childhood when we are more in touch with nature and beauty.

D. Wordsworth wrote about a childhood more in touch with nature and beauty.

E. Nature and beauty were endlessly part of the childhood of William Wordsworth.

B. The additional information about Wordsworth—his birth and death and the term *Romantic*—are inconsistent with the degree of information about the other writers discussed in the passage, and the verb *were* is correctly in past tense. Choice C adds even more extraneous information, choice D eliminates necessary information, and choice E alters the sentence's meaning.

2. In context, what is the best version of the underlined portion of sentence 9 in paragraph 2 (reproduced below)?

   The folks at Disney figure that adults who experienced Disneyland or Disney World as children have a strong attraction to a past associated with <u>their experiences going there, and a strong desire to recreate those experiences</u>.

   A. (As it is now)
   B. Disney, and a desire to have that again
   C. recreating the Disney experience
   D. the Disney experience, and a strong desire to recreate that experience
   E. the Disney experience, and a strong desire to give that experience to others

   D. This choice contains clear and complete information, and avoids the vagueness of "going there."

3. What is the best ordering of ideas for the underlined portion of sentence 10 (reproduced below)?

   There's nothing necessarily wrong with that, and sometimes good can even come from it (<u>suppose you become an environmental activist in order to return air quality to a more pristine state, motivated by nostalgia for your childhood when the air was cleaner</u>); however, it's smart to notice that the "Remember the Magic" slogan effectively appeals to that part of each of us that lives in that love-the-past-more-than-the-present mental space.

   A. (As it is now)
   B. in order to return air quality to a more pristine state, suppose you become an environmental activist, motivated by nostalgia for your childhood when the air was cleaner
   C. suppose you become an environmental activist, motivated by nostalgia for your childhood when the air was cleaner, in order to return air quality to a more pristine state
   D. suppose that, motivated by nostalgia for your childhood when the air was cleaner, you become an environmental activist in order to return air quality to a more pristine state
   E. suppose that, motivated by nostalgia for your childhood when the air was cleaner, in order to return air quality to a more pristine state, you become an environmental activist

D. This choice emphasizes nostalgia earlier than choices B and C, and therefore maintains a stronger connection with the subject of the sentence. Choice E suffers from a confusing sentence structure.

4. Which choice represents the best way to express the content of sentences 11 and 12 (reproduced below)?

   However, we should all sit up and take notice whenever we hear or see ads that invoke a more ideal past. As Billy Joel reminds us in his song "Keeping the Faith," our memories of the past are sometimes more positive than what we actually experienced.

   A. No change
   B. However, as Billy Joel says, we should all sit up and take notice whenever we hear or see ads that invoke a more ideal past, because we may not have experienced what we think we did.
   C. If you sit up and take note whenever you hear or see ads that invoke a more ideal past, new insights often emerge from just observing such things, such as in Billy Joel's "Keeping the Faith."
   D. However, we should all sit up and take notice whenever we hear or see ads that invoke a more ideal past, because, as Billy Joel sings in "Keeping the Faith."
   E. However, we should all sit up and take notice whenever we hear or see ads that invoke a more ideal past, whereas Billy Joel sings in "Keeping the Faith" and in other popular songs.

A. Choices B and C incorrectly make Billy Joel's song a cause of the advice in sentence 3. Choices D and E are grammatically incorrect.

5. What phrase should be added at the beginning of sentence 6 in paragraph 2, to create a stronger transition between paragraphs?

   A. As if there wasn't enough nostalgia already,
   B. Realizing Walt's desire for an ideal past,
   C. Just for adults who can afford tickets to a Disney theme park,
   D. To capitalize on this nostalgia,
   E. Just like Wordsworth and Wolfe,

D. The use of *this nostalgia* creates a clear connection to the previous sentence.

6. Which sentence below makes the best conclusion for the essay?

   A.   That ideal past that we sometimes desire, and even pay to revisit, could be a figment of our imagination.
   B.   Even though a return to the past is never really possible, we all like to imagine that it is.
   C.   Therefore, the past can never be recaptured.
   D.   Billy Joel and William Wordsworth have a lot in common.
   E.   The old Disney World, like Wordsworth's "celestial light," can no longer be seen.

A. Both paragraphs discuss the human desire for a past that never really existed, and the second paragraph discusses Disney's campaign to use this nostalgia to attract customers.

Sentence/Text Completion

Sentence/Text completion questions—found on both the SAT and GRE—test your ability to understand words and evaluate their meanings in the context of sentences or short passages, and also to grasp the appropriateness and logic of their use in sentences.

Directions

These questions—called "Sentence Completion"—ask you to fill in one, two, or three blanks with the correct word or words. The SAT lists five choices, labeled A through E, underneath each sentence. Choose the words that, when inserted in the sentence, best fit the meaning of the sentence as a whole.

Examples for SAT Questions

As you read each sentence, you might first ask yourself (before looking at the answer choices) which words *you* would insert in the blank(s). Study the following sentence:

1. Public _____ for exercise has grown over the last ten years, so that now fitness is a top _____ for the majority of American adults.

How would you fill in the blanks? The positive associations with *fitness* in the second half the sentence (particularly the word *top*) suggest that the first half contains a positive-attitude word in the blank—for instance, "liking" or "support." Consequently, you might guess that those who like exercise make it a top "interest," or "activity," or "value," perhaps. With such guesses in mind, consider the answer choices:

- A. fondness . . . drawer
- B. enthusiasm . . . priority
- C. patience . . . concern
- D. strength . . . achievement
- E. substitution . . . evasion

The terms closest to the proposed guesses are *enthusiasm* and *priority* from choice **B**. None of the other choices suits the meaning, logic, and word choice of the original sentence so well.

Words surrounding the blank(s) can provide clues. Study the following example:

2. At her most combative, Rachel was too self-absorbed to recognize how _____ she could be.

- A. docile
- B. balmy
- C. antiquated
- D. belligerent
- E. facetious

D. *belligerent* A clue word here is *combative*. The sentence indicates that a synonym (word of like meaning) for *combative* is needed. A *combative* person would naturally be *belligerent*, which means confrontational and argumentative. Rachel is neither *docile* (choice A), which means tame and quiet, nor *facetious* (choice E), which means light-hearted and playful.

There are other special words in sentences that, although they may not necessarily surround the blanks, nonetheless can provide important clues to the meaning or connotation of the missing words, such as *but, although, nevertheless, despite, though, in spite of, however,* etc. Study the following example:

3. Although he was a friendly man, Bob continually _____ my sister.

    A.   called
    B.   surprised
    C.   avoided
    D.   complimented
    E.   rewarded

C. *avoided* Notice the word *although*. This signal word establishes that the first part of the sentence must contrast with (be opposite of) the second part of the sentence. Since *avoiding* someone contrasts with being *friendly,* choice C is the correct answer. None of the other choices directly contrasts with *friendly.* Look for these signal words because they commonly establish opposite connotations within sentences.

Consider whether the correct choice(s) should have positive or negative connotations. Study the following example:

4. Those who prefer Shakespeare's plays to his poems sometimes argue that many of the poems are _____ compositions.

    A.   distinctive
    B.   courtly
    C.   lucid
    D.   dramatic
    E.   mediocre

E. *mediocre* Because the sentence presents the poems as less preferred, we expect the word describing them to have a negative connotation. The only word with a clearly negative connotation is *mediocre* (E).

Examples for GRE Questions

The GRE—which calls this type of question "Text Completion"—uses a slightly different format, as the question below indicates. In this case, select one word from each corresponding column of choices. Examples follow:

1. Some ads for cosmetic surgery suggest that a(n) (i) _____ face can give a false impression of the inner self; for instance, people with drooping eyelids are said to look angry, sad, or tired. In answer, cosmetic surgeons claim to make the outside of the body reflect more positive inner (ii) _____.

Blank (i)	Blank (ii)
A. impeccable	D. statuses
B. imperfect	E. shapes
C. classic	F. states

B and F. *imperfect . . . states.* Those who attribute negative inner feelings to those with drooping eyelids find such people's faces to be *imperfect.* Cosmetic surgeons claim then to remake faces into manifestations of positive *inner states. Impeccable* (choice A) and *classic* (choice C) would describe faces that are far from imperfect.

2. New job responsibilities that come without additional pay can still be viewed as (i) _____. They can be extremely (ii) _____ for building your resume and expanding your career prospects in a climate that favors those employees who have the capacity and energy to (iii) _____ themselves.

Blank (i)	Blank (ii)	Blank (iii)
A. brash	D. valuable	G. digress
B. ideal	E. efficient	H. disperse
C. opportune	F. hoary	I. stretch

C, D, and I. *opportune . . . valuable . . . stretch.* While new job responsibilities without additional pay can be *opportune* (providing opportunity), they would hardly be *ideal* (choice B). Since they are opportune, they would naturally be *valuable.* To *stretch* oneself is to expand, in this case to become more than one was before. One would not, however, want to stretch to the point of being *dispersed* (choice H), which is to become dissolved or diffused.

3. Blinders restrict a horse's vision to what lay straight ahead, so it won't become distracted or (i) _____ by things going on alongside or behind it. It's no surprise that the idea of having "blinders on" refers to people whose view of the world around them is (ii) _____, people who cannot see "the big picture."

Blank (i)	Blank (ii)
A. soothed	D. contracted
B. mollified	E. spacious
C. spooked	F. dilatory

C and D. *spooked . . . contracted Spooked* means startled or agitated, and thus fits well with *distracted*. *Soothed* (choice A) and *mollified* (choice B) have the opposite meanings, and are thus antonyms. Someone who is not a big-picture thinker would have a *contracted* (narrowed) view of the world. *Spacious* (choice E) means just the opposite.

4. Nature is most (i) _____ where rain falls (ii) _____. Some of the world's most luxuriant vegetation is (iii) _____ in the forests of the Amazon, where more than six feet of rain falls each year.

Blank (i)	Blank (ii)	Blank (iii)
A. harsh	D. horizontally	G. honored
B. lush	E. copiously	H. generated
C. genial	F. opaquely	I. branded

B, E, and H. *lush . . . copiously . . . generated Lush* and *luxuriant* are synonyms that both indicate abundance, and such vegetation relies on a substantial amount of rainfall. *Copiously* means plentifully or bountifully. *Horizontally* (choice D) would not work in any case, since rain falls downward, not side to side! The logic of the passage stresses that much rainfall produces or *generates* lush plant life.

Sentence Equivalence

Also found on the GRE, "Sentence Equivalence" questions ask you not only to employ the skills used for sentence/text completion, but also to understand words that are defined in the same way—commonly called synonyms.

Directions

Select <u>two</u> answer choices, each of which can be used to complete the sentence correctly. Each word should fit the sentence's meaning as a whole.

1. Ethan was _____ when it was proven that the next-door neighbor was the one who broke the window.

   A. impeached
   B. indicted
   C. deified
   D. vindicated
   E. cleared
   F. tapered

D and E. *vindicated . . . cleared* Someone who has been proven not to have committed a negative or unlawful act is *vindicated* (held blameless), or *cleared* of any wrongdoing. *Impeached* (choice A) and *indicted* (choice B) mean denounced and accused, respectively, and are antonyms (words of opposing meaning). This is a good example of a test-maker's strategy: selecting words of whose meanings you may be unsure in an effort to confuse you.

2. The mayor was admired for her keen ability to make _____ speeches; she always seemed to know just how to make the essential points without engaging in undue elaboration.

   A. pithy
   B. complicated
   C. sophisticated
   D. convoluted
   E. tortuous
   F. concise

A and F. *pithy . . . concise* A key here is the idea of making *essential points* without undue (unnecessary or gratuitous) elaboration (lengthiness or expansion). *Pithy* means brief yet full of substance, and *concise* means stating much in few words, so both of these fit the sentence very well. *Complicated* (choice B) and *convoluted* (choice D) are antonyms of pithy and concise, while a *sophisticated* (choice C) speech might be elaborate or brief.

3. We should not equate the narrator of *The Great Gatsby*—Nick Carraway—with that novel's author—F. Scott Fitzgerald—since a narrator is always, at least in part, a(n) _____ entity.

   A. imaginary
   B. fictitious
   C. true
   D. ghostly
   E. real
   F. effervescent

A and B. *imaginary . . . fictitious* A key to the logic of this sentence are the words *should not equate,* which signal a difference between the narrator and author. Authors, we know, are actual people, while characters are *imaginary* or *fictitious.*

4. People often use the word *rhetoric* in a _____ way—for instance, when they say, "The governor's speech was all rhetoric and no substance."

   A. loose
   B. scanty
   C. dismissive
   D. foolish
   E. trivializing
   F. oblivious

C and E. *dismissive . . . trivializing* Rhetoric is the art of speaking or writing persuasively. Politicians are often accused, as in this sentence, of making general and vague promises without offering any details; thus, rhetoric has a bad name, and is often used in a *dismissive* or *trivializing* way.

In the Grammar and Usage Review following the diagnostic test, you will find other kinds of errors of grammar, sentence structure, usage, or diction that appear in the verbal ability sections of many tests.

Chapter 2
Grammar and Usage Diagnostic Test

Answer Sheet

1 Ⓐ Ⓑ Ⓒ Ⓓ Ⓔ	
2 Ⓐ Ⓑ Ⓒ Ⓓ Ⓔ	
3 Ⓐ Ⓑ Ⓒ Ⓓ Ⓔ	
4 Ⓐ Ⓑ Ⓒ Ⓓ Ⓔ	
5 Ⓐ Ⓑ Ⓒ Ⓓ Ⓔ	
6 Ⓐ Ⓑ Ⓒ Ⓓ Ⓔ	
7 Ⓐ Ⓑ Ⓒ Ⓓ Ⓔ	
8 Ⓐ Ⓑ Ⓒ Ⓓ Ⓔ	
9 Ⓐ Ⓑ Ⓒ Ⓓ Ⓔ	
10 Ⓐ Ⓑ Ⓒ Ⓓ Ⓔ	
11 Ⓐ Ⓑ Ⓒ Ⓓ Ⓔ	
12 Ⓐ Ⓑ Ⓒ Ⓓ Ⓔ	
13 Ⓐ Ⓑ Ⓒ Ⓓ Ⓔ	
14 Ⓐ Ⓑ Ⓒ Ⓓ Ⓔ	
15 Ⓐ Ⓑ Ⓒ Ⓓ Ⓔ	
16 Ⓐ Ⓑ Ⓒ Ⓓ Ⓔ	
17 Ⓐ Ⓑ Ⓒ Ⓓ Ⓔ	
18 Ⓐ Ⓑ Ⓒ Ⓓ Ⓔ	
19 Ⓐ Ⓑ Ⓒ Ⓓ Ⓔ	
20 Ⓐ Ⓑ Ⓒ Ⓓ Ⓔ	

Sentence Correction
Type 2

21 Ⓐ Ⓑ Ⓒ Ⓓ Ⓔ
22 Ⓐ Ⓑ Ⓒ Ⓓ Ⓔ
23 Ⓐ Ⓑ Ⓒ Ⓓ Ⓔ
24 Ⓐ Ⓑ Ⓒ Ⓓ Ⓔ
25 Ⓐ Ⓑ Ⓒ Ⓓ Ⓔ
26 Ⓐ Ⓑ Ⓒ Ⓓ Ⓔ
27 Ⓐ Ⓑ Ⓒ Ⓓ Ⓔ
28 Ⓐ Ⓑ Ⓒ Ⓓ Ⓔ
29 Ⓐ Ⓑ Ⓒ Ⓓ Ⓔ
30 Ⓐ Ⓑ Ⓒ Ⓓ Ⓔ
31 Ⓐ Ⓑ Ⓒ Ⓓ Ⓔ
32 Ⓐ Ⓑ Ⓒ Ⓓ Ⓔ
33 Ⓐ Ⓑ Ⓒ Ⓓ Ⓔ
34 Ⓐ Ⓑ Ⓒ Ⓓ Ⓔ
35 Ⓐ Ⓑ Ⓒ Ⓓ Ⓔ
36 Ⓐ Ⓑ Ⓒ Ⓓ Ⓔ
37 Ⓐ Ⓑ Ⓒ Ⓓ Ⓔ
38 Ⓐ Ⓑ Ⓒ Ⓓ Ⓔ
39 Ⓐ Ⓑ Ⓒ Ⓓ Ⓔ
40 Ⓐ Ⓑ Ⓒ Ⓓ Ⓔ

Sentence Correction
Type 3

41 Ⓐ Ⓑ Ⓒ Ⓓ
42 Ⓕ Ⓖ Ⓗ Ⓙ
43 Ⓐ Ⓑ Ⓒ Ⓓ
44 Ⓕ Ⓖ Ⓗ Ⓙ
45 Ⓐ Ⓑ Ⓒ Ⓓ
46 Ⓕ Ⓖ Ⓗ Ⓙ
47 Ⓐ Ⓑ Ⓒ Ⓓ
48 Ⓕ Ⓖ Ⓗ Ⓙ
49 Ⓐ Ⓑ Ⓒ Ⓓ
50 Ⓐ Ⓑ Ⓒ Ⓓ
51 Ⓕ Ⓖ Ⓗ Ⓙ
52 Ⓐ Ⓑ Ⓒ Ⓓ
53 Ⓕ Ⓖ Ⓗ Ⓙ
54 Ⓐ Ⓑ Ⓒ Ⓓ
55 Ⓕ Ⓖ Ⓗ Ⓙ
56 Ⓐ Ⓑ Ⓒ Ⓓ
57 Ⓕ Ⓖ Ⓗ Ⓙ
58 Ⓐ Ⓑ Ⓒ Ⓓ
59 Ⓕ Ⓖ Ⓗ Ⓙ
60 Ⓐ Ⓑ Ⓒ Ⓓ
61 Ⓕ Ⓖ Ⓗ Ⓙ
62 Ⓐ Ⓑ Ⓒ Ⓓ
63 Ⓕ Ⓖ Ⓗ Ⓙ
64 Ⓐ Ⓑ Ⓒ Ⓓ
65 Ⓕ Ⓖ Ⓗ Ⓙ

CUT HERE

Improving Paragraphs	Sentence/Text Completion	Sentence Equivalence
66 Ⓐ Ⓑ Ⓒ Ⓓ Ⓔ	78 Ⓐ Ⓑ Ⓒ Ⓓ Ⓔ	93 Ⓐ Ⓑ Ⓒ Ⓓ Ⓔ Ⓕ
67 Ⓐ Ⓑ Ⓒ Ⓓ Ⓔ	79 Ⓐ Ⓑ Ⓒ Ⓓ Ⓔ Ⓕ Ⓖ Ⓗ Ⓘ	94 Ⓐ Ⓑ Ⓒ Ⓓ Ⓔ Ⓕ
68 Ⓐ Ⓑ Ⓒ Ⓓ Ⓔ	80 Ⓐ Ⓑ Ⓒ Ⓓ Ⓔ Ⓕ	95 Ⓐ Ⓑ Ⓒ Ⓓ Ⓔ Ⓕ
69 Ⓐ Ⓑ Ⓒ Ⓓ Ⓔ	81 Ⓐ Ⓑ Ⓒ Ⓓ Ⓔ Ⓕ Ⓖ Ⓗ Ⓘ	96 Ⓐ Ⓑ Ⓒ Ⓓ Ⓔ Ⓕ
70 Ⓐ Ⓑ Ⓒ Ⓓ Ⓔ	82 Ⓐ Ⓑ Ⓒ Ⓓ Ⓔ	97 Ⓐ Ⓑ Ⓒ Ⓓ Ⓔ Ⓕ
71 Ⓐ Ⓑ Ⓒ Ⓓ Ⓔ	83 Ⓐ Ⓑ Ⓒ Ⓓ Ⓔ Ⓕ	98 Ⓐ Ⓑ Ⓒ Ⓓ Ⓔ Ⓕ
72 Ⓐ Ⓑ Ⓒ Ⓓ Ⓔ	84 Ⓐ Ⓑ Ⓒ Ⓓ Ⓔ	99 Ⓐ Ⓑ Ⓒ Ⓓ Ⓔ Ⓕ
73 Ⓐ Ⓑ Ⓒ Ⓓ Ⓔ	85 Ⓐ Ⓑ Ⓒ Ⓓ Ⓔ Ⓕ Ⓖ Ⓗ Ⓘ	100 Ⓐ Ⓑ Ⓒ Ⓓ Ⓔ Ⓕ
74 Ⓐ Ⓑ Ⓒ Ⓓ Ⓔ	86 Ⓐ Ⓑ Ⓒ Ⓓ Ⓔ	101 Ⓐ Ⓑ Ⓒ Ⓓ Ⓔ Ⓕ
75 Ⓐ Ⓑ Ⓒ Ⓓ Ⓔ	87 Ⓐ Ⓑ Ⓒ Ⓓ Ⓔ Ⓕ	102 Ⓐ Ⓑ Ⓒ Ⓓ Ⓔ Ⓕ
76 Ⓐ Ⓑ Ⓒ Ⓓ Ⓔ	88 Ⓐ Ⓑ Ⓒ Ⓓ Ⓔ	103 Ⓐ Ⓑ Ⓒ Ⓓ Ⓔ Ⓕ
77 Ⓐ Ⓑ Ⓒ Ⓓ Ⓔ	89 Ⓐ Ⓑ Ⓒ Ⓓ Ⓔ Ⓕ Ⓖ Ⓗ Ⓘ	104 Ⓐ Ⓑ Ⓒ Ⓓ Ⓔ Ⓕ
	90 Ⓐ Ⓑ Ⓒ Ⓓ Ⓔ	105 Ⓐ Ⓑ Ⓒ Ⓓ Ⓔ Ⓕ
	91 Ⓐ Ⓑ Ⓒ Ⓓ Ⓔ Ⓕ Ⓖ Ⓗ Ⓘ	106 Ⓐ Ⓑ Ⓒ Ⓓ Ⓔ Ⓕ
	92 Ⓐ Ⓑ Ⓒ Ⓓ Ⓔ	107 Ⓐ Ⓑ Ⓒ Ⓓ Ⓔ Ⓕ

Quick Reference Guide

Sentence Correction – Type 1 (p. 27): SAT, PPST, PSAT/NMSQT

Sentence Correction – Type 2 (p. 30): ACT

Sentence Correction – Type 3 (p. 36): GMAT, SAT, PPST, PSAT/NMSQT

Improving Paragraphs (p. 43): SAT, PSAT/NMSQT

Sentence/Text Completion (p. 49): GRE, SAT, PSAT/NMSQT

Sentence Equivalence (p. 54): GRE

Remember to work with *all* of the question types above, even if some will not appear on your particular test. All questions test the same range of grammar and usage knowledge. The more you answer questions, the stronger your overall knowledge will become.

Sentence Correction – Type 1

Directions: Some of the following sentences are correct. Others contain errors in grammar, usage, or word choice. There is not more than one error in any sentence. If there is an error, it will be underlined and lettered. Find the one underlined part that must be changed to make the sentence correct, and choose the corresponding letter on your answer sheet. Mark E if the sentence contains no error.

The Answer Key for the Sentence Correction – Type 1 section is on p. 58, and the explanatory answers begin on p. 61.

1. The mayor <u>continually</u> asserted that one of the crucial strengths of
   A
   the political system <u>is</u> each <u>individual</u> having the right to determine
   BC
   which way <u>he or she</u> will vote. <u>No error</u>.
   DE

2. The concept of hypocrisy <u>applies</u> to morals; a person should be
   A
   good and <u>not merely</u> seem <u>so,</u> and a bad person <u>is little mended</u> by
   BCD
   pretense of goodness. <u>No error</u>.
   E

3. We should support those proposals for increasing <u>or redistributing</u>
   A
   tax money <u>that</u> <u>will raise</u> the per pupil expenditure in our cities and
   BC
   <u>equalize them</u> throughout the public school system. <u>No error</u>.
   DE

4. <u>Like Faulkner,</u> Porter's short stories <u>give</u> the reader a vivid sense of
   AB
   what life in New Orleans <u>must have been</u> <u>like</u> in the twenties and
   CD
   thirties. <u>No error</u>.
   E

5. His intention was not to establish a new sect or in any way
                                                        A
   to decrease the power of Canterbury but in hope of making the
       B   C
   bishops cut back their lavish outlay of church funds. No error.
                                      D   E

6. Despite his poor start, Williams is the player whom I think is most
   A   B   C
   likely to win the batting crown. No error.
                             D   E

7. Most all the instruments in the orchestra are tuned just before the
   A   B   C
   concert begins; the piano, of course, is an exception. No error.
                             D   E

8. The fall in wheat prices, together with a decline in the demands for
       A
   beef, have effected a significant drop in the value of Swenson
         B   C   D
   Company stock. No error.
                   E

9. The number of Irish immigrants in Boston was larger than Italian or
   A   B   C
   Scottish, but it was not until 1900 that Boston's first Irish mayor

   was elected. No error.
   D   E

10. The trustees of the fund which determine the awarding of the grants
                             A   B
    are expected to meet in New York, not Washington. No error.
    C   D   E

11. The increasing number of predators that carry infectious diseases to
                          A   B   C
    the herds of zebra and gnu are a serious concern of park rangers.
                             D
    No error.
    E

12. The humor of the fable <u>on which</u> these questions <u>are based</u> <u>derive</u>
A B C
from a logical problem <u>relating</u> to the drawing of conclusions from
D
evidence. <u>No error</u>.
E

13. Everybody stationed at the American embassy in Moscow

<u>have been</u> <u>affected</u> in some way by the radio waves, but there is not
A B
yet any certainty about <u>just what</u> the <u>effects</u> have been. <u>No error</u>.
C D E

14. The speaker discussed the difficulty of finding a <u>single job</u> <u>that</u>
A B
combines financial security, creativity, personal growth, and

<u>opportunities to help others</u> and <u>effect</u> social change. <u>No error</u>.
C D E

15. Unaffected <u>by neither hunger nor cold</u>, Scott covered up to twenty
A
miles on each of the days <u>that</u> the weather <u>permitted him</u> to travel
B C
<u>at all</u>. <u>No error</u>.
D E

16. Among the pleasures <u>of the film is</u> the subtle performance <u>by</u> W. C.
A B
Fields and the <u>more boisterous antics</u> <u>of</u> the youthful Mae West.
C D
<u>No error</u>.
E

17. I had no sooner picked up my spoon <u>to begin my soup</u> <u>when</u> the waiter
A B
<u>descended on</u> me with <u>my</u> salad, main course, and coffee. <u>No error</u>.
C D E

18. Hoping <u>to lie</u> as close <u>to</u> the water as possible, I <u>laid</u> my towel on
A B C
the sand, unpacked my sun lotion, and <u>settled down for</u> the
D
afternoon. <u>No error</u>.
E

19. <u>Seen from above</u>, the island and the mainland together are shaped
        A

    <u>something</u> <u>like</u> a droopy, spreading oak tree <u>as</u> a child might draw
         B   C   D

    it. <u>No error</u>.
       E

20. The altitude, temperature, and wind conditions of the plain <u>make</u>
                                               A

    cattle raising impossible, and <u>this is why</u> protein deficiency <u>is</u> <u>so</u>
                                B   C D

    common among the villagers. <u>No error</u>.
                                    E

Sentence Correction – Type 2

Directions: Some part of each sentence below is underlined; sometimes the whole sentence is underlined. Five choices for rephrasing the underlined part follow each sentence; the first choice A repeats the original, and the other four are different. If choice A seems better than the alternatives, choose answer A; if not, choose one of the others.

For each sentence, consider the requirements of standard written English. Your choice should be a correct and effective expression, not awkward or ambiguous. Focus on grammar, word choice, sentence construction, and punctuation. If a choice changes the meaning of the original sentence, do not select it.

The Answer Key for the Sentence Correction – Type 2 section is on p. 58, and the explanatory answers begin on p. 62.

21. The reason the cat won't eat is <u>because he likes only liver-flavored cat food</u>.

    A.   because he likes only liver-flavored cat food
    B.   that he liked cat liver-flavored food only
    C.   on account of he only likes liver-flavored cat food
    D.   that he likes only liver-flavored cat food
    E.   because of liking only liver-flavored cat food

22. No sooner had the mayor announced that she would run for president <u>than the governor threw her hat</u> into the ring.

    A.   than the governor threw her hat

    B.   when the governor threw her hat

    C.   than the governor throws her hat

    D.   then the governor would throw her hat

    E.   but the governor threw her hat

23. <u>If you would have been more careful,</u> you would have broken fewer plates.

    A.   If you would have been more careful

    B.   If you had been more careful

    C.   If you would be more careful

    D.   Were you more careful

    E.   If you would have taken more care

24. Madame Arnot insisted <u>on me speaking only</u> in French.

    A.   on me speaking only

    B.   on me only speaking

    C.   on my speaking only

    D.   upon me speaking only

    E.   that only I speak

25. <u>There are considerations of passenger safety which prevent</u> the crew from drinking while they are working.

    A.   There are considerations of passenger safety which prevent

    B.   There are considerations of passenger safety which prevents

    C.   There are considerations of passenger safety that prevent

    D.   Considerations of passenger safety prevent

    E.   Considerations of passenger safety prevents

26. One of the characteristics of the earliest settlers of Massachusetts <u>consisted in their willingness to endure hardships</u>.

    A.   consisted in their willingness to endure hardships

    B.   were their willingness to endure hardships

    C.   consisted of their willingness to endure hardships

    D.   was their willingness to endure hardships

    E.   was in their being willing to endure hardships

27. <u>Like many groups,</u> the aims of the Signet Society have changed in the last ten years.

    A.   Like many groups

    B.   Like those of many groups

    C.   Like many group's

    D.   Like those of many other groups

    E.   Like those of many other group's

28. <u>When she was only five, Janet's mother married for the third time.</u>

    A.   When she was only five, Janet's mother married for the third time.

    B.   When only five, Janet's mother married for the third time.

    C.   When Janet was only five, her mother married for the third time.

    D.   When Janet's mother married for the third time, she was only five.

    E.   Janet's mother married, when Janet was only five, for the third time.

29. We asked him about not only <u>how he expected to reduce taxes, but his plans to increase employment</u>.

    A.   how he expected to reduce taxes, but his plans to increase employment

    B.   how he expected to reduce taxes, but also how he planned to increase employment

    C.   how he expects to reduce taxes, but also his plans to increase employment

    D.   how he plans to reduce taxes, but also about his plans to increase employment

    E.   how he expected to reduce taxes, but also about his plans to increase employment

30. Although England and France once believed the Concorde to be the plane of the future, other countries, such as the United States, <u>was beginning to become concerned about the Concorde's effect on</u> the environment, long before it was retired in 2003.

   A. was beginning to become concerned about the Concorde's effect on
   B. became concerned about the Concorde's affect on
   C. immediately began to become concerned about the Concorde's affect on
   D. became concerned about the Concorde's effect on
   E. is beginning to be concerned about the Concorde's effect on

31. <u>After he graduated from college, his parents gave him a new car, ten thousand dollars, and sent him on a trip around the world.</u>

   A. After he graduated from college, his parents gave him a new car, ten thousand dollars, and sent him on a trip around the world.
   B. After graduating from college, his parents gave him a new car, ten thousand dollars, and sent him on a trip around the world.
   C. After he had graduated from college, his parents gave him a new car, ten thousand dollars, and a trip around the world.
   D. After he had graduated from college, his parents gave him a new car, ten thousand dollars, and sent him on a trip around the world.
   E. After graduating from college, his parents gave him a new car, ten thousand dollars, and a trip around the world.

32. The difficulty with an inflated grading system is that everyone <u>believes he or she is as good or better than everyone else as a student</u>.

   A. believes he or she is as good or better than everyone else as a student
   B. believes he or she is as good as or better than every other student
   C. believes he or she is as good as or better than every student
   D. believes they are as good as or better than every other student
   E. believes they are as good as or better than everyone else as a student

33. <u>To learn to write well is more difficult than learning to read well.</u>

   A. To learn to write well is more difficult than learning to read well.
   B. Learning to write well is more difficult than learning to read well.
   C. It is more difficult to learn to write well than it is to learn to read well.
   D. Learning to write well is more difficult than it is to learn to read well.
   E. To learn to write well is more difficult than it is to learn to read well.

34. When that halfback played for the New York Jets, <u>their records he set lasted fifteen years</u>.

   A. their records he set lasted fifteen years
   B. his records lasted fifteen years
   C. he set records that lasted fifteen years
   D. the records set lasted fifteen years
   E. he set records, and they would have lasted fifteen years

35. <u>The shortstop threw late to the second baseman and missed the runner, which</u> allowed the batter to reach first base safely.

   A. The shortstop threw late to the second baseman and missed the runner, which
   B. The shortstop's late throw to the second baseman missed the runner, and
   C. By throwing late to the second baseman, the shortstop missed the runner which
   D. The shortstop throwing late to the second baseman missed the runner, and it
   E. The shortstop threw late to the second baseman and missed the runner, and this

36. His ability to work steadily, to accept criticism, and to retain his sense of humor made O'Hara the most valued man in Sherman's army and, when the war was over, <u>made him</u> the obvious choice for governor.

    A.   made him

    B.   it made him

    C.   it also made him

    D.   this made him

    E.   this also made him

37. The group of composers who were in Vienna in the 1790s <u>includes Mozart, Gramm, and Hummel, and though the younger</u>, Mozart, wrote the lasting works.

    A.   includes Mozart, Gramm, and Hummel, and though the younger

    B.   include Mozart, Gramm, and Hummel, and though the youngest

    C.   included Mozart, Gramm, and Hummel, though the youngest

    D.   included Mozart, Gramm, and Hummel, and though he was the youngest in the group

    E.   included Mozart;

38. <u>When you pass the first two tests, it</u> does not guarantee that you will pass the course.

    A.   When you pass the first two tests, it

    B.   Because you pass the first two tests, it

    C.   You passing the first two tests

    D.   That you have passed the first two tests

    E.   Passing the tests

39. <u>How a woman who has had every advantage can marry a man as unsavory as him</u> is beyond my understanding.

    A.   How a woman who has had every advantage can marry a man as unsavory as him

    B.   How a woman whom has had every advantage can marry a man as unsavory as him

    C.   How a woman who has had every advantage can marry a man so unsavory as him

    D.   How a woman who has had every advantage can marry a man as unsavory as he

    E.   How a woman whom has had every advantage can marry a man so unsavory as he

40. <u>The new innovations at Shoppers' Mall are</u> a children's theater and live musical entertainment.

    A.   The new innovations at Shoppers' Mall are

    B.   The new innovation at Shoppers' Mall is

    C.   The innovation at Shoppers' Mall is

    D.   The innovations at Shoppers' Mall are

    E.   Shoppers' Mall has two new innovations,

Sentence Correction – Type 3

Directions: In the left-hand column, you will find passages with various words and phrases underlined. In the right-hand column, you will find a set of responses corresponding to each underlined portion. If the underlined portion is correct as it stands, mark the letter indicating "NO CHANGE." If the underlined portion is incorrect, decide which of the choices best corrects it. Consider only underlined portions; assume that the rest of the passage is correct as written.

The Answer Key for the Sentence Correction – Type 3 section is on p. 59, and the explanatory answers begin on p. 63.

Passage I

Theodore Roosevelt was vice president when McKinley was assassinated in 1901. As the Republican candidate, he was elected <u>to be the president</u> in
41

41. A.   NO CHANGE
    B.   to be president
    C.   to the presidency
    D.   to president

<u>1904, and</u> he declined to run for a
42
third term. He supported Taft, the

42. F.   NO CHANGE
    G.   1904 and
    H.   1904, and then
    J.   1904, but

Republican nominee in <u>1908, and he</u>
43
was elected by a wide margin. By

43. A.   NO CHANGE
    B.   in 1908; who
    C.   in 1908 who
    D.   in 1908, he

1912, Roosevelt <u>became dissatisfied</u>
44

44. F.   NO CHANGE
    G.   had become dissatisfied
    H.   dissatisfied
    J.   was unsatisfied

with Taft, and <u>ran in opposition to</u>
45
Taft and Wilson as the candidate of a third party, the Progressives.

45. A. NO CHANGE
    B.   ran opposed to
    C.   ran as opposition of
    D.   opposed to

Wilson, the Democratic candidate, was the winner of the election of 1912, and he was to win again in the

46.
- F. NO CHANGE
- G. (DO NOT begin new paragraph) The Democratic candidate, Wilson,
- H. (DO NOT begin new paragraph) The Democratic candidate, Wilson
- J. Wilson, the Democratic candidate

election of 1916. Known best, perhaps, for his failure to persuade the Senate to join the League of Nations, Wilson's first term as president was marked by reform. Wilson's management of the war was efficient and tactful, and he won the

47.
- A. NO CHANGE
- B. Perhaps known best for his
- C. Best remembered, perhaps, for the
- D. Best known, perhaps, for his

backing both of business and labor. He suffered the third of three strokes

48.
- F. NO CHANGE
- G. both of labor as well as business
- H. of both business and labor
- J. both of business as well as of labor

in 1919, and thereafter he is without any significant political influence.

49.
- A. NO CHANGE
- B. was of no significant
- C. had no significant
- D. was without any significant

Passage II

For two years—ever since a Turkish sponge diver first spotted it—a joint Turkish-American team has been excavating a shipwreck 150 feet below the surface <u>off the southern coast</u> of Turkey. The

50. A. NO CHANGE
    B. of the southern coast
    C. off of the southern coast
    D. off of the south coast

wrecked <u>ship, its</u> salvagers surmise, was Greek. It probably set sail from Syria with a cargo of tin and glass from farther east and stopped in Cyprus to load three tons of copper ingots and several crates of pottery.

51. F. NO CHANGE
    G. ship, so its
    H. ship, it's
    J. ship, so it's

It was headed for Greece when <u>it was driven onto the rocks and sank</u>. The cargo wasn't salvaged at the time because the ship's owners didn't have the technology <u>to do it</u>. That was about 3,400 years ago.

52. A. NO CHANGE
    B. when it was driven onto the rocks and was sunk
    C. when it was driven onto the rocks and was sunken
    D. sinking, when it was driven onto the rocks

53. F. NO CHANGE
    G. to do that
    H. to do so
    J. to do this

Up to the present point in time,
54
the salvagers have brought up

much of the cargo and of the artifacts,
55
as well as part of the keel and some

planking from the vessel itself.

"These bones of the wreck push back

our knowledge of Mediterranean

ship-building by nearly a millennium,"

an archeologist writes. He believes the

copper and tin brought west for the
56
express purpose of manufacturing

bronze weapons and tools. His team is

salvaging history itself. The evidence
57
of a flourishing international trade;

the mystery of eight stone anchors

each weighing 600 to 800 pounds,

somehow loaded on board before the

invention of block and tackle; the

54. A. NO CHANGE
B. So far
C. So far,
D. Up to this time,

55. F. NO CHANGE
G. many cargo and artifacts
H. much of the artifacts and cargo
J. much of the cargo and many artifacts

56. A. NO CHANGE
B. were brought west
C. were being brought west
D. was being brought west

57. F. NO CHANGE
G. itself; the
H. itself: the
J. itself, the

artifacts of the maritime industry that was at the heart of ancient Greek civilization. They will keep scholars and onlookers enthralled for years.

Passage III

The Electoral College came most into question after such close presidential elections as 1960 between
58
John Kennedy and Richard Nixon,

in which the alternation of a few
59
votes would of changed the outcome. The system works as the Founding Fathers intended, but what they intended was a buffer against the popular vote.

That, in fact, remains the problem. The Electoral College system doesn't reflect the popular vote. Fifteen

58. A. NO CHANGE
    B. like 1960
    C. as that of 1960
    D. like that of 1960

59. F. NO CHANGE
    G. in which the alternation of a few votes would have changed
    H. in which the changing of a few votes would have altered
    J. in which changing a few votes would of altered

presidents <u>who had not received</u> a
₆₀
majority of the popular votes have

been elected, and the list includes

three presidents who actually trailed

their nearest opponent in the popular

vote. Some of these were chosen not

by the Electoral College <u>but the</u>
₆₁
<u>House of Representatives,</u> which

decides when no candidate wins an

electoral majority—and does so by

giving one vote to each state <u>regardless</u>
₆₂
<u>of their population</u>.

The major cause of this disparity

is the unit system <u>that count</u> all of a
₆₃
state's electoral votes as blocs,

ignoring second-party votes. The

procedure is far less than

representative. In 1969, following a

close contest between Richard

Nixon and Hubert Humphrey, the

60. A. NO CHANGE
B. that have not received
C. not receiving
D. who have not received

61. F. NO CHANGE
G. but chosen by the House of Representatives
H. but instead, by the House of Representatives
J. but by the House of Representatives

62. A. NO CHANGE
B. irregardless of population
C. irregardless of their population
D. regardless of population

63. F. NO CHANGE
G. which count
H. that counts
J. counting

House <u>voted overwhelmingly</u> for a constitutional amendment in favor of direct popular election of presidents, and a runoff election if no candidate received at least 40 percent of the total vote. The proposal was done in by the Senate filibuster of some southerners and small-state senators, but the time will undoubtedly come again when the risk of defeating the will of the people <u>rises</u> new voices for reform.

64. A. NO CHANGE
B. decided by an overwhelming vote
C. overwhelmingly votes
D. voted overwhelming

65. F. NO CHANGE
G. arises
H. raised
J. raises

Improving Paragraphs

Directions: Carefully read the excerpt below, which represents writing one might find in drafts of student papers. Here, you will find questions that ask you to address not only grammar and usage within individual sentences, but also questions that deal with the excerpt more globally, asking you to address features such as organization and the development of ideas.

The Answer Key for the Improving Paragraphs section is on p. 59, and the explanatory answers begin on p. 65.

Passage I

(1) When is a gift not a gift? (2) When it's a Trojan Horse! (3) The story of the Trojan Horse originated in Homer's *Aeneid,* an epic poem written in the first century BCE. (4) This incident has led to the well-known saying roughly translated as "Beware of Greeks bearing gifts." (5) In the *Aeneid,* the Greek army pretends to sail away from Troy after a ten-year attempt to conquer the city, leaving an enormous wooden horse (a "steed of monstrous height") at the city gates, as a "gift." (6) After the Trojans take the horse into the city, thirty Greek soldiers who have been hiding inside appear, open the gates to let in the soldiers, and the siege of Troy ends with a Greek victory.

(7) These days, "Trojan Horse" is also used to refer to a computer virus—installation by a malicious hacker—that "hides" inside an apparently harmless program. (8) It can attach itself to email, music and video files, and software. (9) Releasing the virus is often as easy as clicking on a hypertext link, one that you presume is "friendly" but which soon proves otherwise. (10) For instance, you might receive an email message that says, "Your inbox has exceeded its capacity, and no further emails will be delivered, unless you click on the link below to increase your email capacity," and following this sort of direction can release viruses that run rampant, infecting not only your own computer but also those of your contacts. (11) The prevalence of these unwanted and destructive invaders has led many computer owners to install anti-virus software that recognizes, isolates, and to eliminate the virus before it can spread.

66. Where should sentence 4 be placed in the essay?

    A. (where it is now)
    B. After sentence 11
    C. After sentence 6 in paragraph 1
    D. As part of sentence 7
    E. Before sentence 7 in paragraph 2

67. The use of the word *Greek* in sentence 6 is an example of which of the following?

    A. correct usage
    B. overuse of a proper noun
    C. redundancy
    D. the author's cultural bias
    E. wordiness

68. What is the best way of writing the underlined portion of sentence 6 (reproduced below)?

After the Trojans take the horse into the city, thirty Greek soldiers who have been hiding inside appear, <u>open the gates to let in the soldiers, and the siege of Troy ends with a Greek victory</u>.

A. (as it is now)
B. open the gates letting in the soldiers, so the siege of Troy ends with a Greek victory
C. open the gates to let in their countrymen, and the siege of Troy ends with a Greek victory
D. open the gates, and the siege of Troy ends with a Greek victory
E. open the gates to a Greek victory that ends the siege of Troy

69. Which of the following is the best version of sentence 7 (reproduced below)?

These days, "Trojan Horse" is also used to refer to a computer virus—installation by a malicious hacker—that "hides" inside an apparently harmless program.

A. (as it is now)
B. These days, "Trojan Horse" is also used to refer to a computer virus—installed by a malicious hacker— that "hides" inside an apparently harmless program.
C. These days, "Trojan Horse" is also used to refer to computer viruses—installed by a malicious hacker—that "hides" inside an apparently harmless program.
D. "Trojan Horse" in these days is also used to refer to a computer virus—installed by a malicious hacker that "hides" inside an apparently harmless program.
E. These days, "Trojan Horse" is also use to refer to a computer virus—installed by a malicious hacker—that "hides" inside an apparently harmless program.

70. How can the information in sentence 10 (reproduced below) be more effectively and correctly expressed?

For instance, you might receive an email message that says, "Your inbox has exceeded its capacity, and no further emails will be delivered, unless you click on the link below to increase your email capacity," and following this sort of direction can release viruses that run rampant, infecting not only your own computer but also those of your contacts.

A. (as it is written)

B. For instance, you might receive an email message. It says, "Your inbox has exceeded its capacity, and no further emails will be delivered unless you click on the link below to increase your email capacity." Following this sort of direction can release viruses that run rampant, infecting not only your own computer but also those of your contacts.

C. For instance, you might receive an email message that says, "Your inbox has exceeded its capacity, and no further emails will be delivered unless you click on the link below to increase your email capacity." Following this sort of direction can release viruses that run rampant, infecting not only your own computer but also those of your contacts.

D. as a separate paragraph

E. as part of paragraph 1

71. What is the best way to write the underlined portion of sentence 11 (reproduced below)?

The prevalence of these unwanted and destructive invaders has led many computer owners to install <u>anti-virus software that recognizes, isolates, and to eliminate the virus before it can spread.</u>

A. (as it is written)

B. anti-virus software products that recognize, isolate, and keep eliminating the virus before it can spread.

C. anti-virus software that recognizes, to isolate and eliminate the virus before it can spread.

D. anti-virus recognition software that isolates and eliminates it before it can spread.

E. anti-virus software that recognizes, isolates, and eliminates the virus before it can spread.

Passage II

(1) Some critics have called the *Twilight* saga sexist because Bella seems needy and is weaker than Edward and Jacob; she is willing to give up her soul for Edward, and would be helpless if Edward or Jacob were to decide to destroy her in a moment of uncontrolled emotion. (2) She is also the object of Edward's "stalking" behavior, which is following her around and visiting her bedroom while she sleeps. (3) While we might want to call these elements potential problems, there are other perspectives to consider as well. (4) Though we might conclude that Bella is willing to give up her soul, and to give it up for love, she does not see herself this way. (5) Further, Edward is not willing to give up his life for Bella. (6) Thus, in terms of their devotion and self-sacrifice, Edward and Bella seem to be equals.

(7) Most of us do not give up our souls or lives for our beloved, but we do come to understanding of that we must both help and protect one another. (8) We see this in Edward, who is both the protector of and protected by Bella. (9) Though Bella is vulnerable to harm and hurt, so is Edward, who is gentle, artistic, and compassionate—not at all the kind of brute that we would associate with a macho male. (10) Hardly the weak female, Bella is strong and fearless, risking her life not only for Edward but also for her father and mother. (11) In this way, she's a kind of super girl. (12) Bella is not replaced by Edward; rather, the limits of her human powers are tested by her love for him.

72. How is sentence 2 (reproduced below) best written?

She is also the object of Edward's "stalking" behavior, which is following her around and visiting her bedroom while she sleeps.

A. (as it is now)

B. And because of Edward's "stalking" behavior as he follows Bella around and visits her bedroom to watch her sleep.

C. Also problematic is Edward's "stalking" behavior as she is followed around and being secretly visited in her bedroom as he watches her sleep.

D. Edward sees that she is followed around and being secretly visited in her bedroom as he watches her sleep.

E. She is also the object of Edward's "stalking" behavior, as he follows her around and visits her bedroom while she sleeps.

73. What is the most concise way to express the information given in sentence 4 (reproduced below)?

Though we might conclude that Bella is willing to give up her soul, and to give it up for love, she does not see herself this way.

A. (as it is now)
B. Bella is not willing to give up her soul, and to give it up for love.
C. Though we might conclude that Bella is willing to give up her soul for love, she does not see herself this way.
D. Bella is not willing to give up her soul for love.
E. Bella is willing to give up her soul for love, though she does not think this to be the case.

74. What is the best version of sentence 5 (reproduced below)?

Further, Edward is not willing to give up his life for Bella.

A. (as it is now)
B. Further, Edward is willing to give up his life for Bella.
C. Further, Edward is unwilling to give up his life for Bella.
D. Further, Edward has the good will to give up his life for Bella.
E. Further, Edward is not willing to change his life for Bella.

75. What is the best way to express the underlined portion of sentence 7 (reproduced below)?

Most of us do not give up our souls or lives for our beloved, but we do come to understanding of that we must both help and protect one another.

A. (as it is now)
B. come to an understanding of
C. understand
D. have the understanding of
E. come to understand

76. What is the best way to express the underlined portion of sentence 12 (reproduced below)?

Bella is not <u>replaced by Edward; rather,</u> the limits of her human powers are tested by her love for him.

- A. (as it is now)
- B. replaced by Edward, rather,
- C. effaced by Edward, rather,
- D. effaced by Edward; rather,
- E. replaced by Edward (rather)

77. What is the best conclusion for this essay?

- A. Edward obviously loves Bella so much that he makes her stronger.
- B. She clearly passes this test.
- C. *New Moon* proves Edward is vulnerable.
- D. Bella looks good compared to Edward because she is more a super girl than he is a super man.
- E. Bella is amazing.

Sentence/Text Completion

Directions: Each sentence or passage below contains one, two, or three blanks to indicate omitted words. Considering the lettered choices beneath each sentence, choose the word or words that best fit(s) the whole sentence. Formats for both GRE and SAT completions are used in the examples below.

The Answer Key for the Sentence/Text Completion section is on p. 59, and the explanatory answers begin on p. 66.

78. Contemporary feminists recognize that we cannot _____ a general, or universal woman, since there are _____ differences among women, depending upon race, ethnicity, class, religion, and individual history.

- A. posit . . . significant
- B. select . . . unnecessary
- C. withhold . . . non-existent
- D. determine . . . prudent
- E. refuse . . . serious

79. In the Old Testament, Joseph was expert at (i) _____ the Pharaoh's dream in which there appeared seven fat cows followed by seven thin ones. Joseph told Pharaoh that the cows were symbols that indicated Egypt would enjoy seven years of (ii) _____, followed by seven years of famine. Because Pharaoh responded by setting aside food during the good times, Egypt was able to withstand the worst of the (iii) _____ period that succeeded them.

Blank (i)	Blank (ii)	Blank (iii)
A. encoding	D. plenty	G. lenient
B. programming	E. want	H. affluent
C. interpreting	F. paucity	I. trying

80. When biologist Alexander Fleming saw that some of the bacteria he was studying had unexpectedly been destroyed by a fungus, he was happy to realize that he had (i) _____ discovered the first (ii) _____.

Blank (i)	Blank (ii)
A. serendipitously	D. microorganism
B. shrewdly	E. antibiotic
C. cannily	F. disease

81. Aesthetics began in ancient Greece as the study of (i) _____ things—as opposed to things not perceptible to the senses, such as God, or ideal essences. For this reason, the early Greeks emphasized the importance of (ii) _____, that is, how well an artistic representation copied nature. For them, the goal of an artist was the accurate (iii) _____ of the world around them.

Blank (i)	Blank (ii)	Blank (iii)
A. unfathomable	D. abstraction	G. enhancement
B. immaterial	E. instinct	H. portrayal
C. material	F. imitation	I. diminishment

82. The Augustan Age was a traditional period in which there was a
_____ of innovation and experimentation.

    A. plethora
    B. surplus
    C. mistrust
    D. certainty
    E. strain

83. Any scientist who does not appreciate the conclusions of an
empirical (i) _____ must be one who does not believe in the
importance of (ii) _____ facts.

Blank (i)	Blank (ii)
A. investigation	D. speculative
B. opinion	E. experiential
C. treatise	F. bald

84. Without complete _____ consumer prices, each of us can only
hope that the will of the majority will both _____ our own will
and affect the price-setting activity of manufacturers.

    A. allegiance to . . . reward
    B. control over . . . reflect
    C. knowledge of . . . enrich
    D. concern about . . . consume
    E. hope for . . . defeat

85. Teachers who make (i) _____ comments on student papers
succeed only in (ii) _____ each student's desire for
(iii) _____ and belief in his or her abilities.

Blank (i)	Blank (ii)	Blank (iii)
A. constructive	D. sharpening	G. alienation
B. tedious	E. dulling	H. annulment
C. derogatory	F. maintaining	I. improvement

86. The theorist and the practitioner cannot be entirely separated; after all, every theory refers to the _____ world and every practitioner bases his or her activity on an intellectual conception of the task. Thus, theory and practice always _____ one another.

A. unseen . . . eliminate
B. practical . . . entail
C. mental . . .prefer
D. invisible . . . reject
E. cosmic . . . attack

87. To understand that change is (i) _____, one need only listen to current high-school slang and (ii) _____ it with that spoken a generation ago.

Blank (i)	Blank (ii)
A. intrusive	D. analogize
B. inevitable	E. regret
C. finite	F. contrast

88. Some believe that the smarter students are those who speak most _____ in class. But until it can be shown that intelligence is _____ only through vocal cord use, I must insist that silence and ignorance are not always partners.

A. frequently . . . revealed
B. safely . . . insinuated
C. ceremoniously . . . dispensed
D. formally . . . concealed
E. angrily . . . heightened

89. (i) _____ his opponent's thrusts repeatedly, Blake seemed unwilling to make a(n) (ii) _____ move, even though the weapons were (iii) _____ and dangerous injury was impossible.

Blank (i)	Blank (ii)	Blank (iii)
A. Parrying	D. offensive	G. uneven
B. Inviting	E. organized	H. jagged
C. Fending	F. backward	I. blunted

90. Everyone else on the dais laced his or her remarks with humor, but Professor Dexter remained stern, even _____, throughout his speech.

    A. comical

    B. droll

    C. solemn

    D. malignant

    E. waggish

91. Sharon argued that if (i) _____ and (ii) _____ are distinct characteristics in a piece of writing, then one's appearance must be distinct from one's identity. Emilio countered, however, that such distinctions cannot be (iii) _____ made, since appearances can often be indications of what lay deeper.

Blank (i)	Blank (ii)	Blank (iii)
A. spelling	D. expression	G. openly
B. ideas	E. imagination	H. cleanly
C. style	F. content	I. delightfully

92. The heroic depiction of Homer's Odysseus in a motion picture will certainly strengthen his image in this age when _____ and nobility are rare. These days, most lead characters in films are _____, exhibiting a mix of positive and negative traits and behaviors.

    A. pomposity . . . scoundrels

    B. condescension . . . angels

    C. glamour . . . stars

    D. spectacle . . . superheroes

    E. courage . . . antiheroes

Sentence Equivalence

Directions: Select <u>two</u> answer choices, each of which can be used to complete the sentence correctly. Each word should fit the sentence's meaning as a whole.

The Answer Key for the Sentence Equivalence section is on p. 60, and the explanatory answers begin on p. 68.

93. Cats are often appreciated for their _____, because they regularly scour their coats with bristly tongues.

   A. lovability
   B. murkiness
   C. hygiene
   D. cleanliness
   E. aptitude
   F. panache

94. Negotiating, rather than _____, is always the ethically better and more effective way to accomplish goals with trying people.

   A. hounding
   B. conciliating
   C. interceding
   D. preening
   E. helping
   F. harrying

95. The last little pig outsmarts the wolf, initially by building a house too strong for the wolf's wind, and then by leaving his house to get food only at times when the wolf is likely to be sleeping and engaging in other kinds of _____.

   A. refusal
   B. passivity
   C. prevarication
   D. deprivation
   E. sustenance
   F. inaction

96. Rising unemployment is yet another symptom of progress toward a time when machines that are both "strong" and "smart" will make human labor _____.

A. cerebral
B. renewable
C. leisurely
D. obsolete
E. outmoded
F. frenetic

97. Many of the critics _____ the film, but their responses did not deter moviegoers, who waited in long lines for every showing.

A. glossed
B. panned
C. commended
D. disparaged
E. applauded
F. appeased

98. Mai's reputation as a decisive business leader puzzled her family, because Mai often _____ when it came to domestic decisions.

A. hustled
B. vacillated
C. misfired
D. hurried
E. jostled
F. equivocated

99. Oksana boasted to everyone about her accomplishments but secretly realized that they were not that _____.

A. noteworthy
B. exceptional
C. public
D. humble
E. modest
F. festooned

100. Mr. Hernandez's _____ knowledge dismays debate opponents who expect to find a chink in his intellectual armor.

    A.   unassailable

    B.   questionable

    C.   unchanging

    D.   unimpressive

    E.   irrefutable

    F.   insipid

101. Many of June's coworkers greeted her cordially, even _____, dispelling her fear that she would be unwelcome.

    A.   cursorily

    B.   perfunctorily

    C.   enthusiastically

    D.   subtly

    E.   tentatively

    F.   eagerly

102. In an attempt to attract _____ professionals to the corporation, members of the hiring committee wrote a job ad that featured higher salaries for those with post-graduate degrees.

    A.   responsible

    B.   hard-working

    C.   learned

    D.   apostolic

    E.   well-educated

    F.   explicable

103. Leroy and Aubrey went through a(n) _____ divorce, involving terrible fights over custody, alimony, and child support that resulted in exorbitant legal fees.

    A.   amicable

    B.   acrimonious

    C.   rancorous

    D.   cordial

    E.   abnormal

    F.   incongruent

104. Theater patrons were in _____ violation when they insistently snapped pictures of the actors, despite the publicly announced house rules against this practice.

- A. covert
- B. lucrative
- C. flagrant
- D. brazen
- E. dormant
- F. sage

105. The couple was so _____ by their lottery win that they hardly knew what to say to eager reporters.

- A. dumbfounded
- B. underwhelmed
- C. lanced
- D. disparaged
- E. vexed
- F. bewildered

106. The car accident was something of a(n) _____, since no one could figure out exactly what had happened.

- A. intrusion
- B. enigma
- C. puzzle
- D. absurdity
- E. incongruity
- F. sovereignty

107. Like most people, I don't have a single, _____ identity.

- A. monolithic
- B. fluctuating
- C. mutable
- D. alterable
- E. uniform
- F. indistinct

Answer Key for the Grammar and Usage Diagnostic Test

Sentence Correction – Type 1

1. C	8. B	15. A
2. E	9. C	16. A
3. D	10. A	17. B
4. A	11. D	18. E
5. C	12. C	19. E
6. B	13. A	20. B
7. A	14. E	

Sentence Correction – Type 2

21. D	28. C	35. B
22. A	29. B	36. A
23. B	30. D	37. C
24. C	31. C	38. D
25. D	32. B	39. D
26. D	33. B	40. D
27. D	34. C	

Sentence Correction – Type 3

Passage I	**Passage II**	**Passage III**
41. C	50. A	58. C
42. J	51. F	59. H
43. A	52. A	60. A
44. G	53. H	61. J
45. A	54. C	62. D
46. F	55. J	63. H
47. C	56. C	64. A
48. H	57. H	65. J
49. C		

Improving Paragraphs

Passage I		
66. C	70. C	74. B
67. A	71. E	75. E
68. C		76. D
69. B	**Passage II**	77. B
	72. E	
	73. C	

Sentence/Text Completion

78. A	83. A, E	88. A
79. C, D, I	84. B	89. A, D, I
80. A, E	85. C, E, I	90. C
81. C, F, H	86. B	91. C, F, H
82. C	87. B, F	92. E

Sentence Equivalence

93. C, D	98. B, F	103. B, C
94. A, F	99. A, B	104. C, D
95. B, F	100. A, E	105. A, F
96. D, E	101. C, F	106. B, C
97. B, D	102. C, E	107. A, E

Charting and Analyzing Your Test Results

One of the most important parts of test preparation is understanding why you missed a question so you can reduce your mistakes. Now that you have taken the diagnostic test and checked your answers, carefully tally your errors by marking them in the proper column. Evaluate your results as you look for trends in the types of mistakes you make, and look for low scores in *specific* topic areas. The answers and explanations following these charts will help you to correctly answer these types of questions in the future.

Grammar and Usage Diagnostic Test Analysis Sheet						
Section	Possible	Total Right	Total in Error	Simple Mistake	Misread Question	Lack of Knowledge
Section 1: Sentence Completion Type 1	20					
Section 2: Sentence Completion Type 2	20					
Section 3: Sentence Completion Type 3	25					
Section 4: Improving Paragraphs	12					
Section 5: Sentence/Text Completion	15					
Section 6: Sentence Equivalence	15					
Overall Grammar and Usage Diagnostic Test Results	107					

Diagnostic Test Answers and Explanations

Sentence Correction – Type 1

1. **C.** The gerund *having* should be preceded by the possessive *individual's*.

2. **E.** The sentence is correct as given.

3. **D.** The singular *expenditure* should be followed by the singular *it*, not *them*.

4. **A.** The sentence should begin *Like Faulkner's* or *Like those of Faulkner* to parallel the possessive *Porter's*.

5. **C.** With the correlatives *not . . . but*, an infinitive must follow *but* to be parallel to the infinitive after *not* (*to establish . . . to make*).

6. **B.** The *whom* should be *who*, subject of the clause *who is most likely to win*. The *I think* is parenthetical.

7. **A.** The adverb *almost* should be used to modify the adjective *all*.

8. **B.** The subject *fall* is singular. The correct verb is *has effected*.

9. **C.** The comparison should be between *the number of Irish* and *the number of Italian or Scottish*.

10. **A.** Since the trustees are humans, the pronoun *who*, not *which*, should be used. You might be tempted to choose B, reasoning that the sentence should read *. . . the fund which determines . . .* ; however, this choice would not use appropriate diction, suggesting that *a fund* (an inanimate thing) could *determine*.

11. **D.** The singular *number* is the subject; the verb should be the singular *is*.

12. **C.** The subject is the singular *humor;* the verb should be the singular *derives*.

13. **A.** The singular *Everybody* should be followed by the singular verb *has been*.

14. **E.** The sentence is correct as given.

15. **A.** With the negative *unaffected*, the correlatives should be *either . . . or*.

16. **A.** The compound subject (*performance* and *antics*) requires the plural verb *are*.

17. B. The idiom is *sooner . . . than.*

18. E. The sentence is correct as given.

19. E. The sentence is correct as given.

20. B. The pronoun *this* has no specific antecedent. A phrase like *and it is for this reason that* would correct the sentence.

Sentence Correction – Type 2

21. D. With the phrase *The reason is,* you must use the pronoun *that,* not the conjunction *because.* Choice D is preferable to choice B because of the two present tenses. Choice B shifts from present to past tense.

22. A. The correct idiom is *sooner . . . than.* The past perfect tense in the first clause requires a past tense in the second.

23. B. The sentence is a contrary-to-fact construction requiring a past subjunctive (*had been*) in the *if* clause.

24. C. The possessive *my* must be used with the gerund *speaking.*

25. D. The use of *There are* is verbose. The plural *prevent* agrees with the plural subject *Considerations.*

26. D. Since the subject of the sentence is the singular *one, was* is preferable to *consist of,* which means *to be made up of parts.* Choice D is the most concise version of the sentence, and the singular *was* agrees with the singular subject.

27. D. The sentence must include both *those* and *other,* since the parallel is between aims and since the Society is a group. With *of,* the possessive in choice E is unnecessary.

28. C. In all but choices C and E, the pronoun *she* seems to apply to Janet's mother. Choice E awkwardly separates elements of the sentence.

29. B. With the correlatives *not only . . . but also,* the structure *how he expected to* should be followed by the same structure, *how he planned to.*

30. D. This version contains the correct verb tense, and correctly uses *effect* rather than *affect.*

31. C. In choices B and E, the participle dangles and seems to suggest that the *parents* have graduated from college. In choices A and D, the three parts of the series are not parallel.

32. B. The singular *everyone* requires the singular *believes he or she is.*

Choice A omits the necessary *as* after *good.* Choice C omits the necessary *other.*

33. **B.** Choices C, D, and E are wordy. Choice B is preferable to choice A because it parallels *Learning* and *learning.*

34. **C.** Only choice C presents a clear and logical relationship to the adverbial clause that introduces the sentence.

35. **B.** The pronouns (*which, it, this*) are all ambiguous. Choice B eliminates the ambiguous pronoun.

36. **A.** Choice A avoids the ambiguous pronouns and is the most concise version of the sentence.

37. **C.** With the past tense *wrote,* the first verb should also be in the past tense (*included*). The comparison with three requires *youngest.* Choice D is wordy, and E is incomplete.

38. **D.** Choices A and B have ambiguous pronouns. Choice C should use *your* before the gerund *passing.* Choice E leaves out an important part of the sentence (*the first two*).

39. **D.** The only error in the original is the use of *him* rather than *he. He* is correct when used as the subject of a verb (*he is*). Each of the other choices either preserves this error or makes unnecessary or erroneous additional changes.

40. **D.** Since *innovation* means *something newly introduced,* the use of *new* is unnecessary. The plural *innovations* and *are* are necessary to agree with the plural *theater* and *entertainment.*

Sentence Correction – Type 3

Passage I

41. **C.** The more concise and more idiomatic phrase with *elected* is *to the presidency.*

42. **J.** The *but* signals the change of direction in meaning more clearly than *and.*

43. **A.** Only choice A has no punctuation error.

44. **G.** The past perfect tense is necessary to indicate an action that took place before the past tense of *ran.*

45. **A.** Only choice A is idiomatic.

46. **F.** A new paragraph is necessary. The subject of the second paragraph is Wilson, not Roosevelt. The appositive after *Wilson* (*the Democratic candidate*) requires two commas to set it off.

47. **C.** Only choice C avoids the dangling participle. The subject of the sentence is *Wilson's first term,* not *Wilson.* The sentence as given suggests that the *term* was *known best.*

48. **H.** The *both . . . and* correlatives are used correctly and concisely in choice H.

49. **C.** Choice C provides the most concise expression.

Passage II

50. **A.** Choice A is both idiomatic and more concise than choices C and D. Choice B distorts the meaning.

51. **F.** Choice F is correct and concise. With the apostrophe, *it's* means *it is.*

52. **A.** Choice A uses the verb tenses correctly.

53. **H.** None of the pronouns *it, that,* or *this* can be used here, since there is no specific antecedent to which they refer.

54. **C.** The phrase *So far* is more concise. It should be followed by a comma.

55. **J.** The phrase *much of the* or *much* should precede *cargo; many* should precede *artifacts.*

56. **C.** The plural subject (*copper* and *tin*) requires a plural verb (*were*). Since the action was incomplete, the correct tense is as given in choice C.

57. **H.** The series should be introduced by a colon.

Passage III

58. **C.** With *such, as* rather than *like* must be used. The pronoun *that* is necessary to make both terms of the comparison (*elections . . . that*) similar. Without *that, elections* are compared to a date.

59. **H.** The passage confuses *alternate* (*to take turns*) and *alter* (*to change*). The verb should be *would have.* The use of the preposition *of* as part of the verb is an error arising from the similar sound of *would've,* the contraction of *would have.*

60. **A.** The past perfect tense is correct.

61. J. With the correlatives *not . . . but,* the *by* after *not* should be repeated after *but.*

62. D. The English word is *regardless.* Since *state* is a singular, the plural *their* is an agreement error.

63. H. Since *system* is singular, the verb should be the singular *counts.*

64. A. A past tense (*voted*) and an adverb (*overwhelmingly*) are needed here. Choice B is wordy.

65. J. The present tense of the transitive verb *raise* is required. Its object is *voices.*

Improving Paragraphs
Passage I

66. C. The phrase *this incident* refers to the siege of Troy, which is not described until sentence 6. Of the other answers, choice E might seem like a good one; however, this sentence acts as a conclusion for paragraph 1, rather than as an introduction to paragraph 2.

67. A. Two instances of *Greek* are not redundant, wordy, or biased, and do provide clarity that the sentence requires.

68. C. The underlined phrase does not clearly identify those who are let in as additional Greek soldiers; choice C does so with the term *countrymen.*

69. B. Sentence 7 uses *installation* instead of the correct verb, *installed.* Choice B corrects this and does not include ungrammatical or awkward writing found in the other choices.

70. C. The information given fits paragraph 2, making choices D and E incorrect. However, sentence 10 as written is a run-on sentence, which can be better expressed as two separate sentences.

71. E. The underlined portion contains faulty parallelism, which choice E corrects without unnecessarily altering the sentence further.

Passage II

72. E. This choice is clearest and most correct. The other choices include awkward or ungrammatical sentence structure and usage. The use of *which is* in the original incorrectly indicates that it is the *stalking behavior,* not Edward, that is following her around.

73. **C.** This is more concise than the original, and—unlike the other choices—also expresses the author's idea that the perspective of the *Twilight* critics who find it sexist differs from that of Bella.

74. **B.** The idea that Edward is not willing to give up his life for Bella is inconsistent with the paragraph's conclusion: that Bella and Edward are equals when it comes to self-sacrifice. Thus, Edward must be willing to give up his life for Bella. Choice D makes Edward's willingness to give up his life less personal, and is also less concise.

75. **E.** This is a grammatically correct and concise way of expressing the content of this sentence. Of the other answers, choice C may seem viable; however, it loses the author's intended meaning, which is that our understanding evolves over time.

76. **D.** The sentence's punctuation is already correct; however, *replaced* is the wrong word choice. To *efface* something is to diminish its existence or influence.

77. **B.** This conclusion follows best from the idea that Bella's love for Edward requires her to stretch beyond her usual limits. Of the other answers, choice A appears to say something similar, yet it makes Bella a more passive recipient of change than the essay as a whole intends.

Sentence/Text Completion

78. **A.** *posit . . . significant.* To *posit* is to propose that something is true or the case. There cannot be a universal woman, since women belong to different racial/ethnic, economic, religious, and experiential groups. It is easy to see then that such differences are *significant,* rather than *unnecessary* (choice B) or *non-existent* (choice C).

79. **C, D, I.** *interpreting . . . plenty . . . trying.* To *interpret* a dream is to explain or decode its meaning. It is precisely the opposite of *encoding* (choice A), in which a meaning is abbreviated as, say, a dream symbol. Since blank ii refers to *the good times,* the appropriate answer is *plenty.* *Want* (choice E) and *paucity* (choice F) mean precisely the opposite. A time of famine would certainly not be *affluent* (choice H), which means wealthy or prosperous.

80. **A, E.** *serendipitously . . . antibiotic.* A key word in the first half of the sentence is *unexpectedly.* *Shrewdly* (choice B) and *cannily* (choice C) cannot be the first blank's answers because both suggest deliberation or planning, while *serendipity* occurs when one makes a favorable discovery by accident. The answer to blank ii is *antibiotic* because this

is what we call substances that kill bacteria. The answer cannot be *microorganism* (choice D) because bacteria are a type of microorganism, of which many were already known.

81. **C, F, H.** *material . . . imitation . . . portrayal. Material,* or tangible things are the opposite of *unfathomable* (choice A) and *immaterial* (choice B) ideas such as God. Since the early Greeks defined aesthetics as the study of material things, they would naturally value imitation of the natural world in art, rather than *abstraction* (choice D). Imitation implies accurate *portrayal,* rather than either *enhancement* (choice G) or *diminishment* (choice I).

82. **C.** *mistrust.* Tradition and innovation are antitheses; thus, in a traditional period there would be a *mistrust* of innovation, rather than a *plethora* (choice A) or a *surplus* (choice B), both of which mean excess or abundance.

83. **A, E.** *investigation . . . experiential.* Working from the second blank first, note that *empirical* refers to conclusions based on experience and is therefore a term consistent with *experiential. Empirical* also can denote the nature of an investigation.

84. **B.** *control over . . . reflect.* If each person has no absolute *control over* price-setting activity, we can only hope that a majority of persons will share our shopping habits in such a way that manufacturers set prices to *reflect* this activity.

85. **C, E, I.** *derogatory . . . dulling . . . improvement.* The first sentence suggests that the teachers' negative comments have a corresponding effect on the students, and the term that most logically expresses such an effect is *dulling. Derogatory* means insulting or belittling and also fits the overall negative assessment of teachers' comments. Such negative comments would hinder student *improvement* as well as belief in their abilities.

86. **B.** *practical . . . entail.* The first sentence begins by indicating that theory and practice cannot be separated, suggesting that the blank referring to theory should indicate its *practical* nature; in other words, the first blank requires a synonym for *practice.* Only choice B satisfies this requirement. If practice and theory go hand-in-hand, they *entail,* or require, one another.

87. **B, F.** *inevitable . . . contrast.* Working from the second blank first, note that a difference between two generations is suggested, so the word *contrast* fits well. The emphasis on *change* suggests that this is bound to occur, or be *inevitable.*

88. **A.** *frequently . . . revealed.* In the second sentence the idea that silence means ignorance is not accepted (they are not automatic *partners*). Thus, *intelligence* is not *revealed* through vocal cord use (i.e., speaking *frequently* in class).

89. **A, D, I.** *parrying . . . offensive . . . blunted.* The word *parrying* means warding off or deflecting and contrasts with an *offensive* (attacking) movement. The word *blunted* means rounded or dulled, so a blunted weapon would prevent dangerous injury.

90. **C.** *solemn.* The word *but* tells us that the sentence requires a word that both contrasts with *humor* and complements *stern,* so the only choice is *solemn.*

91. **C, F, H.** *style . . . content . . . cleanly.* We are looking for two words that are comparable to *appearance* and *identity. Appearance* is comparable to *style* (outer characteristics of writing), and *identity* (the "substance" of a person) is comparable to content (the ideas expressed in writing). Emilio complicates Sharon's view, however, by blurring the lines between style and content, and between appearance and identity. In other words, Emilio says, these distinctions cannot be made *cleanly,* that is, without qualifications.

92. **E.** *courage . . . antiheroes.* The terms *heroic* and *courage* are consistent with the term *nobility,* and further, *courage* and *nobility* define the characteristics of someone who is *heroic.* Lead characters that are neither complete scoundrels nor absolute angels are called *antiheroes.*

Sentence Equivalence

93. **C, D.** *hygiene . . . cleanliness. Bristly tongues that scour coats* tells us that cats' grooming habits are being described; thus, *hygiene* and *cleanliness* fit the sentence well. Of the other answers, *aptitude* (choice E) might seem like a possible choice; however, it is too general, and doesn't indicate what kind of aptitude cats are known for. *Panache* (choice F) means flair or style.

94. **A, F.** *hounding . . . harrying.* The words *rather than* suggest that the answers will be words whose meanings are in contrast to negotiating. *Hounding* and *harrying* are done by those who harass or hassle others, so these fit the blank very well. *Conciliating* (choice B) and *interceding* (choice C) have the opposite meanings (resolving differences through dialogue or mediation), and are thus synonyms for negotiating. *Preening* (choice F) means grooming or tidying up.

95. **B, F.** *passivity . . . inaction.* Sleeping is an act of *passivity* or *inaction* with respect to catching the little pig.

96. **D, E.** *obsolete . . . outmoded.* The sentence suggests that machines will replace humans, and both *obsolete* and *outmoded* refer to something that is no longer useful or necessary.

97. **B, D.** *panned . . . disparaged.* Since the moviegoers' action contrasts with that of the critics, we are looking for words that describe a negative critical response. Both *panned* and *disparaged* do this. *Commended* (choice C) and *applauded* (choice E) are antonyms, or opposite terms.

98. **B, F.** *vacillated . . . equivocated.* Those who *vacillate* or *equivocate* can't make up their minds. These words contrast appropriately with *decisive.*

99. **A, B.** *noteworthy . . . exceptional.* The word *but* indicates that Oksana's accomplishments were nothing about which to boast—that is, they were not *noteworthy* (worth taking note of) or *exceptional* (special; out of the ordinary).

100. **A, E.** *unassailable . . . irrefutable.* To find a chink in someone's armor is a figurative way of saying to find a weakness in that person's knowledge. Mr. Hernandez's debate opponents can find no weakness because his knowledge is both *unassailable* and *irrefutable* (impossible to dispute or question). *Questionable* (choice B) has precisely the opposite meaning. *Insipid* (choice F) means bland or trite.

101. **C, F.** *enthusiastically . . . eagerly.* The sentence requires a positive term consistent with the meaning of *cordially. Enthusiastically* and *eagerly* are the appropriate choices.

102. **C, E.** *learned . . . well-educated.* The attainment of a graduate degree indicates higher learning; therefore, *learned* and *well-educated* are the right choices.

103. **B, C.** *acrimonious . . . rancorous. Terrible fights* reveal that the divorce was full of anger and antagonism. Such a divorce could be described as *acrimonious* or *rancorous* (hostile, uncooperative, mean-spirited). *Amicable* (choice A) and *cordial* (choice D) mean friendly or cooperative, and are therefore antonyms.

104. **C, D.** *flagrant . . . brazen.* People who do something *insistently* and *against rules* of which they are clearly aware are in *flagrant* or *brazen* (shameless, obvious) violation of such rules. They are certainly not behaving in a *covert* (choice A), or hidden, manner.

105. **A, F.** *dumbfounded . . . bewildered.* Since the couple is rendered speechless by their good fortune, the correct word choices are *dumbfounded* and *bewildered* (astonished, dazed). We would hardly expect lottery winners to be either *underwhelmed* (choice B), which means unimpressed, or *vexed* (choice E), which means irritated.

106. **B, C.** *enigma . . . puzzle.* An unexplained accident remains an *enigma* or *puzzle* (a mystery, a thing unresolved).

107. **A, E.** *monolithic . . . uniform.* *Monolithic* and *uniform* are both synonyms for *single.* All other choices are antonyms. *Indistinct* (choice F) means blurry or vague.

Chapter 3

Grammar and Usage Review

The topics that will help guide your understanding of grammar and usage are below.

As you read through the topics with examples in this chapter, you should improve your ability to avoid some of the common departures from the conventions of standard written English. Research shows that repeated and structured practice is a key to your success on standardized tests, so be sure to take advantage of the practice exercises at the end of each topic area and to take the Grammar and Usage Review Test at the end of this chapter on p. 151.

Grammar and Usage Topics			
Section	Topic	Review Page Number	Review Checklist
Section 1	**Basic Parts of Speech**	pp. 75-80	❏ Basic Parts of Speech ❏ Adjectives and Adverbs ❏ Linking Verbs ❏ Comparatives & Superlatives
Section 2	**Case**	pp. 80-87	❏ Subject and Object Errors ❏ Pronouns in Apposition ❏ Who and Whom ❏ Possessive Errors
Section 3	**Agreement**	pp. 87-95	❏ Subject and Verb Agreement ❏ Pronoun Agreement
Section 4	**Verbs**	pp. 95-104	❏ Verb Tenses ❏ Subjunctives ❏ Lie/Lay, Rise/Raise, Sit/Set
Section 5	**Misplaced Parts and Dangling Modifiers**	pp. 105-112	❏ Dangling Modifiers ❏ Participles ❏ Gerunds ❏ Infinitives ❏ Prepositional Phrases and Elliptical Clauses
Section 6	**Parallelism**	pp. 112-120	❏ Shifts in Verb Tenses ❏ Shifts from Active to Passive ❏ Shifts in Person ❏ Errors in a List or Series ❏ Errors in Correlatives

continued

Section	Topic	Review Page Number	Review Checklist
Section 7	**Ambiguous Pronouns**	pp. 120-122	❏ Ambiguous Pronouns
Section 8	**Other Errors of Grammar**	pp. 122-131	❏ Sentence Fragments ❏ Double Negatives ❏ Omission of Necessary Words ❏ Direct and Indirect Questions ❏ Like and As ❏ Who, Which, and That—Restrictive and Nonrestrictive Clauses
Section 9	**Errors of Diction, Idiom, and Style**	pp. 132-139	❏ Fewer/Less, Many/Much, Number/Amount ❏ Between/Among ❏ Affect/Effect ❏ Idiom ❏ Style
Section 10	**Punctuation**	pp. 140-148	❏ Comma ❏ Semicolon ❏ Colon ❏ Dash ❏ Apostrophe
Review	**Vocabulary Skills Review**	pp. 149-151	❏ Prefixes ❏ Suffixes ❏ Roots

Introduction to Grammar and Usage Review

None of the multiple-choice verbal ability tests will ask a test-taker to explain a dangling participle or to pick out the adjectives and adverbs in a sentence. But to make the best use of this book, it will be useful to know the meaning of several of the more important grammatical terms, and to recognize their distinctive features. With this information, you will be better able to tell a noun from a verb and an adverb from an adjective. Most of the tests ask you either to find an error in a sentence or to recognize that a sentence is correct. For example, one of the most common types of questions will ask if the following sentence is correct and, if not, which underlined part contains an error.

Example:

<u>Freshened</u> by rain <u>that fell</u> during the night, the garden smelled
   A   B

<u>fragrantly</u> and <u>glistened brightly</u>. <u>No error.</u>
  C   D   E

Faced with this question, most students will see that the problem is in the word *fragrantly*. Should it be *fragrantly* or *fragrant?* (In fact, it should be *fragrant.*) Even when you ask those who rightly select choice C as the error why they picked choice C instead of choice D, the usual answer is C sounds wrong, and D sounds right. Sometimes we have to depend on the it-sounds-right/ it-sounds-wrong approach. But most of the time this method will not work. To perform well on tests of standard written English, you must be able to see what grammatical question the test is really asking.

In the example above, the real issue is not which sounds better—*smelled fragrant* or *smelled fragrantly*—but whether we use an adverb or an adjective with the verb *smelled*. And so we have to begin at the beginning—with a review of the parts of speech on which questions will be based.

Practice Exercises: Charting and Analyzing Your Results

As you work through the practice exercises that follow each topic area in the Grammar and Usage Review, use the chart below to identify your strengths, as well as areas that need improvement. Once you complete all ten practice exercises, evaluate your results as you look for patterns in the types of errors you make, and look for low scores in *specific* topic areas. One of the most important parts of test preparation is analyzing why you missed a question so you can reduce the number of mistakes on the actual exam.

Practice Exercise Analysis Sheet						
Section	Possible	Total Correct	Total in Error	Simple Mistake	Misread Question	Lack of Knowledge
Section 1: Basic Parts of Speech	15					
Section 2: Case – Part A Section 2: Case – Part B	10 10					
Section 3: Agreement	20					
Section 4: Verbs	16					
Section 5: Misplaced Parts and Dangling Modifiers	12					
Section 6: Parallelism	15					
Section 7: Ambiguous Pronouns	8					
Section 8: Other Errors of Grammar – Part A	5					
Section 8: Other Errors of Grammar – Part B	20					
Section 9: Errors of Diction, Idiom, and Style – Part A	8					
Section 9: Errors of Diction, Idiom, and Style – Part B	10					
Section 10: Punctuation	9					
Overall Grammar and Usage Test Results	158					

Section 1: Basic Parts of Speech

Basic Parts of Speech	Definition	Examples
Noun	a word used as a person, a place, or a thing	woman, boy, hope, Boston, car, noun
Pronoun	a word used as a substitute for a noun	I, you, he, she, it, me, him, her, we, they, who, whom, which, what, this, that, one, none, someone, somebody, myself, anything, nothing
Verb	a word used to assert action or state of being	kill, eat, is, are, remain, think, study, become
Adjective	A word used to modify a noun or pronoun. To modify is to describe, to qualify, or to limit or restrict in meaning. In the phrase *a large, red barn*, both *large* and *red* are adjectives that modify the noun *barn*.	loud, quiet, hot, cold, old, new, red
Adverb	A word used to modify a verb, an adjective, or another adverb. In the phrase *to eat a very large meal very slowly*, *very* and *slowly* are adverbs. The first *very* modifies an adjective *(large)*, the second modifies an adverb *(slowly)*, and *slowly* modifies the verb *(eat)*.	very, rather, quickly, quite, easily, hopelessly
Conjunction	a connector that links two words, phrases, or clauses	Coordinating conjunctions: and, but, for, or, yet Correlative conjunctions: either . . . or, not only . . . but also, both . . . and Subordinating conjunctions: after, although, before, since, unless, while
Preposition	a word that indicates a logical, temporal, or spatial relationship with its object	over, under, above, below, to, for, in, with

Adjectives and Adverbs

A common error in the sentences on the exams is the misuse of an adjective or an adverb. Adjectives modify nouns and pronouns; adverbs modify verbs, adjectives, and other adverbs. Errors occur when an adjective is used to do an adverb's job or an adverb to do an adjective's.

Example:

Which of the following sentences have adjective or adverb errors?

1. As the debate progressed, the defenders of tax reform grew more and more excited.
2. As the debate progressed, the defenders of tax reform spoke more and more excited.
3. Asleep awkwardly on his side, the man snored noisily enough to shake the bedroom.
4. Lying awkward on his side, the sleeper snored loudly enough to shake the bedroom.

Sentences 1 and 3 are correct. Sentences 2 and 4 have adjective/adverb errors. In Sentence 1, the adjective *excited* correctly modifies the noun *defenders.* In sentence 2, the adjective *excited* incorrectly modifies the verb *spoke,* describing how they spoke. It should instead be the adverb *excitedly* (many words that end with *-ly* are adverbs). The adjective *excited* is correct in the first sentence because it modifies the noun *defenders,* not the verb *grew.* In sentence 3, the adverb *awkwardly* is properly used to modify the adjective *asleep,* and the adverb *noisily* is used correctly to modify the verb *snored.* Sentence 4 correctly uses the adverb *loudly* but mistakenly uses the adjective *awkward* to modify the verbal adjective *lying.*

Be careful not to confuse *most* and *almost. Most* is an adjective, related to *much* or *many,* as in *most children like ice cream,* but *most* may be used as an adverb to modify another adjective or adverb as in *most beautiful* or *most quickly. Almost* is an adverb meaning *nearly.* You can write *most people* or *most men,* but you must write *almost every person* or *almost all men.* A phrase such as *most every person* or *most all men* is incorrect because the adjective *most* cannot modify the adjectives *every* or *all.*

Linking Verbs

It is easy enough to remember that adjectives modify nouns and adverbs modify adjectives, verbs, and other adverbs. The hard part is deciding which word the adjective or adverb modifies. Why must we say *the defenders grew more and more excited* when we also must say *the defenders spoke more and more excitedly?* We do so because there are a number of verbs, called *linking verbs* that express a state of being rather than an action. These verbs are followed by an adjective, not an adverb. The most common linking verb is the verb *to be* in all its forms (for example: *am, is, are, was, were*). Many other linking verbs are equivalent in meaning to the verb *to be,* including:

to seem   *to become*   *to remain*   *to appear*

In addition, the verbs *to feel, to taste, to smell,* and *to look* are usually linking verbs and will be followed by an adjective rather than an adverb.

"To be" verbs can also be followed by a noun, forming a predicate nominative.

Examples:

Barack Obama was elected President.

The caterpillar became a butterfly.

In each of the sentences below, the adjective modifies the noun or pronoun subject of the sentence.

Examples:

I am sad.   The cloth feels soft.

She became sad.   The food tastes bad.

They remain happy.   The garden smells sweet.

He appears happy.

When you see a linking verb in a sentence on an exam, be alert to the possibility of an adverb-for-adjective error. But do not assume that the verbs on this list will never have adverbial modifiers.

Examples:

The detective looks *carefully* at the footprints.

The butler looks *suspicious.*

The detective looks *suspiciously* at the butler.

As these sentences illustrate, *looks* may or may not be a linking verb. If the verb expresses an action rather than describes a state, and the modifier describes that action, use an adverb. In sentence 2, the butler is not taking action; rather, *looks* expresses the butler's state of being.

Comparatives and Superlatives

Adjectives and adverbs have three forms: positive (*quick, quickly*), comparative (*quicker, more quickly*), and superlative (*quickest, most quickly*). Many comparatives and superlatives are formed by adding -*er* and -*est* to the adjective stem, though some words (*good, better, best; well, better, best*) change altogether, and some simply add *more* or *most* (*eager, more eager, most eager; quickly, more quickly, most quickly*).

When it is clear that only two are compared, use a comparative, not a superlative. When the comparison involves more than two, use a superlative.

Examples:

> Compared to Smith, Jones is *richer.* (comparative)
>
> Of all the oil-producing countries, Saudi Arabia is the *richest.* (superlative)
>
> Of the two finalists, Smith hits *harder.*
>
> Of the eight boxers, Jones hits *hardest.*
>
> Of the eight boxers, Jones hits *harder* than Smith, but Williams hits *hardest* of all.

Practice Exercise 1: Basic Parts of Speech

Choose the correct form in each of the following sentences.

1. (Most, Almost) every person in the stadium was wearing an orange cap.

2. After $2,500 worth of cosmetic surgery, she appears quite (different, differently) from the woman we had known.

3. The ship appeared (sudden, suddenly) out of the fog.

4. Of all the players in the tournament, Smith has the (better, best) volley.

5. Of the two finalists, Jones has the (better, best) serve.

6. The pie tasted so (bad, badly) that he left the piece uneaten.

7. Dickens has a (noticeable, noticeably) more inventive imagination than Gaskell.

8. I feel (sad, sadly) about his losing so much money on the lottery.

9. It is impossible to take his claims (serious, seriously).

10. The forest smells most (aromatic, aromatically) when the wind is from the south.

11. I don't believe him (most, almost) any time he talks about money.

12. If you look very (careful, carefully), the scratches on the car are (clear, clearly) visible.

13. The eland is the (larger, largest) of all of the antelopes but not the (slower, slowest).

14. Early in the century, the supply of bison (sure, surely) seemed (inexhaustible, inexhaustibly).

15. From a distance, the hill appears to rise (steep, steeply), but it does not look (steep, steeply) from here.

Answers – Practice Exercise 1: Basic Parts of Speech

1. *almost*—an adverb, modifying the adjective *every*

2. *different*—an adjective, with the linking verb *appears*

3. *suddenly*—an adverb, modifying *appeared*. In this sentence, *appeared* means *made an appearance* rather than *looked* and is not a linking verb.

4. *best*—the superlative. There are more than two players.

5. *better*—the comparative, with only two compared

6. *bad*—an adjective, modifying *pie*. *Tasted* here is a linking verb.

7. *noticeably*—an adverb, modifying the adverb *more*

8. *sad*—an adjective, with the linking verb *feel*

9. *seriously*—an adverb, modifying the verb *take*

10. *aromatic*—an adjective, with the linking verb *smells*

11. *almost*—an adverb, modifying the adjective *any*

12. *carefully*—an adverb. In this sentence *look* means *examine* not *appear* and is not a linking verb.

    clearly—an adverb, modifying the adjective *visible*

13. *largest*—the superlative. There are many antelopes.

    slowest—the superlative. Again, there are more than two.

14. *surely*—an adverb, modifying the verb *seemed*

    inexhaustible—an adjective, modifying the noun *supply*

    seemed is a linking verb.

15. *steeply*—an adverb, modifying the verb *rise*

    steep—an adjective, modifying the pronoun *it,* with the linking verb *look*

Section 2: Case

Case refers to the way in which a word or phrase functions in a sentence.

Subject and Object Errors

Nouns and pronouns in English may be used as *subjects* (The *garden* is large. *I* am tired.), as *objects* (David weeded the *garden*. David hit *him*.), and as *possessors* (*David's* garden is large. *His* arm is broken.). Nouns and pronouns, then, have a subjective case, an objective case, and a possessive case.

Since the form of a noun in the subjective case is no different from the form of the same noun in the objective case (The *bat* hit the *ball*. The *ball* hit the *bat*.), errors of case are not a problem with nouns. But several pronouns have different forms as subjects and objects.

Subject	Object
I	me
he	him
she	her
we	us
they	them
who	whom
whoever	whomever

Where are the errors of case (confusions of the subjective and objective form of the pronoun) in the following sentences?

1. I am going to the play with her.
2. Me and her are going to the games.
3. The committee gave prizes to my brother, my sister, and I.
4. For we Americans, July fourth is a special day.
5. Mary invited my cousin, her sister, a friend from New York, and I to the party.

Sentence 1 is correct, but there are case errors in sentences 2, 3, 4, and 5. In sentence 2, *me* and *her,* the subjects of the sentence, should be *I* and *she* (or better, *She* and *I*). In sentence 3, *I* should be *me,* the object of the preposition *to,* and in sentence 4, *we* should be *us,* the object of the preposition *for.* In sentence 5, *I* should be *me,* the object of the verb *invited.* It would be easy to spot the error if the sentences simply said, *The committee gave prizes to I,* or *Mary invited I,* but when the sentence contains elements that separate the verb or the preposition from the pronoun object, it becomes harder to see the error at once. The question writers know this fact and exploit it in all exams. When you see a compound subject or object (that is, two or more subjects or objects joined by *and*), look carefully at the case of the pronouns. Imagine how the sentence would read with just the pronoun (*Mary invited I*).

Pronouns in Apposition

An *appositive* is a word, phrase, or clause in apposition—that is, placed next to another so that the second explains the first.

> Margaret, my sister, and my oldest brother, Hugh, are in New York.

In this sentence, *sister* is in apposition to *Margaret* and *Hugh* is in apposition to *brother.* A pronoun in apposition is in the same case as the noun or pronoun to which it is in apposition. Thus in a sentence such as *The outfielders, Jack, Joe, and I, are ready to play,* the *I,* which is in apposition to the subject *outfielders,* is subjective. But in a sentence such as *The class elected three representatives, Jack, Joe, and me,* the objective *me* is correct because it is in apposition to *representatives,* which is the object of the verb *elected.*

Who and Whom

The demons of case are *who* and *whom.* Your test may not ask you to choose between them at all, but it also may do so more than once. If you understand how to deal with *who* and *whom,* questions about the case of other pronouns should give you no trouble. The problem is always the same: Is the pronoun a subject or an object? Is it *I, he, she, who* or *me, him, her, whom?*

Use *who* for a subject, *whom* for an object:

> *Who* is going to the store? (subject of sentence)
>
> With *whom* are you going? (object of preposition *with*)
>
> *Whom* did they choose? (object of verb *choose; they* is the subject of the sentence)

If you have trouble with sentences that are questions, it may help to rephrase the sentence as a statement:

> You are going with whom.
>
> They did choose whom.

And it may also help if you substitute *he/him* for *who/whom.*

> *He* is going to the store.
>
> Are you going with *him?*
>
> Did they choose *him?*

Before going on to tougher examples of *who* and *whom,* we need to define three more terms: *clause, independent clause,* and *dependent clause.* A *clause* is a group of related words containing a verb and its subject. An *independent clause* can stand by itself as a sentence. A *dependent clause,* though it has a subject and a verb, cannot stand by itself as a complete sentence.

> I spoke. (one independent clause with a subject and a verb)
>
> I spoke and she listened. (two independent clauses—*I spoke/she listened* could be complete sentences)
>
> I spoke while she listened. (one independent clause—*I spoke*—and one dependent clause—*while she listened*—which, though it has a subject and a verb, is not a complete sentence due to *while*)
>
> The girl who is dressed in red is rich. (one independent clause—*The girl . . . is rich*—and one dependent clause—*who is dressed in red*)

The easier questions involving *who* and *whom* occur in sentences with only one clause. In sentences with more than one clause, the case of the pronoun (*who* or *whom*) is determined by its use in its own clause. Before you can decide between *who* and *whom,* you must be able to isolate the clause in which the pronoun appears.

Examples:

1. He will give the book to whoever wants it.
2. He will give the book to whomever Jane chooses.
3. He will give the prize to whoever deserves it.
4. He will give the prize to whomever he likes.

In sentence 1, there are two clauses: *He will give the book to* and *whoever wants it.* The whole second clause (*whoever wants it*), not the pronoun *whoever,* is the object of the preposition. In this second clause, *whoever* is the subject, *wants* is the verb, and *it* is the object. If you find this sort of sentence difficult, isolate the clause and substitute *he/him* for *who/whom* or *whoever/whomever.* Here, *he wants it* should be easy to recognize as preferable to *him wants it.*

In sentence 2, there are again two clauses: *He will give the book to* and *whomever Jane chooses.* Again, the whole clause is the object of the preposition, but the subject of the second clause is *Jane,* the verb is *chooses,* and *whomever* is the object of the verb *chooses.* (Jane chooses *him,* not Jane chooses *he.*) Sentences 3 and 4 follow the same principles. In sentence 3, *whoever* is the subject of the second clause; in sentence 4, *he* is the subject and *whomever* is the object of *likes.*

Remember that *whom* by itself is the object of a preposition like *to* (*to whom* did he give the book?), but in this sentence there is only *one* clause.

There is one more complication. You will sometimes find sentences in which a parenthetical expression occurs with the *who/whom* clause. Phrases like *I think, we know, they believe, he supposes, they say,* and *one imagines* are, in fact, independent clauses and do not affect the case of *who/whom* in a separate clause.

Examples:

1. He is a man who I think should be in prison.
2. He is a man, one assumes, who is sick.
3. Her husband is a man whom I think she has misunderstood.
4. He is a student whom we know the teachers dislike.
5. They will pay a large fee to whoever they decide is most qualified.

All of these sentences have three, not two, clauses. When deciding on the case of *who* or *whom,* pay no attention to the parenthetical phrases *I think, one assumes,* and *we know.* The *who/whom* clauses are *who should be in prison, who is sick, whom she has misunderstood,* and *whom the teachers dislike.* In the first two, *who* is the subject. In sentences 3 and 4, *whom* is the object of the verbs *has misunderstood* and *dislike.* There are two traps in sentence 5, the preposition *to* and the phrase *they decide,* but the clause is *whoever is most qualified.* The whole clause is the object of the preposition *to,* and *they decide* is a separate clause. Therefore, it must be *whoever* (*he* is most qualified) because *whoever* is the subject of the clause.

Possessive Errors

The third case of English nouns and pronouns is the possessive, which is used, logically enough, to show possession: *my, your, his, her, its, our, their, whose.* Remember that the possessive form of the pronoun *it* is *its* without an apostrophe. With the apostrophe, *it's* is a contraction and means *it is.* Remember, too, that *their* is the possessive form of the pronoun *they,* while *there* is an adverb meaning *in that place.*

As a rule, use the possessive case before a gerund, that is, a verb used as a noun. Gerunds are formed by adding *-ing* to verb stems: *going, eating, writing, borrowing.* Like nouns, they are used as both subjects and objects.

Examples:

1. I don't like my brother's borrowing so much money.
2. I don't mind his eating so much ice cream.
3. I don't approve of his driving with such worn-out tires.
4. I recommend his seeing a doctor.

In these sentences, *borrowing, eating, driving,* and *seeing* are gerunds preceded by possessive forms. If the first sentence had said *brother* rather than *brother's,* it would seem to say *I don't like my brother* rather than *I don't like his borrowing so much.* Similarly, if sentence 2, 3, or 4 had used *him* instead of *his,* the meaning of the sentences would be changed. If an exam question offers you a choice between a possessive and an objective pronoun before a gerund, look carefully at what the sentence is saying. It is likely that the possessive is the better choice.

Practice Exercise 2: Case

Choose the correct form in each of the following sentences.

Part A

1. The study suggests that (we, us) New Englanders are not practical.

2. Everybody at the table chose steak except Tom and (I, me).

3. I don't mind (him, his) using the car.

4. It was (I, me) who telephoned the fire department.

5. Why does he object to (us, our) standing here?

6. It is difficult to imagine how such an invention will affect you and (I, me).

7. Let's you and (I, me) invest together in this project.

8. I'm going to complain about (him, his) talking so loudly.

9. The Secret Service is worried about the (president, president's) riding in an open car.

10. They will award the trophy to one of the finalists, either Jack or (I, me).

Part B

1. The woman (who, whom) was recently elected to the board of directors has been with the company for some years.

2. The accountant (who, whom) we understand did not wish to be interviewed has been asked to appear at the trial.

3. (Who, Whom) do you suppose will buy this car?

4. (Who, Whom) do you suppose the company will choose?

5. Let me speak to (whoever, whomever) is waiting for the general.

6. Let me speak to (whoever, whomever) the general hopes to convince to join his campaign.

7. (Whoever, Whomever) I think deserves the prize always seems to lose.

8. They will give the job to (whoever, whomever) they decide is most likely to support their position.

9. They will give the job to (whoever, whomever) they decide they can agree with about prices.

10. Do you really care about (who, whom) you choose?

Answers – Practice Exercise 2: Case

Part A

1. *we*—subject of the clause *we are not*

2. *me*—object of the preposition *except*

3. *his*—possessive, before the gerund *using*

4. *I*—subjective case, agreeing with the subject *it*

5. *our*—possessive, before the gerund *standing*

6. *me*—object of the verb *affect*

7. *me*—objective case, in apposition to the objective *us* (*Let's = Let us*)

8. *his*—possessive, before the gerund *talking*

9. *president's*—possessive, before the gerund *riding*

10. *me*—objective case, in apposition to *finalists,* the object of the preposition

Part B

1. *who*—subject of the clause *who was elected*

2. *who*—subject of the clause *who did not wish to be interviewed.* The *we understand* is parenthetical.

3. *Who*—subject of the clause *Who will buy this car*

4. *Whom*—object of the verb *will choose.* The subject of the clause is *company.*

5. *whoever*—subject of the clause *is waiting for the general*

6. *whomever*—object of the verb *convince*

7. *Whoever*—subject of the clause *deserves the prize*

8. *whoever*—subject of the clause *is most likely to support their position*

9. *whomever*—object of the preposition *with*

10. *whom*—object of the verb *choose*

Section 3: Agreement

An agreement error is the faulty combination of a singular and a plural. Agreement errors occur between subjects and verbs, between pronouns and their *antecedents* (the word, phrase, or clause to which a pronoun refers), and between two nouns.

Subject and Verb Agreement

Use a singular verb with a singular subject and a plural verb with a plural subject. The key to seeing errors of subject-verb agreement is identifying the subject correctly. Often, the sentences will try to mislead you by separating the subject and verb.

Examples:

1. The *sound* is beautiful. (singular subject/singular verb)

2. The *number seems* to increase. (singular subject/singular verb)

3. The *sound* of birds singing and crickets chirping all about the sunlit lakes and woods is beautiful. (singular subject/singular verb)

4. The *number* of boats pulling water skiers on the lakes *seems* to increase every summer. (singular subject/singular verb)

Sentences 1 and 2 here are easy, but in sentences 3 and 4, the plurals that come between the singular subjects and the verbs may make the reader forget that the verbs must be singular to agree with the singular subjects.

In sentences where there are two or more subjects joined by *and,* use a plural verb. Do not confuse compound subjects (two subjects joined by *and*) with prepositional or parenthetical phrases introduced by such words or phrases as *with, as well as, in addition to, along with, in the company of, not to mention,* and the like. A singular subject followed by a phrase of this sort still takes a singular verb.

Examples:

1. The actress and the director *are* in the dressing room.
2. The chairman of ExxonMobil, as well as the president of Texaco and the vice president of Chevron, *is* attending the meeting.
3. The fullback, accompanied by two ends, two guards, and the 340-pound tackle, *is* leaving the field.
4. The conductor, with his 125-piece orchestra, two small brass bands, and the Mormon Tabernacle Choir, *is* ready to begin the concert.

In sentence 1, there are two subjects (*actress* and *director*) joined by *and,* so the verb is plural. But in sentences 2, 3, and 4, the subject is singular (*chairman, fullback, conductor*), and all the plurals that intervene between the subject and the verb do not change the rule that the verb must be singular to agree with the singular subject.

Two singular subjects joined by *and* (a compound subject) must have a plural verb, but two singular subjects joined by *or, nor, either . . . or,* or *neither . . . nor* take singular verbs.

Examples:

> Mary *and* Jill *are* in the play.
> Mary *or* Jill *is* in the play.
> *Neither* Mary *nor* Jill *is* in the play.

In sentences with *either . . . or, neither . . . nor,* if one subject is singular and one is plural, the verb agrees with the subject nearer the verb.

Examples:

1. Neither the hunter nor the *rangers are* in sight.
2. Neither the rangers nor the *hunter is* in sight.
3. Either the dog or the *cats are* in the yard.
4. Either the cats or the *dog is* in the yard.

In sentences 1 and 3, the subjects nearer the verb are the plurals *rangers* and *cats,* so the verb is plural. In sentences 2 and 4, the singular subject is nearer the verb, and the verb is singular.

When the following words are used as subjects, use a singular verb: *anyone, anybody, anything, someone, something, everyone, everybody, everything, no one, nobody, nothing, either, neither, each, another, many a.*

Examples:

> *Everyone* in the class of six hundred students *is* going on the field trip.
>
> *Everybody* in the four western states *is* concerned about the election.
>
> *Either* of the answers *is* correct.
>
> *Neither* of the teams *has* won a game.
>
> *Each* of the contestants *has* won a prize.
>
> *Many a* man *has* gone astray.

Notice that many of these sentences begin with a singular subject followed by a prepositional phrase with plurals. The exam sentences will often use this structure to test whether the plurals in the prepositional phrase will distract you from the real point—that the subject is singular. The sentences on the exam may be much longer than these examples so that the verb is even farther away from the singular subject.

Example:

> *Everybody* in the crowded shopping center, in the food stores, and in the specialty shops, as well as those who filled the department stores down the street, *was* looking for bargains.

When the subject is *none,* and the meaning is *not one* or *no one else,* use a singular verb. In some instances, the rest of the sentence will make it clear that the plural is more appropriate, but it is more likely that a sentence on the exam that uses *none* as the subject is testing your ability to see that *none* is usually singular.

Examples:

1. None of the players *is* ready.
2. None of the twenty-two starting players on the two teams *is* ready.
3. None *is* so foolish as a man who will not listen to advice.
4. None *are* so foolish as men who will not listen to advice.

In the first three examples, *none* means *no one* and the verb is singular. In sentence 4, the plural *men* makes it clear that *none* must also be a plural.

Collective nouns like *jury, team, orchestra, crowd,* and *family*—that is, nouns in which a singular form denotes a collection of individuals—usually take a singular verb. If the collection is thought of as a whole (*the jury is deliberating*), the verb is singular. If the sentence makes it clear that the members are thought of as acting separately, the verb is plural (*my family have settled in five different states*).

Watch carefully for agreement errors in sentences with the phrases *the number* or *a number* as subjects. *The number* is singular, but it is likely to be followed by a prepositional phrase with plurals. So long as *the number* is the subject, use a singular verb.

Examples:

> *The number* of bugs in my gardens and lawns *is* enormous.
>
> *The number* of tests in my classes this semester *is* larger than last year's.
>
> *The number* of people killed every year in highway accidents, drownings, and airplane crashes *has* increased every year since 1942.

A number can take either a singular or plural verb. Use a plural when *a number* means *many.*

Examples:

1. *A number* of tests *are* given in this class.
2. *A number* of bugs *are* crawling on my roses.
3. *A number* of theories to account for the high incidence of lung disease *have* been discussed in the study.
4. *A number* that many people consider to be unlucky *is* thirteen.

In the first three examples, *a number* means *many* and the verbs are plural. In sentence 4, *a number* refers to one number (thirteen), and the verb is singular.

Be wary of nouns based on Latin and Greek that form their plurals with *a* at the end. *Criteria* is a plural (one criterion, two criteria) as are *data* (one datum), *phenomena* (one phenomenon), and *media* (one medium).

Examples:

> The media *are* guilty of sensationalism.
>
> The criteria for admission *are* listed in the catalog.

The tests can include agreement errors in sentences in which the verb precedes the subject, often by using an opening of *There is* or *There are.*

Examples:

> There are hidden away in a lonely house out on the heath a brother and sister living alone.
>
> There is in London and New York newspapers a self-satisfaction not found in the papers of smaller cities.

Both of these sentences are correct, though it would be easy to miss the agreement error if the first had used *is* and the second, *are.* Do not let the singular nouns in the prepositional phrases in the first sentence or the plurals in the second distract you from finding the subjects of the verbs—the compound subject *brother and sister* in the first and the singular *self-satisfaction* in the second. The test writer's technique here is like that in those sentences that pile up plurals between a singular subject at the beginning of the sentence and the verb at the end. But in this case, the verb comes first.

Pronoun Agreement

Since personal pronouns have distinctive singular and plural forms (*he/ they, his/their, him/them*), pronoun agreement errors are as common as noun-verb agreement errors. The number (that is, singular or plural) of a pronoun is determined by its *antecedent* (the word, phrase, or clause to which it refers), and pronouns must agree in number with their antecedents. Most of the rules that apply to the agreement of nouns and verbs also apply to the agreement of pronouns and their antecedents.

Examples:

1. The *workers* finished *their* job on time.
2. The *group* of workers finished *its* job on time.
3. The *men* earn *their* money.
4. The *man* earns *his* money.
5. The *men* who earn *their* money are tired.

In sentence 1 here, the plural *their* agrees with the plural *workers*. In sentence 2, the singular *its* agrees with the singular subject, the collective noun *group*. In sentences 3 and 4, the antecedents are *men* and *man,* so the pronouns are *their* and *his.* In sentence 5, the antecedent to the pronoun *their* is *who.* To determine whether *who* is singular or plural, we must look at its antecedent. In this sentence, it is the plural *men.*

In the subject-verb agreement questions, as long as you know whether the subject is singular or plural, you should have no trouble. In pronoun agreement questions, you must know which word is the antecedent of the pronoun and whether that word is singular or plural. As the following sentences will demonstrate, these questions are more difficult.

> Rosen is the only one of the five American musicians *who have entered* the competition *who is* likely to win a medal.
>
> The leader of the senators *who are* gathered to discuss the tax on oil is the only one *who represents* an oil-producing state.

In the first sentence, the antecedent of the first *who* is the plural *musicians.* Therefore, *who* is plural and the correct verb is *have.* But the antecedent of the second *who* is *one* (and the antecedent of *one* is *Rosen*), and so the verb in this clause must be the singular *is.* In the second sentence, the antecedent of the first *who* is the plural *senators* (thus, *are*) while the antecedent of the second *who* is the singular *one* (thus, *represents* not *represent*).

Use a singular pronoun when the antecedent is *anyone, anybody, anything, someone, somebody, something, everyone, everybody, everything, no one, nobody, either, neither, each, another, one, person, man, woman, kind,* and *sort.*

Examples:

> *None* of the girls in the class finished *her* assignment on time.
>
> *Everybody* on the men's team has *his* weaknesses.
>
> *Neither* of the women paid *her* bills.
>
> *Each* of the boys ate *his* ice cream.
>
> *One* of the twenty men in the upper balcony dropped *his* program into the orchestra.

When two or more antecedents are joined by *or* or *nor,* the pronoun should agree with the nearer antecedent.

Examples:

> Neither the mother nor the *daughters* brought *their* cars.
>
> Neither the daughters nor the *mother* brought *her* car.

Noun agreement is necessary when a noun should be similar in number to an antecedent noun.

Examples:

> The employees in the Community Relations department donated their paychecks to charity.

The correct word here is *paychecks,* not *paycheck*.

Practice Exercise 3: Agreement

Choose the correct form in each of the following sentences.

1. None of the candidates who (is, are) campaigning in New Hampshire (is, are) willing to speak to that organization.

2. Either the general or the sergeant-at-arms (is, are) responsible for greeting the new Greek minister.

3. None of the applicants who (has, have) failed to submit photographs (is, are) likely to be called for an interview.

4. Mr. Lombardi, as well as his wife and three children, (was, were) found before midnight.

5. The newly discovered evidence, together with the confirming testimony of three eyewitnesses, (make, makes) his conviction certain.

6. The criteria for admission to Yale Law School in New Haven (includes, include) a score above 170 on the LSAT.

7. Precise and symmetrical, the basalt columns of the Devil's Postpile in the Sierras (looks, look) as if (it, they) had been sculpted in an artist's studio.

8. Neither the teacher nor the student (is, are) in the classroom.

9. Mr. and Mrs. Smith, in addition to their four children, (is, are) vacationing in Orlando.

10. Jack is one of eight quarter-milers who (has, have) reached the final heat.

11. The number of penguins that (is, are) killed by DDT (increases, increase) each year.

12. Either Harry or Mary Jane (is, are) going to Detroit.

13. Everyone in the theater, filled with more than six hundred people, (was, were) bored.

14. Neither Sally nor the twins (has, have) finished (her, their) practice teaching.

15. Neither Louisa nor Sally (has, have) finished (her, their) practice teaching.

16. Neither she nor I (was, were) dancing, for we felt tired.

17. The President, no less than all the other members of the First Family, (enjoy, enjoys) bowling.

18. The number of books about corruption in the government written by participants in the Watergate affair (seem, seems) to grow larger every month.

19. A number of the books about Watergate (has, have) been translated into Russian.

20. The data used in determining your federal tax (is, are) to be submitted with your letter of appeal.

Answers – Practice Exercise 3: Agreement

1. *are, is*—The antecedent of *who* is the plural *candidates;* the subject of *is* is the singular *None.*

2. *is*—For two singular subjects joined by *or,* the verb should be singular.

3. *have, is*—The antecedent of *who* is the plural *applicants;* the subject of *is* is the singular *None.*

4. *was*—The subject is the singular *Mr. Lombardi.*

5. *makes*—The subject is the singular *evidence.*

6. *include*—The subject is the plural *criteria.*

7. *look, they*—The subject is the plural *columns,* which is also the antecedent of *they.*

8. *is*—For two singular subjects joined by *nor,* the verb should be singular.

9. *are*—The subject is compound, *Mr. and Mrs. Smith.*

10. *have*—The antecedent of *who* is *quarter-milers.*

11. *are, increases*—The antecedent of *that* is the plural *penguins;* the subject of *increases* is the singular *number.*

12. *is*—For two singular subjects joined by *or,* the verb is singular.

13. *was*—The subject is the singular *Everyone.*

14. *have, their*—For a sentence with a compound subject, the subject closest to the verb governs the verb. In this case, *twins* is plural.

15. *has, her*—For two singular subjects joined by *nor,* the verbs should be singular.

16. *was*—The subject is the singular *I.*

17. *enjoys*—The subject is the singular *President.*

18. *seems*—The singular *The number* is the subject.

19. *have*—A number here means *many,* so the verb is plural.

20. *are*—The subject *data* is plural.

Section 4: Verbs

When you look up a verb in the dictionary, you will find an entry like the following:

    eat, v.t. (ate, eaten, eating)
    chop, v.t. (chopped, chopping)
    be, v.i. (was or were, been, being)
    go, v.i. (went, gone, going)
    run, v.i., t. (ran, run, running)

The *v.* indicates that the word is a verb, and the *t.* or *i.* that it is transitive (takes an object) or intransitive (does not take an object). Some verbs, like *run,* can be either intransitive (I run faster than David) or transitive (I run a factory in Kansas City).

The forms of the verb given in the parentheses are the past tense (*ate, chopped*), the past participle (*eaten, chopped*), and the present participle, or *-ing* form of the verb.

Verb Tenses

To deal more fully with verb errors, we will need to review and define some additional terms. Each verb has *number, person, voice,* and *tense. Number* is simply singular or plural. The three *persons* of a verb are first (*I, we*), second (*you*), and third (*he, she, it, they*). Active (*I hit the ball*) and passive (*The ball was hit by me*) are the *voices* of verbs. If the subject of a verb performs the action of the verb, the verb is *active,* while if the subject receives the action, the verb is *passive. The tenses* of a verb are the forms that show *the time* of its action or state of being. Most of the verb errors that appear on the exams are errors of agreement or errors of tense.

The following charts give the tenses of the verbs *to be* and *to chop.*

Present Tense: Action or State of Being in the Present		
	Singular	**Plural**
first person	I am/I chop	we are/we chop
second person	you are/you chop	you are/you chop
third person	he, she, it is/he, she, it chops	they are/they chop

Past Tense: Action or State of Being in the Past		
	Singular	**Plural**
first person	I was/I chopped	we were/we chopped
second person	you were/you chopped	you were/you chopped
third person	he, she, it was/he, she, it chopped	they were/they chopped

Future Tense: Action or State of Being in the Future		
	Singular	Plural
first person	I will be/I will chop	we will be/we will chop
second person	you will be/you will chop	you will be/you will chop
third person	he, she, it will be/he, she, it will chop	they will be/they will chop

There should be no trouble with the present, past, and future tenses, but some examples of the perfect tenses may be helpful. Remember that the *present perfect* tense is used to describe action in *past* time in relation to the present. An example of a *past* tense is *I chopped wood last week.*

An example of a *present perfect* tense is *I have chopped wood every Tuesday for three years.* That is, the wood chopping is an action begun in the past and continuing to the present. An example of a *past perfect* tense is *I had chopped wood every Tuesday until I bought a chain saw.* That is, the wood chopping was an action in the past that preceded another past action, buying a chain saw. In this sentence, *had chopped* is a *past perfect tense,* and *bought* is a *past* tense. An example of the future perfect tense is *By 2020, I will have chopped enough wood to heat six houses.* That is, the wood chopping will continue into the future but will be past in 2020.

Present Perfect Tense: Action in Past Time in Relation to Present Time		
	Singular	Plural
first person	I have been/I have chopped	we have been/we have chopped
second person	you have been/you have chopped	you have been/you have chopped
third person	he, she, it has been/he, she, it has chopped	they have been/they have chopped

Past Perfect Tense: Action in Past Time in Relation to Another Past Time		
	Singular	Plural
first person	I had been/I had chopped	we had been/we had chopped
second person	you had been/you had chopped	you had been/you had chopped
third person	he, she, it had been/he, she, it had chopped	they had been/they had chopped

97

Future Perfect Tense: Action in a Future Time in Relation to Another Time Even Further in the Future		
	Singular	**Plural**
first person	I will have been/I will have chopped	we will have been/we will have chopped
second person	you will have been/you will have chopped	you will have been/you will have chopped
third person	he, she, it will have been/he, she, it will have chopped	they will have been/they will have chopped

Almost all verb tense errors on the exam occur in sentences with two verbs. Always look carefully at the tenses of the verbs in a sentence. Does the time scheme make sense? Is it consistent and logical? Since tense reflects the time of the actions, there can be no single rule about which tenses should be used—the action's time scheme will determine tense. But sometimes the meaning will require a change of tense. For example:

> Yesterday, I ate breakfast at seven o'clock, and tomorrow I will eat at nine.

We have both a past (*ate*) and a future (*will eat*) in this sentence, but other words that explain the time scheme (*yesterday, tomorrow*) make it clear that both a past and a future tense are necessary. On the other hand, consider this example:

> In the seventeenth century, the performances at public theatres took place in the afternoon, and the actors dress in splendid costumes.

In this sentence, the change from the past (*took*) to the present (*dress*) makes no sense. Both verbs refer to past actions (in *the sixteenth century*); both should be in the past tense (*took, dressed*).

To spot errors in verb tense, you must look carefully at the verbs and the other words in the sentence that establish the time scheme. Adverbs like *then, subsequently, before, yesterday,* and *tomorrow,* and prepositional phrases like *in the dark ages* and *in the future,* work with the verbs to make the time of the actions clear.

The following are sentences very much like those used on examinations to test verb tenses. Which of the italicized verbs are incorrect?

1. The winds blew sand in the bathers' faces, so they gathered up their towels and *will leave* the beach quickly.

2. The new variety of plum was developed by Burbank, who *begun* to work with fruits after the Civil War.

3. In the year 2030, I *am* fifty years old.

4. I *had spoke* with her briefly many times before, but today's conversation was the first in which she *spoke* frankly about her political ambitions.

All but one of the italicized verbs are incorrect. In sentence 1, the shift to the future tense (*will leave*) makes no sense after the two other verbs in the past tense. The verb should be *left*. In sentence 2, the past tense, *began,* or better, the past perfect, *had begun,* is necessary. The *am* of sentence 3 should be *will be,* a future tense. In sentence 4, *had spoke* incorrectly tries to form the past perfect tense using the past tense (*spoke*) instead of the past participle *spoken*. The second *spoke* is a correct use of the past tense.

In general, be sure that sentences have a coherent time sequence. A sentence like *Eating my lunch, I took the car to the gas station* makes sense if you eat and drive at the same time. If your meaning is *after lunch,* you must write *Having eaten my lunch, I took the car to the gas station.*

We expect a simple sentence that begins in the past tense to continue to refer to action in the past.

Greek sailors in the first century *thought* that their ships *traveled* faster with light ballasts and small sails.

Egyptian astronomers *believed* that the sun *rose* when the jackal *howled.*

In both of these sentences, all the verbs are, rightly, in the past tense. But there is one kind of sentence that occasionally appears on advanced grammar exams that works differently.

Greek sailors in the first century *discovered* that the prevailing winds in the Ionian Sea *blow* from east to west.

A handful of ancient astronomers *realized* that the earth *revolves* about the sun and the moon *circles* the earth.

In these sentences, though the main verbs are in the past tense (*discovered, realized*), the verbs in the subordinate clauses are in the present tense (*blow, revolves, circles*). Because the action or state the clauses describe continues to be true (the earth still revolves around the sun), the present tense is correct. Logical meaning is the key to tense. Sentences like these will occur infrequently and are likely to appear in the sentence correction form of question.

Subjunctives

In dependent clauses, a subjunctive expresses a condition that is untrue or contrary to fact: The phrase *if I were sick* indicates that I'm *not* sick; the phrase *if he had arrived five minutes earlier* indicates that he *did not*. The following are examples of subjunctive forms of the verb.

If I *were* sick . . . If I *arrive* on time . . .	present tense
If I *had been* sick . . . If I *had arrived* on time . . .	past tense
If he *were* here . . . If he *arrives* on time . . .	present tense
If he *had been* here . . . If he *had arrived* on time . . .	past tense

For standardized exams, what you must remember about subjunctive verbs is that *would have* should never be used in the *if* clause. The question will probably be like one of the following:

1. If Holmes <u>would have arrived</u> a few minutes sooner, the murderer would not have escaped.

   A.   would have arrived
   B.   did arrive
   C.   had arrived
   D.   arrives
   E.   would arrive

2. If the economic situation <u>would have improved</u> in the first three
A

months of this fiscal year, the banks <u>would not have had</u>
B

<u>to foreclose on</u> so many mortgages. <u>No error.</u>
C   D

In question 1, choice **C** is the correct answer. The contrary-to-fact clause
(*if*) requires a past subjunctive form. In question 2, the error is choice **A.**
(Never use *would have* in the *if* clause.) The correct form of the verb in this
clause is *had improved.*

Lie/Lay, Rise/Raise, Sit/Set

Lie is an intransitive verb (it takes no object) meaning *to rest* or *to recline.*
Lay is a transitive verb (it must have an object) meaning *to put* or *to place.*
The confusion between the two verbs probably arose because the past tense
of the verb *to lie* (*to recline*) is the same as the present tense of the verb *to
lay* (*to place*).

Examples:

> Yesterday I *lay* in bed till noon.
>
> intransitive verb-past tense-no object

> I *lay* the paper on the table.
>
> transitive verb-present tense-object (*paper*)

Definition	Present Tense	Past Tense	Past Participle	Present Participle
to rest, to recline *intransitive*	lie	lay	lain	lying
to place, to put *transitive*	lay	laid	laid	laying

Examples:

> I like *laying* my head in a pile of sand when I am *lying* on the beach.
>
> I *laid* the book on the table and *lay* down on the couch.
>
> I have *laid* the book on the table.
>
> I have *lain* in bed all morning.

Like *lie,* the words *rise,* and *sit* are intransitive verbs. Like *lay,* the words *raise* and *set* are transitive verbs.

Definition	Present Tense	Past Tense	Past Participle	Present Participle
to go up, to ascend *intransitive*	rise	rose	risen	rising
to lift *transitive*	raise	raised	raised	raising
to be seated *intransitive*	sit	sat	sat	sitting
to put *transitive*	set	set	set	setting

Examples:

> I *raise* the window shade and watch the sun *rise.*
> I *raised* the shade after the sun had *risen.*
> The sun *rose* before I had *raised* the shade.
> *Raising* the shade, I watched the sun *rising.*

Practice Exercise 4: Verbs

Choose the correct verb form in the following sentences.

1. If you (had, would have) eaten fewer potato chips, you would not be ill now.

2. In 1620, Philips discovered that a candle lighted at only one end (lasts, lasted) longer than one lighted at both ends.

3. I (waited, have waited) for her on the platform.

4. I (have waited, had waited) for her for two hours when she arrived at noon.

5. He (will go, will have gone) to the city tomorrow.

6. If I (were, was) thinner, I would buy a new wardrobe.

7. The thief climbed up the trellis, opened the window, and (steps, stepped) quietly into the room.

8. The letters (lying, laying) on the table have been (lying, laying) there for a week.

9. I (lay, laid) my briefcase on the table and (lay, laid) down on the couch.

10. In this car, the windows (rise, raise) at the press of a button.

11. (Sitting, Setting) the flowers on the table, she noticed the cat (setting, sitting) on the chair nearby.

12. At nine o'clock, a grill (rises, raises) to prevent any entry into the vault.

13. When I reach retirement age in 2025, I (will be, will have been) sixty years old.

14. When I reach retirement age in 2025, I (will work, will have worked) for the post office for thirty years.

15. If you (had been, were) more careful, you would not have dented the fender of the car.

16. If you (had been, were) more careful, you would make fewer mistakes.

Answers – Practice Exercise 4: Verbs

1. *had*—Never use *would have* in the *if* clause.

2. *lasts*—Since the discovery is a fact that continues to be true, use the present tense.

3. *waited*—There is nothing in the sentence to suggest a present time to which a present perfect tense is related, so only the past tense makes sense.

4. *had waited*—Here the other verb in the sentence is the past tense *arrived*. Action in past time in relation to another past time is expressed by the past perfect tense.

5. *will go*—The sentence expresses a simple future (*tomorrow*). The future perfect would be used only if the action were related to another time even further in the future.

6. *were*—Since the condition expressed in the *if* clause is untrue (I am not thinner), the present subjunctive should be used. *Was* is the past tense and not a subjunctive.

7. *stepped*—The first two verbs (*climbed, opened*) are in the past tense. There is no reason to change tenses, so the third verb should also be in the past tense.

8. *lying, lying*—The verb here is the intransitive *lie* (*to rest*). The participial form of *lie* is *lying*.

9. *laid, lay*—The first verb is the transitive verb *lay* (*to place*) in the past tense. The second verb is the intransitive verb *lie* (*to recline*) in the past tense. The first verb has an object (*briefcase*); the second has none.

10. *rise*—The intransitive verb *rise* in the present tense is correct here.

11. *Setting, sitting*—The first verb is the transitive *set* with *flowers* as the object; the second verb, the intransitive *sit,* has no object.

12. *rises*—The intransitive verb *rise* in the present tense is correct here.

13. *will be*—The future tense, not the future perfect, is correct here. There is no time even further in the future to which this verb is related.

14. *will have worked*—Here the future perfect is correct because the opening clause defines a time even further in the future. In sentence 13, 2025 is in the future but not further in the future than the time at which I will be sixty. But in the second sentence, 2025 will come at the end of the period of thirty years' work.

15. *had been*—The verb in the first clause is subjunctive because it describes a contrary-to-fact situation. The past tense of the verb in the second clause requires a subjunctive in the past tense of the first. In the present tense, this sentence would read *If you were more careful, you would not dent the fender of the car.*

16. *were*—The correct verb here is the present subjunctive.

Section 5: Misplaced Parts and Dangling Modifiers

The first part of this section discusses misplaced parts of the sentence. Since a misplaced part is often awkward but not, strictly speaking, grammatically incorrect, the questions testing for misplaced parts usually present five versions of the same sentence and ask you to select the sentence that is not only grammatically correct but also clear and exact, free from awkwardness and ambiguity. This form of question may also, of course, be used to test for the kinds of error already discussed.

A well-written sentence will be clear and concise. Given a choice between two sentences that say all that must be said and are error free, choose the shorter version. This is *not* to say that any shorter sentence is the right answer. Sometimes a shorter sentence will have a grammatical error, omit part of the original thought, or change the meaning.

Example:

> Fifteen women have formally protested their <u>being overlooked for promotion</u>.
>
> A. their being overlooked for promotion
> B. themselves being overlooked for promotion
> C. their overlooking for promotion
> D. overlooking themselves for promotion
> E. themselves as overlooked for promotion

Choice C is the shortest of the five choices here, but it is the wrong answer. It changes the meaning by leaving out *being*. The right answer is choice **A,** for a reason you already know—the possessive (*their*) before the gerund (*being overlooked*). The shorter version, then, is not always the best answer, but the right answer will be as short as it can be without sacrificing grammatical correctness and clarity of content.

The basic rule for dealing with misplaced parts of the sentence is *Keep related parts together.* Avoid any unnecessary separation of closely related parts of the sentence. Avoid odd or unnatural word order. Keep modifiers as near as possible to the words they modify.

Be especially careful with the adverbs *only, just, almost, nearly, even, hardly,* and *merely.* Their placement can be crucial to the meaning of a sentence. Look closely at the following two sentences.

1. I almost walked to the park.
2. I walked almost to the park.

There may, at first, appear to be no difference between sentence 1 and sentence 2. But in sentence 1, *almost* clearly modifies *walked.* In sentence 2, it modifies the phrase *to the park.* The meaning of sentence 1 is either *I almost walked* (rather than rode, hopped, or ran) or *I almost walked* (but then decided not to). The meaning of sentence 2 is *I did walk* (but not quite as far as the park).

Place modifying words, phrases, and clauses in positions that make clear what they modify.

Examples:

1. I bought a jacket in a Westwood shop *made of leather.*
1. I bought a jacket *made of leather* in a Westwood shop.

2. The soprano had dreamed of singing at the Met *for many years.*
2. *For many years,* the soprano had dreamed of singing at the Met.

3. The committee decided *after the next meeting* to hold a dance.
3. The committee decided to hold a dance *after the next meeting.*

4. The ice cream cone I licked *rapidly* melted.
4. The ice cream cone I licked melted *rapidly.*
4. The ice cream cone I *rapidly* licked melted.

In the first version of sentences 1, 2, and 3, the placement of the italicized phrases makes the meaning of the sentence unclear, but the revisions place the phrases closer to the words they modify. In the first version of sentence 4 the adverb *rapidly* may modify either *licked* or *melted,* but it is not clear which meaning is intended. The two revised versions are clear, with two different meanings.

The normal word order in an English clause or sentence is subject-verb-object: *The dog bit the boy.* Although there are bound to be times when another word order is necessary, keep in mind that the clearest sentences will move from subject to verb to object and keep the three elements as close as possible. One type of question that appears on several exams presents the problem of lack of sentence clarity when there are several modifiers of the same word. Normally we want to keep the subject close to the verb, but if the subject has modifiers we also must keep these modifiers close to the subject. The following is a typical question of this sort.

Example:

Which is the best version of the underlined portion of the sentence?

The tuba player, unlike the drummer, whose arms and hands must be strong, relying upon the power of his lungs, is likely to have an unusually well developed chest.

A.   The tuba player, unlike the drummer, whose arms and hands must be strong, relying upon the power of his lungs, is likely

B.   Unlike the drummer, whose arms and hands must be strong, and relying upon the power of his lungs, the tuba player is likely

C.   Relying upon the power of his lungs unlike the drummer, whose arms and hands must be strong, the tuba player is likely

D.   Because of relying upon the power of his lungs, unlike the drummer, whose arms and hands must be strong, the tuba player is likely

E.   Unlike the drummer, whose arms and hands must be strong, the tuba player, relying upon the power of his lungs, is likely

The subject here is *player* and the verb is *is*. There are two units modifying the subject (*player*): *unlike the drummer, whose arms and hands must be strong* and *relying upon the power of his lungs*. How can we place both of these elements close to the subject and at the same time avoid separating the subject from the verb? The best we can do is to put the subject between the two modifiers. By putting the longer of the two modifiers at the beginning, we reduce the length of the separation of subject and verb. The best choice, then, is **E**.

Dangling Modifiers

Dangling modifiers are phrases that have nothing to modify. They most frequently occur at the beginning of a sentence and are usually verbals: participles (verbal adjectives), gerunds (verbal nouns), and infinitives.

Participles

A participle is a verb used as an adjective. The present participle ends in -*ing* (*eating, seeing, writing*), while the past participle is that form of the verb used to form the perfect tense (*eaten, seen, written*). Whenever you see a sentence that begins with a participle, check to be sure that the participle logically modifies the subject that immediately follows the comma that sets off the participial phrase. In the following sentences, the first version begins with a dangling participle. The revised versions correct the sentence to eliminate the error.

Examples:

1. *Waiting* for the bus, the sun came out.

   While we were waiting for the bus, the sun came out.

2. *Fishing* for trout, our canoe overturned.

   While we were fishing for trout, we overturned our canoe.

   Fishing for trout, we overturned our canoe.

3. *Having finished* chapter one, chapter two seemed easy.

   After I had finished chapter one, chapter two seemed easy.

   Having finished chapter one, I found chapter two easy.

4. *Having had* no soup, the salad was welcome.

   Because I had no soup, the salad was welcome.

   Having had no soup, I found the salad welcome.

Sentences 1 and 2 use present participles; sentences 3 and 4 use past participles. The second of the two revisions of these sentences illustrates that a sentence can begin with a participle that does not dangle, and the exams will probably contain sentences that begin with a participle used correctly. But you may be sure that they will also contain sentences with dangling participles to test your ability to recognize this error.

Gerunds

Gerunds, verbal nouns, look like participles, but they are used as nouns rather than adjectives. In the sentence *Waiting for the bus is very boring, waiting* is a *gerund* used as a *noun* and the subject of the sentence. But in the sentence *Waiting for the bus, I became bored, waiting* is a *participle* used as an *adjective* and modifying the subject *I*. The following sentences contain dangling gerunds, corrected in the revision that follows each.

Examples:

1. By changing the oil regularly, your car will run better.

   By changing the oil regularly, you can make your car run better.

2. By working very hard, better grades will result.

   By working very hard, you will get better grades.

3. After sneezing, my handkerchief was useful.

   After sneezing, I found my handkerchief useful.

   After I sneezed, my handkerchief was useful.

Infinitives

An *infinitive* is the simple, uninflected form of a verb, usually written with the preposition *to; to go* is an infinitive, while *goes* or *going* are inflected forms with additional sounds (*-es, -ing*) added to the infinitive. Dangling infinitives show up much less frequently on the exams than dangling participles or gerunds, but the principle of the error is the same. As with dangling participles and gerunds, you can correct a sentence with a dangling infinitive by making sure that the subject of the sentence that follows the comma is what the infinitive really modifies.

Examples:

The first version of the following sentences contains a dangling infinitive, corrected in the revisions.

1. To play the violin well, constant practicing is necessary.

   To play the violin well, you must practice constantly.

2. To make cookies, sugar and flour are needed.

   To make cookies, you need sugar and flour.

Prepositional Phrases and Elliptical Clauses

An *ellipsis* is the omission of a word or words. An *elliptical clause* or *phrase* is one in which the subject and verb are implied, but omitted. For example, in the sentence *When in New York, I stay at the Plaza,* the implied subject and verb of *When in New York* are *I am,* but they have been omitted. It is acceptable to use an ellipsis like this, but if the implied subject does not follow, the phrase will dangle.

Examples:

1. Though rich and beautiful, her marriage was a failure.
2. While on guard duty, her rifle was lost.
3. When a very young child growing up in Brooklyn, his father sent him to summer camp in New Hampshire.
4. On the ship's observation deck, three gray whales were sighted.

The first three of these sentences begin with dangling elliptical clauses. Adding *she was* in the first and second clause and *he was* in the third—that is, filling in the ellipsis—will correct the sentences. Sentence 4 illustrates that even a prepositional phrase may dangle. An observer, not the three whales, is much more likely to be on this ship's observation deck. Dangling modifiers are, like this one, often not only incorrect but ridiculous too. Whenever you see a sentence that begins with a participle, gerund, elliptical phrase, or infinitive, look very carefully to see whether or not the phrase dangles. And remember that some will be correct.

Practice Exercise 5: Misplaced Parts and Dangling Modifiers

All of the following sentences contain misplaced parts or dangling modifiers. Rewrite each sentence to eliminate the errors.

1. After making a par despite a very bad drive, the crowd cheered loudly for Nancy Lopez.

2. Having failed to read the book carefully, his remarks in class were either imperceptive or irrelevant.

3. By keeping your eye on the ball and not on your partner, the overhead may become your most consistent shot.

4. Hoping to win a place on the team, her free-skating performance must be first-rate.

5. To do well in this exam, both stamina and concentration are absolutely essential.

6. For months we had anticipated seeing Carrie Underwood's performance, and to get the best possible view of the stage, our seats were on the center aisle in the front row.

7. When only eight years old, he sent his son to boarding school in Arizona.

8. Though only five feet four, his quickness of reflex and the uncanny accuracy of his volley have made him the best doubles player on the team.

9. At temperatures below 250 degrees, you should stir the boiling syrup very briskly.

10. I have never, if I remember correctly, been in Venice in October.

11. By applying the insecticide carefully, damage to the environment can be avoided.

12. I just have enough money to pay my telephone bill.

Answers – Practice Exercise 5: Misplaced Parts and Dangling Modifiers

There are several ways to rewrite these sentences and eliminate the errors. The following are a few of the possible revisions.

1. As it stands now, the participial phrase at the beginning of the sentence dangles and appears to modify *crowd* rather than *Nancy Lopez*. One can correct the sentence by beginning *After she made a par* or by leaving the participial phrase unchanged and writing *Nancy Lopez was cheered* after the comma.

2. This sentence also beings with a dangling participle. It can be corrected by beginning with *Because he failed* or by writing *he made remarks in class that were* after the comma.

3. Again, the error is a dangling participle. Revise the sentence to begin with *If you keep* or write something like *you may make the overhead* after the comma.

4. A dangling participle once more. The corrected sentence could begin *If she hopes to win* or could say *she must give a first-rate free-skating performance* after the comma.

5. The error here is a dangling infinitive, which makes it appear that *stamina* and *concentration* are taking the exam. Either add a human agent in the first phrase (*For you to do well*) or begin the second with *you must have.*

6. This is a very difficult sentence because the dangling infinitive is not at the beginning of the sentence but in the middle (*to get the best possible view*). As it stands, the *seats,* not the ticket holders, are getting the best view. By revising the last clause of the sentence to read *we bought seats on the center aisle,* we eliminate the error.

7. The elliptical phrase here dangles, so the sentence suggests that the father is eight years old. To remove the error, we can remove the ellipsis and write *When his son was only eight years old.* If we wish to keep the opening unchanged, we must write *his son was sent* after the comma.

8. Like sentence 7, this sentence opens with a dangling elliptical phrase. The simplest way to correct the error is to write *Though he is only.*

9. Here the prepositional phrase that begins the sentence seems to modify *you.* Beginning the sentence with the *you* clause and putting the prepositional phrase at the end will correct the error.

10. To avoid the unnecessary separation of the parts of the verb, begin the sentence with *If I remember correctly.*

11. The opening elliptical phrase dangles. Write *By applying the insecticide carefully, you can avoid damage to the environment.*

12. The *just* is misplaced. Write *I have just enough* so that *just* is next to the word it modifies.

Section 6: Parallelism

Errors of parallelism will occur when two or more linked ideas are expressed in different grammatical structures. In a sentence such as *I am interested in nuclear physics, to play tennis, and going to the theatre,* each of the three elements of the series is in a different grammatical form: a noun, an infinitive, and a gerund phrase. To make the series parallel, one would use any one of the forms three times.

Examples:

I am interested in nuclear physics, tennis, and theatre.
(three nouns)

I am interested in studying nuclear physics, playing tennis, and going to the theatre.
(three gerunds)

I like to study nuclear physics, to play tennis, and to go to the theatre.
(three infinitives)

To find errors of parallelism, look first to be sure there are two or more ideas, words, or phrases that are similar; then check to see that the coordinate ideas are expressed by the same part of speech, verb form, or clause or phrase structure.

Examples:

The first version of the following sentences is *not* parallel. The revisions that follow each sentence correct the parallelism errors.

1. I admire *his cheerfulness* and *that he perseveres.*
   I admire his cheerfulness and his perseverance.

2. *To dance* and *singing* were his favorite pastimes.
   Dancing and *singing* were his favorite pastimes.
   To dance and *to sing* were his favorite pastimes.

3. *Her cleverness* and *that she looks innocent* helped her escape.
   Her cleverness and innocent appearance helped her escape.

4. *To ship* a package by air freight is more expensive than *if you send* it by parcel post.
   To ship a package by air freight is more expensive than *to send* it by parcel post.

Common Parallelism Errors

The following are common parallelism errors in standardized examinations. In the examples, the first version is in error; the revision or revisions correct the sentence.

Unnecessary Shifts in Verb Tenses

1. She *bought* her ticket at the box office and *sits* in the first row.
   She *bought* her ticket at the box office and *sat* in the first row.

2. Every day he *runs* five kilometers and *swam* half a mile.
   Every day he *runs* five kilometers and *swims* half a mile.
   Every day he *ran* five kilometers and *swam* half a mile.

Unnecessary Shifts from an Active to a Passive Verb

1. John *plays* tennis well, but Ping-Pong *is played* even better by him.
   John *plays* tennis well, but he *plays* Ping-Pong even better.

2. The editor *wrote* his article in thirty minutes, and it *was typed* by him in five.
   The editor *wrote* his article in thirty minutes and *typed* it in five.

Unnecessary Shifts in Person

We divide personal pronouns into three classes: the first person (singular, *I;* plural, *we*), the second person (*you*), and the third person (singular, *he, she, it, one;* plural, *they*). Though it is possible that a sentence will refer to more than one person (*I went to Florida, and she went to Georgia*), in sentences where the change of person is not part of the meaning, the pronouns should be consistent. The first version of each of the following sentences is incorrect.

1. *One* should drive slowly and *you* should keep your eyes on the road.
   One should drive slowly and keep *one's* eyes on the road.
   You should drive slowly and keep *your* eyes on the road.

2. To win at poker, *a player* must know the odds and *you* must observe your opponents carefully.
   To win at poker, *you* must know the odds and observe your opponents carefully.
   To win at poker, *a player* must know the odds and observe *his or her* opponents carefully.

Parallelism Errors in a List or Series

Parallelism errors are likely to occur in a list or series. In the following examples, the second version of the sentences corrects the parallelism errors.

1. The game has three steps: *getting* your pieces to the center, *capturing* your opponent's pieces, and you must *end* with a throw of double six.

   The game has three steps: *getting* your pieces to the center, *capturing* your opponent's pieces, and *ending* with a throw of double six.

2. I talked on, trying to be *charming, gracious,* and *to keep* the conversation going.

   I talked on, trying *to be* gracious and charming and *to keep* the conversation going.

The second example begins with a series of two adjectives (*charming, gracious*), but the expected third adjective is an infinitive. The revised version eliminates the series and makes the two infinitives (*to be, to keep*) parallel.

Sentences incorporating a series set up expectations of parallel structures. In a series of three or more, the first two elements will establish a pattern. Assume a series is to include three parts: mow the grass, weed the garden, and empty the trash. One can say: (1) I want you to mow the lawn, weed the garden, and empty the trash or (2) I want you to mow the lawn, to weed the garden, and to empty the trash. In (1), the series begins with the infinitive using *to,* and the *to* is understood in the next two parts. The series is *mow, weed, empty.* In (2), the *to* is used with all three verbs. But if the sentence read *I want you to mow the lawn, weed the garden, and to empty the trash,* the parallelism would be lost.

Do not expect every element in parallel structures to be identical all the time. It is proper, for example, to say *I want you to wash the kitchen and the bathroom, go to the store, and cash a check at the bank.* The parallel elements here are *to wash,* (to) *go,* and (to) *cash,* but other elements within the series are different.

Parallelism Errors in Correlatives

One sure sign of a sentence that must have parallel grammatical constructions is the use of correlatives. Correlatives are coordinating conjunctions used in pairs to express similarity or equality in thought. Whenever any of the following correlatives are used, they should be followed by similar grammatical constructions. Memorize this list, and whenever you see these words in a sentence on the exam, you can be very sure that parallelism is one of the problems in the question.

both . . . and	first . . . second
not only but also	not merely . . . but
not only but	not so much . . . as
not but	as much . . . as
either or	more . . . than
neither nor	less . . . than

In a sentence with *both . . . and,* look first to see exactly what the grammar is immediately after *both;* then make sure the same structure follows *and.*

Examples:

In the following examples, the first version illustrates an error, corrected in the revision or revisions that follow.

1. The opera is *both* a complex work *and* original.

   The opera is *both* complex *and* original.
   both, adjective; *and,* adjective

   The opera is *both* a complex *and* an original work.
   both, article, adjective; *and,* article adjective

2. He *not only* is selfish *but also* deceitful.

   He is *not only* selfish *but also* deceitful.
   not only, adjective; *but also,* adjective

   He *not only* is selfish *but also* is deceitful.
   not only, verb, adjective; *but also,* verb, adjective

3. The book is *not only* about pigs *but also* flowers.

   The book is *not only* about pigs *but also* about flowers.
   not only, preposition, noun; *but also,* preposition, noun

4. The letter is *either* for you *or* your husband.

The letter is for *either you—or* your husband.

either, pronoun; *or,* pronoun, noun

The letter is *either* for you *or* for your husband.

either, preposition, pronoun; *or,* preposition, pronoun, noun

Note that in sentence 4 the corrected versions are not identical (for *you/for your husband*). The parallel must be in structure, but one part may contain additional words. It is correct to write *The letter is either for you or for your husband* since both *either* and *or* are followed by prepositional phrases beginning *with for.*

Practice Exercise 6: Parallelism

If there is an error in the following sentences, choose the underlined lettered part in which the error occurs. Some of the sentences will contain no errors.

1. <u>Because</u> I <u>grew up</u> in Switzerland, I read and <u>speak</u> <u>both French</u>
     A   B   C   D
   and German. <u>No error</u>.
               E

2. <u>It is</u> not his reckless spending of my money but <u>that he spends</u> <u>it</u> on
    A   B   C
   other women <u>that has led</u> me to file for divorce. <u>No error</u>.
              D   E

3. Educational reform is now <u>being brought about</u> by students who
                              A
   are more concerned with the value of <u>their</u> education than <u>getting a</u>
                                        B   C
   <u>piece</u> of paper with B.A. <u>written on it</u>. No error.
    D   E

4. <u>A person's aptitude</u> for foreign languages <u>is</u> important to State
         A   B
   Department examiners, but on this exam, <u>it</u> is your ability to read
                                              C
   French <u>that will make</u> the difference. <u>No error</u>.
          D   E

5. Law school <u>not only enables</u> one to practice law, <u>but also teaches</u>
                   A   B

    <u>you</u> to <u>think more clearly</u>. <u>No error</u>.
    C   D   E

6. I want you <u>not only</u> <u>to paint</u> and sand the screens <u>but also</u> <u>to put</u>
                A   B   C   D

    them in the cellar. <u>No error</u>.
                    E

7. What <u>one expects</u> <u>to get out</u> of a long-term investment <u>should be</u>
         A   B   C

    considered carefully <u>before</u> you see your broker. <u>No error</u>.
                          D   E

8. <u>Come</u> to the next class meeting <u>prepared</u> to take notes, to speak
    A   B

    <u>briefly</u>, and <u>with some questions to ask</u>. <u>No error</u>.
    C   D   E

9. Her grace and charm, <u>her ability to see</u> both sides of a question,
                           A

    and <u>her willingness</u> to accept criticism <u>are</u> qualities <u>that</u> I especially
          B   C   D

    admire. <u>No error</u>.
          E

10. We <u>must look</u> <u>closely</u> <u>both at the data</u> in this <u>year's</u> report and the
      A   B   C   D

    results of last year's analysis. <u>No error</u>.
                          E

11. The process of natural selection <u>requires that</u> animals be able to
                                     A

    adapt <u>to changing climates</u>, to discover new foods, <u>and defend</u>
           B   C

    <u>themselves</u> against <u>their</u> enemies. <u>No error</u>.
             D   E

12. The new employee <u>soon</u> <u>proved himself</u> <u>to be</u> not only capable but
                      A   B   C

    also <u>a man who could be trusted</u>. <u>No error</u>.
                D   E

13. <u>As soon as</u> school <u>ended</u>, he jumped into his car, drove to the pool,
     A   B

    <u>changes</u> his clothes, and <u>swam</u> twenty laps. <u>No error</u>.
    C   D   E

14. To complete your application, <u>you</u> must fill out three forms, <u>pay</u> the
$\qquad\qquad\qquad\qquad\qquad\qquad\ \ $ A $\qquad\qquad\qquad\qquad\qquad\qquad\qquad$ B

enrollment fee, <u>submit</u> a recent photograph, and <u>enclose</u> a copy of
$\qquad\qquad\qquad\ \ $ C $\qquad\qquad\qquad\qquad\qquad\qquad\qquad$ D

your high-school transcript. <u>No error</u>.
$\qquad\qquad\qquad\qquad\qquad\qquad$ E

15. I must remember <u>to buy</u> soap and a toothbrush, <u>to have</u> the car
$\qquad\qquad\qquad\qquad\quad\ $ A $\qquad\qquad\qquad\qquad\qquad\ $ B

washed, <u>to order</u> my Christmas cards and gift subscriptions, and
$\qquad\quad\ $ C

<u>cash</u> a check before the bank closes. <u>No error</u>.
D $\qquad\qquad\qquad\qquad\qquad\qquad\ $ E

Answers – Practice Exercise 6: Parallelism

1. **E.** The parallelism here is correct.

2. **B.** With the correlatives *not . . . but,* the words after *but* should be parallel to those after *not: not his reckless spending . . . but his spending.*

3. **C.** The phrase *more concerned with* should have a parallel after *than: than with getting.*

4. **A.** Since the pronoun *your* is used later in the sentence (and cannot be changed, since it is not underlined) the first phrase in the sentence should read *Your aptitude.*

5. **C.** Since the pronoun *one* is used earlier in the sentence, *you* should be *one.*

6. **E.** The parallelism here is correct.

7. **A.** Since the pronoun *you* is used at the end of the sentence, *one* should be *you.*

8. **D.** The series of infinitives (*to take, to speak*) should be completed with another infinitive (*to ask some questions*).

9. **E.** The series in this sentence maintains parallelism.

10. **C.** With the correlatives *both . . . and,* the structure following should be parallel. The correct version is *at both the data.*

11. **C.** To maintain the series of infinitives, the sentence should read *and to defend.*

12. **D.** With the correlatives *not only . . . but also,* the sentence should read *not only capable but also trustworthy.*

13. C. The past tense should be used in all the verbs—*ended, jumped, drove, changed, and swam.*

14. E. The parallelism here is correct.

15. D. The final verb in this series should be an infinitive (*to cash*) to be parallel with the others.

Section 7: Ambiguous Pronouns

In conversation and in informal writing, we often use pronouns that have no single word as their antecedent. *This* happens all the time—for example, the *this* that begins this sentence. It refers to the general idea of the preceding sentence but not to a specific noun. In the exams, you should regard as an error a pronoun that does not have a specific noun or word used as a noun as its antecedent. This sort of error is more likely to occur in the kind of question that gives you a choice of revisions. The correct answer will either get rid of the ambiguous pronoun or supply a specific antecedent.

Examples:

Which is the best version of the following sentence?

1. The sun was shining brightly, *which* pleased me.
2. The sun was shining brightly, and *this* pleased me.
3. The sun was shining brightly, and *that* pleased me.
4. Because the sun was shining brightly, *this* pleased me.
5. There was bright sunshine, and *this* pleased me.

Sentence 5 is the best version, for the pronoun *this* has a specific antecedent (*sunshine*). In the first four sentences, none of the pronouns has a specific antecedent. A revision such as *That the sun was shining brightly pleased me* would also be correct since this version simply removes the ambiguous pronoun. The four wrong answers demonstrate that you cannot correct an ambiguous pronoun by substituting another pronoun. The ambiguity will remain until you revise to supply a specific antecedent or to get rid of the pronoun altogether.

Be careful with sentences that have a pronoun and a choice of antecedents. In a sentence such as *Mark told Luke that he owed him five dollars,* we cannot know for certain who owes money to whom. A sentence with an ambiguity of this sort may appear in a question asking you to select an underlined error.

Example:

For many years, the American consumer <u>preferred</u> <u>a cola</u> to a
                                         A   B
lemon, orange, or grapefruit flavored drink; recent surveys <u>show</u> a
                                                              C
surprising rise in the consumption <u>of it</u>. <u>No error</u>.
                                      D   E

The error here is choice **D,** the ambiguous pronoun *it,* which may refer to anyone of four flavors.

Practice Exercise 7: Ambiguous Pronouns

All of the following sentences contain ambiguous pronouns. Identify the ambiguous pronoun and revise the sentence to eliminate the error.

1. I came in fifteen minutes late, which made the whole chemistry class incomprehensible to me.

2. I want to go to law school because this is the best way to prepare myself for a career in politics.

3. I wrote checks for my phone bill, gas bill, and union dues, and this made my account overdrawn.

4. He ate a salad, pizza, order of chili, and large wedge of apple pie in only seven minutes, and, needless to say, this gave him indigestion.

5. I bought a radio and a record player at the second-hand store, but when I plugged it in, it would not work.

6. Both Dave and Vince were scheduled to work Saturday morning, but because his car wouldn't start, he didn't appear until noon.

7. I am told that I think clearly and write well, and these are important in historical studies.

8. Marine iguanas have armored skin, strong claws, and sharp teeth, and this makes them seem ferocious, though they are harmless vegetarians.

Answers – Practice Exercise 7: Ambiguous Pronouns

All of the following are *possible* answers, but certainly not the only right response.

1. The *which* has no specific antecedent. To avoid the ambiguous pronoun, one might write *My coming in fifteen minutes late made . . .* or *I came in fifteen minutes late and found. . . .* One cannot correct the error by substituting another pronoun for the ambiguous *which*.

2. The ambiguous pronoun is *this*. The sentence can be corrected by simply omitting the phrase *because this is* and adding a comma after *school*.

3. The ambiguous pronoun is *this*. Effectively revised, the sentence would read *By writing checks for . . . I overdrew my account*.

4. The ambiguous pronoun is *this*. It can be eliminated by concluding the sentence with *and, needless to say, had indigestion*. The sentence could also be corrected by adding a noun after the ambiguous pronoun: *this overeating gave him indigestion*.

5. The antecedent of *it* could be either the radio or the record player. The simple solution is to say *when I plugged in the radio* (or *the record player), it would not work*.

6. The antecedent of *his* and *he* is unclear. As in sentence 5, the solution is to use the noun (*Dave* or *Vince*) in place of *he*.

7. The *these* is ambiguous. One solution is to write *these abilities*.

8. The *this* is ambiguous. One could write *this appearance makes them seem ferocious* or *and they appear ferocious, though. . . .*

Section 8: Other Errors of Grammar

Sentence Fragments

A complete sentence must be an independent clause. Do not assume that a subject and a verb automatically make a complete sentence. *I go,* though it is only two words long, is a complete sentence, while *When he had finished eating his dinner, had pushed back his chair, placed his napkin by his empty wine glass, and risen from the table* is not. It is a dependent clause, a sentence fragment.

Examples:

All of the following are sentence fragments.

1. Hoping to be elected on either the first or second ballot
2. Because the jurors had very carefully examined the evidence presented in the twenty-two days of testimony
3. The runners from six South American countries, together with the volleyball teams from Canada, Cuba, and the United States

To complete sentence 1, we must add a subject and verb either in an independent clause following this dependent clause or by changing *Hoping* to *He hoped, She hoped, Carol hoped,* or something of the kind. *Because* at the beginning of sentence 2 marks it as a dependent clause. Sentence 3 has no main verb.

Double Negatives

It's hard to miss the double negative in a sentence such as *I don't want no peas.* The errors are much less obvious with other negative adverbs such as *hardly, but, scarcely, seldom, rarely,* and the like.

Examples:

When you see these words in a sentence, be on the lookout for a double negative like the following.

1. I spent ten dollars on gasoline, and now I don't have hardly any money.
   (Correct to: *I have hardly any money.*)

2. In the twilight, a batter can't hardly see a fastball.
   (Correct to: *can hardly see*)

3. I don't have but a dollar, and that will not scarcely pay my check.
   (Correct to: *I have but . . . will scarcely pay*)

Omission of Necessary Words

Good writing is concise. Given a choice on the exam between two grammatically correct sentences whose meanings are the same, you should choose the shorter version. But be sure there are no necessary words missing.

Examples:

When we read carelessly, sentences like these (which are *not* correct) appear to be complete.

> People who read rapidly can easily and often have overlooked important details.
>
> He always has and, I'm afraid, always will eat like a pig.

Both of these sentences need two main verbs but try to do the work with one. The verbs *have overlooked* and *will eat* are complete, but we cannot say *can overlooked* or *has eat*. We must write *can easily overlook and often have overlooked* and *always has eaten and . . . always will eat.* In a sentence like *He always does and always will eat like a pig,* we need not repeat the verb *eat,* but when the auxiliary verbs require different forms of the verb, the sentence must include both forms.

Watch very carefully for a missing preposition in sentences with two adjectives joined by a conjunction and followed by prepositions, phrases like *bored by and hostile to* or *fearful of and concerned about.*

Examples:

There are prepositions missing in the following sentences.

> He doesn't like watching football games, but he is impressed and enthusiastic about some of the cheerleaders.
>
> I am uninterested and bored by shopping for clothes.

We cannot say *impressed about* or *uninterested by*. So we must say *impressed by* and *enthusiastic about* and *uninterested in* and *bored by*.

Be especially wary with comparisons. Be certain that the two elements that are compared are equivalent. You cannot say, *The man's time in the hundred meters was much faster than the woman,* because the two elements being compared are *different*—*time* versus *woman.* The sentence must read *The man's time in the hundred meters was much faster than that of the woman* or *The man's time in the hundred meters was much faster than the woman's.*

Examples:

What words must be added to correct the following sentences?

1. He is, sensibly, more interested in getting a good job than a rich wife.
2. The amount of vitamin C in eight ounces of tomato juice is much greater than eight ounces of milk.
3. There are far fewer single parents in Maine, Vermont, and New Hampshire than Massachusetts or Connecticut.

Sentence 1 needs a phrase like *than in getting a rich wife.*

Sentence 2 should end with *than that in eight ounces of milk.*

Sentence 3 should read *than in Massachusetts or Connecticut.*

You must often include *any* or *any other* after comparisons using *than* or the phrase *different from.*

Examples:

Your exam may ask you to choose among the five versions of a sentence like this.

The poetry of Keats is <u>different from any English poet</u>.

A. different from any English poet
B. different than any English poet
C. different from that of any English poet
D. different from that of any other English poet
E. different from any English poet's

There are several problems here. To begin with, the preferred English idiom is *different from* rather than *different than.* And both choices A and B have missing words, since, as they stand, they make a comparison between *poetry* and a *poet.* The right answer must add *that of* or make *poet* possessive. The difference between choices C and D is the addition of *other* in choice D. The *other* is necessary, since Keats was also a poet. For this reason, choice **D** is the correct answer. Choice E would also need to add *other* to be correct.

The difference between *any* and *any other* is a difference in meaning. Had the sentence been about a Latin poet, say Virgil, it might read, *The poetry of Virgil is different from that of any English poet* without the *other.* If I say, *Evans is faster than any other runner at Yale, and Jones is faster than any runner at Yale,* I am also telling you that Evans is a runner at Yale and Jones is not. Any sentence appearing on the exam will make its meaning clear.

Another favorite form of question testing the same error is a sentence with *like* or *unlike* at the beginning or end.

Examples:

1. Like Shelley, Byron's poetry is sensuous.
2. Like New York, Chicago's traffic is snarled on Friday afternoons.
3. The market in Boston never closes, like New York.
4. Her bank account is never overdrawn, unlike her husband.

In all of these sentences, the two compared elements are not parallel. Sentence 1 compares *Byron's poetry* with *Shelley,* not with *Shelley's poetry,* and sentence 2 compares *New York* and the *traffic* in Chicago. Any of the following revisions will correct sentence 1.

Like Shelley, Byron wrote sensuous poetry.

(Shelley = Byron)

Like Shelley's, Byron's poetry is sensuous.

(Shelley's poetry = Byron's poetry)

Like that of Shelley, Byron's poetry is sensuous.

(Shelley's poetry = Byron's poetry)

Similarly, sentence 4, which compares a *bank account* to a *husband,* must be revised. Either of the following is correct.

Her bank account is never overdrawn, unlike her husband's.

Her bank account is never overdrawn, unlike that of her husband.

Direct and Indirect Questions

Direct questions are followed by question marks. Indirect questions are questions within a sentence that is not a question.

Direct: Did you hear my new record?

Indirect: I asked if you heard my new record.

Direct: The premier asked, "How can we save Venice?"

Indirect: The question is how we can save Venice.

In direct questions, the verb usually precedes the subject. In indirect questions, the subject should precede the verb. Thus, in a sentence like *I wonder how I can afford to buy a new car,* where the question is indirect, the subject (*I*) comes before the verb (*can afford*). In a direct question such as *How can I afford a new car?,* the verb (*can*) precedes the subject.

Like and As

Like is a preposition, that is, a word used to connect a noun or pronoun to another element of the sentence. We speak of the noun or pronoun as the object of the preposition and phrases such as *like me* or *like New York* as prepositional phrases. *Like* should be followed by a noun (*like the wind*) or a pronoun (*like her*). It should not be used in place of the conjunction *as* to introduce a clause with a subject and verb or an implied verb.

Examples:

All of the following are correct.

1. As you said, he is overweight, like me.
2. Like zinnias, marigolds are easy to grow.
3. Marigolds are easy to grow, as zinnias are.
4. He is as fast as I. (The verb *am* is understood.)
5. He is fast, like me.
6. As I said, peaches taste good, as summer fruits should.

Who, Which, and That—Restrictive and Nonrestrictive Clauses

Given a choice among *who, which,* or *that,* use *who* when the antecedent is a single human being (*the man who; John Smith, who*) or a group thought of as individuals (*the lawmakers who, the players who, the jurors who*). Use *that* or *which* for a group thought of as a group (*the senate that; the team, which; the jury that*).

Conservative grammarians distinguish between *which* and *that,* using *that* in defining or restrictive clauses and *which* in non-defining or nonrestrictive clauses. A restrictive clause identifies or defines the noun it modifies, while a nonrestrictive clause merely describes or adds information.

Examples:

> The novel *that he wrote in 1860* was not published until 1900.
> (restrictive clause)

> The novel *The Guardian, which he wrote in 1860,* was not published until 1900.
> (nonrestrictive clause)

> The musicians *who missed two rehearsals* played badly.
> (restrictive clause)

> The musicians, *who rehearse every day,* are on stage.
> (nonrestrictive clause)

The pronoun *who* can introduce either a restrictive or a nonrestrictive clause. If the clause is nonrestrictive, it should be set off by commas. Though it is extremely unlikely that a test will ask you to discriminate between the use of *that* and *which,* the point may appear in a sentence with a second and more obvious sort of error. But you should be alert to the possibility of a question that asks you to decide about the use of commas with a *who* clause, especially on the ACT exams, which test punctuation more frequently. Sentences with a human antecedent wrongly using *which* or *that* instead of *who* are common.

Practice Exercise 8: Other Errors of Grammar

Part A

Identify the sentence fragments in the following.

1. Representing the farm belt attitude toward price subsidies, the delegations from Kansas, Nebraska, and Iowa, as well as food processors from Texas, Louisiana, and Georgia.

2. So David wept.

3. The Colt Company, a leader in the industry, and celebrated for introducing the first energy-efficient nine-room house at a cost under sixty thousand dollars.

4. Is he?

5. When glaciers ground extensive tracts of the granite to a highly polished finish.

Part B

All of the following sentences contain errors described in Section 8. Identify the error and correct the sentence.

1. The price of meat has gone up steeply in the past six months, according to an unofficial government survey, but there is some consolation for yogurt eaters: yogurt prices haven't risen hardly at all.

2. While calculating their income tax returns, people can and often have made mistakes.

3. During the Renaissance, Venice was wealthier and more important than any city in the world.

4. I wonder how can we finish both the painting and the window washing in a single day.

5. People have and probably will say for many years to come that Mead's *Coming of Age in Samoa* should be required reading for anyone interested in anthropology.

6. I invested my money in the bank, which pays a higher rate of interest than any other in the city.

7. What Congress decides today will determine the kind of world people must live in the future.

8. The Orsinis hoped to establish their influence throughout Tuscany like the Borgias did in Rome.

9. The embassy claimed that the rights of Soviet Jewish citizens are no different from any Russians.

10. If you use two tablespoons of soy sauce, you will not need scarcely any salt.

11. Scientists argue that water plants can be as effective, if not more effective than chemicals in water purification.

12. The question is when can we afford to take the time to finish the report.

13. He never has and never will be able to play left field as well as Williams.

14. He bought the turkey at Jack's Ranch Market that offered a special price on poultry.

15. Despite their inventive plots and catchy melodies, the musical plays of Sondheim are less popular and less frequently recorded than Cole Porter.

16. As Spain, France was eager to send its navigators to Africa and America.

17. Her trills are as good or better than those of any other soprano.

18. The predators follow the herds of zebra who migrate more than fifteen hundred miles each year.

19. Like the senator explained, what transpired in Chicago in the 1930s now happens all over the country.

20. I am puzzled about how can he afford to make the payments on his cars and a boat while his income is so small.

Answers – Practice Exercise 8: Other Errors of Grammar

Part A

1. A fragment. There is no main verb, only a participle.

2. A complete sentence. *David* (subject) *wept* (verb).

3. A fragment. There is no verb.

4. A complete sentence. *Is* (verb) *he* (subject).

5. A fragment. The clause is dependent.

Part B

1. Double negative—*haven't risen <u>hardly</u>*

2. Omission of necessary word—*can <u>make</u>*

3. Omission of necessary word—since Venice is a city, *any <u>other</u> city*

4. Word order in indirect question—*how <u>we can</u>*

5. Omission of necessary word—*have <u>said</u>*

6. *Which* for *that*—the clause is restrictive, *bank <u>that</u>* (with no comma)

7. Omission of necessary word—*must live in <u>in</u> the future*

8. *Like* for *as*—the clause has a subject and *verb*—*<u>as</u> the Borgias*

9. Omission of necessary words—*different from <u>those</u> of any <u>other</u>*

10. Double negative—*<u>not</u> need <u>scarcely</u>*

11. Omission of necessary word—*as effective <u>as</u>*

12. Word order in indirect *question*—*when <u>we can</u>*

13. Omission of necessary word—*never has <u>been</u>*

14. *That* for *which*—the clause is nonrestrictive—*Jack's Ranch Market, <u>which</u>*

15. Omission of necessary words—*than <u>those of</u> Cole Porter*

16. *As* for *like*—the sentence should begin with a prepositional phrase *<u>Like</u> Spain*

17. Omission of necessary word—*as good <u>as</u>*

18. *Who* for *which*—zebras are not humans—*zebra, <u>which</u> migrate*

19. *Like* for *as*—the clause has a subject and a verb—*<u>As</u> the senator explained*

20. Word order in indirect question—*how <u>he can</u> afford*

Section 9: Errors of Diction, Idiom, and Style

Diction

A diction error, which is the choice of the wrong word, is caused by not knowing exactly what each word means. Obviously, the more words you know, the fewer diction errors you will make. Sometimes the words with which you are presented are not obscure or difficult. They are much more likely to be words we all know—or think we know—but confuse with words that look or sound similar. A list of words that are easily mixed up can go on for pages. You should be aware of the following examples, but don't try to memorize the list. Just be sure when you are taking a test to read *each word* carefully.

allude (refer to)—elude (escape from)

allusion (reference)—illusion (false or misleading appearance)

invoke (ask solemnly for)—evoke (summon)

afflict (cause suffering to)—inflict (impose)

aggravate (intensify)—irritate (annoy)

anxious (apprehensive)—eager (ardent)

fortuitous (accidental)—fortunate (lucky)

detain (confine, delay)—retain (keep, hire)

precede (go before)—proceed (advance, continue)

there (in that place)—their (belonging to them)—they're (they are)

its (of it)—it's (it is)

Fewer/Less, Many/Much, Number/Amount

Use *fewer* (not *less*), *many* (not *much*), and *number* (not *amount*) with items that can be counted or numbered.

fewer gallons, *many* gallons, the *number* of gallons

Use *less, much,* and *amount* with items that cannot be counted or numbered.

less gasoline, *much* gasoline, the *amount* of gasoline

Between/Among

Use *among* with three or more people or things. When there are only two, use *between*.

> The estate was divided between his wife and his daughter.
>
> The vote was split among the three candidates.

Affect/Effect

Affect is a verb meaning to influence. As a verb, *effect* means to bring about, but as a noun *effect* means a result or an influence.

> The *effect* (result) of his decision was to *effect* (bring about) a change in the voting laws that have *affected* (influenced) every candidate for office.
>
> Her decision will not *affect* single taxpayers, but it will have some *effect* on married couples.

In the second sentence, both *affect* and *effect* mean *influence,* but *affect* is a verb and *effect* a noun.

As a noun, *affect* refers to an expressed or observed emotional response:

> A flat or numbed *affect* can result from anti-depressant medications.

Idiom

This Grammar and Usage Review began by saying that you must not choose your answers according to it-sounds-right/it-sounds-wrong principles. However, unless you have memorized every idiom in the English language (and no one has), there is nothing on which to rely in choosing among idioms except the it-sounds-right principle. Should I say *agree with, agree to,* or *agree upon?* Depending upon the sentence, any one of the three may be right.

Examples:

> I *agree with* your opinion.
>
> The plaintiff *agreed to* pay damage of one hundred dollars.
>
> The committees have *agreed upon* a compromise.

Idioms are the usual way in which educated people put words together to express thought. Careful speakers or writers say *different from,* not *different than,* and *other than,* not *other from.* Most idiom problems arise from the use of prepositions. Since prepositions are so often insignificant words (*to, from, of, by*), it is easy to miss an obvious idiom error if you read carelessly.

There are no rules for idioms, and as the example of *agree* illustrates, idioms often will depend upon meaning. The more advanced tests will occasionally use an idiom uncertainty to distract you from a real error. Which is the better of these two sentences?

> The issue is how can we make our streets free of crime.

> The issue is how we can make our streets free from crime.

Is *it free from* or *free of?* Neither sounds wrong, and in fact, either is acceptable. The sentence is really testing word order with an indirect question; sentence 2 (*we can*) is the better sentence.

You may be asked to choose between a three-word phrase made up of a noun or adjective followed by a preposition and a gerund (a word ending in *-ing*) or a similar phrase with the same noun or adjective followed by an infinitive (the preposition *to* and the verb): *hope of going* or *hope to go; ability in running* or *ability to run; afraid of jumping* or *afraid to jump.* You must, finally, depend upon your ear and the context, but if neither version sounds clearly right or wrong, choose the infinitive. It is the better percentage play.

> Apes have demonstrated some ability *for reasoning* deductively.

> Apes have demonstrated some ability *to reason* deductively.

There are some established English idioms that appear regularly on standardized examinations. Below, the correct idioms are given first.

> *different from,* not *different than*
>
> *die of,* not *die from*
>
> *try to,* not *try and*
>
> *except for,* not *excepting for*
>
> *in regard to,* not *in regards to*
>
> *plan to,* not *plan on*
>
> *prior to,* not *prior than*
>
> *type of,* not *type of a*
>
> *bored by,* not *bored of*

Style

To this point, we have been concerned with errors of grammar, usage, diction, and idiom. With errors of this sort, you can point to a problematic single word or phrase and identify an error. In some questions, you will be asked to choose between several versions of a sentence, none of which contains a specific error of grammar or usage. One of the answers will be better than the others for reasons of style because it conveys meaning with superior precision, conciseness, clarity, or grace.

Between an awkward sentence that is grammatically correct and a smoother sentence with a grammatical error, always choose the correct version. But when neither of the two sentences has an error, base your decision on style. *Verbosity,* or unnecessary wordiness, is a common stylistic error.

Example:

<u>After the shipment of bananas had been unloaded, a tarantula's nest was discovered by the foreman</u> in the hold of the ship.

A.   After the shipment of bananas had been unloaded, a tarantula's nest was discovered by the foreman

B.   After unloading the shipment of bananas, a tarantula's nest was discovered by the foreman

C.   Having unloaded the shipment of bananas, a tarantula's nest was discovered by the foreman

D.   After the shipment of bananas had been unloaded, the foreman discovered a tarantula's nest

E.   After the shipment of bananas had been unloaded, the foreman discovers a tarantula's nest

Choices B, C, and E cannot be right—choices B and C because of the dangling gerund and dangling participle, and choice E because of the improper verb tenses (a past perfect and a present). Both choices A and D are grammatical, but because it uses the passive voice, choice A is wordier than choice **D.** Given a choice like this, prefer the sentence in the active voice. It is impossible to write the same sentence using a passive verb without using at least two more words than the active voice requires.

I hit the ball. (four words, active)

The ball was hit by me. (six words, passive)

You should note also the ambiguity in choice A in that you are not sure if the *foreman,* the *nest,* or both are in the *hold* of the ship.

In our eagerness to be expressive, we sometimes waste words by saying the same thing twice.

Examples:

> His prose is *clear* and *lucid.*
>
> The *annual* celebration *takes place every year.*
>
> Her argument was *trivial,* and it *had no importance.*

There are many phrases that take two or more words to say what one word can say equally well. *Due to the fact that* takes five words to say what *because* says in one. A verbose sentence will use a phrase like *his being of a generous nature* using six words where a phrase like *his generous nature* would say the same thing in three and *his generosity* in two. The following are examples of verbose phrases and formulas with a concise alternative.

Verbose	Concise
due to the fact that	because
owing to the fact that	because
inasmuch as	because
which was when	when
for the purpose of + gerund for the purpose of eating	to + verb to eat
in order to + verb in order to fly	to + verb to fly
so they can + verb so they can appreciate	to + verb to appreciate
not + negative adjective not useless	positive adjective useful
each and every	every
he is a man who	he is
. . . is a . . . that soccer is a game that	is soccer is
the truth is that the truth is that I am tired	often omit altogether I am tired
the fact is that the fact is that you were late	often omit altogether you were late
it is it is money that talks	often omit altogether money talks

Verbose	Concise
there are there are some flowers that are poisonous	often omit altogether some flowers are poisonous
in a situation where	where
in a condition where	where

Practice Exercise 9: Errors of Diction, Idiom, and Style

Part A

All of the following sentences contain an error of diction or idiom. Identify the error and correct the sentence.

1. Led by the oldest graduate present, with classes more or less in chronological order, the alumni parade winds it's way from Weld Hall to the Ford Theatre, where the annual meeting is held.

2. Governor Smith's way of running the state is noticeably different than Governor Eliot's.

3. There are fewer cars on the road, less accidents, and a lower death rate since the gasoline shortage.

4. Since his speeches usually have considerable affect on the Senate, the president will speak tonight.

5. The squabbles between the four original New England states delayed the calling of a convention.

6. I will plan on attending the meeting if I am not delayed.

7. Inflicted with poor eyesight and hearing as a result of her indigent childhood, she nevertheless rose to be the top money winner in women's badminton.

8. By calling her client's widowed mother, the lawyer hoped to effect the jury, but the strategy had no effect.

Part B

All of the following sentences are verbose. Cross out all the unnecessary words without changing the meaning of the sentences.

1. Though trailing thirty-one to ten, the team showed great resiliency and an ability to bounce back; when the fourth quarter ended, the score was thirty-one to thirty.

2. She is so compulsive about avoiding noise that she refuses to begin to do her homework until there is total and complete silence in the dorm.

3. When I look back in retrospect on all that has happened, it is clear that I made the right decision.

4. At the present moment in history, there are now over two thousand unregistered handguns in Alpine County alone.

5. Raised in a well-to-do and affluent suburb of New York, she was unable to adjust to the lack of physical comforts in rural Saskatchewan.

6. Unless the president presents a workable and practicable program to conserve and keep energy from being wasted, none of the New England states is likely to support him.

7. The true facts of the case made it clear that he was obviously a victim of a hideous injustice.

8. The subtle distinctions and nice discriminations of her philosophical essays are too fine for any but the most learned and erudite to understand, even with several re-readings.

9. Many dramatists and playwrights, Congreve among them, wrote about the elegance and corruption of the Restoration society.

10. The photography of the mountainous hill regions where the peasants live is beautiful; unfortunately, the film opened when the potential audience to whom it might have appealed had sated its appetite for travelogues.

Answers – Practice Exercise 9: Errors of Diction, Idiom, and Style

Part A

1. *it's*—should be *its*. *It's* means *it is*.

2. *than*—The correct idiom is *different from*.

3. *less*—Since accidents can be numbered, it should be *fewer accidents*.

4. *affect*—*Affect* is a verb; the noun *effect,* as the object of *have,* should be used here.

5. *between*—Since there are four states, use *among*.

6. *plan on attending*—The correct idiom is *plan to attend*.

7. *Inflicted*—The required word here is *afflicted*.

8. *effect*—The first *effect* should be the verb *affect*. The second *effect* is correct.

Part B

1. *Resiliency* and *ability to bounce back* mean the same thing.

2. One could omit *to do. Total* and *complete* mean the same thing.

3. Since *retrospect* means *a looking back,* the prepositional phrase *in retrospect* is unnecessary.

4. The phrase *At the present moment in history* is unnecessary with the use of *now*.

5. *Well-to-do* and *affluent* mean the same thing.

6. *Workable* and *practicable* mean the same thing. You also do not need both *conserve* and *keep from being wasted*.

7. Both *true* and *obviously* are unnecessary words here.

8. Either *subtle distinctions* or *nice discriminations* and either *learned* or *erudite* can be eliminated.

9. A *dramatist* is a *playwright.* One or the other is sufficient.

10. With *mountainous, hill* is unnecessary, and *potential* is equivalent to *to whom it might have appealed.*

Section 10: Punctuation

This section will certainly not tell you all you ought to know about punctuation to write well. It will describe the kind of punctuation errors that tend to appear in examination questions. You are not likely to find sentences that ask you whether to put the comma inside or outside a parenthesis. But you will find it useful to know the difference between a comma and a semicolon.

The comma is used to indicate a slight separation of sentence elements. The semicolon indicates a greater degree of separation, and the period marks the end of a sentence. The punctuation errors that will appear most frequently on the exams are the use of a comma where a semicolon is needed and the use of a semicolon where a comma is needed. In compound sentences (sentences with two independent clauses), a semicolon and a comma are not interchangeable.

Examples:

Punctuate the following sentences with either a comma or a semicolon.

1. I had come to China to buy silk and I was not planning to buy anything else.

   I had come to China to buy silk I was not planning to buy anything else.

2. I got my needles from Frankfurt but my threads came from London.

   I got my needles from Frankfurt my threads came from London.

In both examples, the first version needs a comma before a coordinating conjunction (*but*). In the second version, a semicolon should follow *silk* and *Frankfurt*. The principle is the same in both. With two independent clauses joined by a conjunction, use a comma. With two independent clauses that are not joined by a conjunction, use a semicolon. ***Note:*** The comma is not often used before a subordinating conjunction: *after, although, before, since, unless, while.*

Examples:

Now punctuate the following sentences with either a comma or a semicolon.

1. I looked for a house for sale on the lake hoping to be able to finish my book there.
2. They bundled themselves into the car waved once and drove away.
3. He was not at all interesting a man who talked endlessly about himself and how much money he had.

All three sentences need commas and only commas: after *lake* in sentence 1, after *car* and *once* in sentence 2, and after *interesting* in sentence 3. None of the segments following the comma is an independent clause that would allow for a semi-colon rather than a comma.

The following is an example of a sentence correction question that tests your knowledge of punctuation.

The editorials in *Ghost Magazine* are infuriating to some <u>readers;</u>
1

1. A. NO CHANGE
   B. readers. And
   C. readers,
   D. readers; or

delightful to others. <u>Nevertheless, its</u>
2
circulation has grown more rapidly than that of any other fantasy magazine.

2. F. NO CHANGE
   G. Nevertheless its
   H. Nevertheless, it's
   J. Nevertheless it's

The correct answers here are 1. **C** and 2. **F.** You must use a comma after *readers.* If you use a period or a semicolon, the phrase *delightful to others* is a sentence fragment. In 2, the punctuation is correct. The possessive of the pronoun *it* is *its; it's* is a contraction of *it is.* The comma marks the slight pause after the introductory word *Nevertheless.*

Commas, Semicolons, and Colons

The following is a brief summary of the rules governing commas, semicolons, and colons.

Comma

Use a comma:

1. in a series of three or more with a single conjunction.

   He bought red, green, and blue neckties.

   I must stop at the bank, have the car washed, and leave my shirts at the laundry.

2. to set off parenthetical expressions.

   The result, I imagine, will be in the paper.

   The check, you will be glad to know, is in the mail.

3. to set off nonrestrictive relative clauses.

   In 1600, when *Hamlet* was first acted, the Globe was London's largest public theatre.

   Montpelier, Concord, and Augusta, which are all small cities, are the capitals of the northern New England states.

4. to separate the two parts of a sentence with two independent clauses joined by a conjunction.

   The film is over, and the audience has left the theatre.

   The mayor is present, but the governor is not here.

5. to set off introductory words, phrases, or clauses.

   Unfortunately, he left his wallet in the car.

   Having looked in the glove compartment, he discovered his wallet was missing.

6. to set off appositives.

   Mr. Smith, the mayor, called the meeting to order.

   The leading batter in the league is John Jones, the first baseman.

Do not use a comma to join two independent clauses not joined by a conjunction. Use a period or a semicolon.

1. Her novels are always best sellers; they are translated into three languages.
2. The boat crossed the lake in fifteen minutes; the canoe took two hours.

Each of these sentences could be written as two sentences with periods at the end. If a conjunction were added, a comma would replace the semicolons.

1. Her novels are always best sellers, *and* they are translated into three languages.
2. The boat crossed the lake in fifteen minutes, *but* the canoe took two hours.

Semicolon

Use a semicolon:

1. to separate two independent clauses in a compound sentence when there is no conjunction between them.

   The hurricane came ashore near Lake Charles; its winds were measured at more than one hundred miles per hour.

   The warnings were broadcast early in the day; thus, there was no loss of life. *Note:* Thus is a conjunctive adverb, not a conjunction.

2. to separate a series when one or more of the elements of the series contains commas.

   He bought a red, a green, and a blue tie; three button-down shirts; and a pair of penny loafers.

   We will stop in Maumee, Ohio; Erie, Pennsylvania; Albany, New York; and Amherst, Massachusetts.

Colon

Use a colon after an independent clause:

1. to introduce a series.

   The following vegetables should be planted in March: radishes, carrots, leeks, turnips, and cabbage.

In this sentence, the clause before the colon is independent. In a sentence such as, *In March, you should plant radishes, carrots, leeks, turnips, and cabbage,* in which there is no independent clause before the series, you should *not* use a colon.

2. to join two independent clauses when the second amplifies or interprets the first.

   A preliminary step is essential to successful whipped cream: you must chill the bowl and the beaters.

3. before an explanation that is not an independent clause.

   He had two goals in life: to make the big leagues and to break his father's record.

4. to introduce a quotation.

   Every English schoolchild knows the opening line of *Twelfth Night:* "If music be the food of love, play on."

Other Marks of Punctuation

Dash

Use a dash to indicate an abrupt break and to set off parenthetical elements already broken up by commas.

I believe—no, I know—he is guilty.

I—er—you—er—forget it!

The general—over decorated, overconfident, overweight—spoke to the troops on the benefits of self-sacrifice.

The speech—the harangue, I should say—lasted for three hours.

Apostrophe

Use an apostrophe to indicate the omission of a letter or letters in a contraction (*I'm, I've, you'd, don't, who's, we're*).

Form the possessive of singular nouns by adding *'s* (*tiger's, cat's, man's*). Form the possessive of plural nouns by adding just the apostrophe if the plural ends in *s* (*tigers', cats', dogs'*). Form the possessive of plural nouns that do not end in *s* by adding *'s* (*mice's, men's, children's*).

Practice Exercise 10: Punctuation

In the left-hand column, you will find a passage in a "spread-out" format with various words and phrases underlined. In the right-hand column, you will find a set of responses corresponding to each underlined portion. If the underlined portion is correct as it stands, mark the letter indicating "NO CHANGE." If the underlined portion is incorrect, decide which of the choices best corrects it. Consider only underlined portions; assume that the rest of the passage is correct.

Anything it seems is worth
1
fighting about when there's money
to be made. How else can we explain
the public-relations war being waged
between the plastics and paper
industries over the best kind of
grocery bag to use. If you've been to
2
the supermarket lately, you know
what we're talking about.

Alongside those tried trusty and
3
true brown paper bags that Americans
have relied on and treasured since
1883, you'll see a lump of limp,
shapeless, non-biodegradable plastic
containers that the plastic lobby would
try to convince you is the way to go.

1. A. NO CHANGE
   B. Anything, it seems is worth
   C. Anything it seems, is worth
   D. Anything, it seems, is worth

2. F. NO CHANGE
   G. bag to use? If
   H. bag to use; if
   J. bag to use! If

3. A. NO CHANGE
   B. tried, trusty, and true, brown
   C. tried, trusty, and true brown
   D. tried, trusty and true brown

Their argument is that plastic bags are more easily <u>portable—at least, for</u> ₄ <u>those who go to the store on foot—</u>

4. F.   NO CHANGE
   G.   portable, at least, for those who go to the store on foot—
   H.   portable—at least for those who go to the store on foot—
   J.   portable, at least, for those, who go to the store on foot,

because they have <u>handles; that</u> they ₅ don't leak all over the place when something wet gets loose; and that they can just as easily be used as garbage containers as the paper variety. They are also cheaper for the supermarket, at about 2.6 cents apiece, compared with 4.4 cents for paper bags, and they require less storage space.

5. A.   NO CHANGE
   B.   handles that
   C.   handles, that
   D.   handles-that

The obvious response to this propaganda barrage is that paper bags stand on their <u>own, so to speak, in your trunk, are bio-degradable, make a better waste container can</u> be cut up and used to wrap books, packages, or parcels, or to make

6. F.   NO CHANGE
   G.   own so to speak in your trunk, are biodegradable, make a better waste container, can
   H.   own, so to speak, in your trunk; are biodegradable; make a better waste container; can
   J.   own, so to speak, in your trunk, are biodegradable, make a better waste container, can

Halloween <u>masks; and—here's the telling punch—are</u> actually cheaper overall because supermarket checkers can pack them 18 percent faster than the plastic.

7. A.   NO CHANGE
   B.   masks; and here's the telling punch; are
   C.   masks, and, heres the telling punch, are
   D.   masks, and—here's the telling punch—are

Surveys have been <u>conducted, of course, and it turns out, not too surprisingly,</u> that those who live alone in city apartments—typically singles, old people, and just about anyone who lives in the middle of

8. F.   NO CHANGE
   G.   conducted, of course, and it turns out not too surprisingly
   H.   conducted of course, and it turns out not too surprisingly
   J.   conducted of course, and it turns out, not too surprisingly

Manhattan or San Francisco—prefer plastic. The rest of <u>us—suburbanites</u>₉ <u>the pro-plastic folks disparagingly call us—</u>are quite happy with our brown paper bags, thank you, and we're still a majority.

9. A. NO CHANGE
   B. us—"suburbanites" the pro-plastic folks disparagingly call us—
   C. us—"suburbanites," the pro-plastic folks disparagingly call us—
   D. us—suburbanites, the pro-plastic folks disparagingly call us

Answers – Practice Exercise 10: Punctuation

1. **D.** The phrase *it seems* is parenthetical and should be set off by two commas.

2. **G.** The sentence is a question.

3. **C.** The words are a series.

4. **H.** The dashes set off an interrupting phrase. One could use commas instead of the dashes, but not one comma and one dash as in choice G. No commas are needed after *least* and *those.*

5. **A.** The semicolon here divides the parts of a series.

6. **H.** The parenthetical *so to speak* should be set off by commas. The series requires semicolons after *trunk, biodegradable,* and *container* because it contains commas within elements of the series.

7. **A.** The dashes set off the interruption. Choice C omits the apostrophe in *here's.* The series has been written using semicolons, so the commas are inconsistent in choices C and D.

8. **F.** The phrases *of course* and *not too surprisingly* are parenthetical and each requires two commas

9. **C.** The word *suburbanites* should be in quotation marks (quoting the pro-plastic folks) and set off from the subject of the clause by a comma.

Vocabulary Skills Review

Verbal ability involves vocabulary skills on many standardized tests. You will see questions that require you to recognize the meaning of given words, identify words with like meanings and unlike meanings, and decide which word or words best fits the overall meaning of the context of sentences and paragraphs.

The level of vocabulary in each of these cases can be challenging. Although there is no way to quickly develop a strong vocabulary, you may increase your vocabulary gradually by reading widely, always checking the definitions of unfamiliar words, and learning the meanings of common prefixes, suffixes, and roots. Rather than explaining the particular types of vocabulary skills tests you may encounter, we suggest learning the general meaning of "word parts" (prefixes, suffixes, and roots) that are useful in all cases.

Prefixes

A *prefix* is the beginning section of a word and tells the partial meaning of the word. For instance, the *pre-* in *prefix* means *before* and tells us that a prefix occurs before the rest of the word. Here are ten common prefixes:

Prefix	Meaning	Example
anti-	against	*antibiotic—against* life (bacteria)
bi-	two	*bilingual—capable of speaking *two* languages
co-, com-, con-	together, with	*cooperation—joint* effort
dia-	through, across, between	*dialogue—conversation *between* two people
dis-	not, opposite of, un-	*disreputable—not* reputable, *not* respectable
equi-	equal, equally	*equinox—when day and night are of *equal* length
mis-	wrongly, bad, badly	*misinterpretation—wrong* interpretation
re-	again, over again	*reiterate—to say or do something *again*
sub-	under, beneath,	*subdue—to bring *under* control
trans-	across, over, beyond	*transcendental—beyond* human experience

If you are in doubt about the prefix of an unfamiliar word, try this:

1. Focus on the beginning section of the word. For instance, if you encounter *malevolence,* focus on *mal.*

2. Recall a word in your vocabulary that contains the same prefix. In this case, one such word might be *malfunction* or *malicious.*

3. Apply your knowledge of the word(s) you know to the word you do not know. In this case, *mal* seems to mean *bad,* so you might conclude that *malevolence* has a bad, or negative, connotation.

Suffixes

A *suffix* is a word ending that affects the meaning of the word.

Here are ten common suffixes:

Suffix	Meaning	Example
-able, -ible	capable of being	*combustible—capable* of burning
-ant, -ent	person who	*aspirant—a person who* aspires, seeks
-ful	full of, with qualities of	*remorseful—full of* remorse, or sadness
-fy	cause to be, make	*emulsify—make* into an emulsion, or milky fluid
-ism	condition of being	*pauperism—the condition of being* a pauper
-ive	having the quality of	*predictive—having the quality of* a prediction
-less	without	*relentless—without* relenting, or giving up
-ness	state of being	*vociferousness—state of being* vociferous, or loud
-ous, -os	full of, like	*curious—full of* curiosity
-tude	state of being	*lassitude—state of being* weary

To practice with common suffixes, try this. For every suffix, list at least five familiar words and define them. For instance, you might practice with *-less* as follows:

Fearless	without fear
Errorless	without error
Hopeless	without hope, and so forth.

Roots

Take away prefixes and suffixes, and you are left with the *root of a word,* the part that holds its essential meaning. Here are ten common roots:

Root	Meaning	Example
belli	war	*belligerent—warlike*
ben, bene	well, good	*benefit—good* result
fac, fic	to do or make	*facile—easy to do*
grad, gress	to go	*regression—going* or moving backward
liber	book, free	*liberty—*freedom
meter	to measure	*barometer—*instrument for *measuring* atmospheric pressure
nov	new	*novel—new*
port	to carry	*deportation—expulsion* from a country
un, uni	one	*disunify—*break apart a *unit*
vid, vis	to see	*visage—*the face

Roots, prefixes, and suffixes work together to make up the meaning of a word. Take *disunify,* for instance: *dis = not, uni = one, fy = make.* Therefore, *disunify* means *make not one,* or as noted above, *break apart a unit.*

Grammar and Usage Review Test

Now that you have reviewed grammar and usage topics, you can practice on your own. Answers and explanations follow the questions.

Some of the following sentences may be correct while others contain errors. Each sentence has no more than one error. Find the one underlined part that must be changed to make the sentence correct. Choose E if the sentence contains no error.

1. No one <u>but</u> the president, secretary, <u>and me</u> <u>was</u> at the meeting, and we
    A   B   C
   voted <u>unanimously to spend</u> all of the money in the treasury. <u>No error.</u>
              D   E

2. Many a young man of twenty-five or thirty <u>have dreamed</u> of
      A
   retiring at fifty, but few, when they reach <u>that age</u>, find that the sum
                                                B
   <u>they had thought</u> <u>could support</u> them is adequate. <u>No error</u>.
       C   D   E

3. <u>Having lived</u> for two years <u>near both the highway</u> and the airport,
       A   B
   I am used to the noises of cars and planes, <u>which</u> no longer
                                                C
   <u>disturb my sleep</u>. <u>No error</u>.
       D   E

4. The book's <u>public-relations prose</u>, <u>its long-windedness</u>, and its
                A   B
   tendency <u>uncritically to list</u> ideas ultimately <u>makes it</u> a wholly
              C   D
   useless study that should never have been published. <u>No error</u>.
                                                            E

5. It is depressing to realize <u>that in</u> a country <u>as rich as this</u>, thousands of
                                 A   B
   people live out <u>their life</u> without <u>ever having</u> enough to eat. <u>No error</u>.
                      C   D   E

6. My family <u>includes</u> several serious and responsible members,
               A
   <u>my sister and I</u>, for example, but <u>even we</u> have had <u>next to no</u>
       B   C   D
   influence on public life. <u>No error</u>.
                                E

7. The result of all the tests, <u>according to</u> the surgeon, <u>was not</u>
                                   A   B
   <u>likely to alarm</u> either her husband <u>or her</u>. <u>No error</u>.
       C   D   E

8. Some smaller players will tackle <u>only</u> <u>whoever</u> comes near them,
                                       A   B
   while others <u>will tackle</u> <u>whoever</u> they can catch. <u>No error</u>.
                   C   D   E

9. Though the first question on the test <u>seemed</u> <u>simple</u>, there were
                                            A   B
   <u>simply</u> too many questions <u>for me to finish</u> on time. <u>No error</u>.
       C   D   E

10. There are several runners on the home team <u>who</u> are <u>faster</u> in the
    AB
    <u>shorter</u> races than the runners of the opposing team, but in the field
    C
    events, the opposing runners are <u>best</u>. <u>No error</u>.
    DE

11. <u>Laying aside</u> his guns, the western hero seems <u>to lose</u> his
    AB
    distinguishing feature, and <u>he became</u> <u>like anyone else</u>. <u>No error</u>.
    CDE

12. Timur's campaigns <u>were initiated</u> less from geopolitical considerations
    A
    <u>than the need</u> to provide plunder for his army, <u>which resembled</u> a vast
    BC
    mobile city <u>existing only for</u> conquest and pillage. <u>No error</u>.
    DE

13. <u>In calling *Vanity Fair* a "novel without a hero,"</u> Thackeray <u>suggests</u>
    AB
    that none of his characters, <u>not even Amelia or Dobbin,</u> <u>is</u> completely
    CD
    admirable. <u>No error</u>.
    E

14. The psychosomatic origin of migraine headaches <u>has been suspected</u>
    A
    for years, but <u>it was not</u> until 1970 that doctors <u>realized</u> that a
    BC
    patient's thinking about pain <u>is</u> likely to prolong an attack. <u>No error</u>.
    DE

15. The fog of myth and superstition <u>was dispelled</u> not by professors
    A
    <u>but men like</u> Prince Henry the Navigator and his captains <u>who went out</u>
    BC
    to explore the globe <u>and to chart</u> the known world. <u>No error</u>.
    DE

16. <u>Raising the window shade slowly,</u> the bright sunshine <u>poured</u> into the
    AB
    room and <u>illuminated</u> the broken crystal <u>lying</u> on the floor. <u>No error</u>.
    CDE

17. <u>Having narrowly missed colliding with another car</u> while trying to
                          A
   change lanes on the freeway, all three of my passengers told <u>me</u> that
                                                  B
   I <u>was</u> <u>a terrible driver</u>. <u>No error</u>.
    C   D   E

18. The prince was <u>embarrassed but not injured</u> when a demonstrator
                              A
   broke through the <u>cordon</u> of security guards <u>and splashes</u> red paint
                    B   C
   on <u>his</u> white suit. <u>No error</u>.
     D   E

19. After beginning at the bottom <u>as a stockboy</u>, <u>he</u> <u>rose</u> to the
                                    A   B C
   presidency of the store <u>in only eight years</u>. <u>No error</u>.
                      D   E

20. You must be very careful to read the instructions <u>on the test booklet</u>,
                                                     A
   to <u>mark</u> the correct space on your answer sheet, and <u>stop</u> writing as
      B   C
   soon as the proctor <u>announces</u> the end of the exam. <u>No error</u>.
                     D   E

21. Gordon's novel, written <u>with an eye to</u> conservative readers, has
                             A
   <u>less scenes</u> of action and more with moral lessons <u>than</u> <u>any other work</u>
    B   C   D
   published this year. <u>No error</u>.
                  E

22. An independent clause can <u>stand alone</u> <u>as a sentence</u>, while a
                            A   B
   dependent clause <u>occupies</u> a subordinate position and cannot
                  C
   <u>by itself</u> be a complete sentence. <u>No error</u>.
    D   E

23. Though his lawyer <u>argued his case</u> cogently, concisely, and <u>forcefully</u>,
                    A   B
   Jones <u>was still</u> found guilty <u>and sentenced</u> to three years in jail.
        C   D
   <u>No error</u>.
    E

24. Since the mountains in California are higher <u>than New York,</u>

                                                    A

<u>those of us</u> who like to ski <u>prefer</u> <u>to spend</u> the winter on the west

   B   C   D

coast. <u>No error.</u>

      E

25. The courtly lover of Provence worshipped both <u>the Virgin</u> and an

                                                  A

earthly lady and <u>paid his</u> tribute <u>to her</u> in <u>ornate</u> lyric poems. <u>No error.</u>

              B   C   D   E

26. Although he <u>took</u> careful notes, <u>studied</u> in the library every night,

              A   B

and <u>wrote</u> two extra papers, this industry <u>did not effect</u> his grade in

     C   D

the class. <u>No error.</u>

          E

27. <u>Like</u> a large room, the American continent once offered <u>an exhilarating</u>

 A   B

<u>spatial freedom</u>, impressing western settlers <u>first with</u> its sublime beauty

                                                C

and afterward with <u>its opportunities for exploitation.</u> <u>No error.</u>

                             D   E

28. When the queen entered, the <u>musicians which were</u> on the stage

                                          A

withdrew quietly, but the actors were <u>too surprised</u> <u>to be able</u>

                                    B   C

<u>to know what to do.</u> <u>No error.</u>

     D   E

29. I have <u>no interest</u> and <u>no intention</u> to become involved with

         A   B

<u>this foolish debate</u> about priorities <u>in</u> Central America. <u>No error.</u>

       C   D   E

30. We will have <u>to start for home</u> much earlier this week, <u>for</u> there are

                 A   B

<u>not but two or three hours</u> of good driving conditions <u>if we leave</u>

            C   D

after two o'clock. <u>No error.</u>

               E

When you take a grammar exam, you must be able to recognize the kind of error or errors that a sentence includes. Certain words or sentence structures should warn you at once of the kind of error likely to occur in the sentence. All of the following words or structures should alert you to one or two likely errors. What are these errors?

31. a sentence beginning with a participle

32. a sentence beginning with *both*

33. a sentence containing a series

34. a sentence beginning with *either*

35. a sentence containing *not*

36. a sentence beginning with a prepositional phrase with *like*

37. a sentence containing the phrase *a number*

38. a sentence beginning with *everybody*

39. a sentence containing *who*

40. a sentence containing the verb *look*

41. a sentence beginning with *one*

42. a sentence beginning with *none*

43. a sentence beginning with an elliptical phrase

44. a sentence containing *criteria*

45. a sentence containing *almost*

46. a sentence containing *hardly*

47. a sentence containing a comparison

48. a sentence containing the verb *lie*

49. a sentence beginning with *if*

50. a sentence containing *as well as*

Answers and Explanations – Grammar and Usage Review Test

1. E. The *me* is the object of the preposition *but;* the subject is the singular *No one,* so *was* is also correct. (see p. 89)

2. A. The phrase *many a young man* is singular, and takes the verb *has.* The plural would be *many men.* (see p. 90)

3. E. The agreement in this sentence is correct. (see p. 89)

4. D. The subject is plural, a compound subject with *and.* (see p. 88)

5. C. Since *thousands* is plural, *life* should be *lives.* (see p. 84)

6. B. The phrase *my sister and I* is in apposition to *members,* the object of *includes. I* should be *me.* (see p. 81)

7. E. The singular *was* is correct with the singular subject *result. Her* is the object of *alarm.* (see p. 88)

8. D. The subject of the last clause is *they,* the verb is *can catch,* and the object should be *whomever.* (see p. 81)

9. E. The adjective *simple* is correct with the linking verb *seemed.* The adverb *simply* modifies the adverb *too.* (see p. 76)

10. D. With a comparison of two teams, *better* not *best* should be used. (see p. 78)

11. C. Since the main verb in the first part of the sentence is in the present tense (*seems*), there is no reason to shift to a past tense. (see p. 96)

12. B. With *less from* followed by *than,* the *from* should be repeated. (see p. 115)

13. E. The sentence is correct as given. (see p. 89)

14. E. The present tense of *is* is correct, since the subject is a medical fact that continues to be true. (see p. 97)

15. **B.** With the correlatives *not . . . but,* the *but* should be followed by the preposition *by* to be parallel. (see p. 115)

16. **A.** *Raising* is the right verb (not *rising*), but the phrase is a dangling participle. It reads as though the *sunshine* raised the shade. (see p. 107)

17. **A.** Another dangling participle. The *I* of the sentence, not the passengers, narrowly missed the collision. (see p. 107)

18. **C.** The other verbs of the sentence (*was, broke*) are in the past tense, so *splashed* would be correct here. (see p. 96)

19. **E.** The beginning phrase modifies *he* and does not dangle. (see p. 107)

20. **C.** The series should have three infinitives: *to read, to mark,* and *to stop.* (see p. 109)

21. **B.** *Less* should be *fewer.* (see p. 132)

22. **E.** The sentence is correct as given. (see p. 96)

23. **B.** *Forcefully* repeats *cogently.* (see p. 135)

24. **A.** The sentence should read *than those in New York.* (see p. 123)

25. **C.** The antecedent of *her* is ambiguous. It could be either *the Virgin* or *an earthly lady.* (see p. 120)

26. **D.** *Effect* should be *affect.* (see p. 133)

27. **E.** There is no error in this sentence. (see p. 108)

28. **A.** Since the musicians are human, the pronoun should be *who.* (see p. 127)

29. **A.** The sentence should read *no interest in becoming.* (see p. 123)

30. **C.** The *not* and *but* are both negatives. Eliminate *not.* (see p. 123)

31. dangling participle (see p. 108)

32. either agreement (the subject will be plural) or parallelism with *both . . . and* (see pp. 87 and 115)

33. parallelism (see p. 115)

34. either agreement (the verb will agree with the word nearer the verb) or parallelism with *either . . . or* (see pp. 87 and 115)

35. double negative or parallelism with *not both . . . but* (see pp. 123 and 115)

36. confusion of *like* and *as* or parallelism with the prepositional phrase (see pp. 127 and 112)

37. agreement—*a number* is singular (see p. 87)

38. agreement—*everybody* is singular (see p. 91)

39. case of *who/whom*—confusion of *who/that/which* (see p. 127)

40. adverb for *adjective,* when *look* is used as a linking verb: *The lion looks hungry.* (see p. 76)

41. agreement—*one* is singular, a change of person, or the incorrect use of *your* later in the sentence (see p. 89)

42. agreement—*none* is singular (see p. 89)

43. dangling elliptical phrase (see p. 109)

44. agreement—*criteria* is plural (see p. 90)

45. placement of related words (see p. 76)

46. double negative (see p. 123)

47. parallelism—be sure like elements are compared, or check for omission of necessary words such as *other* (see pp. 78 and 123)

48. *lie* versus *lay* (see p. 101)

49. tense of subjunctive verbs (see p. 100)

50. agreement—*as well as* is parenthetical and will not make a singular subject plural (see p. 88)

Chapter 4

English Grammar and Usage Practice Test

Answer Sheets

(Remove these sheets and use them to mark your answers.)

Section 1: Sentence Correction – Type 1

Set 1	Set 2	Set 3	Set 4

CUT HERE

Set 1	Set 2	Set 3	Set 4
1 Ⓐ Ⓑ Ⓒ Ⓓ Ⓔ	16 Ⓐ Ⓑ Ⓒ Ⓓ Ⓔ	31 Ⓐ Ⓑ Ⓒ Ⓓ Ⓔ	46 Ⓐ Ⓑ Ⓒ Ⓓ Ⓔ
2 Ⓐ Ⓑ Ⓒ Ⓓ Ⓔ	17 Ⓐ Ⓑ Ⓒ Ⓓ Ⓔ	32 Ⓐ Ⓑ Ⓒ Ⓓ Ⓔ	47 Ⓐ Ⓑ Ⓒ Ⓓ Ⓔ
3 Ⓐ Ⓑ Ⓒ Ⓓ Ⓔ	18 Ⓐ Ⓑ Ⓒ Ⓓ Ⓔ	33 Ⓐ Ⓑ Ⓒ Ⓓ Ⓔ	48 Ⓐ Ⓑ Ⓒ Ⓓ Ⓔ
4 Ⓐ Ⓑ Ⓒ Ⓓ Ⓔ	19 Ⓐ Ⓑ Ⓒ Ⓓ Ⓔ	34 Ⓐ Ⓑ Ⓒ Ⓓ Ⓔ	49 Ⓐ Ⓑ Ⓒ Ⓓ Ⓔ
5 Ⓐ Ⓑ Ⓒ Ⓓ Ⓔ	20 Ⓐ Ⓑ Ⓒ Ⓓ Ⓔ	35 Ⓐ Ⓑ Ⓒ Ⓓ Ⓔ	50 Ⓐ Ⓑ Ⓒ Ⓓ Ⓔ
6 Ⓐ Ⓑ Ⓒ Ⓓ Ⓔ	21 Ⓐ Ⓑ Ⓒ Ⓓ Ⓔ	36 Ⓐ Ⓑ Ⓒ Ⓓ Ⓔ	51 Ⓐ Ⓑ Ⓒ Ⓓ Ⓔ
7 Ⓐ Ⓑ Ⓒ Ⓓ Ⓔ	22 Ⓐ Ⓑ Ⓒ Ⓓ Ⓔ	37 Ⓐ Ⓑ Ⓒ Ⓓ Ⓔ	52 Ⓐ Ⓑ Ⓒ Ⓓ Ⓔ
8 Ⓐ Ⓑ Ⓒ Ⓓ Ⓔ	23 Ⓐ Ⓑ Ⓒ Ⓓ Ⓔ	38 Ⓐ Ⓑ Ⓒ Ⓓ Ⓔ	53 Ⓐ Ⓑ Ⓒ Ⓓ Ⓔ
9 Ⓐ Ⓑ Ⓒ Ⓓ Ⓔ	24 Ⓐ Ⓑ Ⓒ Ⓓ Ⓔ	39 Ⓐ Ⓑ Ⓒ Ⓓ Ⓔ	54 Ⓐ Ⓑ Ⓒ Ⓓ Ⓔ
10 Ⓐ Ⓑ Ⓒ Ⓓ Ⓕ	25 Ⓐ Ⓑ Ⓒ Ⓓ Ⓔ	40 Ⓐ Ⓑ Ⓒ Ⓓ Ⓔ	55 Ⓐ Ⓑ Ⓒ Ⓓ Ⓔ
11 Ⓐ Ⓑ Ⓒ Ⓓ Ⓔ	26 Ⓐ Ⓑ Ⓒ Ⓓ Ⓔ	41 Ⓐ Ⓑ Ⓒ Ⓓ Ⓔ	56 Ⓐ Ⓑ Ⓒ Ⓓ Ⓔ
12 Ⓐ Ⓑ Ⓒ Ⓓ Ⓔ	27 Ⓐ Ⓑ Ⓒ Ⓓ Ⓔ	42 Ⓐ Ⓑ Ⓒ Ⓓ Ⓔ	57 Ⓐ Ⓑ Ⓒ Ⓓ Ⓔ
13 Ⓐ Ⓑ Ⓒ Ⓓ Ⓔ	28 Ⓐ Ⓑ Ⓒ Ⓓ Ⓔ	43 Ⓐ Ⓑ Ⓒ Ⓓ Ⓔ	58 Ⓐ Ⓑ Ⓒ Ⓓ Ⓔ
14 Ⓐ Ⓑ Ⓒ Ⓓ Ⓔ	29 Ⓐ Ⓑ Ⓒ Ⓓ Ⓔ	44 Ⓐ Ⓑ Ⓒ Ⓓ Ⓔ	59 Ⓐ Ⓑ Ⓒ Ⓓ Ⓔ
15 Ⓐ Ⓑ Ⓒ Ⓓ Ⓔ	30 Ⓐ Ⓑ Ⓒ Ⓓ Ⓔ	45 Ⓐ Ⓑ Ⓒ Ⓓ Ⓔ	60 Ⓐ Ⓑ Ⓒ Ⓓ Ⓔ

Section 2: Sentence Correction – Type 2

| Set 1 | Set 2 | Set 3 |

1 Ⓐ Ⓑ Ⓒ Ⓓ Ⓔ   16 Ⓐ Ⓑ Ⓒ Ⓓ Ⓔ   31 Ⓐ Ⓑ Ⓒ Ⓓ Ⓔ
2 Ⓐ Ⓑ Ⓒ Ⓓ Ⓔ   17 Ⓐ Ⓑ Ⓒ Ⓓ Ⓔ   32 Ⓐ Ⓑ Ⓒ Ⓓ Ⓔ
3 Ⓐ Ⓑ Ⓒ Ⓓ Ⓔ   18 Ⓐ Ⓑ Ⓒ Ⓓ Ⓔ   33 Ⓐ Ⓑ Ⓒ Ⓓ Ⓔ
4 Ⓐ Ⓑ Ⓒ Ⓓ Ⓔ   19 Ⓐ Ⓑ Ⓒ Ⓓ Ⓔ   34 Ⓐ Ⓑ Ⓒ Ⓓ Ⓔ
5 Ⓐ Ⓑ Ⓒ Ⓓ Ⓔ   20 Ⓐ Ⓑ Ⓒ Ⓓ Ⓔ   35 Ⓐ Ⓑ Ⓒ Ⓓ Ⓔ

6 Ⓐ Ⓑ Ⓒ Ⓓ Ⓔ   21 Ⓐ Ⓑ Ⓒ Ⓓ Ⓔ   36 Ⓐ Ⓑ Ⓒ Ⓓ Ⓔ
7 Ⓐ Ⓑ Ⓒ Ⓓ Ⓔ   22 Ⓐ Ⓑ Ⓒ Ⓓ Ⓔ   37 Ⓐ Ⓑ Ⓒ Ⓓ Ⓔ
8 Ⓐ Ⓑ Ⓒ Ⓓ Ⓔ   23 Ⓐ Ⓑ Ⓒ Ⓓ Ⓔ   38 Ⓐ Ⓑ Ⓒ Ⓓ Ⓔ
9 Ⓐ Ⓑ Ⓒ Ⓓ Ⓔ   24 Ⓐ Ⓑ Ⓒ Ⓓ Ⓔ   39 Ⓐ Ⓑ Ⓒ Ⓓ Ⓔ
10 Ⓐ Ⓑ Ⓒ Ⓓ Ⓔ   25 Ⓐ Ⓑ Ⓒ Ⓓ Ⓔ   40 Ⓐ Ⓑ Ⓒ Ⓓ Ⓔ

11 Ⓐ Ⓑ Ⓒ Ⓓ Ⓔ   26 Ⓐ Ⓑ Ⓒ Ⓓ Ⓔ   41 Ⓐ Ⓑ Ⓒ Ⓓ Ⓔ
12 Ⓐ Ⓑ Ⓒ Ⓓ Ⓔ   27 Ⓐ Ⓑ Ⓒ Ⓓ Ⓔ   42 Ⓐ Ⓑ Ⓒ Ⓓ Ⓔ
13 Ⓐ Ⓑ Ⓒ Ⓓ Ⓔ   28 Ⓐ Ⓑ Ⓒ Ⓓ Ⓔ   43 Ⓐ Ⓑ Ⓒ Ⓓ Ⓔ
14 Ⓐ Ⓑ Ⓒ Ⓓ Ⓔ   29 Ⓐ Ⓑ Ⓒ Ⓓ Ⓔ   44 Ⓐ Ⓑ Ⓒ Ⓓ Ⓔ
15 Ⓐ Ⓑ Ⓒ Ⓓ Ⓔ   30 Ⓐ Ⓑ Ⓒ Ⓓ Ⓔ   45 Ⓐ Ⓑ Ⓒ Ⓓ Ⓔ

Section 3: Sentence Correction – Type 3

| Set 1 | Set 2 | Set 3 | Set 4 |

1 Ⓐ Ⓑ Ⓒ Ⓓ Ⓔ   17 Ⓐ Ⓑ Ⓒ Ⓓ Ⓔ   35 Ⓐ Ⓑ Ⓒ Ⓓ Ⓔ   50 Ⓐ Ⓑ Ⓒ Ⓓ Ⓔ
2 Ⓐ Ⓑ Ⓒ Ⓓ Ⓔ   18 Ⓐ Ⓑ Ⓒ Ⓓ Ⓔ   36 Ⓐ Ⓑ Ⓒ Ⓓ Ⓔ   51 Ⓐ Ⓑ Ⓒ Ⓓ Ⓔ
3 Ⓐ Ⓑ Ⓒ Ⓓ Ⓔ   19 Ⓐ Ⓑ Ⓒ Ⓓ Ⓔ   37 Ⓐ Ⓑ Ⓒ Ⓓ Ⓔ   52 Ⓐ Ⓑ Ⓒ Ⓓ Ⓔ
4 Ⓐ Ⓑ Ⓒ Ⓓ Ⓔ   20 Ⓐ Ⓑ Ⓒ Ⓓ Ⓔ   38 Ⓐ Ⓑ Ⓒ Ⓓ Ⓔ   53 Ⓐ Ⓑ Ⓒ Ⓓ Ⓔ
5 Ⓐ Ⓑ Ⓒ Ⓓ Ⓔ   21 Ⓐ Ⓑ Ⓒ Ⓓ Ⓔ   39 Ⓐ Ⓑ Ⓒ Ⓓ Ⓔ   54 Ⓐ Ⓑ Ⓒ Ⓓ Ⓔ

6 Ⓐ Ⓑ Ⓒ Ⓓ Ⓔ   22 Ⓐ Ⓑ Ⓒ Ⓓ Ⓔ   40 Ⓐ Ⓑ Ⓒ Ⓓ Ⓔ   55 Ⓐ Ⓑ Ⓒ Ⓓ Ⓔ
7 Ⓐ Ⓑ Ⓒ Ⓓ Ⓔ   23 Ⓐ Ⓑ Ⓒ Ⓓ Ⓔ   41 Ⓐ Ⓑ Ⓒ Ⓓ Ⓔ   56 Ⓐ Ⓑ Ⓒ Ⓓ Ⓔ
8 Ⓐ Ⓑ Ⓒ Ⓓ Ⓔ   24 Ⓐ Ⓑ Ⓒ Ⓓ Ⓔ   42 Ⓐ Ⓑ Ⓒ Ⓓ Ⓔ   57 Ⓐ Ⓑ Ⓒ Ⓓ Ⓔ
9 Ⓐ Ⓑ Ⓒ Ⓓ Ⓔ   25 Ⓐ Ⓑ Ⓒ Ⓓ Ⓔ   43 Ⓐ Ⓑ Ⓒ Ⓓ Ⓔ   58 Ⓐ Ⓑ Ⓒ Ⓓ Ⓔ
10 Ⓐ Ⓑ Ⓒ Ⓓ Ⓔ   26 Ⓐ Ⓑ Ⓒ Ⓓ Ⓔ   44 Ⓐ Ⓑ Ⓒ Ⓓ Ⓔ   59 Ⓐ Ⓑ Ⓒ Ⓓ Ⓔ

11 Ⓐ Ⓑ Ⓒ Ⓓ Ⓔ   27 Ⓐ Ⓑ Ⓒ Ⓓ Ⓔ   45 Ⓐ Ⓑ Ⓒ Ⓓ Ⓔ   60 Ⓐ Ⓑ Ⓒ Ⓓ Ⓔ
12 Ⓐ Ⓑ Ⓒ Ⓓ Ⓔ   28 Ⓐ Ⓑ Ⓒ Ⓓ Ⓔ   46 Ⓐ Ⓑ Ⓒ Ⓓ Ⓔ   61 Ⓐ Ⓑ Ⓒ Ⓓ Ⓔ
13 Ⓐ Ⓑ Ⓒ Ⓓ Ⓔ   29 Ⓐ Ⓑ Ⓒ Ⓓ Ⓔ   47 Ⓐ Ⓑ Ⓒ Ⓓ Ⓔ   62 Ⓐ Ⓑ Ⓒ Ⓓ Ⓔ
14 Ⓐ Ⓑ Ⓒ Ⓓ Ⓔ   30 Ⓐ Ⓑ Ⓒ Ⓓ Ⓔ   48 Ⓐ Ⓑ Ⓒ Ⓓ Ⓔ   63 Ⓐ Ⓑ Ⓒ Ⓓ Ⓔ
15 Ⓐ Ⓑ Ⓒ Ⓓ Ⓔ   31 Ⓐ Ⓑ Ⓒ Ⓓ Ⓔ   49 Ⓐ Ⓑ Ⓒ Ⓓ Ⓔ
16 Ⓐ Ⓑ Ⓒ Ⓓ Ⓔ   32 Ⓐ Ⓑ Ⓒ Ⓓ Ⓔ
                   33 Ⓐ Ⓑ Ⓒ Ⓓ Ⓔ
                   34 Ⓐ Ⓑ Ⓒ Ⓓ Ⓔ

CUT HERE

Section 4: Improving Paragraphs

Set 1   Set 2   Set 3

Set 1	Set 2	Set 3
1 Ⓐ Ⓑ Ⓒ Ⓓ Ⓔ	13 Ⓐ Ⓑ Ⓒ Ⓓ Ⓔ	25 Ⓐ Ⓑ Ⓒ Ⓓ Ⓔ
2 Ⓐ Ⓑ Ⓒ Ⓓ Ⓔ	14 Ⓐ Ⓑ Ⓒ Ⓓ Ⓔ	26 Ⓐ Ⓑ Ⓒ Ⓓ Ⓔ
3 Ⓐ Ⓑ Ⓒ Ⓓ Ⓔ	15 Ⓐ Ⓑ Ⓒ Ⓓ Ⓔ	27 Ⓐ Ⓑ Ⓒ Ⓓ Ⓔ
4 Ⓐ Ⓑ Ⓒ Ⓓ Ⓔ	16 Ⓐ Ⓑ Ⓒ Ⓓ Ⓔ	28 Ⓐ Ⓑ Ⓒ Ⓓ Ⓔ
5 Ⓐ Ⓑ Ⓒ Ⓓ Ⓔ	17 Ⓐ Ⓑ Ⓒ Ⓓ Ⓔ	29 Ⓐ Ⓑ Ⓒ Ⓓ Ⓔ
6 Ⓐ Ⓑ Ⓒ Ⓓ Ⓔ	18 Ⓐ Ⓑ Ⓒ Ⓓ Ⓔ	30 Ⓐ Ⓑ Ⓒ Ⓓ Ⓔ
7 Ⓐ Ⓑ Ⓒ Ⓓ Ⓔ	19 Ⓐ Ⓑ Ⓒ Ⓓ Ⓔ	
8 Ⓐ Ⓑ Ⓒ Ⓓ Ⓔ	20 Ⓐ Ⓑ Ⓒ Ⓓ Ⓔ	
9 Ⓐ Ⓑ Ⓒ Ⓓ Ⓔ	21 Ⓐ Ⓑ Ⓒ Ⓓ Ⓔ	
10 Ⓐ Ⓑ Ⓒ Ⓓ Ⓔ	22 Ⓐ Ⓑ Ⓒ Ⓓ Ⓔ	
11 Ⓐ Ⓑ Ⓒ Ⓓ Ⓔ	23 Ⓐ Ⓑ Ⓒ Ⓓ Ⓔ	
12 Ⓐ Ⓑ Ⓒ Ⓓ Ⓔ	24 Ⓐ Ⓑ Ⓒ Ⓓ Ⓔ	

Section 5: Sentence/Text Completion

Set 1   Set 2   Set 3

Set 1	Set 2	Set 3
1 Ⓐ Ⓑ Ⓒ Ⓓ Ⓔ	16 Ⓐ Ⓑ Ⓒ Ⓓ Ⓔ	31 Ⓐ Ⓑ Ⓒ Ⓓ Ⓕ
2 Ⓐ Ⓑ Ⓒ Ⓓ Ⓔ	17 Ⓐ Ⓑ Ⓒ Ⓓ Ⓔ	32 Ⓐ Ⓑ Ⓒ Ⓓ Ⓔ
3 Ⓐ Ⓑ Ⓒ Ⓓ Ⓔ	18 Ⓐ Ⓑ Ⓒ Ⓓ Ⓔ	33 Ⓐ Ⓑ Ⓒ Ⓓ Ⓔ
4 Ⓐ Ⓑ Ⓒ Ⓓ Ⓔ	19 Ⓐ Ⓑ Ⓒ Ⓓ Ⓔ	34 Ⓐ Ⓑ Ⓒ Ⓓ Ⓔ
5 Ⓐ Ⓑ Ⓒ Ⓓ Ⓔ	20 Ⓐ Ⓑ Ⓒ Ⓓ Ⓔ	35 Ⓐ Ⓑ Ⓒ Ⓓ Ⓔ
6 Ⓐ Ⓑ Ⓒ Ⓓ Ⓔ	21 Ⓐ Ⓑ Ⓒ Ⓓ Ⓔ	36 Ⓐ Ⓑ Ⓒ Ⓓ Ⓔ
7 Ⓐ Ⓑ Ⓒ Ⓓ Ⓔ	22 Ⓐ Ⓑ Ⓒ Ⓓ Ⓔ	37 Ⓐ Ⓑ Ⓒ Ⓓ Ⓔ
8 Ⓐ Ⓑ Ⓒ Ⓓ Ⓔ	23 Ⓐ Ⓑ Ⓒ Ⓓ Ⓔ	38 Ⓐ Ⓑ Ⓒ Ⓓ Ⓔ
9 Ⓐ Ⓑ Ⓒ Ⓓ Ⓔ	24 Ⓐ Ⓑ Ⓒ Ⓓ Ⓔ	39 Ⓐ Ⓑ Ⓒ Ⓓ Ⓔ
10 Ⓐ Ⓑ Ⓒ Ⓓ Ⓔ	25 Ⓐ Ⓑ Ⓒ Ⓓ Ⓔ	40 Ⓐ Ⓑ Ⓒ Ⓓ Ⓔ
11 Ⓐ Ⓑ Ⓒ Ⓓ Ⓔ	26 Ⓐ Ⓑ Ⓒ Ⓓ Ⓔ	41 Ⓐ Ⓑ Ⓒ Ⓓ Ⓔ
12 Ⓐ Ⓑ Ⓒ Ⓓ Ⓔ	27 Ⓐ Ⓑ Ⓒ Ⓓ Ⓔ	42 Ⓐ Ⓑ Ⓒ Ⓓ Ⓔ
13 Ⓐ Ⓑ Ⓒ Ⓓ Ⓔ	28 Ⓐ Ⓑ Ⓒ Ⓓ Ⓔ	43 Ⓐ Ⓑ Ⓒ Ⓓ Ⓔ
14 Ⓐ Ⓑ Ⓒ Ⓓ Ⓔ	29 Ⓐ Ⓑ Ⓒ Ⓓ Ⓔ	44 Ⓐ Ⓑ Ⓒ Ⓓ Ⓔ
15 Ⓐ Ⓑ Ⓒ Ⓓ Ⓔ	30 Ⓐ Ⓑ Ⓒ Ⓓ Ⓔ	45 Ⓐ Ⓑ Ⓒ Ⓓ Ⓔ

CUT HERE

Set 4

| 46 Ⓐ Ⓑ Ⓒ Ⓓ Ⓔ Ⓕ Ⓖ Ⓗ Ⓘ |
| 47 Ⓐ Ⓑ Ⓒ Ⓓ Ⓔ Ⓕ Ⓖ Ⓗ Ⓘ |
| 48 Ⓐ Ⓑ Ⓒ Ⓓ Ⓔ Ⓕ Ⓖ Ⓗ Ⓘ |
| 49 Ⓐ Ⓑ Ⓒ Ⓓ Ⓔ Ⓕ Ⓖ Ⓗ Ⓘ |
| 50 Ⓐ Ⓑ Ⓒ Ⓓ Ⓔ Ⓕ Ⓖ Ⓗ Ⓘ |
| 51 Ⓐ Ⓑ Ⓒ Ⓓ Ⓔ Ⓕ Ⓖ Ⓗ Ⓘ |
| 52 Ⓐ Ⓑ Ⓒ Ⓓ Ⓔ Ⓕ Ⓖ Ⓗ Ⓘ |
| 53 Ⓐ Ⓑ Ⓒ Ⓓ Ⓔ Ⓕ Ⓖ Ⓗ Ⓘ |
| 54 Ⓐ Ⓑ Ⓒ Ⓓ Ⓔ Ⓕ Ⓖ Ⓗ Ⓘ |
| 55 Ⓐ Ⓑ Ⓒ Ⓓ Ⓔ Ⓕ Ⓖ Ⓗ Ⓘ |
| 56 Ⓐ Ⓑ Ⓒ Ⓓ Ⓔ Ⓕ Ⓖ Ⓗ Ⓘ |
| 57 Ⓐ Ⓑ Ⓒ Ⓓ Ⓔ Ⓕ Ⓖ Ⓗ Ⓘ |
| 58 Ⓐ Ⓑ Ⓒ Ⓓ Ⓔ Ⓕ Ⓖ Ⓗ Ⓘ |
| 59 Ⓐ Ⓑ Ⓒ Ⓓ Ⓔ Ⓕ Ⓖ Ⓗ Ⓘ |
| 60 Ⓐ Ⓑ Ⓒ Ⓓ Ⓔ Ⓕ Ⓖ Ⓗ Ⓘ |

Set 5

| 61 Ⓐ Ⓑ Ⓒ Ⓓ Ⓔ Ⓕ Ⓖ Ⓗ Ⓘ |
| 62 Ⓐ Ⓑ Ⓒ Ⓓ Ⓔ Ⓕ Ⓖ Ⓗ Ⓘ |
| 63 Ⓐ Ⓑ Ⓒ Ⓓ Ⓔ Ⓕ Ⓖ Ⓗ Ⓘ |
| 64 Ⓐ Ⓑ Ⓒ Ⓓ Ⓔ Ⓕ Ⓖ Ⓗ Ⓘ |
| 65 Ⓐ Ⓑ Ⓒ Ⓓ Ⓔ Ⓕ Ⓖ Ⓗ Ⓘ |
| 66 Ⓐ Ⓑ Ⓒ Ⓓ Ⓔ Ⓕ Ⓖ Ⓗ Ⓘ |
| 67 Ⓐ Ⓑ Ⓒ Ⓓ Ⓔ Ⓕ Ⓖ Ⓗ Ⓘ |
| 68 Ⓐ Ⓑ Ⓒ Ⓓ Ⓔ Ⓕ Ⓖ Ⓗ Ⓘ |
| 69 Ⓐ Ⓑ Ⓒ Ⓓ Ⓔ Ⓕ Ⓖ Ⓗ Ⓘ |
| 70 Ⓐ Ⓑ Ⓒ Ⓓ Ⓔ Ⓕ Ⓖ Ⓗ Ⓘ |
| 71 Ⓐ Ⓑ Ⓒ Ⓓ Ⓔ Ⓕ Ⓖ Ⓗ Ⓘ |
| 72 Ⓐ Ⓑ Ⓒ Ⓓ Ⓔ Ⓕ Ⓖ Ⓗ Ⓘ |
| 73 Ⓐ Ⓑ Ⓒ Ⓓ Ⓔ Ⓕ Ⓖ Ⓗ Ⓘ |
| 74 Ⓐ Ⓑ Ⓒ Ⓓ Ⓔ Ⓕ Ⓖ Ⓗ Ⓘ |
| 75 Ⓐ Ⓑ Ⓒ Ⓓ Ⓔ Ⓕ Ⓖ Ⓗ Ⓘ |

Section 6: Sentence Equivalence

Set 1

| 1 Ⓐ Ⓑ Ⓒ Ⓓ Ⓔ Ⓕ |
| 2 Ⓐ Ⓑ Ⓒ Ⓓ Ⓔ Ⓕ |
| 3 Ⓐ Ⓑ Ⓒ Ⓓ Ⓔ Ⓕ |
| 4 Ⓐ Ⓑ Ⓒ Ⓓ Ⓔ Ⓕ |
| 5 Ⓐ Ⓑ Ⓒ Ⓓ Ⓔ Ⓕ |
| 6 Ⓐ Ⓑ Ⓒ Ⓓ Ⓔ Ⓕ |
| 7 Ⓐ Ⓑ Ⓒ Ⓓ Ⓔ Ⓕ |
| 8 Ⓐ Ⓑ Ⓒ Ⓓ Ⓔ Ⓕ |
| 9 Ⓐ Ⓑ Ⓒ Ⓓ Ⓔ Ⓕ |
| 10 Ⓐ Ⓑ Ⓒ Ⓓ Ⓔ Ⓕ |
| 11 Ⓐ Ⓑ Ⓒ Ⓓ Ⓔ Ⓕ |
| 12 Ⓐ Ⓑ Ⓒ Ⓓ Ⓔ Ⓕ |
| 13 Ⓐ Ⓑ Ⓒ Ⓓ Ⓔ Ⓕ |
| 14 Ⓐ Ⓑ Ⓒ Ⓓ Ⓔ Ⓕ |
| 15 Ⓐ Ⓑ Ⓒ Ⓓ Ⓔ Ⓕ |

Set 2

| 16 Ⓐ Ⓑ Ⓒ Ⓓ Ⓔ Ⓕ |
| 17 Ⓐ Ⓑ Ⓒ Ⓓ Ⓔ Ⓕ |
| 18 Ⓐ Ⓑ Ⓒ Ⓓ Ⓔ Ⓕ |
| 19 Ⓐ Ⓑ Ⓒ Ⓓ Ⓔ Ⓕ |
| 20 Ⓐ Ⓑ Ⓒ Ⓓ Ⓔ Ⓕ |
| 21 Ⓐ Ⓑ Ⓒ Ⓓ Ⓔ Ⓕ |
| 22 Ⓐ Ⓑ Ⓒ Ⓓ Ⓔ Ⓕ |
| 23 Ⓐ Ⓑ Ⓒ Ⓓ Ⓔ Ⓕ |
| 24 Ⓐ Ⓑ Ⓒ Ⓓ Ⓔ Ⓕ |
| 25 Ⓐ Ⓑ Ⓒ Ⓓ Ⓔ Ⓕ |
| 26 Ⓐ Ⓑ Ⓒ Ⓓ Ⓔ Ⓕ |
| 27 Ⓐ Ⓑ Ⓒ Ⓓ Ⓔ Ⓕ |
| 28 Ⓐ Ⓑ Ⓒ Ⓓ Ⓔ Ⓕ |
| 29 Ⓐ Ⓑ Ⓒ Ⓓ Ⓔ Ⓕ |
| 30 Ⓐ Ⓑ Ⓒ Ⓓ Ⓔ Ⓕ |

Set 3

| 31 Ⓐ Ⓑ Ⓒ Ⓓ Ⓔ Ⓕ |
| 32 Ⓐ Ⓑ Ⓒ Ⓓ Ⓔ Ⓕ |
| 33 Ⓐ Ⓑ Ⓒ Ⓓ Ⓔ Ⓕ |
| 34 Ⓐ Ⓑ Ⓒ Ⓓ Ⓔ Ⓕ |
| 35 Ⓐ Ⓑ Ⓒ Ⓓ Ⓔ Ⓕ |
| 36 Ⓐ Ⓑ Ⓒ Ⓓ Ⓔ Ⓕ |
| 37 Ⓐ Ⓑ Ⓒ Ⓓ Ⓔ Ⓕ |
| 38 Ⓐ Ⓑ Ⓒ Ⓓ Ⓔ Ⓕ |
| 39 Ⓐ Ⓑ Ⓒ Ⓓ Ⓔ Ⓕ |
| 40 Ⓐ Ⓑ Ⓒ Ⓓ Ⓔ Ⓕ |
| 41 Ⓐ Ⓑ Ⓒ Ⓓ Ⓔ Ⓕ |
| 42 Ⓐ Ⓑ Ⓒ Ⓓ Ⓔ Ⓕ |
| 43 Ⓐ Ⓑ Ⓒ Ⓓ Ⓔ Ⓕ |
| 44 Ⓐ Ⓑ Ⓒ Ⓓ Ⓔ Ⓕ |
| 45 Ⓐ Ⓑ Ⓒ Ⓓ Ⓔ Ⓕ |

CUT HERE

These practice exercises will cover all of the grammar and usage principles discussed in the Grammar and Usage Review, and all of the question types that appear in Chapter 1: Grammar and Usage Question Types. Work on *every* question, even if it is not a type that appears on the test for which you are preparing. The more questions you attempt, and the more answers you fully understand, the better equipped you will be to deal with the full range of grammar and usage questions on any particular test.

Pay close attention to the explanations that follow this practice test. They will reinforce the concepts made in the Grammar and Usage Review. For questions that test your vocabulary knowledge (Sentence/Text Completion and Sentence Equivalence), make sure to look up unfamiliar words in all of the answer choices in your dictionary. That way, you'll be prepared if any of them show up on your test.

Quick Reference Guide

Section 1: Sentence Correction – Type 1 (p. 166): SAT, PPST, PSAT/NMSQT

Section 2: Sentence Correction – Type 2 (p. 176): ACT

Section 3: Sentence Correction – Type 3 (p. 188): GMAT, SAT, PPST, PSAT/NMSQT

Section 4: Improving Paragraphs (p. 208): SAT, PSAT/NMSQT

Section 5: Sentence/Text Completion (p. 221): GRE, SAT, PSAT/NMSQT

Section 6: Sentence Equivalence (p. 241): GRE

Section 1: Sentence Correction – Type 1

Directions

Some of the following sentences are correct. Others contain errors in grammar, usage, or word choice. There is no more than one error in any sentence.

If there is an error, it will be underlined and lettered. Find the one underlined part that must be changed to make the sentence correct and choose the corresponding letter on your answer sheet. Mark E if the sentence contains no error.

The Answer Key for the Sentence Correction – Type 1 section is on p. 253, and the explanatory answers begin on p. 260.

Set 1

1. <u>Had you</u> paid very close attention to the shape of the gem, or had
      A

   you <u>looked</u> carefully at the <u>allegedly</u> sterling silver setting, you
        B   C

   <u>would of suspected</u> that the ring was not an antique. <u>No error</u>.
        D   E

2. If the election results are <u>as</u> Harris predicted, the new senator will
                  A

   be the man <u>whom</u> the people <u>believed</u> made the <u>better</u> showing in
         B   C   D

   the televised debate. <u>No error</u>.
                    E

3. None of sixty-five students <u>majoring in</u> economics <u>were prepared for</u>
                         A   B

   the <u>teacher's</u> <u>laying a trap</u> for them in the comprehensive exam.
       C   D

   <u>No error</u>.
     E

4. If they <u>simply gave</u> the prize <u>to whoever</u> really deserves it, the
             A   B

publishers who pay for publicity <u>would withdraw</u> their support, and
                                     C

<u>there would be</u> no award at all. <u>No error.</u>
    D   E

5. It must be <u>she</u> <u>whom</u> he had in mind when he spoke of a "well-trained,
           A   B

superbly conditioned athlete <u>who</u> <u>might have captured</u> a spot on the
                            C   D

Olympic team." <u>No error.</u>
             E

6. The reasons for his success are <u>that he works hard,</u> <u>his good looks,</u>
                                A   B

<u>that he exercises regularly,</u> and <u>that his grandmother left him</u> four
        C   D

million dollars. <u>No error.</u>
              E

7. <u>You'd think</u> that people <u>smart and intelligent enough</u> to be in
    A   B

business <u>by themselves</u> would have the sense to know the value of
            C

monthly savings <u>at a guaranteed</u> high interest rate. <u>No error.</u>
                 D   E

8. The jury must first decide <u>whether or not</u> the defendant <u>was</u> in New
                         A   B

York on August third, and then how <u>can he</u> have had the strength
                                  C

<u>to carry</u> a 200-pound body. <u>No error.</u>
  D   E

9. The art of American morticians <u>paints</u> death <u>to look like life,</u>
                              A   B

sealing <u>it</u> up in watertight caskets <u>and spiriting</u> it away to graveyards
      C   D

camouflaged as gardens. <u>No error.</u>
                     E

10. <u>Anyone</u> of the compounds that can be <u>produced from</u> the leaves
     A   B

of this plant <u>is</u> dangerous, but the plant <u>itself</u> is not poisonous.
            C   D

<u>No error.</u>
  E

11. None of the survivors <u>who have</u> now recovered consciousness
A

remember <u>hearing</u> any unusual sound in the motor <u>just before</u> the
B C D

plane crashed. <u>No error.</u>
E

12. *The Destructors* is an <u>unusually</u> powerful film about a group of
A

cruel and idle young boys <u>who destroy</u> an old man's home for no
B

other reason <u>but because</u> it is beautiful. <u>No error.</u>
C D E

13. <u>Hoping to both cut taxes and reduce unemployment</u>, the Senate
A

has recommended a bill <u>that allows</u> married couples <u>not to declare</u>
B C

the income of either the husband or the wife, depending upon

<u>which income is the lowest.</u> <u>No error.</u>
D E

14. <u>It seems increasingly obvious</u> that men's clothes are designed not to
A

please the men who will wear <u>them,</u> <u>but as status symbols that impress</u>
B C

the people <u>who will see them.</u> <u>No error.</u>
D E

15. <u>Unlike Monet,</u> Graham's oil paintings have <u>few</u> bright colors,
A B

<u>are small,</u> <u>and depict</u> only urban scenes. <u>No error.</u>
C D E

Set 2

16. <u>While I was out of action with a broken arm,</u> the nurses <u>tried to teach</u>
A B

me <u>to eat, write, and to shave</u> with my left hand, but I was never able
C

<u>to write</u> or shave very well. <u>No error.</u>
D E

17. <u>If I had my way</u>, that driver <u>would be</u> charged <u>for criminal</u> negligence
     A   B   C
 and drunken driving <u>and spend</u> at least six months in jail. <u>No error</u>.
                D   E

18. Most schools require <u>students to take</u> standardized tests <u>that</u> are used
                         A   B
 by admissions committees to evaluate one student <u>against another</u>
                                                 C
 with common <u>criteria</u>. <u>No error</u>.
                 D   E

19. If westerners <u>acknowledge that</u> the eastern United States
                    A
 <u>has wilderness areas,</u> <u>one probably thinks</u> of the Blue Ridge
         B   C
 Mountains or <u>perhaps</u> western Maine. <u>No error</u>.
            D   E

20. Paul Ramsey, a theologian at Princeton University, as well as Edward

 Leon, a philosopher and physician at the University of Chicago,

 <u>have argued</u> that test-tube fertilization is <u>a form of experimentation</u>
    A   B
 <u>that is</u> unethical, since the potential child cannot <u>consent to</u> the risks
  C   D
 of the experiment. <u>No error</u>.
                 E

21. Though in <u>only her</u> first year of research, Dr. Gomez <u>has discovered</u>
           A   B
 a formula <u>that may effect</u> the study of mathematics <u>all over</u> the
               C   D
 world. <u>No error</u>.
      E

22. <u>By buying</u> the economy-size packages of pasta, of muffin mix,
   A
 <u>and detergent</u>, shoppers can save <u>as much</u> as two dollars in <u>less than</u>
    B   C   D
 one month. <u>No error</u>.
         E

23. As <u>they</u> crossed the Atlantic, <u>colonists</u> probably <u>made cheeses</u>
      A   B   C

<u>in the galley of</u> the *Mayflower.* <u>No error.</u>
    D   E

24. Hospital patients <u>prefer homemade recipes</u> <u>that</u> are <u>lower</u> in calories
                         A   B   C

and cost, <u>which</u> is important to those with high medical bills and
        D

weight problems. <u>No error.</u>
              E

25. The focus of the new <u>newspaper and television advertisements</u>
                                   A

will be the claim <u>that prunes</u> are not only low in fat <u>but also are</u>
               B   C

<u>the highest in fiber.</u> <u>No error.</u>
    D   E

26. When the Baseball <u>Writers'</u> Association announced that Willie
                    A

McCovey, then the <u>top</u> left-handed home run hitter in National
                 B

League history, <u>had been elected</u> to the Hall of Fame, nobody
             C

<u>was</u> at all surprised. <u>No error.</u>
  D   E

27. Public-opinion surveys <u>commissioned as part of</u> a federal anti-noise
                         A

program at the airport <u>indicates</u> that no resident of the surrounding
                    B

area <u>is</u> <u>seriously disturbed</u> by aircraft noise. <u>No error.</u>
     C   D   E

28. It was Cardinal <u>Richelieu who decided</u> to found the French
                 A

Academy <u>when he learned</u> that an <u>eminent</u> group of grammarians
         B   C

and intellectuals <u>will meet in secret</u> to exchange views on literature.
                  D

<u>No error.</u>
  E

29. <u>More than thirty countries from around the world</u> <u>have submitted</u>
                   A   B

    entries for the Best Foreign Language Film Award <u>being presented</u>
                                                    C

    at the ceremony <u>six weeks from today</u>. <u>No error</u>.
                         D   E

30. <u>Like President Clinton</u>, President Obama's cabinet <u>was chosen from</u>
          A   B

    former allies <u>in state politics</u>, national party leaders, personal
                      C

    friends, and <u>seasoned political professionals</u>. <u>No error</u>.
                        D   E

Set 3

31. The <u>decline in</u> the industrial average was much smaller
         A

    <u>in comparative terms</u> <u>to</u> the 1929 decline because the Dow
            B   C

    index <u>stands</u> at a much higher level today. <u>No error</u>.
           D   E

32. <u>To safeguard wildlife</u>, the state of Florida will line <u>its</u> highways with
            A   B

    high fencing, <u>forcing</u> panthers <u>to scoot</u> beneath the roads through
                  C   D

    specially designed animal underpasses. <u>No error</u>.
                                     E

33. The discovery of the existence of a fifth force <u>could have</u> enormous
                                              A

    impact <u>on</u> theoretical physicists <u>who</u> are trying to develop a unified
           B   C

    theory to explain <u>the interactions of matter</u>. <u>No error</u>.
                     D   E

34. If the team <u>is</u> to qualify for the state championship, <u>it</u> cannot afford
           A   B

    <u>to make</u> <u>those</u> kind of mental error. <u>No error</u>.
      C   D   E

35. <u>Neither the violinists</u> nor the harpist <u>were accustomed to</u> playing
    　　　A　　　　　　　　　　　　　　B

modern music, <u>and so</u> the performance of the concerto was a <u>total</u>
　　　　　　　　C　　　　　　　　　　　　　　　　　　　　　　　D

failure. <u>No error.</u>
　　　　　E

36. <u>Missing the forehand volley</u>, a <u>relative easy shot</u>, Kita fell behind
    　　　A　　　　　　　　　　　　　B

early in the match, and <u>he</u> never <u>recovered</u>. <u>No error.</u>
　　　　　　　　　　　　C　　　　　D　　　　　E

37. The writer of allegory <u>commonly</u> invents a world <u>in order to talk</u>
    　　　　　　　　　　　　　　A　　　　　　　　　　　B

about <u>the world in which we live</u>; the symbolist uses the real world
　　　　C

to reveal <u>a world we cannot see</u>. <u>No error.</u>
　　　　　　D　　　　　　　　　　　E

38. When <u>it is</u> five o'clock in New York, it is <u>only four</u> in most of Texas,
    　　　　A　　　　　　　　　　　　　　　　　B

and <u>it will be</u> two o'clock in California, Washington, <u>and</u> Oregon.
　　　　C　　　　　　　　　　　　　　　　　　　　　　D

<u>No error.</u>
E

39. <u>Some</u> begonias have huge flowers, <u>wonderfully colored;</u> <u>some have</u>
    　　A　　　　　　　　　　　　　　　B　　　　　　　　C

glorious foliage; and <u>some</u> provide a blaze of color, with large
　　　　　　　　　　　D

clusters of small flowers. <u>No error.</u>
　　　　　　　　　　　　　E

40. The highest profits <u>are</u> likely <u>to be earned</u> by those investors
    　　　　　　　　　　A　　　　　B

<u>whom brokers claim</u> are willing to take risks <u>early in the year</u>. <u>No error.</u>
　C　　　　　　　　　　　　　　　　　　D　　　　　E

41. Northerners seem to believe that <u>we</u> Texans talk <u>oddly</u>, but we think
    　　　　　　　　　　　　　　　A　　　　　　　B

<u>it</u> is <u>them</u> who have the strange accents. <u>No error.</u>
　C　　D　　　　　　　　　　　　　　E

42. <u>To encourage better reading skills</u>, students in the public schools
             A

    <u>are now required</u> by teachers to submit weekly reports
        B

    <u>of the books, magazines, and newspapers</u> <u>they have read</u>. <u>No error</u>.
            C   D   E

43. The legislators insist <u>that</u> charitable foundations have the
             A

    <u>same, identical moral obligations</u> <u>as</u> private citizens or
        B   C

    <u>publicly owned corporations</u>. <u>No error</u>.
        D   E

44. University libraries across the nation use different methods to control

    crime, and the electronic system <u>that emits a signal</u> <u>if a person leaves</u>
             A   B

    the library with a book that has not been checked out <u>was</u> one of
             C

    <u>them</u>. <u>No error</u>.
     D   E

45. The notion that Americans are conventional and Europeans are

    <u>free-spirited</u> <u>is</u> not only a dubious thesis <u>but also a trivial</u> <u>one</u>.
        A   B   C   D

    <u>No error</u>.
     E

Set 4

46. <u>Like Friedman warned</u> in the early seventies, taxes and the cost
        A

    of living <u>have risen</u> steadily <u>while</u> the value of the dollar abroad
          B   C

    <u>has steadily declined</u>. <u>No error</u>.
        D   E

47. Those musicians <u>having studied</u> under masters like Baker and Hess
            A

    are the ones who <u>ought</u> to become teachers when <u>their</u> performing
          B   C

    careers <u>have ended</u>. <u>No error</u>.
        D   E

48. Either to bemoan the death of the counterculture or <u>to insist</u> that <u>it</u>
 A B

still exists is <u>to commit</u> the same error, for a counterculture never
 C

really <u>existed</u>. <u>No error</u>.
 D E

49. <u>Woven from fronds of cabbage palms and palmettos</u>, the natives of
 A

the islands <u>constructed</u> huts <u>that</u> are both rainproof in winter and
 B C

cool in the <u>summertime</u>. <u>No error</u>.
 D E

50. <u>Though raised in conservative New Hampshire</u>, June <u>leads</u> a
 A B

remarkably unconventional life in an environment <u>totally</u> <u>unlike that</u>
 C D

of her childhood. <u>No error</u>.
 E

51. <u>Quicker at the net than any other player in the tournament</u>, his weak
 A

returns of service and <u>his tendency to double fault under pressure</u>
 B

<u>have</u> prevented Simmons <u>from reaching</u> the quarterfinals. <u>No error</u>.
 C D E

52. Neither the British archaeologists nor the American, Asha Bello,

<u>have</u> discovered anything <u>with a</u> significance comparable <u>to that of</u>
A B C

the artifacts <u>unearthed</u> here twenty years ago. <u>No error</u>.
 D E

53. <u>Using the inland roads</u>, you will have to travel far <u>less</u> miles, but the
 A B

scenery, <u>such as it is</u>, is markedly inferior to <u>what you can see</u> on the
 C D

coast. <u>No error</u>.
 E

54. <u>Unwilling to depend on you</u>, your brother, or even <u>I</u>, she <u>has rented</u>
 A B C

a car at the airport and <u>has already driven</u> to Cleveland. <u>No error</u>.
 D E

55. If you want to get ahead in this world, <u>one</u> must be ready <u>to make</u>
    A   B
sacrifices, <u>to compromise</u>, and, when the situation is unavoidable,
        C
<u>to tell</u> half-truths. <u>No error</u>.
    D   E

56. Between 1930 and 1945, most jazz improvisers played <u>not only the</u>
                                            A
songs of Gershwin, Rodgers, and Berlin, <u>but also those</u> <u>of</u> less well
                                    B   C
known writers <u>like</u> Wilder, Arlen, and Hunter. <u>No error</u>.
            D   E

57. Tommy Jones, together with Keeter Betts <u>on bass</u> and Jimmy Smith
                                        A
on drums, <u>are</u> performing at Newport <u>in</u> an oblique, original, and
        B   C
<u>unwearyingly inventive</u> concert program. <u>No error</u>.
    D   E

58. The easiest way to get to Cnidus from Athens is not, <u>as would seem</u>
                                                A
likely, to fly to Istanbul but <u>as a passenger</u> on the ships <u>that</u>
                        B   C
<u>ply between</u> Rhodes and the Turkish coast. <u>No error</u>.
    D   E

59. Although the <u>councilman</u> had promised to support rent control, it
                A
was <u>with no hesitation</u> and apparently with some pleasure <u>when</u> he
    B   C
cast his vote on the side of the <u>landlords</u>. <u>No error</u>.
                            D   E

60. The quarterback, <u>with the trainer</u> and two doctors, <u>were slowly walking</u>
                    A   B
toward the bench <u>while</u> the crowd groaned <u>audibly</u>. <u>No error</u>.
            C   D   E

Section 2: Sentence Correction – Type 2

Directions

Some part of each sentence below is underlined; sometimes the whole sentence is underlined. Five choices for rephrasing the underlined part follow each sentence; the first choice (A) repeats the original, and the other four are different. If choice A seems better than the alternatives, choose answer choice A; if not, choose one of the others.

For each sentence, consider the requirements of standard written English. Your choice should be a correct and effective expression, not awkward or ambiguous. Focus on grammar, word choice, sentence construction, and punctuation. If a choice would change the meaning of the original sentence, do not select it.

The Answer Key for the Sentence Correction – Type 2 section is on p. 254, and the explanatory answers begin on p. 263.

Set 1

1. The series of articles is not only about the sicknesses of a violent and materialistic society, <u>but also how these ills can be remedied</u>.

   A. but also how these ills can be remedied
   B. but also remedies for these ills
   C. but also their remedy
   D. but also about remedies for these ills
   E. but also how a remedy for these ills can be made possible

2. Carrying the warm water across the yard to melt the ice on the birdbath, <u>the sparrows were gathered</u> only a few feet from me.

   A. the sparrows were gathered
   B. the sparrows gathered
   C. the groups of sparrows were
   D. the group of sparrows was gathered
   E. I saw that the sparrows were gathered

3. This year's alumnae differ from last year's in the way <u>they believe and give support to fund raising</u>.

    A.   they believe and give support to fund raising
    B.   it believes and gives support to fund raising
    C.   it believes in and gives support to fund raising
    D.   they believe in and support fund raising
    E.   they believe in fund raising, and support it

4. In addition to higher costs for gasoline and sugar, <u>the consumer is plagued by higher wheat prices</u>.

    A.   the consumer is plagued by higher wheat prices
    B.   the consumer is plagued by more expensive wheat
    C.   higher wheat prices are also plaguing the consumer
    D.   higher wheat prices also plague the consumer
    E.   the wheat consumer is plagued by higher prices

5. When you see, instead of read, a play, <u>it sometimes reveals new strengths and weaknesses</u>.

    A.   it sometimes reveals new strengths and weaknesses
    B.   ncw strengths and weaknesses are sometimes revealed to you
    C.   you sometimes see new strengths and weaknesses
    D.   sometimes new strengths and weaknesses are revealed
    E.   new strengths and weaknesses are seen sometimes

6. The doctor visits her patients once every three hours, <u>which can be decreased</u> as the danger lessens.

    A.   which can be decreased
    B.   a schedule that can be altered
    C.   which can be altered
    D.   to be decreased
    E.   and can be altered

7. She desperately wanted, <u>and in the second set nearly did, to win.</u>

    A.   wanted, and in the second set nearly did, to win.

    B.   wanted to win, and in the second set, she nearly did win.

    C.   wanted to, and in the second set nearly did, win.

    D.   wanted to win, and in the second set nearly did.

    E.   wanted to win, in the second set she nearly did.

8. <u>The appearance of a musical play—its sets, costumes, and lighting— is</u> as important as enjoying its songs.

    A.   The appearance of a musical play—its sets, costumes, and lighting—is

    B.   The appearance of a musical play—its sets, costumes, and lighting—are

    C.   Enjoying the appearance of a musical play—its sets, costumes, and lighting—is

    D.   In a musical play, the sets, costumes, and lighting are

    E.   The sets, costumes, and lighting of a musical play are

9. <u>Like many composers,</u> the operas of Mozart are more frequently performed in Italy than in France.

    A.   Like many composers

    B.   Like many other composers

    C.   Like the operas of many composers

    D.   Like those of many other composers

    E.   As many composers

10. Many people admire his lectures, but to me, <u>he is nothing else, in my opinion,</u> only a bore.

    A.   he is nothing else, in my opinion,

    B.   he is

    C.   he is nothing else except

    D.   he is nothing but,

    E.   he is nothing except

11. All of this trouble could have been avoided if you <u>would have planned who to ask</u> to speak before you rented the hall.

    A. would have planned who to ask
    B. planned who to ask
    C. had planned whom to ask
    D. had planned who to ask
    E. planned whom to ask

12. Some young people work until they are <u>exhausted; and this</u> will surely prove injurious to their physical well-being later on in life.

    A. exhausted; and this
    B. exhausted; it
    C. exhausted, which
    D. exhausted, a practice that
    E. exhausted, and it

13. I <u>am both afraid and awed by her ability</u> to reach important decisions and take action so quickly.

    A. am both afraid and awed by her ability
    B. both am afraid and awed by her ability
    C. am both afraid of and awed by her ability
    D. am both afraid and in awe of her ability
    E. am afraid and also awed by her ability

14. The book contends <u>that *Othello* is not a better play but more carefully constructed</u> than *King Lear.*

    A. that *Othello* is not a better play but more carefully constructed
    B. *Othello* is not a better play but is more carefully constructed
    C. not that *Othello* is better but a more carefully constructed play
    D. not that *Othello* is a better play, but that it is more carefully constructed
    E. not that *Othello* is better, but it is more carefully constructed

15. The house we rented had no garage, <u>which means we had to keep</u> our boat on the front lawn.

    A. which means we had to keep
    B. which meant keeping up
    C. and this means we had to keep
    D. so we had to keep
    E. so we keep

Set 2

16. <u>That your horse won at Bowie</u> is not an indication of Kentucky Derby quality.

    A. That your horse won at Bowie
    B. Because your horse won at Bowie
    C. Your horse winning at Bowie
    D. If your horse won at Bowie
    E. Winning results at Bowie

17. Every one of the tickets <u>that was reserved for parents has</u> been sold.

    A. that was reserved for parents has
    B. reserved for parents have
    C. that were reserved for parents have
    D. that were reserved for parents has
    E. reserved for parents had

18. Neither salad oils nor butter <u>has less calories than</u> margarine.

    A. has less calories than
    B. has fewer calories than
    C. have fewer calories than
    D. are less in calories than
    E. are fewer in calories than

19. Manning's article on *Nicholas Nickleby* <u>is both the most dependable account and shortest guide to</u> this difficult novel.

    A.   is both the most dependable account and shortest guide to

    B.   is both the shortest and most dependable account to

    C.   both is the most dependable account and shortest guide to

    D.   is both the most dependable account of and shortest guide to

    E.   is the most dependable account of and shortest guide to

20. Every one of the Democrat candidates <u>have promised to support whoever wins</u> the primary.

    A.   have promised to support whoever wins

    B.   has promised to support whomever wins

    C.   has promised to support whoever wins

    D.   have promised to support whomever wins

    E.   had promised to support whoever wins

21. The symbolical and experimental nature of modern fiction frequently <u>relegates them to publication in magazines that have limited circulation</u>.

    A.   relegates them to publication in magazines that have limited circulation

    B.   relegate them to publication in magazines with limited circulation

    C.   relegates them to publication in magazines of limited circulation

    D.   relegates it to publication in magazines, which have limited circulation

    E.   relegates it to publication in magazines with limited circulation

22. Lured by the Florida sun, <u>Canadians by the thousands descend annually into St. Petersburg each year</u>.

    A.   Canadians by the thousands descend annually into St. Petersburg each year

    B.   St. Petersburg receives thousands of Canadians each year

    C.   St. Petersburg annually receives thousands of Canadians

    D.   Canadians by the thousands descend on St. Petersburg each year

    E.   thousands of Canadians descend into St. Petersburg each year

23. <u>Like Switzerland,</u> the mountains of Colorado and Wyoming keep their snow for ten months.

    A. Like Switzerland,
    B. As Switzerland,
    C. Like those in Switzerland,
    D. Like the mountains which are in Switzerland,
    E. Switzerland, like

24. At the door to the kitchen, he stopped to wipe the mud from his boots and run a comb through his hair, <u>and then knocks loudly at the door</u>.

    A. and then knocks loudly at the door
    B. and then knocks loud at the door
    C. and then knocked loudly at the door
    D. and then knocks loudly at the door
    E. and then knocking at the door loudly

25. <u>Whoever makes the least mistakes or whoever</u> the wind reaches first is likely to win the sailing trophy.

    A. Whoever makes the least mistakes or whoever
    B. Whoever makes the least mistakes or whomever
    C. Whoever makes the fewest mistakes or whomever
    D. Whoever can make the least mistakes or whoever
    E. Whoever makes the fewest mistakes or whoever

26. I especially admire <u>her eagerness to succeed, that she is willing to work hard, and her being optimistic</u>.

    A. her eagerness to succeed, that she is willing to work hard, and her being optimistic
    B. that she is eager to succeed, willing to work hard, and that she is optimistic
    C. her eagerness to succeed, her willingness to work hard, and that she is optimistic
    D. her eagerness to succeed, her willingness to work hard, and her optimism
    E. her being eager to succeed, her being willing to work hard, and her being optimistic

27. <u>Where the main purpose of the greenhouse is</u> to raise half-hardy plants for planting out in the garden or to grow flowering plants in pots for cut flowers and for bringing into the house.

    A.   Where the main purpose of the greenhouse is

    B.   When the main purpose of the greenhouse is

    C.   The main purpose of the greenhouse is

    D.   The main purpose of the greenhouse are

    E.   Where the main purpose of the greenhouse are

28. With his new knowledge of the processes of cell formation and reproduction, <u>nurserymen have now learned to induce sports</u> or mutations in plants.

    A.   nurserymen have now learned to induce sports

    B.   science has now learned to induce sports

    C.   the nurseryman has now learned to induce sports

    D.   science has now learned how to induce sports

    E.   scientists have now learned how to induce sports

29. The city plans to dismantle and move a fourteenth-century English church to Arizona <u>which will give it</u> the oldest church in the Western Hemisphere.

    A.   which will give it

    B.   and this will give it

    C.   which will give the state

    D.   and this will give the state

    E.   so that the state will have

30. Banking regulators have seized a savings bank in Georgia and charged that the institution <u>both used deceptive lending and business practices and it misled</u> its stockholders.

    A.   both used deceptive lending and business practices and it misled

    B.   both used both deceptive lending and business practices and that it misled

    C.   used both deceptive lending and business practices, misleading

    D.   used deceptive both lending and business practices, and misled

    E.   both used deceptive lending and business practices and misled

Set 3

31. More children are held in the Belmont City Jail <u>than in any lockup</u> in the state.

    A. than in any lockup
    B. than in any other lockup
    C. than any
    D. than any other
    E. than any other lockup

32. For three years, the rock group White Flag <u>has virtually ignored Chicago, the city where they started in</u>.

    A. has virtually ignored Chicago, the city where they started in
    B. have virtually ignored Chicago, the city where they started in
    C. has virtually ignored Chicago, the city in which it started
    D. has virtually ignored Chicago, the city where it started in
    E. have virtually ignored Chicago, the city in which it started

33. To whet the appetite for next week's Super Bowl, <u>NBC will show film clips of this year's best plays</u>.

    A. NBC will show film clips of this year's best plays
    B. NBC will show film clips of this years' best plays
    C. this year's best plays will be shown in film clips by NBC
    D. film clips of this year's best plays will be shown by NBC
    E. this year's best plays in film clips will be shown by NBC

34. Neither of the state's senators <u>is supportive or interested in</u> a constitutional amendment.

    A. is supportive or interested in
    B. is supportive of or interested in
    C. are supportive of or interested in
    D. support or are interested in
    E. supports or are interested in

35. This semester I will <u>try and do my work as well or better</u> than anyone else in the class.

   A.   try and do my work as well or better
   B.   try and do my work better
   C.   try to do my work as well or better
   D.   try to do my work as well as or better
   E.   try and do my work as well as or better

36. Unlike savings bonds, <u>government mortgage certificates have a fluctuating principle value, but may earn higher interest</u>.

   A.   though their principle value fluctuates, you may earn higher interest with government mortgage certificates
   B.   though their principal value fluctuates, you may earn higher interest with government mortgage certificates
   C.   government mortgage certificates have a fluctuating principle value, but they may pay higher interest
   D.   though their principle value fluctuates, government mortgage certificates may pay you higher interest
   E.   government mortgage certificates have a fluctuating principal value, but may earn higher interest

37. <u>Personally, I believe that we all will be happier</u> if there were no cars at all in the downtown area of the city.

   A.   Personally, I believe that we all will be happier
   B.   I believe we all would be happier
   C.   I personally believe that all of us will be happier
   D.   I believe that all of us would be more happy
   E.   I believe we will all be happier

38. To lose weight quickly on this diet, one must weigh every food portion carefully, exercise regularly, <u>and you should only drink</u> water, black coffee, or diet soda.

   A.   and you should only drink
   B.   drinking only
   C.   only drinking
   D.   and drink only
   E.   and one should drink only

39. <u>Different from any designs in the show</u>, Orlando Fashions Company exhibited a collection made entirely of nylon.

    A.   Different from any designs in the show

    B.   Different from any other designs in the show

    C.   With designs different from any in the show

    D.   With designs different from any others in the show

    E.   With designs different from any other designs in the show

40. As Gordon's army advanced farther into the interior, <u>its supply line from the coast became more and more threatened</u>.

    A.   its supply line from the coast became more and more threatened

    B.   it's supply line from the coast became more and more threatened

    C.   it's supply line from the coast became more and more of a threat

    D.   its supply line on the coast became more threatening

    E.   its supply line from the coast became more of a threat

41. The drug appears to have <u>no affect whatsoever in regards to</u> a patient's cold symptoms.

    A.   no affect whatsoever in regards to

    B.   no affect whatsoever in regard to

    C.   no affect whatsoever upon

    D.   no effect whatsoever on

    E.   no effect whatsoever regarding

42. He has been cheated several times <u>because of his being of a credulous nature</u>.

    A.   because of his being of a credulous nature

    B.   because of his credibility

    C.   because of his credible nature

    D.   because he is credulous

    E.   because he is credible

43. A very old plant in our gardens, <u>cornflowers appear in paintings made as early as in the fourth century</u>.

   A. cornflowers appear in paintings made as early as in the fourth century

   B. paintings of cornflowers were made as early as the fourth century.

   C. fourth century made paintings show cornflowers

   D. the cornflower appears in paintings made as early as the fourth century

   E. paintings of cornflowers have been made as early as in the fourth century

44. None of the <u>terrorists who were seen in Libya in June has</u> been connected to the latest bomb threat.

   A. terrorists, who were seen in Libya in June, has

   B. terrorists, who were seen in Libya in June, would have

   C. terrorists who were seen in Libya in June has

   D. terrorists, who was seen in Libya in June, must have

   E. terrorists, who were seen in Libya in June, will have

45. Paging through the cookware catalog, <u>Jerry chose a matching skillet, teakettle, and saucepan as a prize for Janice and I or for whoever wins the contest</u>.

   A. Jerry chose a matching skillet, teakettle, and saucepan as a prize for Janice and I or for whoever wins the contest.

   B. Jerry chose a matching skillet, teakettle, and saucepan as a prize for Janice and me or for whoever wins the contest.

   C. Jerry chose a matching skillet, teakettle, and saucepan as a prize for Janice and me or for whomever wins the contest.

   D. a matching skillet, teakettle, and saucepan were chosen by Jerry as a prize for Janice and me or for whoever wins the contest.

   E. Jerry chose a matching skillet, teakettle, and saucepan for a prize for us or the contest winners.

Section 3: Sentence Correction – Type 3

Directions

In the left-hand column, you will find passages with various words and phrases underlined. In the right-hand column, you will find a set of responses corresponding to each underlined portion. If the underlined portion is correct as it stands, mark the letter indicating "NO CHANGE." If the underlined portion is incorrect, decide which of the choices best corrects it. Consider only underlined portions; assume that the rest of the passage is correct as written.

The Answer Key for the Sentence Correction – Type 3 section is on p. 254, and the explanatory answers begin on p. 267.

Set 1: Passages I and II

Passage I

Before the Summer Games of 1984, optimists believed the Los Angeles Olympiad <u>would produce</u> a small profit. But no one guessed just how well the plan for private-sector financing would work. Audits have shown that the Summer Games generated a whopping surplus of two hundred and <u>fifteen million dollars,</u> this sum grew to two

1. A.   NO CHANGE
    B.   will produce
    C.   would deduce
    D.   to produce

2. F.   NO CHANGE
    G.   fifteen million dollars
    H.   fifteen million dollars;
    J.   fifteen million dollars:

hundred and fifty million dollars as Olympic coin sales continued and two million dollars in interest was added to the total each month.

All of this money went to good causes. The U.S. Olympic Committee, youth and athletic programs, and amateur American sports groups. In addition, the Los Angeles committee's board voted to donate seven million dollars to foreign Olympic committees, reimbursing them for their delegations' housing costs in Los Angeles.

All of this stands in stark contrast to the financing fiasco in Montreal eight years before. Citizens there did

3. A.   NO CHANGE
   B.   causes; the
   C.   causes, including the
   D.   causes including the following;

4. F.   NO CHANGE
   G.   the costs for housing their committee delegations
   H.   their delegations housing costs
   J.   their delegation's housing costs

5. A.   NO CHANGE
   B.   in contrast starkly with
   C.   contrasting to
   D.   contrasting with

not pay off their one-billion-dollar public debt until 2006, more than thirty years later. And <u>there was no surplus</u> funds to help sustain amateur athletics in Canada and Olympic committees elsewhere in the world. For this reason, we have seen <u>fewer and fewer city</u> governments willing to take on the financial risk of sponsoring the Olympic Games single-handed. The huge success of the 1984 Summer Games in Los Angeles made <u>private-sector financing</u> more attractive than ever.

6. F. NO CHANGE
   G. they're were no surplus
   H. there were no surplus
   J. their were no surplus

7. A. NO CHANGE
   B. less and less
   C. a smaller and smaller number of
   D. a lesser and lesser number of

8. F. NO CHANGE
   G. privatization options
   H. private financing
   J. the private financing

Passage II

A crucial political change seemed imminent when three of Canada's most important provinces' premiers, Rene Levesque of Quebec, William Davis of Ontario, and Peter Lougheed of Alberta, all announced their retirements. It may have been just a coincidence; a series of independent decisions by long-time political leaders to yield the responsibilities of power. But it also seemed to signal the end of a long period of estrangement between the national government in Ottawa and Canada's relative autonomous provinces.

Levesque once led Quebec's separatist movement. But with as little as four percent of the province's voters favoring separatism, Levesque

9. A. NO CHANGE
   B. just have been a coincidence; a
   C. have been just a coincidence, a
   D. just have been a coincidence— a

10. F. NO CHANGE
    G. relatively autonomous
    H. relatedly autonomous
    J. relative

abandoned <u>it as</u> the key plank in his
11
platform. Meanwhile, Quebec voters

appeared at the time to be leaning

more toward the mainline national

parties, with polls showing the

Liberals in the lead. In national

elections, half of the province's vote

went to the Progressive-Conservative

Party, <u>which had been led</u> by
12
French-speaking Quebecer Brain

Mulroney. In effect, Mulroney's rise

to power in Ottawa left Levesque

with <u>neither cause nor a future</u> in
13
Quebec City.

The one resignation that seemed

to spell trouble for Mulroney

<u>was Davis</u>. With his departure,
14
Ontario's normally Conservative

11. A. NO CHANGE
B. them as
C. it to be
D. OMIT

12. F. NO CHANGE
G. lead
H. which had been lead
J. led

13. A. NO CHANGE
B. neither cause or future
C. neither a cause nor a future
D. neither a cause nor future

14. F. NO CHANGE
G. was Davis's resignation
H. was Davis's
J. was that of Davis's

Legislature came under the control
15
of a newly formed coalition of
Liberals and third-party New
Democrats. Provincial politics in
Canada haven't necessarily reflected
national trends, and the Ontario
alliance was not extendable
nationwide. Having fared very badly
in prior elections, new strength in
16
national opinion polls was shown by
the Liberals. Ironically, Mulroney
had the middle slip out from under
him just as his political flanks were
being secured by the retirements of
two of Canada's more contentious
provincial premiers.

15. A.   NO CHANGE
   B.   will have come under
   C.   are now under
   D.   has come under

16. F.   NO CHANGE
   G.   national opinion polls
        show new Liberal
        strength
   H.   national opinion polls
        show new strength in the
        Liberal Party
   J.   the Liberals showed new
        strength in national
        opinion polls

Set 2: Passages III, IV, and V

Passage III

On your last camping vacation or

fishing trip far from the bright lights

of the urban American city, perhaps
     17
you gazed upward on a breathtakingly

clear night and were struck by awe at
                             18

the starry panorama. If so, you may
                      19
be able to appreciate the elation of

scientists at the California Institute

of Technology in 1985, when the

Institute was given seventy million

dollars to construct the world's largest

telescope.

17. A. NO CHANGE
    B. of the American city
    C. of urban American cities
    D. of the urban city

18. F. NO CHANGE
    G. with awe
    H. awesomely
    J. in awe

19. A. NO CHANGE
    B. If this is so,
    C. If so
    D. So

The generous donor was the W. M. Keck Foundation of Los Angeles, whose grant paid for all but fifteen million dollars of the cost of building the telescope and an observatory to house it atop a dormant volcano in Hawaii. The telescope has thirty-six mirrors with a total diameter of about thirty-three feet, which permit study of a volume of space eight times greater <u>than the second largest telescope,</u> on Palomar Mountain in California.

A telescope is more than just an instrument <u>to look at stars</u>. It's also a time <u>machine, the</u> light it captures may have left a distant star billions of years earlier. The Keck scope can pick up light from matter that is

20. F.   NO CHANGE
    G.   than the second largest telescope's
    H.   than that visible with the second largest telescope
    J.   than that of the second largest telescope's

21. A.   NO CHANGE
    B.   to look for stars
    C.   for looking at stars
    D.   for the purpose of looking at stars

22. F.   NO CHANGE
    G.   machine—the
    H.   machine the
    J.   machine; the

twelve billion years old, three quarters the estimated age of the universe. Small wonder, then, that the scientists <u>were happy and gleeful</u>. The Keck donation put much more of the universe within their view.

23. A. NO CHANGE
    B. were gleeful, and happy
    C. were gleeful
    D. were happily gleeful

Passage IV

I often wish that the phrase "applied science" had never been invented, for it suggests that there is a sort of scientific knowledge of direct practical use, which can be studied <u>apart from another sort</u> of scientific knowledge, which has no practical use, and which is termed "pure science." But there <u>is no more total and complete</u> fallacy than this.

24. F. NO CHANGE
    G. as a part of
    H. apart and separate from
    J. as part

25. A. NO CHANGE
    B. are no more total
    C. is no more complete
    D. is no fallacy that is a more complete

What people call "applied science" is nothing but the application of pure science to particular classes of problems. They consist of deductions
26
from those general principles, established by the reasoning and observation that constitute pure science. No one can safely make these deductions until he has a firm grasp of the principles.
27

26. F. NO CHANGE
    G. It consists
    H. Classes consist
    J. Problems consist

27. A. NO CHANGE
    B. principles, happen to be involved.
    C. principals that are involved.
    D. principals.

Passage V

These paragraphs may or may not be in the most logical order. The last item of this passage will ask you to choose the most logical order.

(1)

Many people mistakenly believe they have insomnia. Because they have not had eight full hours of sleep, they think that they are insomniacs. But there is no evidence to support the common belief that everyone has to get eight hours of
<u>everyone has</u>
28

sleep nightly. <u>In fact,</u> a few people
29
habitually sleep as little as two hours a night and wake up feeling fine. A much larger number of people <u>requires only</u> five hours of sleep
30
each night, while others must have ten hours to feel refreshed.

28. F. NO CHANGE
   G. everyone have
   H. everybody have
   J. that everybody have

29. A. NO CHANGE
   B. OMIT and begin sentence with *A few*
   C. Move to after *habitually*
   D. Move to after *as little as*

30. F. NO CHANGE
   G. requires
   H. only requires
   J. require only

(2)

Another type of insomnia occurs when something exciting or something upsetting happens, or is about to happen, in someone's life. Fortunately, this sort of insomnia is likely to disappear naturally after the crisis has passed. When insomnia does not go away, it is possible that sleeplessness is a sign of physical or emotional illness. Awakening early in the morning, for example, is sometimes a sign of depression, and this is a potentially serious mental illness.

(3)

There is a type of insomnia in which people believe that they have had only a few minutes of sleep, or no sleep at all. Though these sufferers

31. A. NO CHANGE
    B. something exciting or something upsetting happens
    C. something exciting or something upsetting happen,
    D. something exciting or upsetting happen

32. F. NO CHANGE
    G. Leave the comma, and omit the rest
    H. ; and this is
    J. for which this is

have not slept well, they have probably had some sleep. Because periods of light sleep and wakefulness are often fused, the insomniac does not realize that <u>they have been</u> asleep.
₃₃
It is harder to judge time in a dark bedroom than in the daylight, so it is easy to overestimate the number of wakeful hours and to underestimate those spent sleeping.

33. A.   NO CHANGE
B.   they were
C.   he or she has been
D.   he or she have been

34. Choose the sequence of paragraph numbers that will make the essay's structure most logical.

F.   NO CHANGE
G.   1, 3, 2
H.   2, 1, 3
J.   3, 1, 2

Set 3: Passages VI and VII

Passage VI

At one time, the home satellite dish industry experienced such explosive growth <u>which today it is</u>
₃₅
<u>being estimated</u> that fifty thousand

35. A.   NO CHANGE
B.   today which it is being estimated
C.   that today it is estimated
D.   which today it is currently estimated

new receivers <u>had installed</u> each year
36
during much of that decade. This
growth brought an expansive range of
programming to more than one
million people <u>every day; many</u> dish
37
owners, however, were getting mixed
signals about the usefulness of home
dishes and the continued availability
of satellite-delivered programming.
At the time, several leading pay TV
programmers began moving ahead
with plans to scramble <u>their service</u>.
38
The large investment in a satellite dish
was a questionable one. Though some
dish owners mistakenly believed that
the scrambling of signals was illegal,
the Cable Communications Act
recognized that satellite programmers
can scramble to protect <u>their services</u>
39
<u>being used</u> without authorization.

36. F. NO CHANGE
G. were being installed
H. will have received installation
J. will have been installed

37. A. NO CHANGE
B. every day. Many
C. every weekday. (Begin new paragraph with *Many*)
D. every day. (Begin new paragraph with *Many*)

38. F. NO CHANGE
G. its services
H. their services
J. each of their services

39. A. NO CHANGE
B. their service being used
C. its services' being used
D. their services from being used

Cable companies have long been concerned <u>by protecting</u> their services from unauthorized use by commercial enterprises <u>as hotels, bars, and restaurants,</u> which in some cases have broken the law by charging customers for the privilege of viewing <u>programs which it has</u> received without charge. Scrambling was the most efficient way to prevent this unlawful activity.

40.
- F.   NO CHANGE
- G.   to protecting
- H.   about protecting
- J.   for protecting

41.
- A.   NO CHANGE
- B.   such as hotels bars and restaurants
- C.   such as hotels, bars, and restaurants
- D.   as hotels, bars and restaurants

42.
- F.   NO CHANGE
- G.   programs that it has
- H.   programs that they have
- J.   programs it has

Passage VII

Larry Harmon was Bozo the Clown for thirty-five years. He played the character on live television <u>and had been providing</u> the voice for twenty years of Bozo cartoons.

Even at age sixty, Harmon was still going strong, and insisting that

43.
- A.   NO CHANGE
- B.   and he provides
- C.   and is
- D.   and provided

202

characters like Bozo were needed more than ever. <u>That is the reason why</u> he was still donning his Bozo costume at age seventy-one, thrilling thousands with an appearance at the Rose Parade.

44. F. NO CHANGE
G. That is why
H. This is why
J. For this reason,

Through Bozo, Harmon <u>not only urged people</u> to do something good for others, but also to be good to themselves.

45. A. NO CHANGE
B. urged people not only
C. urged not only people
D. both urged people

<u>For example, he</u> warned schoolchildren about the danger of drugs and at the same time cheered them up.

46. F. NO CHANGE
G. He, as an example,
H. As an example, he
J. Hc, as an example,

<u>In his own way to make</u> the world a safer, happier place to live.

47. A. NO CHANGE
B. He tried to make in his own way
C. To try in his own way, he made
D. In his own way, he tried to make

<u>Interviewed at his home in Silver Lake,</u> I once asked him about

48. F. NO CHANGE
G. When interviewed at his home in Silver Lake
H. Interviewing him at his home in Silver Lake
J. Being interviewed at his home in Silver Lake

retiring. <u>"Bozo will never retire," he</u>₄₉ <u>said.</u> He'd go smiling and in makeup

to that big circus in the sky.

49. A. NO CHANGE
B. He said Bozo will never retire.
C. Bozo will never retire he said.
D. "Bozo will never retire"; he said.

Set 4: Passages VIII and IX

Passage VIII

The Voyager 2 spacecraft, racing

toward an encounter with Uranus

years ago, <u>had already discovered a</u>₅₀ <u>number</u> of tiny moons orbiting

the planet. Ranging in size from

twenty to thirty miles in diameter,

<u>the spacecraft also discovered new</u>₅₁ <u>moons</u> that scientists had not been

able to see with high-powered

<u>telescopes. Because</u> Uranus is so far₅₂ from the sun and so dimly lighted.

50. A. NO CHANGE
B. has already discovered the number
C. have already discovered the number
D. have already discovered a number

51. F. NO CHANGE
G. the spacecraft discovered new moons
H. new moons were also visible to the spacecraft
J. new moons also discovered by the spacecraft

52. A. NO CHANGE
B. telescopes, due to the fact that
C. telescopes.
D. telescopes because

Most scientists had expected additional moons <u>to be discovered</u>.
₅₃

53. F. NO CHANGE
G. discovered
H. to have been discovered
J. will have been discovered

Prior to this Voyager flight, <u>only five moons were detected</u>, and
₅₄

54. A. NO CHANGE
B. five moons only were detected
C. only five moons had been detected
D. only five moons have been detected

these were much larger <u>than the new</u>
₅₅
<u>discovered</u> satellites. None of the moons was in an area that would endanger Voyager <u>being they are</u> in
₅₆
orbits fifty thousand miles from the planet's center. No photographs of the new moons were immediately released when the spacecraft was still so far from Uranus that satellites <u>appeared only as tiny specks of</u>
₅₇
<u>light</u>.

55. F. NO CHANGE
G. than new discovered
H. than newly discovered
J. than the newly discovered

56. A. NO CHANGE
B. being it is
C. because it is
D. because they are

57. F. NO CHANGE
G. are tiny specks of light only
H. appears only as tiny specks of light
J. will appear only as tiny specks of light

205

Passage IX

Born only a week ago, <u>according to a spokesman for World Seas Theme Park,</u>⁵⁸ a killer whale died last night. When the whale was born, it weighed three hundred pounds and it appeared healthy. <u>And three days later, however,</u>⁵⁹ it displayed symptoms of a respiratory ailment; it was moved to an intensive-care pool but did not respond to treatment.

There is a high mortality rate for whales born in captivity. None of the four killer whales <u>which</u>⁶⁰ <u>were given birth to</u> at World Seas <u>have survived</u>.⁶¹ One of the only killer whales born in captivity to survive was born in an aquarium in Europe.

58. A. NO CHANGE
B. according to a World Seas spokesman,
C. Move phrase to beginning of sentence
D. Move phrase to end of sentence

59. F. NO CHANGE
G. And three days later,
H. Three days later, however,
J. Three days after,

60. A. NO CHANGE
B. that were born
C. , that had been born,
D. , that were given birth to,

61. F. NO CHANGE
G. has survived
H. survive
J. are surviving

Named Triumph, the whale is now

eight years <u>old; and is featured</u> daily

62

62.	A.	NO CHANGE
	B.	old and is featured
	C.	old, and the whale is featured
	D.	old; featured

with dolphins <u>in an aquatic show</u>

63
<u>each day</u>.

63.	F.	NO CHANGE
	G.	each day in an aquatic show
	H.	in an aquatic show
	J.	every day in an aquatic show

Section 4: Improving Paragraphs

Directions

Carefully read the excerpts below, which represent writing one might find in drafts of student papers. Here, you will find questions that require you not only to address grammar and usage within individual sentences but also to address questions that deal with the excerpt more globally by asking you to attend to features such as organization and the development of ideas.

The Answer Key for the Improving Paragraphs section is on p. 256, and the explanatory answers begin on p. 271.

Set 1: Passages I and II

Passage I

(1) Realizing that the Watergate scandal could damage his chances for re-election, Nixon engaged in a cover-up of his own ties to the break-in. (2) On June 17, 1972, it so happens that five men associated with the Committee to Re-elect the President (CREEP) decided to break into the Democratic National Committee headquarters, but they were caught. (3) The headquarters were at the Watergate Hotel in Washington, D.C. (4) The CREEPs were working on behalf of Nixon's re-election campaign, trying to gather intelligence that might assure Nixon a second term in office.

(5) On August 15, 1973, Richard Nixon gave a televised address to the nation in which he denied any personal wrongdoing in the Watergate scandal. (6) Nixon claimed to take responsibility for whatever went on in his administration, and he denied that anything about the break-in had been known by him, saying, "I neither authorized nor encouraged subordinates to engage in illegal or improper campaign tactics."

(7) In the same speech, Nixon also claimed that he "neither took part in nor knew about any of the subsequent cover-up activities." (8) But the speech really was part of the cover-up. (9) Shortly afterward, new information and evidence showed that Nixon did in fact know about and was aware of the whole scheme. (10) Nixon tried to place the blame elsewhere, implying in the August 15 speech that there were bad guys were the ones who wanted him to hand over tape recordings proving he was part of the plot. (11) Facing possible impeachment in light of the tapes, Nixon became the only U.S. president ever to resign from office.

1. Where does sentence 1 belong in the essay?

   A. where it is now
   B. after sentence 2 in paragraph 1
   C. after sentence 3 in paragraph 1
   D. after sentence 4 in paragraph 1
   E. as the last sentence of paragraph 2

2. Which of the following is the best way to combine and revise sentences 2 and 3 (reproduced below)?

   On June 17, 1972, it so happens that five men associated with the Committee to Re-elect the President (CREEP) decided to break into the Democratic National Committee headquarters, but they were caught. The headquarters were at the Watergate Hotel in Washington, D.C.

   A. On June 17, 1972, it so happens that five men associated with the Committee to Re-elect the President (CREEP) decided to break into the Democratic National Committee headquarters at the Watergate Hotel in Washington, D.C., but were caught.
   B. On June 17, 1972, five men associated with the Committee to Re-elect the President (CREEP) decided to break into the Democratic National Committee headquarters at the Watergate Hotel in Washington, D.C., but were caught.
   C. On June 17, 1972, five men associated with the Committee to Re-elect the President (CREEP) were caught breaking into the Democratic National Committee headquarters at the Watergate Hotel in Washington, D.C.
   D. On June 17, 1972, it so happens that five men associated with the Committee to Re-elect the President (CREEP) were caught breaking into the Democratic National Committee headquarters at the Watergate Hotel in Washington, D.C.
   E. On June 17, 1972, five CREEPs were caught breaking into the Democratic National Committee headquarters at the Watergate Hotel in Washington, D.C.

3. In context, which is the best version of the underlined portion of sentence 6 (reproduced below)?

   Nixon claimed to take responsibility for whatever went on in his administration, <u>and he denied that anything about the break-in had been known by him</u>, saying, "I neither authorized nor encouraged subordinates to engage in illegal or improper campaign tactics."

   A. as it is now
   B. yet he denied that anything about the break-in had been known by him
   C. yet he denied having known various details and facts about the break-in
   D. and he denied having known about the break-in
   E. yet he denied having known anything about the break-in

4. What is the best way to combine and revise sentences 8 and 9 (reproduced below)?

   But the speech really was part of the cover-up. Shortly afterward, new information and evidence showed that Nixon did in fact know about and was aware of the whole scheme.

   A. But the speech was really part of the cover-up: shortly afterward, new information and evidence showed that Nixon did in fact know about and was aware of the whole scheme.
   B. But the speech was really part of the cover-up: shortly afterward, new information and evidence showed that Nixon did in fact know about the whole scheme.
   C. But the speech was really part of the cover-up, because, shortly afterward, new information and evidence showed that Nixon did in fact know about and was aware of the whole scheme.
   D. But the speech was really part of the cover-up; shortly afterward, new information and evidence showed that Nixon did in fact know about and was aware of the whole scheme.
   E. But the speech was really part of the cover-up: it was only shortly afterward that new information and evidence showed that Nixon did in fact know about and was aware of the whole scheme.

5. In context, which is the best version of the underlined portion of sentence 10 (reproduced below)?

Nixon tried to place the blame elsewhere, implying in the August 15 speech that <u>there were bad guys were the ones who wanted him to hand over tape recordings, proving he was part of the plot</u>.

A. as it is now

B. there were bad guys, and they were the ones who wanted him to hand over tape recordings proving he was part of the plot

C. the bad guys were the ones who wanted him to hand over tape recordings, proving he was part of the plot

D. the bad guys were those who wanted him to hand over tape recordings that proved he was part of the plot

E. the bad guys were those that wanted him to hand over tape recordings, proving he was part of the plot

6. Which is the best conclusion for this essay?

A. Nixon was a crook.

B. Crime doesn't pay.

C. Politicians are often in denial.

D. Though he left behind a legacy of important achievements, Nixon's denial of Watergate involvement irretrievably scarred his reputation.

E. The Watergate scandal was a sad chapter in Nixon's political life.

Passage II

(1) In my creative writing class, we learned that good writers use figurative language both to get their point across and to make readers see what is being said. (2) Similes are easier to recognize as figures of speech than metaphors, because the "like" or "as" provides a hint.

(3) Figurative language can include metaphors, similes, and unusual verbs and adjectives. (4) When you use a metaphor, you describe one thing in terms of another. (5) If I say, "My boss is a thief because he pays me only minimum wage," I am using a metaphor, since my boss is not literally a thief. (6) However, by calling him a "thief," I make it seem like he is acting in a criminal or immoral manner. (7) This metaphor overstates the case, but is a more colorful and interesting way of complaining than if I had said, "My boss won't give me a raise, and this makes me angry enough to consider his behavior immoral."

(8) Metaphors can be hard to invent. (9) One approach is to ask yourself whether the metaphor you want is positive or negative. (10) For example, if I

love texting my friends, I might think of other kinds of positive experiences that can be compared to texting, and write, "Texting with my friends is like going to a great party without leaving home." (11) The main difference between a metaphor and a simile is that a simile requires the use of "like" or "as." (12) An example of a simile might be, "The sunset was like a ring of fire." (13) Another example might be, "I am as hungry as a bear that's just come out of hibernation."

7. Which of the following is the best version of the underlined portion of sentence 1 (reproduced below)?

   In my creative writing class, we learned that good writers use figurative language <u>both to get their point across and to make readers see what is being said</u>.

   A. Leave it as it is.
   B. both to get their point across and to be interesting
   C. to express their ideas through imagery that allows readers to picture what is being said
   D. to put more figures into their language
   E. to make readers think

8. In context, which is the best way to rephrase sentence 10 (reproduced below)?

   For example, if I love texting my friends, I might think of other kinds of positive experiences that can be compared to texting, and write, "Texting my friends is like going to a great party without leaving home."

   A. Leave it as it is.
   B. For example, if I love texting my friends, I might think of other kinds of experiences that are unlike texting, and write, "Texting with my friends is like going to a great party without leaving home."
   C. For example, if I love texting my friends, I might think of other kinds of positive experiences that can be compared to texting, and write, "Texting my friends is like being at a great party without leaving home."
   D. For example, if I love texting my friends, I might think of other kinds of positive experiences that can be compared to texting, and write, "Texting my friends is a word party."
   E. For example, if I love texting my friends, I might think of other kinds of positive experiences that can be compared to texting, before writing, "Texting my friends is like going to a great party without leaving home."

9. Where should sentence 2 be placed in the passage?

    A.   where it is
    B.   following sentence 12
    C.   It isn't necessary anywhere in the passage.
    D.   replacing sentence 11
    E.   following sentence 7

10. Which of the following is one of the ways in which sentence 8 functions?

    A.   as the overall point of the entire passage
    B.   as an example of the thesis of the second paragraph.
    C.   as a transition from the first paragraph to the second
    D.   as a fact
    E.   as an anecdote

11. Which is the best way to write the underlined portion of sentences 12 and 13 (reproduced below)?

    <u>An example of a simile might be, "The sunset was like a ring of fire."</u> <u>Another example might be,</u> "I am as hungry as a bear that's just come out of hibernation."

    A.   No change is necessary.
    B.   An example of a simile might be, "The sunset was like a ring of fire," or
    C.   Two examples of similes are "The sunset was like a ring of fire," and
    D.   Two similes to use are "The sunset was like a ring of fire," in addition to
    E.   First, "The sunset was like a ring of fire," and second,

12. How is it best to deal with sentence 11 (reproduced below)?

    The main difference between a metaphor and a simile is that a simile requires the use of "like" or "as."

    A.   No change is necessary.
    B.   Replace it with "The main difference between a metaphor and a simile is that the second one requires the use of 'like' or 'as.'"
    C.   Replace it with "The main difference between a metaphor and a simile is the use of 'like' or 'as.'"
    D.   Replace it with sentence 2.
    E.   Replace it with "Simile not metaphor requires the use of 'like' or 'as.'"

Set 2: Passages III and IV

Passage III

(1) In this century, television doctors are portrayed more realistically than they were in earlier decades. (2) This is apparent in medical dramas such as *House, ER* and *Grey's Anatomy*, which stand worlds apart from shows of earlier decades such as *Marcus Welby, MD* and *Medical Center*. (3) These earlier shows depicted doctors as saint-like and nearly unfailing in their ability to heal the sick both physically and emotionally. (4) Today's TV doctors are flawed. (5) They have real lives. (6) They make mistakes that sometimes cost patients their lives. (7) They question their abilities. (8) They get sued. (9) They weep. (10) In other words, they're more like the rest of us: struggling and vulnerable, unable to perform miracles, and on the other hand able to enjoy the occasional success that comes from hard work that often involves imperfection and error along the way.

(11) At times efforts at realism have led to distortion. (12) *Nip/Tuck*, a medical show that ran from 2003-2010, depicted only the seamiest side of the plastic surgery profession. (13) Plastic surgeons Christian Troy (Julian McMahon) and Sean McNamara (Dylan Walsh) were far from perfect. (14) They were not even moral most of the time. (15) Christian took patients who were not good candidates for surgery in order to make a buck. (16) While Sean tried to run a more ethical practice, he too was drawn into the seediness on occasion. (17) The medical procedures shown were often graphic and grotesque. (18) This is just one example of how television reflects certain developments in the culture of medicine, both its practice and the public's perception of it.

13. Which of the following best replaces the word *realistically* in sentence 1?

A. No replacement is needed.
B. optimistically
C. mythologically
D. currently
E. than ever

14. How are sentences 4-9, reproduced below, best expressed?

Today's TV doctors are flawed. They have real lives. They make mistakes that sometimes cost patients their lives. They question their abilities. They get sued. They weep.

A. No changes are necessary.

B. Today's TV doctors are flawed, with real lives, mistakes that take lives, questionable abilities, lawsuits, and weeping.

C. Today's TV doctors are flawed: their lives, mistakes, abilities, lawsuits, and emotions are real.

D. Today's TV doctors are flawed: they have real lives; they make mistakes; they question their abilities; they get sued; and they weep.

E. Today's flawed TV doctors make mistakes that take lives, call their abilities into question, cause lawsuits, and make them weep.

15. What is the best replacement for the underlined portion of sentence 10 (reproduced below)?

In other words, they're more like the rest of us: struggling and vulnerable, unable to perform <u>miracles, and on the other hand able</u> to enjoy the occasional success that comes from hard work that often involves imperfection and error along the way.

A. No change is needed.

B. miracles, and by contrast able

C. miracles, and yet able

D. miracles, and able

E. miracles with the ability

16. What should be added following sentence 16?

A. Nothing should be added.

B. an example

C. at least two examples

D. an analogy

E. a metaphor

17. Where should sentence 17 be located?

    A.   where it is now

    B.   following sentence 12

    C.   following sentence 13

    D.   following sentence 14

    E.   following sentence 15

18. What is the best way to deal with sentence 18?

    A.   Leave it as it is.

    B.   Delete it.

    C.   Move it to another place in the passage.

    D.   Rewrite it to better summarize the overall point of the passage.

    E.   Make it shorter.

Passage IV

(1) We can sometimes become lesser than honest with ourselves, especially when it comes to fledgling love relationships. (2) When we meet someone who could become, or has just become, a life partner, we want nothing more than to fulfill that person's expectations and dreams. (3) I'm not just thinking about your partner's beloved worn-out easy chair, or even about critical in-laws. (4) I'm referring to being swept up into a whole new life consisting of features you never knew you didn't want, or for which you feel wholly unprepared! (5) So we may find ourselves creating experiences and lifestyles that make our partner happy, without consciously realizing that these things aren't making *us* happy.

(6) This is exactly what happened to Elizabeth Gilbert, as she tells us in her runaway bestseller, *Eat, Pray, Love*. (7) Some years into her first marriage, she was so unhappy that she found herself hiding in the bathroom night after night. (8) She tells us that she was sobbing "a great lake of tears" there. (9) She had expected by this time that she'd want to settle down and have children but to her chagrin found that this was not the case. (10) It was painful for her to tell her husband the truth: that she did not want to have a baby, and that she did not want to continue to be married. (11) At one point, she blames herself for helping to fashion a life that didn't suit her, saying "How could I be such a criminal jerk as to proceed this deep into a marriage, only to leave it?" (12) Gilbert was struck by the fact that she "had actively participated in every moment of the creation of this life," yet did not feel that it "resembled" her. (13) The problem can be chalked up to the strong need to mirror the wishes and desires of one's life partner, to keep the relationship pleasant and seemingly without conflict.

19. Which is the best way to reword the underlined portion of sentence 1 (reproduced below)?

    We can sometimes <u>become lesser than honest</u> with ourselves, especially when it comes to fledgling love relationships.

    A. No change.
    B. be the lesser of those who are honest
    C. be less than honest
    D. become less rather than more honest
    E. have less honesty

20. Where should sentence 5 be placed in the passage?

    A. where it is now
    B. following sentence 2
    C. following sentence 3
    D. at the beginning of the second paragraph
    E. as the concluding sentence of the passage

21. Which word or phrase belongs at the beginning of sentence 4?

    A. Instead
    B. Whereupon
    C. For instance
    D. Therefore
    E. By contrast

22. How should sentences 7 and 8 (reproduced below) be changed to improve the structure of the passage?

    Some years into her first marriage, she was so unhappy that she found herself hiding in the bathroom night after night. She tells us that she was sobbing "a great lake of tears" there.

    A. No change is necessary.
    B. Sentence 8 should come before sentence 7.
    C. Sentence 8 should be eliminated.
    D. The two sentences should be combined into one.
    E. Change *there* to *in the bathroom*.

23. What is one reason to revise sentence 13?

    A.   The sentence is too long.

    B.   *Chalked up to* is a slang term.

    C.   Gilbert is not mentioned by name.

    D.   It is not clearly related to the preceding sentence.

    E.   It includes irrelevant information.

24. What would be an appropriate title for this passage?

    A.   Honesty Is the Best Policy

    B.   *Eat, Pray, Love*

    C.   Coping with a Life Partner

    D.   Leaving Well Enough Alone

    E.   None of the above

Set 3: Passage V

Passage V

(1) Many of you have problems facing up to our mistakes. (2) At its worst, this problem could be characterized as the "Frankenstein Flaw." (3) In the classic novel *Frankenstein,* Victor Frankenstein unwittingly creates a monster, and instead of destroying it before it can do harm, Victor flees without telling anyone what he has done. (4) The monster begins roaming the countryside, and eventually becomes a murderer. (5) We could say, then, that Victor's decision not to correct or admit his mistake has fatal consequences.

(6) The economic recession that began in 2008 has been widely recognized as nearly as serious as the Great Depression. (7) It has also been recognized as the result of serious mistakes by corporate executives and government leaders who contributed to the proliferation of high-risk mortgage loans that resulted in a wave of defaults that contributed to a collapse in the housing industry. (8) However, no one has admitted responsibility for these mistakes, even though millions have lost their jobs and their homes as a consequence. (9) This is a modern instance of the Frankenstein Flaw, with no one taking the blame for a monstrous result.

25. What is the best way to correct sentence 1 (reproduced below)?

Many of you have problems facing up to our mistakes.

A. No correction is needed.
B. Change *our* to *our many.*
C. Change *you* to *us.*
D. Change *many* to *all.*
E. Change mistakes to errors.

26. What is the best way of rewriting sentence 3 (reproduced below)?

In the classic novel *Frankenstein,* Victor flees without telling anyone what he has done, after he unwittingly creates a monster instead of destroying it.

A. No change is necessary.
B. In the classic novel *Frankenstein,* Victor Frankenstein unwittingly creates a monster, and instead of destroying it before it can do harm, Victor flees without telling anyone what he has done.
C. Frankenstein flees without telling anyone that he's created a monster rather than destroying one.
D. Without destroying it before it can do harm, Victor Frankenstein flees from the monster he creates in the classic novel, *Frankenstein.*
E. In the classic novel *Frankenstein,* Victor Frankenstein creates a monster rather than destroying one before it can do harm, and flees without telling anyone.

27. Adding *After Victor flees* to the beginning of sentence 4 would be

A. unnecessary.
B. a clarification.
C. a transition.
D. an improvement.
E. an obfuscation.

28. Which of the following would improve sentence 6?

A. No improvement is needed.
B. shortening the sentence
C. deleting *economic*
D. adding a transition
E. replacing *that* with *which*

29. Which is the best version of the underlined portion of sentence 7 (reproduced below).

    It has also been recognized as the result of serious mistakes by corporate executives and government leaders who contributed to the proliferation of <u>high-risk mortgage loans that resulted in a wave of defaults that contributed to a collapse in the housing industry</u>.

    A. The current version is best.
    B. high-risk mortgage loans that resulted in some defaults that contributed to a collapse in the housing industry.
    C. high-risk mortgage loans that could have resulted in a wave of defaults that contributed to a collapse in the housing industry.
    D. highly risky mortgage loans that resulted in a wave of defaults that contributed to a collapse in the housing industry.
    E. high-risk mortgage loans, resulting in a wave of defaults that contributed to a collapse in the housing industry.

30. The use of *monstrous* in sentence 9 is

    A. appropriate, since it indicates the magnitude of the collapse, and reinforces its connection with the Frankenstein Flaw.
    B. inappropriate, since no one involved in the recession was really a monster.
    C. inappropriate, because it is a metaphor.
    D. inappropriate, because the recession has no relationship to *Frankenstein*.
    E. appropriate, because it strongly criticizes those who were responsible for the economic collapse.

Section 5: Sentence/Text Completion

Directions

Following the Sentence Completion format for the SAT, each sentence in Sets 1 through 3 contains one or two blanks to indicate omitted words. Following the Text Completion format for the GRE, each sentence or passage in Sets 4 and 5 contains two or three blanks to indicate omitted words.

Considering the lettered choices beneath each sentence, choose the word or set of words that best fits the whole sentence or passage.

The Answer Key for the Sentence/Text Completion section is on p. 257, and the explanatory answers begin on p. 274.

Set 1

1. Even though we buy most of our groceries weekly, we visit the market _____ to pick up an item or two.

   A. reluctantly
   B. daily
   C. hungrily
   D. locally
   E. together

2. Paradoxically, all the local residents demonstrating for world peace _____ gun control.

   A. need
   B. condone
   C. miss
   D. represent
   E. oppose

3. The panel leader was responsible for dividing the speaking time evenly among the participants, and so he _____ each one fifteen minutes.

   A. averaged
   B. matched
   C. performed
   D. allotted
   E. obtained

4. Most of the merchants have overstocked shelves and do not welcome the manufacture of new _____.

   A. ideas
   B. necessities
   C. products
   D. stores
   E. policies

5. The local _____ is represented by the work of neighborhood _____, whose creations are unique, beautiful, and useful.

   A. mood . . . businessmen
   B. renaissance . . . artisans
   C. traits . . . energy
   D. facility . . . aficionados
   E. consensus . . . dissenters

6. With a _____ hope that the erratic path of the economy would stabilize and begin moving along a(n) _____ course, the prime minister continued those government programs in effect since his election.

   A. squelched . . . unending
   B. persistent . . . steady
   C. high . . . better
   D. sincere . . . patriotic
   E. false . . . winning

7. Everyone at the PTA meeting was encouraged by the news that, although national test scores had fallen, local scores _____ even more sharply than officials had _____.

   A. rose . . . predicted
   B. spoke . . . spoken
   C. spiked . . . explained
   D. remained . . . planned
   E. increased . . . feared

8. History has taught us that crises that seem _____ and portend ultimate _____ often end not in destruction but in an unforeseen technological advance.

   A. placid . . . deviation
   B. beneficial . . . chaos
   C. interesting . . . involvement
   D. minor . . . harm
   E. insoluble . . . doom

9. One's inclination to remain a _____ is often _____ by a hard economic fact: those without a specialized and thorough understanding of a subject will not find a good job.

   A. vagrant . . . repulsed
   B. martinet . . . distinguished
   C. worker . . . salted
   D. dilettante . . . thwarted
   E. thief . . . undercut

10. Nuclear technology has _____ the task of _____ human forces; now the power of many battalions can be activated with the touch of a button.

    A. simplified . . . mobilizing
    B. bluffed . . . eradicating
    C. mitigated . . . naturalizing
    D. emphasized . . . restraining
    E. checked . . . determining

11. Although the most important cause of World War II remains a matter of _____, we can be certain that changing economic conditions _____ to the eventual conflict.

    A. speculation . . . contributed
    B. nationalism . . . added
    C. power . . . proceeded
    D. interpretation . . . speeded
    E. obscurity . . . led

12. At its best, informative writing is clear, direct, and never _____.

   A. personalized
   B. terse
   C. esoteric
   D. interesting
   E. fresh

13. Maintaining one's psychological equilibrium may mean resisting both _____ emotion and callous _____.

   A. moderate . . . reason
   B. calculated . . . rage
   C. nullified . . . love
   D. extreme . . . insensitivity
   E. false . . . uncertainty

14. _____ becoming a star, Lela realized that she would not attain that goal unless all of her activities were _____.

   A. Tending toward . . . major
   B. Looking at . . . limited
   C. Asking about . . . curious
   D. Intent upon . . . purposeful
   E. Flirting with . . . calculated

15. His _____ was reflected by the books he chose to read; every author on his shelf advanced a sneering and _____ view.

   A. pretentiousness . . . servile
   B. image . . . idealistic
   C. generosity . . . parsimonious
   D. literacy . . . licentious
   E. cynicism . . . morose

Set 2

16. While a nuclear holocaust will never become _____, we can help to make it less _____ by advising the superpowers to change their hawkish attitudes.

    A. desperate . . . routine
    B. serious . . . powerful
    C. impossible . . . probable
    D. predestined . . . devastating
    E. real . . . imaginary

17. Because he acted _____ whenever he was in public, most people concluded that he was a rather _____ adult.

    A. stupid . . . famous
    B. silly . . . immature
    C. angry . . . secretive
    D. secretive . . . backwards
    E. uppity . . . mysterious

18. Poetry is not the favorite study of most modern college students because they believe in the utilitarian function of education and do not think poetry has any _____ value.

    A. literary
    B. artistic
    C. practical
    D. timeless
    E. imaginative

19. Because we had eaten turkey on Thanksgiving for so many years, we never wondered whether some other _____ might be an equally _____ alternative.

    A. dish . . . tasty
    B. bird . . . expensive
    C. holiday . . . enjoyable
    D. delicacy . . . exotic
    E. pursuit . . . familiar

20. Responding to the _____ that he hoards a _____ share of the wealth of the community, Sandoval described at length his charitable contributions.

    A.   question . . . questionable

    B.   charge . . . disproportionate

    C.   implication . . . marginal

    D.   threat . . . fractional

    E.   fact . . . growing

21. A memorial in Washington, D. C. _____ Vietnam War _____ by listing all who were killed in battle or missing in action.

    A.   protests . . . philosophy

    B.   disavows . . . heroes

    C.   predicts . . . intervention

    D.   immortalizes . . . casualties

    E.   describes . . . supporters

22. The singer's cynicism was disclosed by _____ lyrics that denied hope, and contrasted sharply with the _____ melody that accompanied them.

    A.   fragmentary . . . brief

    B.   standard . . . complex

    C.   garbled . . . clear

    D.   passionate . . . throbbing

    E.   bitter . . . pleasant

23. When _____ an unpopular viewpoint, one must expect that many will not listen and that an equal number will listen and

_____.

    A.   demonstrating . . . languish

    B.   propagating . . . sneer

    C.   disclaiming . . . leave

    D.   denying . . . extrapolate

    E.   crucifying . . . watch

24. Police science has advanced quickly over the past decade, but the incidence of crime has remained _____.

   A.   unconsidered
   B.   decreasing
   C.   malevolent
   D.   inconsequential
   E.   substantial

25. Hume was the most _____ of the eighteenth-century philosophers; while others looked to God as the source of truth, he proposed that truth was a variable.

   A.   ornery
   B.   ignorant
   C.   skeptical
   D.   scholarly
   E.   optimistic

26. Utopian theories have been repeatedly _____; experimental communities eventually fail when the eternal human _____ enter the picture.

   A.   undervalued . . . spirit
   B.   disproven . . . vices
   C.   attempted . . . beings
   D.   praised . . . optimistic
   E.   studied . . . scholars

27. Although he was criticized by some for being overly _____, those closest to Wilson insisted that his sense of humor was sharp and delightful.

   A.   authoritarian
   B.   somber
   C.   proud
   D.   neat
   E.   foppish

28. Recognizing once again that competition is the life blood of a capitalist society, the federal government has lifted restrictions placed on banks so that they are on a(n) _____ with thrift institutions.

    A. par
    B. basis
    C. era
    D. edge
    E. capacity

29. Those who _____ Byron's poetry as satanic have been replaced today by critics with less moral _____ and more appreciation for unorthodox viewpoints.

    A. minced . . . appetite
    B. bowdlerized . . . staunchness
    C. destroyed . . . turpitude
    D. condemned . . . inflexibility
    E. recited . . . knowledge

30. Rather than propose a budget that is both balanced and austere, the state legislators have opted to continue _____ spending.

    A. sharply curtailed
    B. red-ink
    C. makeshift
    D. voting
    E. over and above

Set 3

31. After observing that hurricanes move in a(n) _____ pattern, Benjamin Franklin was able to predict that such a storm coming from the east would not continue directly _____.

    A. standard . . . seaward
    B. circular . . . west
    C. destructive . . . unseen
    D. unpredictable . . . north
    E. original . . . longitudinally

32. Any candidate for office, no matter how _____, cannot win if he or she is discovered to have substituted _____ for truth.

   A.   pejorative . . . praise
   B.   eloquent . . . facts
   C.   personable . . . artifice
   D.   execrable . . . candor
   E.   distracting . . . virtue

33. Some studies indicate that young children stop being _____ as soon as they reach school age because the classroom is a place where facts rather than imagination predominate.

   A.   creative
   B.   understanding
   C.   cooperative
   D.   mischievous
   E.   restive

34. Socrates' seeming _____ fooled many of his opponents, who mistook the wise man's hesitant stance for ignorance.

   A.   persistence
   B.   despair
   C.   wit
   D.   diffidence
   E.   indifference

35. Every incidence of social injustice sets Mack out on a _____; he cannot learn of any inequity without attempting to correct it.

   A.   crusade
   B.   tantrum
   C.   limb
   D.   dilemma
   E.   lark

36. Many business leaders complain that students graduating with business degrees have had a _____ education, and are urging college entrants to major in fields that _____ rather than focus their knowledge.

    A.   marketable . . . blur
    B.   conventional . . . change
    C.   useful . . . employ
    D.   dreadful . . . ridicule
    E.   narrow . . . broaden

37. An amateur athlete who becomes a professional gets more than _____ compensation; there are also the _____ rewards associated with representing American ideals.

    A.   fancy . . . questionable
    B.   monetary . . . intangible
    C.   extraordinary . . . fringe
    D.   over . . . possible
    E.   legendary . . . mythic

38. The professor's great learning _____ Bill while it also encouraged him; so he approached each class meeting both with _____ and the desire to enrich his own knowledge.

    A.   threatened . . . understanding
    B.   repulsed . . . zeal
    C.   frightened . . . trepidation
    D.   heartened . . . suspicion
    E.   puzzled . . . clarity

39. By _____ all of the more difficult questions posed by the press, the senator aroused suspicion that he was not well informed on the issues.

    A.   deflecting
    B.   rehearsing
    C.   considering
    D.   answering
    E.   requesting

40. Universities that previously had ignored students deficient in basic skills are now instituting _____ programs designed to _____ the mathematical and verbal literacy of entering freshmen.

   A. elitist . . . challenge
   B. experimental . . . eradicate
   C. pretentious . . . disguise
   D. remedial . . . ameliorate
   E. new . . . maintain

41. The keynote speaker's address can be dismissed as simply _____; some potentially interesting points were lost in a garble of _____ jargon.

   A. fascinating . . . short-lived
   B. basic . . . apt
   C. wonderful . . . delightful
   D. dull . . . esoteric
   E. brief . . . clipped

42. Although his pursuit of Sarah's love was _____, Charles Smithson tried to remain _____ each time they met.

   A. forbidden . . . uninterested
   B. central . . . dignified
   C. magnified . . . troubled
   D. feeble . . . aloof
   E. desperate . . . calm

43. There are those who excuse their unwillingness to help the unfortunate by claiming that interfering in another's life is a violation of _____.

   A. selfishness
   B. law
   C. privacy
   D. benevolence
   E. human rights

44. Many poets have claimed that their work was the spontaneous product of _____, but their original manuscripts reveal the close and painstaking attention paid to _____.

    A.   chance . . . contrition

    B.   inspiration . . . revision

    C.   indifference . . . popularity

    D.   collaboration . . . isolation

    E.   education . . . rebellion

45. Leaving aside her _____, the department chair responded objectively to the issues raised in the meeting.

    A.   authority

    B.   biases

    C.   facts

    D.   knowledge

    E.   ability

Set 4

46. The movie was so (i) _____ that my frightened niece (ii) _____ fled the theater.

Blank (i)	Blank (ii)
A. insipid	D. languidly
B. gory	E. casually
C. banal	F. abruptly

47. To revise a paper is to see it with new eyes, and to (i) _____ it substantially. A revision, compared to the draft, should be markedly (ii) _____ in form and content.

Blank (i)	Blank (ii)
A. alter	D. similar
B. alleviate	E. unorthodox
C. continue	F. different

48. In this post-Bernie Madoff world, Gordon Gekko's "Greed Is Good" speech from the movie *Wall Street* would likely get a chorus of boos rather than (i) _____. Corporate ethics, we hope, have moved away from a (ii) _____ focus on the bottom line, to the recognitions that social responsibility gains public trust, and that trust is what makes a business (iii) _____.

Blank (i)	Blank (ii)	Blank (iii)
A. depreciation	D. shrill	G. sustainable
B. censure	E. venerable	H. invalid
C. approbation	F. hollow	I. accessible

49. Fleas can be a real (i) _____ for cats. If a cat is sensitive to their bite, even a single flea can cause the cat (ii) _____ itching and redness.

Blank (i)	Blank (ii)
A. escapade	D. superlative
B. nuisance	E. affable
C. boon	F. insufferable

50. Fictional characters tell us a great deal about our human (i) _____, and we often admire their integrity and (ii) _____. But characters also involve us in another kind of (iii) _____: we see our own flaws, weaknesses, and misdeeds in them and in their behavior.

Blank (i)	Blank (ii)	Blank (iii)
A. fitness	D. contusion	G. rudeness
B. infirmity	E. valor	H. mirroring
C. potential	F. potage	I. splendor

51. Political power in this country is always (i) _____; the support of each elected official's (ii) _____ wanes all too soon.

Blank (i)	Blank (ii)
A. overemphasized	D. components
B. underestimated	E. constituents
C. fleeting	F. fundamentals

52. Those in the humanities hope that the popularity of business and engineering is (i) _____, and look toward a(n) (ii) _____ when love for art and literature will (iii) _____ itself.

Blank (i)	Blank (ii)	Blank (iii)
A. transient	D. allegory	G. reassert
B. succinct	E. revival	H. bury
C. ostentatious	F. abacus	I. distend

53. When asked to (i) _____ the oil industry, government responded (ii) _____ so that neither oil magnates nor consumer advocates could claim to have Uncle Sam on their side.

Blank (i)	Blank (ii)
A. deregulate	D. ambiguously
B. consecrate	E. stringently
C. desecrate	F. implausibly

54. Anthropologists have suggested that only those who can stand (i) _____ a culture will ever recognize its flaws, and thus one (ii) _____ whether they can see flaws in their own.

Blank (i)	Blank (ii)
A. within	D. examines
B. alongside	E. postulates
C. outside	F. wonders

55. Before (i) _____ against consumer fraud were (ii) _____ during the 1970s, government seemed to have little interest in reducing (iii) _____ business practices.

Blank (i)	Blank (ii)	Blank (iii)
A. sentiments	D. legislated	G. excessive
B. safeguards	E. characterized	H. temperate
C. opinions	F. quelled	I. unfair

56. While we all love to hear about new discoveries, we should not (i) _____ the (ii) _____ of well-established information.

Blank (i)	Blank (ii)
A. discount	D. capriciousness
B. contemplate	E. reliability
C. undertake	F. meticulousness

57. We often admire the (i) _____ of those who engage in charitable giving. But one wonders whether donations to (ii) _____ causes would decrease if (iii) _____ were no longer deductible.

Blank (i)	Blank (ii)	Blank (iii)
A. goodness	D. undistinguished	G. contributions
B. burden	E. estimable	H. subscriptions
C. cunning	F. flagship	I. settlements

58. Those who advocate nuclear (i) _____ believe that strong American missile power will prevent other countries from making a first strike. Some wonder, however, whether this is a (ii) _____ policy.

Blank (i)	Blank (ii)
A. diminution	D. halfhearted
B. fission	E. random
C. deterrence	F. sound

59. Resistance to Darwin's theory of evolution came mainly from those who believed that man was created almost (i) _____. By nature, evolution suggests gradual (ii) _____ from simpler to more (iii) _____ forms.

Blank (i)	Blank (ii)	Blank (iii)
A. dogmatically	D. development	G. poignant
B. instantaneously	E. stasis	H. inert
C. ineptly	F. equipoise	I. complex

60. Of the six lead characters on the long-running sitcom *Friends*, Monica may be the most (i) _____. She is a controlling neat freak who cleans and organizes (ii) _____.

Blank (i)	Blank (ii)
A. progressive	D. unwillingly
B. sensible	E. obsessively
C. neurotic	F. discreetly

Set 5

61. In an interview on PBS television's *Nova* series, legendary scientist Carl Sagan (i) _____ his interest in time travel. But he was never a time travel (ii) _____: he was simply trying to understand how the universe works, and the question of how time works is part of (iii) _____ that understanding.

Blank (i)	Blank (ii)	Blank (iii)
A. proclaimed	D. paramour	G. affronting
B. withheld	E. devotee	H. eluding
C. decanted	F. constable	I. attaining

62. Those with (i) _____ syndrome falsely believe that they are not qualified to do their jobs or that they don't truly merit their accomplishments, despite the fact that they are trained, credentialed, and experienced at their work. They believe their (ii) _____ will be discovered at any moment.

Blank (i)	Blank (ii)
A. rectitude	D. acumen
B. encumbrance	E. astuteness
C. imposter	F. incompetence

63. Citing the work of Mark Schaller, social psychologist Alain Morin (i) _____ that celebrities can suffer from "fame-induced self-consciousness," a condition of self-monitoring and (ii) _____ that causes undue stress, as well as the tendency toward substance abuse as a "solution."

Blank (i)	Blank (ii)
A. uncovers	D. self-possession
B. observes	E. self-confidence
C. precludes	F. self-awareness

64. Morality is largely (i) _____, meaning that we shouldn't apply general principles to our lives and then follow them (ii) _____— that is, without reference to a particular set of circumstances. For instance, it may be good to protect a brother, but not when that brother has (iii) _____ a crime.

Blank (i)	Blank (ii)	Blank (iii)
A. status quo	D. blindly	G. disbursed
B. situational	E. sagely	H. perpetrated
C. monotonous	F. judiciously	I. expended

65. In Eastern spiritual traditions, to be mindful is to be fully in the present, to not think about past and future. Mindfulness training can involve an array of (i) _____—including yoga, meditation, musicianship, and conscious eating—that (ii) _____ stress reduction.

Blank (i)	Blank (ii)
A. stipulations	D. disseminate
B. arrangements	E. propagate
C. practices	F. cultivate

66. When you apologize to someone, do not point out that the other person (i) _____ your bad behavior, by saying something such as, "If you hadn't said or done X, I wouldn't have said Y." While it may be true that he or she did contribute in some way, your (ii) _____ this will mean your apology will fall flat. If you *do* manage to offer a pure apology, the other person may do some looking inward, and see his or her own (iii) _____.

Blank (i)	Blank (ii)	Blank (iii)
A. instigated	D. implying	G. shortcomings
B. stifled	E. portending	H. recompenses
C. overpowered	F. repressing	I. fortes

67. Saul wanted so badly to make a(n) (i) _____ point that he was just plain overbearing or hurtful in his remarks. He didn't even (ii) _____ the full impact of what he'd said until months later when he was less swept up in his (iii) _____ aims.

Blank (i)	Blank (ii)	Blank (iii)
A. altruistic	D. classify	G. stodgy
B. self-serving	E. register	H. declining
C. exalted	F. catalog	I. immediate

68. In psychology, projection occurs when something you believe about another person actually (i) _____ with you. Sigmund Freud said projection is a defense mechanism people use in order not to face (ii) _____ truths about themselves. For instance, one person may say to another, "You seem angry," when in fact it's the speaker who's angry. She projects her anger onto the other person so that she doesn't have to (iii) _____ negative emotion in herself!

Blank (i)	Blank (ii)	Blank (iii)
A. dissipates	D. reassuring	G. recognize
B. originates	E. disquieting	H. dispute
C. beckons	F. patronizing	I. negate

69. It's difficult for us to allow others to have their own likes and dislikes. Their differences often mean we have to (i) _____ experiences we don't enjoy, and we just seem naturally (ii) _____ to consider our own taste to be the best. But it's important—for our social lives and for our own inner growth—to respect and even (iii) _____ differences in others.

Blank (i)	Blank (ii)	Blank (iii)
A. shirk	D. inclined	G. abominate
B. escalate	E. dissuaded	H. clinch
C. stomach	F. levied	I. embrace

70. When we're young, we tend to think of our parents as gods. In our teens, we often (i) _____, and decide that they're the biggest idiots ever to walk the planet! At the same time, we hold them up to a very high standard of behavior, sometimes looking down on them as tainted and flawed. It may not be until we ourselves are middle aged—and have made many (ii) _____ and observed our own limitations and weaknesses—that we realize our parents are or were only human, and deserve our compassion rather than our (iii) _____.

Blank (i)	Blank (ii)	Blank (iii)
A. vary	D. gaffes	G. reproach
B. shift	E. antagonists	H. ovation
C. amend	F. nemeses	I. barrenness

71. Researchers believe that John Merrick suffered from a horribly (i) _____ condition called "Proteus Syndrome" (named for the Greek god Proteus, who was a shape-shifter), which causes bone abnormalities, skin overgrowth, and extensive tumors, among other problems. In Merrick's case, grayish, overgrown skin and facial tumors made him look to other people something like an elephant, hence the (ii) _____, "Elephant Man".

Blank (i)	Blank (ii)
A. shoddy	D. autograph
B. ornamental	E. moniker
C. disfiguring	F. epithet

72. In Virginia Woolf's novel *Mrs. Dalloway,* the main character, Clarissa, understands that every individual has a vibrant and (i) _____ inner life that cannot (and should not) be fully known by others. Clarissa believes in what she calls "the privacy of the soul," people's right to think and exist (ii) _____, without being pressured to think, act, or feel the way others want them to.

Blank (i)	Blank (ii)
A. comparable	D. independently
B. diverse	E. impartially
C. consonant	F. demonstrably

73. Retreating from areas of difficulty into imaginary ideal (i) _____ accomplishes nothing. But (ii) _____ in the struggle to make positive changes in the world's problematic (iii) _____ puts us on the path we are meant to travel.

Blank (i)	Blank (ii)	Blank (iii)
A. realms	D. partaking	G. circumstances
B. nadirs	E. meddling	H. ambiances
C. variances	F. disbanding	I. firmaments

74. Movie-goers often glamourize the (i) _____ in which many movie characters engage, and fail to reflect on the consequences characters must (ii) _____ for their actions.

Blank (i)	Blank (ii)
A. turnover	D. emulate
B. mayhem	E. bear
C. civility	F. forgo

75. At the end of James Joyce's novella *The Dead,* the main character, Gabriel Conroy, enters a visionary state in which he abandons his ego and sees into a formless world of (i) _____ between himself and all of humanity. Thinking of relatives long gone or destined soon for the grave, Gabriel recognizes the (ii) _____ fate of mortal humans and feels love and compassion toward everyone and everything. Gone are thoughts of self-image and self-importance; the lesser concerns of the ego have (iii) _____ the higher instincts.

Blank (i)	Blank (ii)	Blank (iii)
A. assemblage	D. sequestered	G. ensued from
B. enmity	E. collective	H. surpassed
C. interconnection	F. compendious	I. yielded to

Section 6: Sentence Equivalence

Directions

Select <u>two</u> answer choices, each of which can be used to complete the sentence correctly. Each word should fit the meaning of the sentence as a whole.

The Answer Key for the Sentence Equivalence section is on p. 258, and the explanatory answers begin on p. 283.

Set 1

1. Last year's flu virus was a particularly _____ strain, causing pneumonia in many sufferers.

   A. philanthropic
   B. innocuous
   C. mild
   D. pernicious
   E. idle
   F. virulent

2. My accountant told me that, after taxes, I _____ quite a bit of salary for the year.

   A. lost
   B. exchanged
   C. cleared
   D. created
   E. netted
   F. bundled

3. When we enter a new life situation—a job, relationship, or living arrangement—we are compelled to change in some way to orient ourselves to its circumstances, conditions, advantages, and _____.

   A. precincts
   B. brinks
   C. quarters
   D. drawbacks
   E. monitors
   F. limitations

4. Juan knew that the English equivalent of his name was "John," but because he _____ his beloved heritage, he asked to be called by his given name.

   A. revered
   B. disdained
   C. abhorred
   D. devoted
   E. admired
   F. mishandled

5. The movie's events were presented in _____ form, meaning that they did not proceed from day one forward in chronological progression.

   A. rudimentary
   B. non-linear
   C. circuitous
   D. straightforward
   E. devious
   F. surly

6. Tom's thoughts were _____ into the future when his friend talked about beginning the college application process.

   A. catapulted
   B. propelled
   C. rebuffed
   D. sheared
   E. warped
   F. appended

7. Klaus had a(n) _____ friend who so loved to chat that he expected Klaus to respond to phone and text messages at all hours of the day and night.

   A. reticent
   B. loquacious
   C. garrulous
   D. taciturn
   E. unwieldy
   F. portly

8. Aisha believes that labeling romantic relationships weighs them down and _____ one's passion.

    A. drenches
    B. relinquishes
    C. dampens
    D. waxes
    E. inhibits
    F. flutters

9. Some greeting card sentiments, with their maudlin prose, are embarrassingly _____.

    A. duplicitous
    B. impassive
    C. syrupy
    D. translucent
    E. leaden
    F. cloying

10. _____ eyelash mites mate, lay eggs, die, and decompose inside our hair follicles.

    A. Minute
    B. Mighty
    C. Bland
    D. Magnified
    E. Diminutive
    F. Wobbly

11. This ethical author of this book in no way intends to _____ on any copyrights.

    A. infringe
    B. pronounce
    C. decide
    D. encroach
    E. pounce
    F. trundle

12. You may be familiar with the various monster creation scenes that occur in film _____ of the nineteenth-century novel *Frankenstein,* in which a man made out of the body parts of the dead is stretched across a table, about to be animated by a bolt of lightning.

   A. prototypes
   B. adaptations
   C. remnants
   D. consummations
   E. rehearsals
   F. renderings

13. Dennis went to the mountains to find _____ after his beloved dog passed away.

   A. solace
   B. stagnation
   C. sloth
   D. seepage
   E. succor
   F. prowess

14. From the birthday boy's crestfallen face, it was clear that the child's parents made a(n) _____ decision to serve a fussy tart, rather than a traditional birthday cake.

   A. no-frills
   B. delectable
   C. ill-advised
   D. misguided
   E. impertinent
   F. embedded

15. One of the most famous literary heroes is the Greek king Odysseus, who fought valiantly over a ten-year period in the Trojan War, and then endured another ten years of _____, bravely conquering the one-eyed Cyclops, the witch Circe, and sea monsters Scylla and Charybdis, in an endeavor to get home to his wife.

   A. consolation

   B. travail

   C. lethargy

   D. adversity

   E. concord

   F. abatement

Set 2

16. As we move through life, encountering and testing old and new ideas against our experience, we inevitably _____ some and embrace others.

   A. adopt

   B. tally

   C. jettison

   D. secrete

   E. discard

   F. caress

17. The investor had a hard time deciding whether to opt out or to invest in the entrepreneur's _____.

   A. enterprise

   B. venture

   C. pandemonium

   D. appendage

   E. frolic

   F. fiasco

18. Sandra thought nothing of reducing others to a(n) _____ stereotype.

    A.   mere

    B.   manifold

    C.   porous

    D.   bare

    E.   impervious

    F.   untimely

19. Carmen acceded _____ to her boss' new initiative because she feared it would have unintended negative effects.

    A.   exultantly

    B.   diffidently

    C.   jovially

    D.   amiably

    E.   dotingly

    F.   reticently

20. When an ex-boyfriend she hadn't seen in years told her she'd aged, Marissa felt utterly _____.

    A.   ebullient

    B.   vivacious

    C.   abject

    D.   pedantic

    E.   mortified

    F.   congested

21. Steve Jobs received countless _____ for his creative brilliance as co-founder of the company that became known as Apple, Inc.

    A.   admonitions

    B.   deprecations

    C.   accords

    D.   accolades

    E.   acclamations

    F.   macrocosms

22. Because the couple had such a(n) _____ relationship, they sought counseling to see if they could get their fighting under control.

    A.   scrupulous

    B.   solicitous

    C.   tempestuous

    D.   turbulent

    E.   inexorable

    F.   iambic

23. Jamila found reading late at night so _____ that she could barely keep her eyes open after half a chapter.

    A.   soporific

    B.   stirring

    C.   strenuous

    D.   strident

    E.   salvific

    F.   somnolent

24. Arturo was such a good piano player by the age of six that many considered him to be a _____.

    A.   calamity

    B.   dawdler

    C.   prodigy

    D.   bureaucrat

    E.   virtuoso

    F.   miscreant

25. Laura was taught to go to confession regularly because her parents believed this was the best way for her to _____ for her sins.

    A.   perish

    B.   atone

    C.   yearn

    D.   entreat

    E.   exfoliate

    F.   compensate

26. The boys were given an old wooden kayak by a neighbor, but because their parents felt it was _____ and could sink, the boys were not allowed to use it.

    A. flimsy
    B. durable
    C. transitory
    D. rickety
    E. grisly
    F. unwavering

27. Peter knew he would have to be _____ during study periods if he were to pass his difficult calculus class.

    A. apathetic
    B. nonchalant
    C. diligent
    D. robust
    E. arrogant
    F. attentive

28. Because Kailani's co-worker was fired for writing personal emails during work hours, Kailani was careful not to _____ her own job in the same way.

    A. jeopardize
    B. reprove
    C. deify
    D. coddle
    E. endanger
    F. insulate

29. The novel's fundamentals were not difficult for Jill to grasp, but she found its _____ of meaning—pointed out by the teacher—more of a challenge.

    A. allocations
    B. nuances
    C. thresholds
    D. shades
    E. pedigrees
    F. contemplations

30. Many people like to honk while driving through tunnels so they can hear the sound _____ all around them.

A. hiss

B. reverberate

C. indemnify

D. grapple

E. echo

F. ripen

Set 3

31. Slamming his fist on the table, the mayoral candidate _____ denied his opponent's accusations.

A. anemically

B. munificently

C. vehemently

D. furtively

E. fervidly

F. pliably

32. The town council voted to keep the park district's parking fees _____ so that everyone could afford them.

A. nominal

B. considerable

C. minimal

D. unrestricted

E. surreptitious

F. systematized

33. The citizens were warned against the inclination to _____ the shopping areas after the hurricane broke the windows on a number of storefronts, exposing their contents to the outside world.

A. replenish

B. loot

C. consolidate

D. ransack

E. abet

F. impede

34. The teacher was dismayed to learn that cheating on the midterm was not limited to the one student he'd identified, because this student relied on the _____ of others to carry out the deed.

    A.   complicity

    B.   scruples

    C.   providence

    D.   frugality

    E.   felicity

    F.   collusion

35. Kaya found the scholar's lecture on global warming so _____ that she wasted no time in sharing the imparted knowledge with her friends.

    A.   edifying

    B.   noxious

    C.   benign

    D.   illuminating

    E.   trifling

    F.   flippant

36. Although the home team was ahead at halftime, the visitors had _____ their rivals by the end of the football game.

    A.   extolled

    B.   quashed

    C.   lionized

    D.   routed

    E.   fabricated

    F.   primed

37. Having given large sums of money to support education and public health, among other causes, the late John D. Rockefeller is known as one of the world's most prominent _____.

    A.   savants

    B.   anarchists

    C.   misanthropists

    D.   philanthropists

    E.   lieges

    F.   benefactors

38. When his boss called him _____, Ben thought it was a compliment, but his wife later told him that this meant Ben was overbearing and intrusive.

    A. unstinting

    B. officious

    C. profuse

    D. preposterous

    E. bureaucratic

    F. fruitful

39. Antonio _____ his inheritance from his grandmother on a pricey sports car and a trip to Las Vegas.

    A. depleted

    B. recouped

    C. lavished

    D. circumvented

    E. sustained

    F. exasperated

40. Since there was a _____ of qualified candidates for the position, the job search committee decided to extend the deadline for applications, in the hope that more time would yield more contenders.

    A. pillar

    B. glut

    C. dearth

    D. salutation

    E. surfeit

    F. shortage

41. Hiroshi considered starting his own construction company, but worried that jobs can sometimes be _____ for the self-employed.

    A. sporadic

    B. blotchy

    C. sumptuous

    D. imperious

    E. intermittent

    F. spindly

42. Carol liked to _____ on Sundays, but her mother often tried to keep her busy with household chores.

    A. leer
    B. loaf
    C. lunge
    D. lounge
    E. lurch
    F. ladle

43. The translator always aimed for the utmost _____ when it came to reproducing the meanings intended by the novel's Spanish author.

    A. imprecision
    B. fidelity
    C. incentive
    D. leniency
    E. charisma
    F. accuracy

44. Julio's father thought that his son's singing ability must have been _____ because Julio could carry a tune without having been taught.

    A. innate
    B. indelible
    C. insensate
    D. inductive
    E. inclement
    F. inborn

45. It was good that Lucy enjoyed finding words with _____ meanings, because her college entrance exam required her to match many terms with their synonyms.

    A. divergent
    B. like
    C. disparate
    D. vague
    E. analogous
    F. obdurate

Answer Key

Section 1: Sentence Correction – Type 1

Set 1	Set 2	Set 3	Set 4
1. D	16. C	31. C	46. A
2. B	17. C	32. E	47. A
3. B	18. E	33. E	48. E
4. E	19. C	34. D	49. A
5. E	20. A	35. B	50. E
6. B	21. C	36. B	51. A
7. B	22. B	37. E	52. A
8. C	23. E	38. C	53. B
9. E	24. D	39. E	54. B
10. A	25. D	40. C	55. A
11. B	26. E	41. D	56. E
12. C	27. B	42. A	57. B
13. D	28. D	43. B	58. B
14. C	29. C	44. C	59. C
15. A	30. A	45. E	60. B

Section 2: Sentence Correction – Type 2

Set 1	Set 2	Set 3
1. D	16. A	31. B
2. E	17. D	32. C
3. D	18. B	33. A
4. D	19. E	34. B
5. C	20. C	35. D
6. B	21. E	36. E
7. D	22. D	37. B
8. C	23. C	38. D
9. D	24. C	39. D
10. B	25. C	40. A
11. C	26. D	41. D
12. D	27. C	42. D
13. C	28. C	43. D
14. D	29. E	44. C
15. D	30. E	45. B

Section 3: Sentence Correction – Type 3

Set 1: Passages I and II

Passage I	Passage II
1. A	9. C
2. H	10. G
3. C	11. A
4. F	12. J
5. A	13. C
6. H	14. H
7. A	15. A
8. F	16. J

Set 2: Passages III, IV, and V

Passage III

17. B
18. G
19. A
20. H
21. C
22. J
23. C

Passage IV

24. F
25. C
26. G
27. A

Passage V

28. F
29. A
30. J
31. A
32. G
33. C
34. G

Set 3: Passages VI and VII

Passage VI

35. C
36. G
37. D
38. H
39. D
40. H
41. C
42. H

Passage VII

43. D
44. J
45. B
46. F
47. D
48. H
49. A

Set 4: Passages VIII and IX

Passage VIII

50. A
51. H
52. D
53. F
54. C
55. J
56. D
57. F

Passage IX

58. D
59. H
60. B
61. G
62. B
63. H

Section 4: Improving Paragraphs

Set 1: Passages I and II

Passage I
1. D
2. C
3. E
4. B
5. D
6. E

Passage II
7. C
8. D
9. C
10. C
11. C
12. A

Set 2: Passages III and IV

Passage III
13. A
14. A
15. C
16. B
17. B
18. D

Passage IV
19. C
20. B
21. A
22. D
23. B
24. E

Set 3: Passage V

Passage V
25. C	27. A	29. E
26. B	28. D	30. A

Section 5: Sentence/Text Completion

Set 1

1. B
2. E
3. D
4. C
5. B
6. B
7. A
8. E
9. D
10. A
11. A
12. C
13. D
14. D
15. E

Set 2

16. C
17. B
18. C
19. A
20. B
21. D
22. E
23. B
24. E
25. C
26. B
27. B
28. A
29. D
30. B

Set 3

31. B
32. C
33. A
34. D
35. A
36. E
37. B
38. C
39. A
40. D
41. D
42. E
43. C
44. B
45. B

Set 4

46. B, F
47. A, F
48. C, F, G
49. B, F
50. C, E, H
51. C, E
52. A, E, G
53. A, D

54. C, F
55. B, D, I
56. A, E
57. A, E, G
58. C, F
59. B, D, I
60. C, E

Set 5

61. A, E, I
62. C, F
63. B, F
64. B, D, H
65. C, F
66. A, D, G
67. B, E, I
68. B, E, G

69. C, D, I
70. B, D, G
71. C, F
72. B, D
73. A, D, G
74. B, E
75. C, E, I

Section 6: Sentence Equivalence

Set 1

1. D, F
2. C, E
3. D, F
4. A, E
5. B, C
6. A, B
7. B, C
8. C, E
9. C, F
10. A, E
11. A, D
12. B, F
13. A, E
14. C, D
15. B, D

Set 2

16. C, E
17. A, B
18. A, D
19. B, F
20. C, E
21. D, E
22. C, D
23. A, F
24. C, E
25. B, F
26. A, D
27. C, F
28. A, E
29. B, D
30. B, E

Set 3

31. C, E
32. A, C
33. B, D
34. A, F
35. A, D
36. B, D
37. D, F
38. B, E
39. A, C
40. C, F
41. A, E
42. B, D
43. B, F
44. A, F
45. B, E

Charting and Analyzing Your Test Results

One of the most important parts of test preparation is understanding why you missed a question so you can reduce your mistakes. Now that you have taken the diagnostic test and checked your answers, carefully tally your errors by marking them in the proper column. As you evaluate, look for trends in the types of mistakes you make, and look for low scores in *specific* topic areas. The answers and explanations following these charts will help you to correctly answer these types of questions in the future.

Grammar and Usage Analysis Sheet						
Section	Possible	Total Right	Total in Error	Simple Mistake	Misread Question	Lack of Knowledge
Section 1: Sentence Correction – Type 1	60					
Section 2: Sentence Correction – Type 2	45					
Section 3: Sentence Correction – Type 3	63					
Section 4: Improving Paragraphs	30					
Section 5: Sentence/Text Completion	75					
Section 6: Sentence Equivalence	45					
Overall Grammar and Usage Test Results	318					

Answers and Explanations

Section 1: Sentence Correction – Type 1

Set 1

1. **D.** The verb should be *would have suspected.*

2. **B.** The correct form is *who,* subject of the clause *who made the better showing in the televised debate.*

3. **B.** The verb should be the singular *was prepared* to agree with the singular subject *None.*

4. **E.** There are no errors in this sentence.

5. **E.** There are no errors in this sentence.

6. **B.** The phrase should be made parallel with the others in the series: *that he is good looking.*

7. **B.** *Smart* and *intelligent* mean the same thing. One of the terms should be deleted.

8. **C.** To be parallel to the first clause, the second clause should be rephrased: *and then, whether or not he had the strength . . .*

9. **E.** The sentence is correct as given.

10. **A.** *Anyone* should be two words: *Any one.*

11. **B.** The verb should be the singular *remembers* to agree with the singular *None.* The plural is correctly used in *who have* to agree with the plural *survivors.*

12. **C.** The idiom is *other than,* so the phrase should read *than that.*

13. **D.** The comparative *lower* should be used with a comparison of only two incomes, those of husband and wife.

14. **C.** With the correlatives *not . . . but,* the structure after *but* should be parallel to *to please,* an infinitive: *but to act as status symbols that impress.*

15. **A.** The correct phrase is *Unlike those of Monet.*

Set 2

16. **C.** The series of *to eat, write, and to shave* should be made up of parallel elements—either *to eat, to write, and to shave* or *to eat, write, and shave*.

17. **C.** In this context, the idiom is *charged with.* To *charge for* is used to mean *to assess a cost.*

18. **E.** The sentence is correct as given.

19. **C.** The pronoun *one* should be the plural *they* to agree with the plural *westerners.*

20. **A.** Because the subject of the sentence is singular, and the phrases following *as well as* are parenthetical and not part of a compound subject, the verb should be *has,* rather than *have.*

21. **C.** The verb *affect* should be used. As a verb, *effect* means *to bring about; affect* means *to influence.*

22. **B.** To keep parallelism in the series (*of pasta, of muffin mix*), you must also say *of detergent.*

23. **E.** This sentence is correct.

24. **D.** The *which* is an ambiguous pronoun.

25. **D.** With *not only . . . but also,* the same structure must follow both correlatives: *not only low in fat . . . but also high in fiber.*

26. **E.** There are no errors in this sentence.

27. **B.** An agreement error. The subject is plural, so the verb should be *indicate.*

28. **D.** A tense error. The future tense makes no sense here where three other verbs are in the past tense.

29. **C.** The present tense of the participle is inappropriate for an action to take place in the future; *to be presented* is better.

30. **A.** The sentence compares a man (*President Clinton*) and a group of people (*cabinet*). It should read *Like President Clinton's.*

Set 3

31. **C.** An error of idiom. With *smaller,* the *to* should be *than.*

32. **E.** The sentence is correct as given.

33. **E.** Remember that roughly one sentence in five on the tests will have no error.

34. **D.** *Kind* is singular. Use *this kind* or *that kind.*

35. **B.** An agreement error. Since the singular *harpist* is nearer the verb in a *neither . . . nor* construction, the verb is singular.

36. **B.** The adverb *relatively* should be used to modify the adjective *easy.*

37. **E.** This sentence contains no errors.

38. **C.** With the present tense used twice already, there is no reason to change to the future tense. Use *it is* three times.

39. **E.** The sentence is correct as given.

40. **C.** The phrase *brokers claim* is parenthetical. The clause should be *who . . . are willing to take risks,* with *who* as the subject of the clause.

41. **D.** The clause here is *it is they; they* is subjective with the verb *is.*

42. **A.** The infinitive at the beginning of the sentence dangles. The word *teachers* (who do the encouraging) should follow *To encourage better reading skills.*

43. **B.** A verbosity error. Since *same* and *identical* mean the same thing, only one of the two should be used.

44. **C.** A verb tense error. The present tense (*is*) should be used here.

45. **E.** There are no errors in this sentence.

Set 4

46. **A.** The clause should begin with the conjunction *As,* not the preposition *Like.*

47. **A.** The phrase *who have studied* is necessary, parallel to *who ought* later in the sentence.

48. **E.** The sentence is correct as given.

49. **A.** The opening participial phrase dangles, modifying *natives* rather than *huts.*

50. **E.** The sentence contains no error.

51. **A.** The opening phrase dangles, modifying *returns* rather than *he* or *Simmons.*

52. **A.** The plural *have* should be singular to agree with the singular nearer the verb after *neither . . . nor.*

53. **B.** The word *fewer* should replace *less.*

54. **B.** The subjective *I* should be *me,* object of the preposition *on.*

55. **A.** Since the sentence begins with *you,* there should be no change of person to *one.*

56. **E.** The sentence is correct as given.

57. **B.** The subject is singular; *are* should be *is.*

58. **B.** With the correlatives *not . . . but,* an infinitive should follow *but* to be parallel with *to fly,* such as *to sail as a passenger.* The phrase *as would seem likely* is parenthetical.

59. **C.** The *when* should be *that.*

60. **B.** The singular subject *quarterback* requires the singular verb *was.*

Section 2: Sentence Correction – Type 2

Set 1

1. **D.** The *not only . . . but also* should both be followed by parallel constructions, *about* and a noun. Choice E adds unnecessary words.

2. **E.** Only choice E supplies an appropriate word (*I*) for the dangling participial phrase (*Carrying the warm water . . .*) to modify.

3. **D.** Since *alumnae* is plural, the pronoun must be *they.* The preposition *in* must follow *believe.*

4. **D.** The opening phrase speaks of *prices,* and unless *prices* follows, the phrase dangles. Choice C, while not incorrect, contains unnecessary words.

5. **C.** Since the sentence begins with *you,* the subject of the main clause should also be *you.*

6. **B.** The pronoun *which* has no clear antecedent; *hours* cannot be *decreased,* choice D, or *altered,* choice E, but a *schedule* can be *altered.*

7. **D.** In choice D, the related words are kept together and the sentence is more concise than choice B.

8. **C.** The beginning of the sentence must parallel *enjoying.*

9. **D.** The prepositional phrase at the beginning of the sentence must refer to *operas* not *composers,* either directly or by a pronoun (*those*). Since Mozart is a composer, *other* is also necessary.

10. **B.** The shortest version here is correct. The word *only* makes the other choices redundant.

11. **C.** The verb in the *if* clause should be *had planned.* The pronoun *whom* is the object of *to ask.*

12. **D.** Only choice D avoids the ambiguous pronoun error.

13. **C.** The correlatives *both . . . and* should be followed by parallel words (the adjectives *afraid* and *awed*). The preposition *of* must follow *afraid.*

14. **D.** This version has parallel clauses.

15. **D.** All other choices change the original meaning or use an incorrect verb tense.

Set 2

16. **A.** *That your horse won* is a noun clause, a proper subject of the verb *is.* In choice C, the gerund requires a possessive. There is an agreement error in choice E.

17. **D.** The antecedent of *that* is the plural *tickets,* but the subject of the sentence is the singular *one.* The verbs should be *were reserved* and *has.*

18. **B.** With *neither . . . nor,* the subject of the verb is the singular *butter.* Since calories can be counted, *less* should be *fewer.*

19. **E.** The first four answers have parallelism errors with the correlatives *both . . . and.* By eliminating the correlatives, choice E avoids the errors and is more concise.

20. **C.** The singular subject (*one*) requires a singular verb (*has promised*). The pronoun should be *whoever,* subject of the clause *whoever wins the primary.* Choice E unnecessarily shifts the verb to past tense.

21. **E.** Though there are two adjectives, the subject of the sentence is the singular *nature,* so the main verb must be *relegates.* Since *fiction* is singular, the correct pronoun is the singular *it.* Both choice D and choice E avoid the agreement errors, but choice D is wordier and uses *which* and a nonrestrictive clause where a restrictive clause with *that* should be used (or the prepositional phrase).

22. **D.** Choice A is wordy (*annually* means *each year*) and misuses the idiom *descend on.* But choices B and C make *lured* a dangling participle. The idiom (*descended into*) in choice E is wrong in this context.

23. **C.** In choices A and B, the two parts of the comparison (*Switzerland* and *mountains*) are not parallel. Choice E makes no grammatical sense. Choices C and D are grammatically correct but choice D is wordy.

24. **C.** With the verb *knocked,* the adverb *loudly,* not the adjective *loud,* should be used. To maintain a logical sequence of verb tenses, the two past tenses (*stopped, run*) should be followed by a third past tense (*knocked*).

25. **C.** The subject of the first clause is *whoever,* but in the clause *whomever the wind reaches, wind* is the subject and *whomever* is the object. The adjective should be *fewest* not *least.*

26. **D.** The problem here is parallelism. The most concise version of the sentence will use three nouns *eagerness, willingness,* and *optimism.* Choice E, though parallel, is wordier than choice D.

27. **C.** Choices A, B, and E are all sentence fragments and dependent clauses. In choice D, the plural verb is an agreement error.

28. **C.** Since the introductory phrase uses the singular *his new knowledge,* the subject must be singular. Since *his* is the possessive case of *he,* the subject must also be a human, a *nurseryman,* not *science.*

29. **E.** The error in choices A, B, C, and D is the same, an ambiguous pronoun (*which* or *this*).

30. **E.** There are parallelism errors with the correlatives *both . . . and* in choices A and B. Choice C, though grammatically correct, changes the meaning of the original sentence slightly. Choice D awkwardly separates the adjective *deceptive* from the words it modifies.

Set 3

31. **B.** To maintain parallelism, *in* must follow *than.* Since the Belmont City Jail is a lockup, the correct phrase is *any other.*

32. **C.** Since *group,* a collective noun, is singular, the correct verb is *has,* and the correct pronoun is *it.*

33. **A.** In choices C, D, and E, the infinitive dangles, since NBC is the subject of the sentence, and is aiming to *whet* the audience's *appetite.* In choice B, *years* is plural.

34. **B.** With the singular subject *Neither,* the verb or verbs must be singular. Choice A omits the necessary word *of.*

35. **D.** The correct idiom is *try to.* Choice C omits the necessary word *as.*

36. **E.** The main clause must begin with *government mortgage certificates.* The correct word here is *principal,* not *principle,* and it is unnecessary to bring the word *you* into the sentence.

37. **B.** With the *if* construction, the correct verb form is *would be.* The word *personally* is unnecessary.

38. **D.** The series here is *one must* followed by a verb controlled by *must: weigh, exercise,* and *drink.*

39. **D.** In choices A and B, *different* modifies *Company.* The word *other* must be included. Choice E adds unnecessary language.

40. **A.** The sentence is correct as given. *Its* (the possessive) is correct here. Choices C, D, and E all change the meaning of the original.

41. **D.** The correct noun here is *effect.* The idiom is *effect on* or *upon.*

42. **D.** The correct word here is *credulous* (trusting, believing) not *credible* (believable). Choice D is better than choice A because it is more concise.

43. **D.** The main clause should begin with a singular plant to agree with the opening phrase *a very old plant.*

44. **C.** The underlined portion of the sentence is correct as is. There is no reason to change the verb *has* into *must have, will have,* or *would have* (choices B, D, and E). The addition of commas in choices A and B changes the meaning of the sentence: with the commas, the sentence allows that there may be other terrorists besides those who were seen.

45. **B.** *Me* is correct as the object of the preposition *for. Whoever* is the subject of the clause *whoever wins the contest.* The correct idiom is *as a prize,* not *for a prize.* While choice D correctly uses *me* and *whoever,* it creates a dangling participial phrase and suggests that the skillet, teakettle, and saucepan are paging through the catalog.

Section 3: Sentence Correction – Type 3

Set 1: Passages I and II

Passage I

1. **A.** No change is needed.

2. **H.** With two independent clauses, the semicolon is correct.

3. **C.** The series of examples should be introduced by a comma, and the word *including*. A colon following the word *causes* would also work were this one of the choices.

4. **F.** Though choice G is not wrong, it uses several additional words, and repeats the word *committee* unnecessarily. The apostrophe here follows the *s,* as *delegations* is plural.

5. **A.** In choices C and D, some meaning is lost by the omission of *stark.* Choice A uses the correct idiom.

6. **H.** With *funds,* the verb must be plural. *There* is correct; *they're* means *they are* and *their* is a possessive form of *they.*

7. **A.** The phrase *fewer and fewer* is correct and concise.

8. **F.** This phrase is fine as it is.

Passage II

9. **C.** The sentence requires a comma. With a semicolon, the second part of the sentence is a fragment without a main verb, and the dash disrupts the flow of ideas.

10. **G.** The adverb *relatively* is needed to modify the adjective *autonomous.*

11. **A.** The singular *separatism* is the antecedent of *it.* Omission of the phrase changes the meaning of the sentence.

12. **J.** The past perfect tense is unnecessary here. The past tense of the verb *to lead* is *led. Lead* is the present tense or the noun for the metal, which is easily confused with *led.*

13. **C.** The article *a* should follow both *neither* and *nor.*

14. **H.** There is no need to repeat *resignation*. One can say either *that of Davis* (with no apostrophe) or, more concisely, *Davis's.*

15. **A.** The simple past tense is required here.

16. **J.** The participial phrase at the beginning modifies *the Liberals,* not *strength* or *national opinion polls*. Without this change, the participle dangles.

Set 2: Passages III, IV, and V

Passage III

17. **B.** Since *urban* means *of the city,* it is unnecessary here.

18. **G.** The idiomatic preposition is *with.*

19. **A.** The briefer *If so* should be followed by a comma.

20. **H.** There must be a parallel to *volume of space* after the comparison. The most concise correct version uses the pronoun *that.* Choices G and I are grammatically incorrect.

21. **C.** The correct idiom for this particular sentence is *instrument for.* Note, though, that in other sentences, the correct idioms may be *instrument to* or *instrument of,* depending on the rest of the sentence.

22. **J.** Use a semicolon between two independent clauses not joined by a conjunction.

23. **C.** The adjective *gleeful* conveys the meaning by itself.

Passage IV

24. **F.** *Apart from* is idiomatic. Choice H includes both *apart* and *separate,* which mean the same.

25. **C.** Since *total* and *complete* mean the same thing, there is no reason to use both. The singular verb agrees with the singular subject, *fallacy.*

26. **G.** The subject of the paragraph is still *applied science.* The antecedent of the pronoun *it* is the singular *science.*

27. **A.** The correct word is *principles.* Choice B adds several unnecessary words.

Passage V

28. F. Either *everyone* or *everybody* can be used, but both are singular so the verb must be *has*.

29. A. The phrase *In fact* should be retained at the beginning of the sentence, since the sentence is correcting the mistaken belief referred to in the first sentence. The phrase *As a matter of fact* is not wrong, but it takes five words to say what *In fact* says in two.

30. J. The phrase *a number of* calls for the plural *require*.

31. A. The comma at the end of the clause is necessary in this case to set off the phrase that follows. While this phrase need not be considered parenthetical, you can be sure that it is treated as such because of the comma after *happen*.

32. G. The phrase that ends the sentence can stand as an appositive. Choice H contains a punctuation error, and choice I is grammatically incorrect.

33. C. The subject of the sentence is the singular *insomniac.* Only in choice C are the pronouns and the verb in agreement with their antecedent.

34. G. Paragraph 2 begins with a reference to *another type* of insomnia, but paragraph 1 has not identified one. Paragraph 2 logically follows only paragraph 3, which does describe types of insomnia.

Set 3: Passages VI and VII

Passage VI

35. C. Only this choice is grammatically correct.

36. G. The verb tense in other choices is incorrect.

37. D. The content of the sentence after the semicolon and the use of *however* signal a change. The sentence is more logically a part of a new paragraph. Choice C changes the meaning of the sentence.

38. H. The antecedent of the pronoun is plural (*programmers*). Choice H is preferable to choice F because multiple programmers provide multiple (plural) *services*.

39. D. Since *programmers* is plural, the correct pronoun is *their.* The meaning of the sentence is not *to protect the services* but *to protect them from being used.*

40. H. The correct idiom here is *concerned about.*

41. C. With the series, there must be at least one comma (after *hotels*), and there can be a comma after *bars.* The preposition *such as* should be used here.

42. H. The clause is a restrictive one. The verb and pronoun should be plural to agree with *commercial enterprises.*

Passage VII

43. D. The consistent sequence of tenses here calls for the past tense.

44. J. Only choice J avoids the use of an ambiguous pronoun.

45. B. Since *but also* is followed by an infinitive, *not only* should also be followed by an infinitive. The correlatives are *not only . . . but also,* not *both . . . but also.*

46. F. This sentence is correct as is. There is no need to change *for example* to *as an example,* placing this language between the sentence's subject and verb disrupts the flow of the sentence.

47. D. Beginning with *in his own way* keeps the subject and verb together. The original is a fragment sentence.

48. H. The subject of the sentence is *I,* so to avoid a dangling phrase, the opening must modify *I,* not *Bozo.*

49. A. The sentence is correctly punctuated.

Set 4: Passages VIII and IX

Passage VIII

50. A. In this context, *a number* (that is, *many*) is correct. The last sentence of the paragraph makes it clear that the number has not yet been determined. The subject is the singular *spacecraft.*

51. H. Since the participial phrase that begins the sentence refers to the *moons,* the *moons* must begin the main clause or the participle will dangle. Choice F has no main verb.

52. D. If the first sentence ends at *telescopes,* the sentence beginning with *Because* is a fragment.

53. F. The expected event will occur in the future; therefore, *to be discovered* is correct.

54. **C.** The past perfect tense is necessary to denote an action in a past time in relation to another past time (*Prior to this flight*).

55. **J.** The article (*the*) is necessary. The adverb *newly* modifies the adjective *discovered*.

56. **D.** The antecedent of *they* is the plural *moons*. The correct conjunction is *because*.

57. **F.** This choice maintains the correct verb tense.

Passage IX

58. **D.** To keep the opening phrase close to the word it modifies, the parenthetical phrase should come at the end of the sentence.

59. **H.** The *and* suggests continuation, but *however* suggests a change of direction in the discourse. The *however* should be used to indicate this change.

60. **B.** Choices C and D add unnecessary words and commas to the phrase.

61. **G.** The subject of the verb is the singular *None*.

62. **B.** The semicolon is not correct because there is no subject in the phrase *and is featured.* Choice C is wordy.

63. **H.** With *daily, each day* or *every day* is unnecessary.

Section 4: Improving Paragraphs

Set 1: Passages I and II

Passage I

1. **D.** *Realizing that the Watergate scandal could damage his chances for re-election, Nixon engaged in a cover-up of his own ties to the break-in* should follow *The CREEPs were working on behalf of Nixon's re-election campaign, trying to gather intelligence that might assure Nixon a second term in office*. Choice B cannot be correct because we don't yet know which president is involved in the discussion.

2. **C.** This is the most succinct combination of the two sentences. In choices A and B, the phrases *decided to break into* and *but they were caught* can be shortened to *were caught breaking into*. In choices A and D, the phrase, *it so happens* is unnecessary to the meaning of the sentence. Choice E does not tell us who the "CREEPs" were.

3. **E.** This is the least wordy version of the underlined portion of the sentence. Since the second part of the sentence provides information that contrasts with the information in the first part, *yet* is a more fitting connector than *and*.

4. **B.** In all answers except choice B, the phrases *knew about* and *was aware of* are redundant. Note that the colon in choice B is a good connector because it indicates that what follows the colon will give specifics to support what precedes the colon.

5. **D.** This is the most concise version of the underlined part of the sentence. Choice E violates the who/that rule, which requires that *who* be used when the phrase refers to people (as opposed to objects). Choices C and E are vague about what *proving* refers to.

6. **E.** The essay focuses on several elements of Nixon's role and denial of the Watergate scandal, and indicates that the outcome was his resignation from office. Choices B and C are not specifically tied to Nixon, choice A is not supported by the focus of the passage, and choice D is incorrect because no details are given in the essay about Nixon's achievements while in office.

Passage II

7. **C.** In the original, *get their point across* is vague. Choice C is both clear and consistent with the passage's overall meaning.

8. **D.** All of the other choices use *like,* which is characteristic of a simile, not a metaphor.

9. **C.** Sentence 2 interrupts the initial points about figurative language and gives information that is well expressed in sentence 11, and therefore is not needed in the passage. This means, though, that the writer should lengthen the opening paragraph by a sentence or two.

10. **C.** This sentence moves us from the overall discussion of metaphor in paragraph one, to the additional points about inventing metaphors in paragraph 2.

11. **C.** This is the most concise and clear of the choices offered.

12. **A.** This is consistent with the correct answer for question 9.

Set 2: Passages III and IV

Passage III

13. **A.** The passage stresses that today's TV doctors are *more like the rest of us,* which is consistent with the use of *realistically.*

14. **A.** Though some readers could deem the several short sentences to be choppy, they arguably provide a degree of emphasis to each idea, and are thus a way of using short sentences to good advantage in this essay.

15. **C.** *On the other hand* introduces a contrast with the first part of the sentence, but uses an incorrect structure (the correct structure is *on one hand . . . on the other hand*). Choice C expresses the contrast in the most concise and correct way.

16. **B.** The sentence could be improved by the addition of an example of how Sean was *drawn into the seediness.*

17. **B.** As it is, the sentence is misplaced amidst points about Christian and Sean. It makes a more general point, connected to the first part of the passage.

18. **D.** This sentence should reflect the overall point of the passage, that today's TV doctors are more realistic than those of earlier decades.

Passage IV

19. **C.** It is both grammatically correct and the most clear and concise choice.

20. **B.** Sentence 5 logically follows the point made in sentence 2.

21. **A.** *Instead* is used to introduce an alternative to a previous point.

22. **D.** The two sentences can be expressed more concisely as one: *Some years into her first marriage, she was so unhappy that she found herself hiding in the bathroom night after night, sobbing "a great lake of tears."*

23. **B.** None of the other choices describes a change that can improve the sentence. The passage does not otherwise use informal tone or diction consistent with slang, and in general, slang terms are not consistent with standard written English.

24. **E.** None of the choices captures the passage's full meaning.

Set 3: Passage V

Passage V

25. **C.** *Us* is grammatically consistent with *our*.

26. **B.** This is the only choice in which the order of events is clear, and in which necessary information has not been removed.

27. **A.** The preceding sentence establishes that Victor has fled.

28. **D.** The relationship of sentence 6 to the preceding paragraph could be made clearer through the addition of a transition.

29. **E.** The problem in the original is the unnecessary repetition of *that: that resulted . . . that contributed.* E is the only choice that corrects this.

30. **A.** Concluding that the term is appropriate allows us to eliminate choices B, C, and D, leaving choice A as a better explanation of the appropriateness of the term than choice E.

Section 5: Sentence/Text Completion

Set 1

1. **B.** *daily.* The phrase *even though* indicates that the blank will contrast with a term in the first half of the sentence—in this case, *weekly.* None of the other terms supplies a contrast.

2. **E.** *oppose.* Opposing gun control seems to be an action that contradicts the desire for world peace. Therefore, these two attitudes have a paradoxical relationship.

3. **D.** *allotted.* To allot is to give a part of something. This choice is consistent with the term *dividing* earlier in the sentence.

4. **C.** *products.* Logically, if shelves are overstocked (presumably with products), merchants will not welcome the existence of even more products.

5. **B.** *renaissance . . . artisans.* A renaissance is a revival, especially of art, and is therefore consistent with the second term, *artisans.* Terms such as *creations, unique,* and *beautiful* suggest the appropriateness of *artisans* (skilled and artistic craftspeople).

6. **B.** *persistent . . . steady.* In this sentence, the correct choices have commonplace associations with the words that follow them: *persistent hope, steady course.* The other choices are either inconsistent or not as appropriate to the meaning of the sentence.

7. **A.** *rose . . . predicted.* The sentence contrasts national scores with local scores, so *rose* is the indicated choice, and *predicted* is its logical partner.

8. **E.** *insoluble . . . doom.* Terms such as *crises* and *destruction* signal two negative blanks, and only choice E supplies them.

9. **D.** *dilettante . . . thwarted.* The first blank describes someone *without a specialized and thorough understanding of a subject.* This definition fits *dilettante,* and *thwarted* (hindered or obstructed) also fits the sentence.

10. **A.** *simplified . . . mobilizing.* The sentence stresses technology, so we expect that the first blank will be a counterpoint term to the value of human forces. *Mobilizing human forces* is the logical equivalent to *power of many battalions.*

11. **A.** *speculation . . . contributed.* The first blank contrasts with *certain,* and *contributed* is also logically and meaningfully related to the sentence as a whole.

12. **C.** *esoteric* (understandable by only a chosen few). This term contrasts with *clear* and *direct* and is therefore the best choice.

13. **D.** *extreme . . . insensitivity.* Each blank should be a threat to psychological equilibrium. Choice D is best because it contains the most extreme and negative terms.

14. **D.** *Intent upon . . . purposeful.* Lela has a goal, and this term signals the equivalent term, *intent,* and the phrase *intent upon.* The term *purposeful* is also appropriate to her goal-oriented attitude.

15. **E.** *cynicism . . . morose. Sneering* indicates that both blanks are similar negative terms.

Set 2

16. **C.** *impossible . . . probable.* Working from the second blank first, note that *less probable* is a logical result of changing hawkish attitudes and that *impossible* makes sense also.

17. **B.** *silly . . . immature.* The sentence points toward human characteristics as appropriate for the blanks, and they should be characteristics that are consistent with each other—his behavior in public is consistent with the assessment of most people. For these reasons, *silly . . . immature* is the best answer choice.

18. **C.** *practical.* The sentence suggests that poetry is not utilitarian—in other words, that it has no practical value.

19. **A.** *dish . . . tasty. Some other* suggests an alternative to turkey. The alternative offered in choice B is too narrow, and those offered in choices C, D, and E are inappropriate.

20. **B.** *charge . . . disproportionate.* The term *hoards* suggests that the blanks surrounding it are negative terms consistent with hoarding. The only choice that offers two negative choices is B.

21. **D.** *immortalizes . . . casualties.* Working from the second blank first, note that *casualties* is the only term appropriate to *all who were killed.* Also, *immortalizes* appropriately describes the function of a memorial.

22. **E.** *bitter . . . pleasant.* The sentence suggests a negative/positive contrast between the blanks—a term consistent with *cynicism* along with one that contrasts with it. The most striking and fitting negative/positive contrast is offered by choice E.

23. **B.** *propagating . . . sneer.* Working from the second blank first, note that *sneer* is a fitting response to an unpopular viewpoint. *Propagating* is another word for *transmitting* or *communicating.*

24. **E.** *substantial. But* signals that the blank contrasts in meaning with the advance of police science. The idea of substantial crime fits that contrast.

25. **C.** *skeptical.* The blank is defined in the second half of the sentence. One who views truth as a variable is a skeptic.

26. **B.** *disproven . . . vices.* Working from the second blank first, note that the correct term must be one consistent with or causing the failure of communities. The only strongly negative term is *vices.*

27. **B.** *somber. Although* signals a contrast, and *somber* (overly serious) contrasts well with *sense of humor.*

28. **A.** *par. Par* means equal status, and noting that equal status makes competition possible, we see that this term is an appropriate choice. Note that *basis* is a more ambiguous term and therefore not the best choice.

29. **D.** *condemned . . . inflexibility.* The first blank contrasts with the *appreciation* noted in the second half of the sentence, and the term that is in contrast to the positive attitude of appreciation is the one expressing a negative *attitude—condemned.* The second term, *inflexibility,* appropriately describes this condemning attitude.

30. **B.** *red-ink.* Red-ink is a standard colloquial term to indicate spending beyond one's budget.

Set 3

31. **B.** *circular . . . west.* The sentence suggests that hurricanes do not move directly, and the term that best expresses indirect movement is *circular;* and a hurricane moving in a circle would not move linearly, from east to west.

32. **C.** *personable . . . artifice.* Working from the second blank first, note that *artifice* (falsehood) is the only term that is a substitute for *truth.* *Personable* means appealing and attractive.

33. **A.** *creative.* The sentence suggests that young children stop something that is inconsistent with facts and consistent with imagination. *Creative* best fits that description.

34. **D.** *diffidence.* To be diffident is to be hesitant and unsure. Thus, *diffidence* describes the *stance* expressed in the sentence.

35. **A.** *crusade.* A crusade is action taken against some injustice or abuse and is therefore a fitting term to describe Mack's action.

36. **E.** *narrow . . . broaden.* Working from the second blank first, note that it requires a contrast *to focus.* Both choices A and E provide this contrast, but the second term offered by choice A, *blur,* is illogical.

37. **B.** *monetary . . . intangible.* The sentence describes two types of rewards. Therefore, the blanks should be filled with contrasting terms.

38. **C.** *frightened . . . trepidation.* The blanks should be filled with terms that are somewhat synonymous with one another, both describing the negative aspect of Bill's response to the professor. Only choice C offers synonymous negative terms; *trepidation* is synonymous with *fear.*

39. **A.** *deflecting.* To arouse suspicion, the senator would have to give an unacceptable response. *Deflecting* (turning away) is the only choice that suggests such a response.

40. **D.** *remedial . . . ameliorate.* *Remedial* (providing a remedy) is a term appropriate to programs that address a deficiency, and *ameliorate* (make better) is consistent with the purpose of such programs.

41. **D.** *dull . . . esoteric.* A speech in which interesting points were lost may best be described as *dull. Esoteric* means understandable only by a few.

42. **E.** *desperate . . . calm. Although* suggests that the correct choices are contrasting terms. The most direct and meaningful contrast is provided by choice E.

43. **C.** *privacy.* Interfering in another's life is logically equivalent to a violation of *privacy.*

44. **B.** *inspiration . . . revision.* Both choices A and B offer terms consistent with *spontaneous,* but B is the better choice because its second term, *revision,* directly contrasts with the idea of spontaneous writing.

45. **B.** *biases.* The term *biases* contrasts with *objectivity* and fits the meaning of the sentence.

Set 4

46. **B, F.** *gory . . . abruptly.* If the niece in the sentence is frightened, the movie must be *gory* (gruesome and bloody), and she would naturally flee the theater in a hurry (i.e., *abruptly*). The movie could of course be *strange* (choice A), but this would be less likely to lead to fearful flights from the theater. *Languidly* (choice D) and *casually* (choice E) do not suggest someone fleeing from something unpleasant.

47. **A, F.** *alter . . . different.* One should always *alter* (modify in the direction of improvement) a draft of, or first pass at, writing a paper. You might also *continue* (choice C), or add to, such a paper, but only with change in mind. Therefore, a revised paper should be substantially *different* from the earlier version. The resultant paper might indeed be *unorthodox* (choice E), or non-conformist, but this would not be required for a revised paper to be different from its predecessor.

48. **C, F, G.** *approbation . . . hollow . . . sustainable.* The opposite of *boos* or disapproval is *approbation,* or praise. A focus on only *the bottom line* would be considered *hollow,* or empty, even cynical. Good values, such as *social responsibility* and *public trust* make a business *sustainable,* or viable. *Censure* (choice B) is a synonym for *boos,* and *venerable* (choice E) is the opposite of *hollow;* thus, these choices do not work.

49. B, F. *nuisance . . . insufferable.* Fleas are quite obviously a *nuisance* (annoyance, irritation) for cats and humans alike. They certainly are not a *boon* (choice C), which means a plus, or advantage. Something impossible to tolerate is said to be *insufferable.* For flea-sensitive cats, the pest's bites would definitely not be *affable* (choice E), which means friendly or agreeable.

50. C, E, H. *potential . . . valor . . . mirroring.* Blanks one and two need positive terms to complement *integrity. Potential* and *valor* fit the bill well. *Fitness* (choice A) is viable, though not as apt as *potential,* since *fitness* usually connotes physical health. *Mirroring* fits blank three since the second sentence talks about seeing ourselves reflected in characters.

51. C, E. *fleeting . . . constituents.* The word *fleeting* is consistent with the description of a political career that *wanes* (fades) all too soon. A *constituent* in political terms is a person who elects someone to represent his or her best interests.

52. A, E, G. *transient . . . revival . . . reassert.* Working from the third blank first, note that those in the humanities—the study of art and literature—would have a positive regard for these subjects. The most positive third term offered in the choices is *reassert. Transient* (not permanent) correctly describes the hope of those in the humanities concerning the other subjects mentioned. What these people would like is a *revival* (renewal or recovery), which complements the hope that love of art and literature will reassert itself.

53. A, D. *deregulate . . . ambiguously.* Working from the second blank first, note that the sentence suggests that the government response was not clearly for one side or the other. A response that is not clear and decisive may be termed *ambiguous. Deregulate* is an appropriate term for describing the lifting of restrictions and is often used in connection with the oil industry.

54. C, F. *outside . . . doubts.* The only term that distinguishes between anthropologists' study of other cultures and the study of their own is *outside.* They are inside their own culture but outside that of others. Since they are inside their own, one *wonders* whether they can recognize its flaws.

55. B, D, I. *safeguards . . . legislated . . . unfair.* Working from the second blank first, note that the term *government* suggests a verb that describes government action. Therefore, *legislated* is a fitting choice, and its forerunner *safeguards* also fits the meaning of the sentence. *Unfair* is the best choice for the third blank because it is more specific than *excessive* (choice G).

56. A, E. *discount . . . reliability.* Working from blank two first, *reliability* is the obvious choice. *Capriciousness* (choice D) means unpredictability and would not fit with *well-established information,* and while such information may indeed be *meticulous* (choice F), there is no saying that new discoveries may not also come from studies that are not meticulous. To not *discount* (choice A) well-established information is consistent with the positive attitude toward it articulated in the sentence.

57. A, E, G. *goodness . . . estimable . . . contributions.* The passage discusses donations to worthy causes, so *estimable* and *contributions* are consistent with this subject. Since the first sentence indicates that charitable giving is thought admirable, engaging in this behavior would naturally be a sign of one's *goodness.* Note that the purpose of sentence two is to undercut the purity of this virtue by suggesting that tax deductions are a part of the story.

58. C, F. *deterrence . . . sound.* The portion of the first sentence following the blank defines *deterrence* as applied to the nuclear issue. The word *however* in the second sentence suggests that people question whether this approach is *sound* (well-reasoned, demonstrating good judgment). *Strong missile power* certainly does not suggest *diminution* (choice A), which would indicate a lessening of nuclear power, and a strong policy could be neither *halfhearted* (choice D) nor *random* (choice E).

59. B, D, I. *instantaneously . . . development . . . complex.* The word that contrasts most clearly with *evolution* is *instantaneously.* *Evolution* always indicates gradual development from simpler to more complex forms. *Stasis* (choice E) and *equipoise* (choice F) are both connotatively antithetical to development. To move from simpler to *inert* (choice H) forms would not indicate evolution but devolution (descending into a lower or less evolved state).

60. C, E. *neurotic . . . obsessively.* Beginning with sentence two first, a *controlling neat freak* would have to be *neurotic* (emotionally or mentally disordered). She would certainly not be *sensible* (choice B), which means levelheaded, or rational. Someone who is neurotic in the area of cleaning and organizing would engage in these activities *obsessively* (compulsively). While she may do this in a way that is controlled by unconscious emotion, we still could not rightly say that she does so *unwillingly* (choice D).

Set 5

61. **A, E, I.** *proclaimed . . . devotee . . . attaining.* To *proclaim* is to declare. Sagan does not *withhold* (choice B) his interest in time travel, since the remainder of the paragraph tells us that he seeks to understand it. A *devotee* is an enthusiastic fan of something, which we're told Sagan is not when it comes time travel; however, we're also told that his seeking knowledge about time travel is a part of *attaining* a larger understanding of how the universe works. A *paramour* (choice D) is a romantic lover, often an adulterous one, and *eluding* (choice H) means avoiding.

62. **C, F.** *imposter . . . incompetence.* An *imposter* is a phony or fraud, so those who are qualified to do their jobs, but feel as if they are not, suffer from *imposter syndrome.* They are always afraid their *incompetence,* or inability will be discovered. *Acumen* (choice D) and *astuteness* (choice E) are positive words, meaning expertise and intelligence, respectively.

63. **B, F.** *observes . . . self-awareness.* To *observe* in this sense is to remark or declare. *Uncovers* (choice A) may seem like a possible answer; however, we don't normally say that someone *uncovers that. Self-awareness* occurs when we are attentive to our own behaviors and characteristics, so this fits well with *self-monitoring* and *self-consciousness.* A *self-possessed* (choice D) person is normally confident and assured, so this word is too positive for the sentence.

64. **B, D, H.** *situational . . . blindly . . . perpetrated.* If we lead our lives according to particular circumstances, we consider *situational* factors when we make decisions. If we ignore specific circumstances and obey general principles, we can be said to do so *blindly.* We would not want to protect a brother who has *perpetrated,* or committed, a crime.

65. **C, F.** *practices . . . cultivate.* Yoga, meditation, musicianship, and conscious eating are all *practices* that promote *mindfulness,* or connection to the present moment. Such practices *cultivate* (promote and nurture) stress reduction. Of the other choices, *propagate* (choice E) almost works, but to *propagate* is really more to circulate or publicize than it is to nurture or promote.

66. **A, D, G.** *instigated . . . implying . . . shortcomings.* To *instigate* is to activate or set off. Your *implying,* or suggesting, that the person to whom you're apologizing set off your bad behavior will likely cancel the good effects of your apology. A real apology may prompt the other person to reflect on his or her own *shortcomings,* or faults.

67. **B, E, I.** *self-serving . . . register . . . immediate.* Working from the third blank first, we can see that *months later* is being contrasted with being swept up in *immediate* aims. If at the time Saul was caught up in immediate aims, he would not have been able to *register* the impact of his discourse. One who is caught up in personal aims, to the point of being overbearing or hurtful, is behaving in a *self-serving* manner. *Altruistic* (choice A) means just the opposite: selfless, acting on behalf of others.

68. **B, E, G.** *originates . . . disquieting . . . recognize.* Working from the third blank first, we can see that the person projecting the anger onto another refuses to *recognize,* or see, it in herself. She does not see that the anger attributed to someone else actually *originates,* or begins, inside herself. She does not wish to recognize *disquieting,* or disturbing, truths about herself.

69. **C, D, I.** *stomach . . . inclined . . . embrace.* We must sometimes *stomach* (endure or tolerate) experiences other people like, but which we don't enjoy. The final sentence, which says we should go beyond mere *respect* and actually *embrace* differences in others, makes clear that we would not *shirk* (choice A), or avoid, disagreeable experiences. *Abominate* (choice G), which means to despise, does not complement *respect.* We tolerate differences in others, even though we are always inwardly *inclined,* or predisposed, to think of our own preferences as best.

70. **B, D, G.** *shift . . . gaffes . . . reproach.* It is a significant *shift* to consider those we once thought of as gods to be idiots. Both *vary* (choice A) and *amend* (choice B) mean something similar, but neither fits the overall grammar of the sentence as well as *shift.* A complementary word for *limitations* and *weaknesses* is *gaffes,* which means mistakes or errors in judgment. An antonym (opposite term) for *compassion* is *reproach,* or criticism and blame.

71. **C, F.** *disfiguring . . . epithet.* A condition that involves bone and skin abnormalities would be *disfiguring,* which means it would alter the body's normal appearance. While Merrick's condition could certainly be said to be *shoddy* (choice A), or substandard, the sentence displays a kind outlook on Merrick, especially through the sympathizing word *horribly,* so it wouldn't insultingly refer to him as *shoddy.* A special name given to someone is a *moniker;* however, *epithet* better suits the passage as a whole since it is commonly used as a synonym for *slur* or *insult.*

72. **B, D.** *diverse . . . independently.* The only appropriate choice for the first blank is *diverse,* or varied. One who maintains personal privacy and acts according to his or her own dictates behaves *independently.*

73. A, D, G. *realms . . . partaking . . . circumstances. Realms* nicely echoes *areas,* and is the only appropriate choice for the first blank. Since a *nadir* (choice B) is a low point, this word does not go well with *ideal realms.* According to the second sentence, we are supposed to be *partaking,* or participating, in the struggle to improve the difficult *circumstances,* or conditions, of the world.

74. B, E. *mayhem . . . bear.* If characters must *bear,* or suffer, consequences for their actions, these actions cannot involve *civility* (choice C), or well-mannered behavior, but instead involve *mayhem,* or violent destruction.

75. C, E, I. *interconnection . . . collective . . . yielded to.* Working with the second sentence first, we can see that if Gabriel feels *compassion toward everyone and everything,* he must see the *interconnection,* or common bond, between himself and all things. This common bond has to do with universal mortality, a *collective* destiny shared by all living things. In such a state, the ego (the interest in one's own self) would have *yielded to* (given way to) compassionate feeling. Gabriel certainly does not feel *enmity* (choice B), or ill will, toward others. It is the higher instincts here that have *surpassed* (choice H), or transcended, the ego, not vice versa. The lesser concerns of the ego do not *ensue from* (choice G), or arise from, the higher instincts.

Section 6: Sentence Equivalence

Set 1

1. D, F. *pernicious . . . virulent.* Both *pernicious* and *virulent* have negative connotations. The first means "causing injury or destruction" and the second means "powerful" and "dangerous." All other choices have a positive connotation.

2. C, E. *cleared . . . netted.* One's *net* pay is what is left, or *cleared,* after taxes. Many of us may certainly feel that we have *lost* (choice A) a lot of salary after paying taxes; however, an accountant would probably not express things in such a way, since our taxes are presumably put to good use. Also, *lost* has no synonyms among the five choices. A person might decide to *bundle* (choice F) his or her money, but this has nothing to do with taxes.

3. D, F. *drawbacks . . . limitations.* The idea of having to conform suggests *drawbacks* and *limitations*—in other words, disadvantages or downsides. None of the other words fit the sentence.

4. **A, E.** *revered . . . admired.* If Juan's heritage is *beloved* by him, he *reveres* or admires his culture. Of the other choices, *disdained* (choice B) and *abhorred* (choice C) mean the opposite (rejected or disliked), and *devoted* (choice D) does not work because the sentence would require additional words to make grammatical sense: "because he *was* devoted *to* his beloved heritage."

5. **B, C.** *non-linear . . . circuitous.* A movie that does not follow a simple chronological progression is often said to be *non-linear,* literally not moving in a straight line. Such movies often seesaw, or move, back and forth in time. Such a movie obviously does not proceed in a *straightforward* (choice D) manner. Though you might find such a movie to be *devious* (choice E), or tricky, most filmmakers are not deliberately aiming to be underhanded, and besides, *devious* has no synonyms among the five choices. *Surly* (choice F) means irritable.

6. **A, B.** *catapulted . . . propelled.* Hearing about a future event or situation will often *catapult* or *propel* (thrust or drive) our minds in that same direction. Since we know about the concept of a time *warp,* you may have selected choice E. However, we do not ordinarily say that something is *warped into the future,* and, again, *warped* has no synonyms among the five choices.

7. **B, C.** *loquacious . . . garrulous.* Klaus' friend is clearly talkative, and this is exactly what both *loquacious* and *garrulous* mean. His friend is neither *reticent* (choice A), which means restrained, nor *taciturn* (choice D), which means reserved.

8. **C, E.** *dampens . . . inhibits.* Since Aisha clearly believes that labeling relationships weighs them down, indicating a negative result, she might also say that labeling *dampens* (dulls) and *inhibits* (subdues) them.

9. **C, F.** *syrupy . . . cloying. Cloying* means overly or sickly sweet, as does *syrupy.* Many greeting cards fit this description. Such cards certainly are not *impassive* (choice B), which means unemotional.

10. **A, E.** *minute . . . diminutive.* If eyelash mites are tiny enough to live inside our hair follicles, they must be very tiny; synonyms for tiny include *minute* and *diminutive.* While we might indeed be required to *magnify* (choice D), or enlarge, eyelash mites to see what they're doing, they need not be enlarged to do what they do!

11. **A, D.** *infringe . . . encroach.* This is a common disclaimer seen in many books. A copyright is a claim to ownership of a book's contents. Therefore, to use a book's contents for one's own purposes,

without both permission and an acknowledgement of ownership, is to *infringe* or *encroach* (overstep or trespass upon) the rights of the book's writer and publisher.

12. **B, F.** *adaptations . . . renderings.* You may know that the original *Frankenstein* is a novel by Mary Shelley. Any film version would be an *adaptation*—a reworking, new *rendering,* or re-interpretation of the novel. A film version certainly would not be a *prototype* (choice A), which is another name for an original work.

13. **A, E.** *solace . . . succor.* Both *solace* and *succor* mean comfort or relief, so these choices fit very well.

14. **C, D.** *ill-advised . . . misguided.* An *ill-advised* act is one that most people would caution against, and it seems fair to say that most children would rather have a traditional birthday cake than a *fussy tart.* The tart can also be said to be a *misguided,* or mistaken, choice of desserts. Clearly, it wasn't a *no-frills* (choice A) sort of treat, since a *fussy* tart is a bit of a frill.

15. **B, D.** *travail . . . adversity.* Both *travail* and *adversity* mean hardship or struggle, so these words fit the sentence well. Odysseus could not have afforded *lethargy* (choice C), which means sluggishness or laziness, when faced with the Cyclops, the witch, and the sea monsters. And *concord* (choice E) means harmony and friendship, and clearly does not work here.

Set 2

16. **C, E.** *jettison . . . discard.* Both *jettison* and *discard* mean to abandon or reject. *Adopt* (choice A) is a synonym for *embrace,* which is not the right choice, since the sentence suggests that some ideas are not embraced. *Caress* (choice F) means to cuddle or hug, something we usually do not do to ideas!

17. **A, B.** *enterprise . . . venture.* Both *enterprise* and *venture* suggest a project or an undertaking, and these are things we would expect an entrepreneur to propose to a potential investor. You might have said *pandemonium* (choice C) because it sounds enough like condominium to suggest a building project; however, *pandemonium* actually means chaos or uproar. An investor undoubtedly would not wish to take a risk on a *frolic* (choice E), since this suggests a playful romp, or a *fiasco* (choice F), which suggests disaster.

18. **A, D.** *mere . . . bare.* A stereotype is a simplistic, often insulting, depiction of a person, reducing him or her to a *mere* or *bare* caricature. A stereotype is therefore not *manifold* (choice B), which means many-sided.

19. **B, F.** *diffidently . . . reticently.* To *accede* is to assent or comply to another's wishes, so already there is some resistance in that word alone. When we add *fear* and possible *negative effects* to the equation, we can see that Carmen agrees to her boss' initiative only diffidently or reticently, both of which mean hesitantly or insecurely. Carmen would agree neither *exultantly* (choice A), which means joyfully, *jovially* (choice C), which means merrily, nor *amiably* (choice D), which means pleasantly. Of course, she might pretend to agree in any of these last three ways, but she would not mean it.

20. **C, E.** *abject . . . mortified.* To be *abject* or *mortified* is to be wretched or humiliated. Marissa certainly did not feel *ebullient* (choice A), which means enthusiastically happy.

21. **D, E.** *accolades . . . acclamations. Creative brilliance* deserves *accolades* and *acclamations* (honors and ovations). It definitely warrants neither *admonitions* (choice A) nor *deprecations* (choice B), both of which refer to reprimands or scoldings.

22. **C, D.** *tempestuous . . . turbulent.* A relationship that involves a lot of fighting would have to be *tempestuous* and *turbulent* (stormy). If their relationship were *inexorable* (choice E), the couple wouldn't bother to seek counseling since *inexorable* means unalterable.

23. **A, F.** *soporific . . . somnolent.* Both *soporific* and *somnolent* mean sleep-inducing. (*Somnolescence,* or sleepiness, is the opposite of *insomnia,* which means the inability to sleep.) Jamila finds nighttime reading neither *stirring* (choice B), which means rousing or stimulating, nor *strenuous* (choice C), which means taxing or labor-intensive.

24. **C, E.** *prodigy . . . virtuoso.* A *prodigy* or *virtuoso* is a person who is exceptionally talented; in the case of *prodigy,* this is often said of children who are talented beyond their years. Arturo was undoubtedly not a *dawdler* (choice B), which describes someone who wastes time or drags his feet. A *miscreant* (choice F) is a criminal or villain.

25. **B, F.** *atone . . . compensate.* The word *atone* is often used in conjunction with the idea of sin. To *atone* is to make amends or do penance, so this fits the sentence perfectly. *Compensate* works well too, since to *compensate* is to pay a cost for something. Laura's parents certainly would not have wanted her to *perish* (choice A), or die for her sins.

26. **A, D.** *flimsy . . . rickety*. An old, unmaintained wooden boat would be *flimsy* (not sturdy) or *rickety* (unsound). It would not be *durable* (choice B), which means sturdy or stable. *Unwavering* (choice F) may have fooled you because the word *wave* is embedded in the longer word; however, unwavering means steady or resolute.

27. **C, F.** *diligent . . . attentive*. Since calculus is a difficult subject, it requires students to study in a *diligent* (intent) and *attentive* (focused) manner. If Peter is *apathetic* (choice A), which means indifferent, he will likely not pass his class. He might decide to put on a nonchalant (choice B), or casual, demeanor, but this has nothing to do with whether or not he passes calculus!

28. **A, E.** *jeopardize . . . endanger*. To *jeopardize* or *endanger* something is to put it at risk, so, unlike any of the other choices, these words fit well.

29. **B, D.** *nuances . . . shades*. *Nuances* and *shades* of meaning describe the subtle aspects of the novel Jill is reading. While the *fundamentals* might refer to general plot elements and character types, a literary work's *nuances* might include the complexities and multiple significances of, say, a symbol, or the irony a character's behavior generates within a particular context.

30. **B, E.** *reverberate . . . echo*. Sounds emitted in cavernous spaces *reverberate* or *echo*, meaning they repeat several times on their own. Car horns do not typically *hiss* (choice A). The sound would not *intensify* (choice C), or increase in volume; rather, it would gradually diminish with each repetition.

Set 3

31. **C, E.** *vehemently . . . fervidly*. Both *vehemently* (insistently) and *fervidly* (vigorously) indicate an aggressive response, so these words key very well with the image of the candidate *slamming his fist on the table*. The candidate certainly did not behave in a *furtive* (choice D) manner, since this means secretive or covert.

32. **A, C.** *nominal . . . minimal*. *Nominal* means token or minor and fits well with *minimal*. The town council wants to keep parking fees affordably low, so *considerable* (choice B) is incorrect, since this indicates a large amount, and fees that are *unrestricted* (choice D) could rise very rapidly.

33. B, D. *loot . . . ransack.* Since the stores' contents are exposed, the citizens are being warned not to *loot* (steal) or *ransack* (raid) those contents. If the citizens were to replenish (choice A), or restock any of the stores' contents, they would actually be doing a nice thing. *Impede* (choice F) means to hinder or block.

34. A, F. *complicity . . . collusion.* When multiple people commit a wrong together, they are said to be in *complicity* (involvement) or *collusion* (collaboration) with one another. Cheating students do not have *scruples* (choice B), which means integrity or moral conscience. Though some students may have cheated in a state of *felicity* (choice E), this mood would not be necessary to carry out the deed.

35. A, D. *edifying . . . illuminating. Edifying* means educational or instructive, and *illuminating* means enlightening or informative; these choices fit the sentence well. If Kaya were to find the scholar's lecture *trifling* (choice E), which means insignificant or unimportant, she would not have thought the imparting knowledge worth sharing.

36. B, D. *quashed . . . routed.* The word *although* suggests that the home team did not win the game in the end. Thus, the visiting team *quashed* (defeated) or *routed* (overpowered) them. Out of kindness, the visitors might have *extolled* (choice A) or *lionized* (choice C) the home team after winning (these words can mean to praise or celebrate), but this is unlikely, and does not accord well with the content of the first part of the sentence.

37. D, F. *philanthropists . . . benefactors.* Those who give to social causes are called *philanthropists* (donors) or *benefactors* (supporters). They would hardly be *misanthropists* (choice C), which is a name for those who dislike people.

38. B, E. *officious . . . bureaucratic.* To be *officious* or *bureaucratic* is to be bossy and inflexible, so these words fit very well with Ben's wife's characterization. Ben would undoubtedly have preferred to be called *unstinting* (choice A)—which means generous—but his boss clearly does not hold this view of him. While a bureaucrat might certainly be *preposterous,* or ridiculous, an employee could be *preposterous* in any number of other ways!

39. A, C. *depleted . . . lavished.* Antonio seems to have spent all of his inheritance from his grandmother, and not on substantial things like an education or home, but on superficial ones. He therefore *lavished* (wasted) or *depleted* (drained) the inheritance. The inheritance was neither *recouped* (choice B), which means regained, nor *sustained* (choice E), which means maintained. Exasperated (choice F) means to annoy or irritate.

40. **C, F.** *dearth . . . shortage.* The job search committee wants to invite more applicants because their pool so far contains a *dearth* (scarcity) or *shortage* (lack) of qualified candidates. Both *glut* (choice B) and *surfeit* (choice E) are antonyms, indicating a surplus or an overabundance of something.

41. **A, E.** *sporadic . . . intermittent.* Hiroshi must be concerned that jobs may be *sporadic* (patchy) or *intermittent* (irregular) if he becomes self-employed.

42. **B, D.** *loaf and lounge.* Here, busyness is opposed to Carol's desire to *loaf* (laze about) or *lounge* (lie around) on Sundays. While loafing and lounging, she would be unlikely to *lunge*—choice C—or to *lurch*—choice E—both of which suggest active movement; she could decide to leer (choice A) at her mother, though!

43. **B, F.** *fidelity . . . accuracy. Fidelity* and *accuracy* both refer to reliability and exactness, so these fit the sentence well. *Imprecision* (choice A) is an antonym.

44. **A, F.** *innate . . . inborn.* A trait that is not, or seems to people not to be, conditioned, is said to be *innate* (instinctive) or *inborn* (inherent).

45. **B, E.** *like . . . analogous.* By now, you know that words with similar meanings are called synonyms. *Like* (comparable) and *analogous* (equivalent) are synonyms for *similar. Divergent* (choice A), or differing, and *disparate* (choice C), or unlike, mean just the opposite, and are thus antonyms (words with opposite meanings). *Obdurate* (choice F) means stubborn.

PART II

READING COMPREHENSION

Chapter 5: Reading Comprehension Review

Reading comprehension is a part of all standardized tests addressed in this book—GRE, GMAT, SAT, ACT, LSAT, CBEST, PPST, and PSAT/NMSQT—and a component of many other tests as well. On each of these tests, you will encounter a section that directs you to answer one or more multiple-choice questions for each of several reading passages.

In this chapter, you will review the types of reading comprehension passages and reading comprehension questions, and learn how to apply specific strategies to successfully respond to each type of passage and question. Several sample problems will provide plenty of practice to help you solidify your skills and your approach to these types of passages and questions. As you study the material in this chapter, it is important to observe your mistakes and take notes about material that requires additional knowledge or understanding. After you review the specific strategies in the sample problems, you should be ready to sharpen your skills by practicing what you have learned in the practice test that follows.

IIere is a quick reference guide that shows what you can expect to encounter on each test.

Quick Reference Guide

Section 1: Brief Passages (pp. 299–315): GMAT, GRE, SAT, PSAT/NMSQT, CBEST, PPST

Brief passages unique to GRE (pp. 306–307)

Brief passages unique to GMAT (pp. 308–309)

Brief passages unique to CBEST (pp. 309–315)

Section 2: Long Passages – Intermediate Difficulty (pp. 315–320): GMAT, GRE, SAT, PSAT/NMSQT, ACT, LSAT

Section 3: Paired (Comparative) Passages (pp. 321–324): SAT, LSAT

Section 4: Long Passages – Challenging (pp. 324–328): GMAT, GRE, LSAT

Though the reference guide provided above is useful, you should still check the official website's description of your exam to determine the passage length and question difficulty you should anticipate. That said, it is advisable that you read and answer questions for *all* passages in the practice test later in this chapter, in which statements and passages of varying lengths and difficulty levels are presented. This way, even if your test includes only briefer passages with fewer questions, you can be sure that you'll be well prepared.

Reading Comprehension Passages

A considerable range of passage lengths and difficulty levels appear across the various tests. On tests such as the CBEST and PPST, reading passages are either one- or two-sentence statements or slightly longer pieces of 100 to 200 words. This is also true of parts of the Reading Comprehension section on the GRE. However, the GRE also includes longer passages (200 to 350 words), as does the GMAT. The SAT contains both short passages (100 to 150 words) and much longer ones (400 to 850 words), while passages on the LSAT are about 400 to 500 words in length. Shorter passages are generally followed by fewer questions (1 to 3), while longer passages are followed by many more questions (as many as 13 in some cases on the SAT). Like passage length and number of questions, difficulty levels also vary both across and within the various tests.

Content of Passages

Reading comprehension passages are based on material from academic and non-academic sources, and they draw from many areas of knowledge, including the sciences and social sciences, arts and humanities, business, education, law, and everyday subjects. However, you need not have any specialized knowledge to answer the questions. All the information you need to answer the questions correctly either will be stated directly or implied within the passages themselves.

Reading Comprehension Questions

Reading comprehension questions are divided into three general categories.

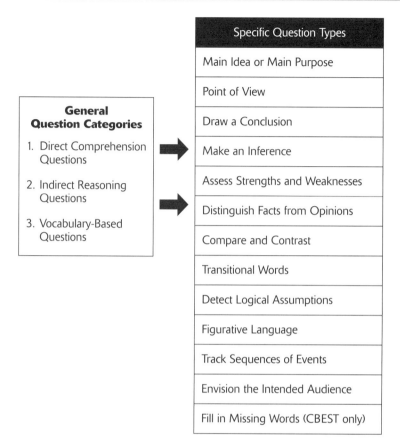

Specific Question Types
Main Idea or Main Purpose
Point of View
Draw a Conclusion
Make an Inference
Assess Strengths and Weaknesses
Distinguish Facts from Opinions
Compare and Contrast
Transitional Words
Detect Logical Assumptions
Figurative Language
Track Sequences of Events
Envision the Intended Audience
Fill in Missing Words (CBEST only)

General Question Categories

1. Direct Comprehension Questions

2. Indirect Reasoning Questions

3. Vocabulary-Based Questions

Direct, literal reading questions ask you for explicit information about the passage. Look for information stated directly in the passage to answer these types of reading comprehension questions, and remember that you can always find the answer somewhere in the passage. Look for specific words, phrases, and facts contained in the passage, and work actively back and forth between the passage and the question.

Indirect, reasoning questions can be slightly more difficult than direct questions. In indirect questions, you will need to make inferences and find a flow of logic to solve the problem as you draw reasonable conclusions from the passage. Some information in this type of question is not directly stated. As you search for the answer in the passage, think about gathering words and phrases to understand what is not stated. Look for supporting proof and evidence among the writer's words. Do not over-think this type of question; the answer is never vague and is always based on evidence from the passage. Once you understand what the writer is communicating in the passage, your inference should make logical sense.

You may encounter an indirect question that requires you to distinguish among *inferences, assumptions,* and *implications.* Here is a definition of each.

Term	Definition
inference	An inference is a conclusion you draw based on stated or evident information. For instance, one can infer that a person who raises his or her voice is angry or upset. (We might, of course, be mistaken: The loud talker might be practicing to give a speech!)
assumption	An assumption is a meaning taken for granted because it corresponds to the usual or normal state of affairs. For example, we assume that the sun will come up each morning or that the people sitting in church on Sunday believe in God. (Again, our assumptions can always be wrong.)
implication	An *implication* is very like an inference, but while an inference is a meaning determined by the receiver of a message, an implication is a meaning sent out or given off, in this case, by the writer of the passage in question. A loud person *implies* that he or she is angry or upset, while a reader or listener *infers* that the loud person is angry or upset. An implicit meaning in a passage is suggested, though not explicitly stated, by the writer, while an *inference* is a conclusion drawn by the reader.

You can see that these three ways of detecting information are quite close in meaning.

Vocabulary in context questions test your skills and knowledge of word meanings in a passage's context. To perform well, you will need to think logically and understand subtle differences in word choices to create a coherent passage. To help yourself with vocabulary in context questions, pay close attention to the word or phrase in the sentence's context. Use the context to figure out the meaning of words, even if you're unfamiliar with them. Sometimes you will need to read the sentence just before and after the word to understand the word's association with the surrounding text. Even if you don't know the word's meaning, the passage will give you good clues. You can also try reading the sentence in the passage, leaving the word space blank, and plugging in each answer to see which answer choice makes the most sense in the sentence.

Computer-based type questions. Some tests—the GRE, GMAT, PPST, and CBEST—offer computer-based versions. For reading comprehension questions in a computer-based format, you will not be able to mark up the passage's important parts as you would on the paper-based version. There are, however, some effective strategies you can employ to make sure you are making the most of "active reading":

- If your test has a "mark and review" feature (the GRE does), questions you choose to skip are marked as "incomplete" in an on-screen grid, so you know which questions you need to reconsider or complete.

- If the online test allows, use your cursor to guide your eyes through the reading passage. This way, you will be less likely to inadvertently miss parts of the passage.

- On the GMAT computer-adaptive test, the questions are based on the skill level you demonstrate as you move through the test. Instead of being faced with a group of questions and the option to skip the more difficult ones and return to them later, you will only see one question at a time on the screen, and must answer it to continue.

The testing organizations that create the GRE, GMAT, PPST, and CBEST offer practice and further information/tutorials about their computer-based versions on their web pages. Refer to p. 3 for these web addresses so you can take full advantage of the additional material they provide.

Specific Types of Questions

Now that we've looked at the general question categories, let's consider specific types of questions that might appear in the reading comprehension sections of standardized tests. Test-taking strategies and sample questions related to specific question types are described in detail starting on p. 299.

You might be asked to do any of the following:

- identify the main idea of the passage
- determine the writer's point of view or attitude toward his or her subject
- draw conclusions or make inferences based on a passage's contents
- recognize a summary of ideas
- assess an argument's strengths and/or weaknesses
- distinguish between facts and opinions
- compare and contrast ideas
- understand the role of transitional words or conjunctions such as *however, yet, but, although, furthermore, also, thus, therefore,* etc.
- detect logical assumptions
- understand the meaning of figurative language
- track sequences of events or pinpoint cause and effect relationships
- envision the intended audience
- fill in missing words, phrases, or sentences (on the CBEST only)

General Strategies for Success

Before you review sample passages, specific types of questions, and practice tests, consider the following useful strategies, techniques, and examples for undertaking each variety of reading comprehension test.

- Read the directions carefully.
- Estimate and allot your time, if possible.
- Sample the questions before reading each passage, if possible. Do not apply any outside knowledge you may have about the subject.
- Eliminate answer choices you find irrelevant, contradictory, or illogical.
- Finish the question set for the passage on which you're working before moving to the next passage.
- If taking a paper-based version of your test, mark each passage as you read. If taking a computer-based version of your test, write notes on scratch paper (or noteboard on the GRE) as you read. Pay attention to any sections of the passage that stand out as important or interesting and always look for:
  1. the passage's main idea
  2. details that support the main idea
  3. the writer's purpose
  4. particular words that are highly significant to the points being made
  5. the language's style and tone
- Practice paraphrasing whenever possible. Read magazines, newspapers, news websites, etc., and jot down the authors' main ideas in whichever articles you happen to read. After you read the full article, turn over the paper and write down what you remember about that author's main idea. Compare your written response to the article itself. As you practice this technique and hone your skills, you will find that you will become more efficient and more accurate at paraphrasing.

Time Management

On reading comprehension tests that combine many brief passages with some longer ones, it is difficult to allot your time for each passage because of the test's irregular structure. However, when you encounter a reading test with passages of approximately equal length, each followed by about the same number of questions, you can estimate the time you should spend on each passage. It is possible to do this on the LSAT and the GMAT, and similar exams. For example, the LSAT's reading comprehension section usually consists of four sets of passages, about 400 to 500 words each, that are followed by five or more questions. (The fourth set, called "Comparative Reading," actually consists of two shorter passages that are to be compared in some way.) You have a total of 35 minutes to complete the section. With this information in mind, you should realize that no more than about eight minutes should be spent on each set of reading passages and questions. "Subdivide" your time, and pace yourself so you are able to attempt all the questions before time is called.

Directions

The following directions are typical of reading comprehension sections on standardized tests:

Each statement or passage in this test is followed by a question or questions based on its content. After reading a statement or passage, choose the best answer to each question from among the five choices given. Answer all questions following a statement or passage on the basis of what is stated or implied in that statement or passage.

Notice that you are to choose the *best* answer of the five choices; in some instances, another answer could be justified, yet it may not be the best of the available choices. Also, realize that your answer should be based only on explicit and/or implicit information from the passage. Those who get low scores on reading comprehension often "read into" a passage, referencing knowledge or beliefs that come from outside the passage itself.

Now that you have a solid overview of the reading comprehension sections of standardized tests, let's look at various passage and question types.

Section 1 – Brief Passages

Read the following strategies and consider the brief passages (under 200 words) of the sort that may appear on the SAT, PSAT/NMSQT, GRE, CBEST, PPST, and other tests.

Suggested Strategies for Brief Passages

These passages require efficient, active reading skills. Typically, a brief passage such as this will be followed by one or two questions. It's a good idea to quickly skim the question(s) before reading the passage (paper-based tests) or write down one or two words (computer-based tests). This way, you can keep in mind the writer's *main idea* and *tone* as you read the passage. After sampling the question(s), read the passage steadily and carefully, marking key words and phrases as you read. Keep the question(s) in mind as you mark, and notate places in the passage that either *address the question* or *stand out as interesting or important.* A sample of a fully marked, longer passage appears later in this section. **Practice reading several short excerpts and passages *before* the day of the test.**

Once you have carefully read and marked the passage, consider each answer choice and pick the best one. *Always read every choice before making a decision, even if one of the early choices seems obviously correct.* As you consider each choice, ask yourself whether it is *irrelevant, contradictory,* or *illogical.* A choice that falls into any of these categories should be eliminated.

Questions 1 and 2 are based on the following passage.

Sample Passage

Norms serve to standardize behavior, bringing order to what otherwise would be a <u>chaotic</u> situation. If some of us drove on the left side of the road and others on the right, or if some of us stopped for red lights while others did not, there would be much confusion and danger. In other words, social life, as we know it, would not be possible without norms. All cultures have systems of norms that provide social order.

Question Type: The Writer's Main Purpose

1. The writer's main purpose in this passage is to

   A. explain the function of norms for maintaining social order.
   B. refute the belief that norms are unimportant.
   C. instruct readers about which norms are appropriate in some cultures.
   D. establish social norms that are especially popular in the United States.
   E. warn reckless drivers to be more careful.

Usually, the primary purpose of any reading passage is not explicitly stated, but becomes evident as you read through the passage. When considering a "primary purpose" question, pay special attention to the first word of every answer choice and eliminate choices if the first word obviously contradicts the passage's purpose. In this case, *refute* (choice B) and *warn* (choice E) do not seem consistent with the passage's overall objective nature. Considering the remaining choices more fully, you should recognize choice A as a possibly correct answer and move on to consider choices C and D. Choice C is irrelevant to the information in the passage because it does not address which *norms* are appropriate and does not focus on some cultures only. Choice D is not altogether irrelevant because it does mention norms that may possibly be popular in the United States, yet the United States is never mentioned explicitly. Also, the description of driving norms is not the writer's primary or overall purpose. If you answered D, you would be mistaking a secondary purpose for a primary purpose. The correct answer is **A.**

Note: Some questions about purpose focus on genre; that is, they ask whether the passage is meant to be persuasive (meaning to convince the reader to believe or do something), narrative (recounting events), descriptive (offering details about events, usually invoking one or more of the five senses), or informative (relating factual information). We will see these categories arise more fully in the next chapter, "Writing Timed Essays."

Question Type: Vocabulary in Context

2. Which of the following is the best definition of the word *chaotic* (underlined) as it is used in the passage?

   A. subject to multiple interpretations
   B. methodical
   C. anarchic
   D. leading to answers
   E. bad for business

The word *chaotic* means anarchic, lawless, or disorderly. (The word comes from the ancient Greek word *anarkhia,* which means without a leader or government.) This definition fits the idea in the sentence that social norms produce social order, since we are looking for a word that expresses the opposite state of affairs. With this information, we can eliminate *methodical* (choice B), which means systematic and is therefore contradictory. Choices D and E are also unrelated. Choice A might be considered; however, the sentence doesn't talk about interpreting, but about chaotic driving behaviors. The correct answer is **C.**

Note: Word meaning choices may include alternative meanings that don't suit the passage's particular context. In other words, you may see multiple meanings for the same word whose meaning in context you are to discern.

Other Specific Types of Questions

We've already seen that you may be asked to identify the main purpose of a passage, and that this may require you to distinguish between a passage's main or primary purpose and its secondary purpose.

We've also seen a question about the meaning of a word in context. In the case of our sample passage, we knew we were looking for a word that expressed the opposite of *order,* since the importance of producing order is the passage's focus, and since a distinction is made between chaotic driving habits and order.

Let's look at a number of other commonly found question types as they apply to a few more brief passages.

Questions 3–5 are based on the following passage.

Passage

The obesity epidemic among children is a serious problem in today's United States. Many blame the ready availability of high-fat processed foods, others the onset of a "couch potato" culture in which kids play video games instead of street ball. Doubtless, both trends are causes.

Question Type: Infer the Writer's Point of View

3. In this statement, the writer is

    A. unconcerned about the obesity epidemic among children.
    B. dissatisfied with explanations for childhood obesity.
    C. resistant to the term *couch potato.*
    D. concerned about the obesity epidemic among children.
    E. angry that kids eat the wrong foods and are inactive.

The writer is clearly concerned about the obesity epidemic since he or she calls it "a serious problem." Therefore, A is not correct. The writer agrees with prevailing theories about childhood obesity's causes in the last sentence; thus B is not correct. The writer gives no indication that the term *couch potato* is problematic, so C is not correct. There are no words or phrases that suggest anger on the part of the writer, who is, in fact, quite objective in tone; therefore, E is not correct. The correct answer is **D.**

Question Type: Identify a Summary of Ideas

4. Which of the following summarizes the passage?

    A. The U.S. has a serious childhood obesity problem.

    B. High-fat, processed foods have caused an obesity epidemic among U.S. children.

    C. Inactivity has caused an obesity epidemic among U.S. children.

    D. Theories abound about the causes of the serious obesity problem in the U.S.

    E. The serious obesity epidemic among children in the U.S. is doubtless caused by both poor nutrition and inactivity.

Choices A, B, and C convey partial information about the passage, and choice D conveys incorrect information. Only choice E is both comprehensive and correct. The correct answer is **E.**

Question Type: Draw Conclusions Based on a Passage's Contents

5. Which sentence below is a fitting addition to the end of the passage?

    A. It would probably be a good idea for us to figure out what to do about this problem.

    B. Ask yourself whether you know any children who are fat.

    C. Thus, a solution to the problem will require keeping potential causes in view.

    D. My second cousin was obese as a child.

    E. It is important to know which of the two causes is more significant.

The style of choice C is consistent with the passage, and is the most logical next statement on the writer's part. Choice A shifts from an objective point of view to making reference to the collective *us.* Choice B similarly shifts voice to address the reader as *you;* also, the writer would likely not use the word *fat,* which has a derogatory connotation. Choice D shifts from an objective point of view to personal example. Choice E does not work because there is no evidence in the passage to suggest that the writer would now become concerned with identifying the bigger of the two cited causes for obesity. The correct answer is **C.**

Questions 6 and 7 are based on the following passage.

Passage

Medieval romance stories often challenge commonly held attitudes about male and female sexuality in their time. In the Middle Ages, women were unfairly defined as temptresses. A man's desire for a woman was generally thought to be the woman's responsibility: she must have seduced him, or wanted him to seduce her. Any illicit activity, then (sex was permissible only for purposes of procreation), could be attributed to the woman. The idea that a woman had any desire at all, let alone illicit desire, was considered inappropriate and, therefore, used to condemn her.

The Wedding of Sir Gawain and Dame Ragnell is a medieval romance that disrupts notions about proper behavior for women. In the story, the primary female character, Dame Ragnell, not only causes two men to spend a year researching women's desire, but also convinces the virtuous Sir Gawain to make love to her. Also, Gawain claims no authority over Ragnell's body, but instead accords her ultimate control over what she does with it.

Question Type: Identify the Main Idea of the Passage

6. Which of the following is the main idea of the passage?

    A. *The Wedding of Sir Gawain and Dame Ragnell* challenges commonly held attitudes about male and female sexuality in the Middle Ages.
    B. Dame Ragnell convinces Sir Gawain to make love to her.
    C. Medieval romances are iconoclastic.
    D. Stories can be revolutionary.
    E. In the Middle Ages, women were unfairly defined as temptresses.

You might have selected choice C, thinking that, since it is short, it must be the main idea. However, the main idea should be a more comprehensive (though not detailed) view of the passage as a whole, and choice C disregards the content in the second paragraph. (By the way, *iconoclastic* means groundbreaking or subversive.) Similarly, choices B and E are mere snippets of the whole. Choice D may be true, but it is far too general to consider it a good descriptor of this particular passage. The correct answer is **A.**

Note: A question about the main idea might be put to you in another way: for instance, you may be asked which answer would make the best title for the passage.

Question Type: Envision the Intended Audience for the Passage

7. In what sort of publication would this passage be most likely to appear?

- A. a newspaper's lifestyle section
- B. a scholarly literary journal
- C. a corporate guide on sexual harassment
- D. an art history book
- E. a popular magazine

The passage's tone suggests that it is written for a scholarly or academic literary journal. Those who write for such publications are usually university professors. The writer, who may be a specialist in medieval studies, knows the historical background of the Middle Ages, and is likely a literary scholar who will go on to interpret *The Wedding of Sir Gawain and Dame Ragnell* in such a way as to show that Ragnell is a subversive character. Perhaps this writer also specializes in gender studies. Choice A is not correct because the lifestyle section of most newspapers contains local events and entertainment, as well as movie and television reviews and feature stories, not the sort of material in this passage. Choice C is an illogical answer, because corporate guides on sexual harassment would not discuss life in the Middle Ages or characters in medieval romances. Choice D is not correct because even though literature is a form of art, art history is generally concerned with painting, sculpture, architectural design, and various decorative pieces. Finally, E cannot be correct, since women's magazines are a popular genre that deals mainly with fashion, health, and dieting tips, and relationship advice, among other topics. The correct answer is **B.**

Note: Passages found on the SAT, PSAT/NMSQT, GRE, and PPST designate line numbers in multiples of five (as do longer passages on the GMAT and LSAT). This assists the test-makers and test-takers in pinpointing particular places in the passage to which questions refer.

GRE Question Types

Reading comprehension is found in the GRE's "Verbal Reasoning" section. Passage lengths range from brief to medium, and difficulty levels from easy to difficult. Many questions conform to the common single-answer choice from among five possibilities. However, there are two other question types that appear on the GRE: one that asks test-takers to choose *all* applicable answers from among three choices, and another—appearing only on the computer-based test—that asks test-takers to select a sentence from within a passage that fits a given description.

Let's look at examples of the two that are unique to the GRE:

Questions 8 and 9 are based on the following passage.

Passage

Midwives refer women to general practitioners or obstetricians when a pregnant woman requires care beyond the midwives' area of expertise. In many parts of the world, these professions work together to provide care for childbearing women. In others, only the midwife is available to provide care. In the latter case, midwives are trained to handle certain more difficult deliveries—including breech births, twin births, and births where the baby is in a posterior position—using non-invasive techniques.

Compared with obstetricians, midwives offer lower maternity care cost, and midwife-led births are associated with lower intervention rates, reduced mortality and morbidity related to interventions, and fewer recovery complications, though this is largely due to the fact that compared to obstetricians they work with more women who have low-risk pregnancies, not because there are lower risks to midwife deliveries.

Source: http://en.wikipedia.org/wiki/Midwifery

Question Type: Select One or More Answers

For question 8, consider each of the choices separately and then select *all* that apply. Be sure to select all of the correct answers, because no partial credit is given.

Note: When this question type appears on the GRE, the answer choices will be in boxes rather than in ovals. When you see answer choices with boxes, realize that you must select one or more answers. In general on the GRE, whenever there is a question type that allows for more than one correct answer, the choice letters will appear within boxes.

8. Which of the following is/are true according to this passage?

   A. Some births are attended by midwives, but not by general practitioners or obstetricians.

   B. In certain parts of the world, midwives are able to serve even in complicated deliveries.

   C. Statistics prove that midwife deliveries are safer.

The second half of the first paragraph clearly states that in some parts of the world, midwives are fully in charge of deliveries, even in cases when conditions are complex. Choice C is not correct because we are told that despite statistics showing lower death rates and recovery complications in midwife-driven births, this is largely due to the fact that, on a worldwide basis, far fewer midwives attend difficult births than do more highly-trained practitioners. The correct answers are **A** and **B.**

Question Type: Select in Passage

Select the sentence that fits the description below.

9. Midwives are not always able to deliver babies.

The answer is the first sentence in the passage. This is the only sentence that informs the reader that midwives refer pregnant women to others in cases that require a more highly trained professional.

On the actual exam, the select-in-passage question type requires that you identify one specific sentence in the passage and click anywhere on that sentence to highlight your answer. When you click on the sentence, your answer will automatically be recorded.

GMAT Question Types

Within the Verbal section of the GMAT are "critical reasoning" questions that consist of brief passages (usually no more than 100 words) offering an argument, a set of statements, or a plan of action. Questions based on these passages are designed to test logical thinking by inviting analysis of the claims or intended actions. (Note that "reading comprehension" questions within the GMAT's Verbal section feature longer passages of approximately 200 to 400 words.) Here are examples:

Question Type: Critical Reasoning

Passage

At regional public universities in California, more than 50 percent of admitted first-year students have not attained entry-level proficiency in writing and mathematics. Those who lack proficiency in writing outnumber those who lack proficiency in mathematics. Proficiency in both areas will improve when high school courses put more emphasis on preparing students for college.

10. Which of the following, if true, would most seriously weaken the conclusion above?

   A. Proficiency in writing and mathematics is low outside California as well.

   B. University expectations in writing and mathematics are lower than they have been in the past.

   C. Writing requirements for high school students have become more rigorous over the last decade.

   D. A small number of first-year California college students have not attended high school in California.

   E. Mathematics skills have changed because of the widespread use of calculators.

The implication of the conclusion is that writing and math are not sufficiently emphasized in high school. Choice C contradicts, and therefore weakens, this conclusion. The correct answer is **C**.

Question Type: Plan of Action

Passage

A company is addressing budget reductions by moving from a workweek that consists of five eight-hour days to a workweek of four ten-hour days. This will reduce energy and maintenance costs by 20 percent, and give workers a three-day weekend. Those who prefer a five-day workweek will have the opportunity to work from home, if their assignment can be accomplished off-site.

11. Which of the following, if true, would strengthen this policy?

    A. The energy costs for a ten-hour day are 20 percent higher than for an eight-hour day.

    B. Most of the work at this company is done via computer.

    C. There is no provision for how to adjust the workweek when a national holiday falls on a Monday or Friday.

    D. The maintenance crew works under a union contract that mandates a five-day workweek.

    E. Eighty percent of the budget for this company is tied to salaries.

Choice B strengthens the provision of the policy that would allow employees to elect to work off-site, since computer work generally allows for this. The correct answer is **B.**

CBEST Question Types

The CBEST contains brief passage question types that involve tables of contents and indexes, as well as graphs, charts, and tables. The CBEST also asks test-takers to insert words, phrases, or sentences in appropriate places within passages, and to recognize summaries of passages in outline form. Let's look at question types particular to the CBEST.

Tables of Contents or Indexes

Use the following excerpt from a Table of Contents to answer questions 12 and 13.

Chapter V: Reading Comprehension

12. On what pages of this book's chapter on reading comprehension would one find approaches to answering questions about longer passages of intermediate difficulty?

    A.   Pages 341–366
    B.   Pages 291–295
    C.   Pages 395–399
    D.   Pages 310–322
    E.   Pages 310–318

The second section, "Reading Comprehension Strategies," is devoted to approaches to skillfully answering questions about longer passages of intermediate difficulty. Choice D cannot be correct, because page 322 cuts well into the material devoted to longer, more challenging passages. The correct answer is **E**.

13. According to what pattern is this part (relating to Chapter V) of the book's Table of Contents organized?

 A. level of difficulty
 B. progression of steps in a process of learning
 C. alphabetically
 D. shortest to longest
 E. answers, followed by questions

One can easily see that this Table of Contents begins by familiarizing the reader with reading comprehension question types and explaining strategies for success, and ends with a practice test followed by answers and explanations. Thus the chapter is organized according to a progression of steps in a process of learning. Choice A might appear to be correct, since brief passages lead to longer passages of intermediate and then challenging difficulty. However, this organizational pattern occurs within subsections of the chapter, but does not organize the chapter as a whole. Choice D is incorrect for the same reason. The correct answer is **B**.

Graphs, Charts, and Tables

Use the graph below to answers questions 14–15.

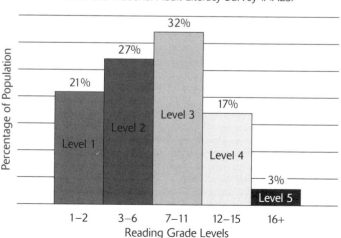

1992 U.S. National Adult Literacy Survey (NALS)

Source: http://commons.wikimedia.org/wiki/File:Nals.jpg

14. The graph above indicates that, in 1992, the majority of U.S. adults were reading

    A. below the level that would be expected of high school graduates.

    B. below the level of a six-year-old.

    C. at levels that corresponded with their ages.

    D. at levels that improved as they got older.

    E. at levels below those of adults in other countries.

The graph indicates that in 1992, 80% (21% + 27% + 32%) of adults were reading at an eleventh grade level or below. The correct answer is **A.**

15. The graph above allows us to draw conclusions about which of the following?

    A. the rate at which reading improves as adults receive additional instruction

    B. the relationship between educational attainment levels and U.S. adults' reading ability

    C. the grade at which many students drop out of school

    D. the effectiveness of reading instruction in elementary and secondary schools

    E. the U.S. regions where reading ability is lowest

The graph compares grade levels, which can correctly be understood as "levels of educational attainment," with the percentage of adults who have reading ability at each level. We cannot conclude from this graph anything about the effectiveness of instruction, dropout patterns, or regional skills, none of which are indicated on the chart. The correct answer is **B.**

Passages with Numbered Sentences

CBEST passages that fall within the "Critical Analysis and Evaluation" part of the reading comprehension section have numbered sentences. This allows for questions to be asked about the strengths and weaknesses of arguments, and about whether particular sentences convey fact, opinion, description, an idea, or another type of utterance.

Questions 16 and 17 are of the sort one would expect to find in the "Critical Analysis and Evaluation" portion of the CBEST, while questions 18 and 19 are of the sort you might find on any reading comprehension section of the various tests we've been addressing.

Questions 16 through 19 are based on the following passage.

Passage

[1] How-to books on creative writing make assorted recommendations about which element of the short story is most important to tackle first. [2] Many advise beginning with character, for instance, arguing that the best stories are those that have characters who come alive, and with whom readers can strongly identify. [3] _____ these aims for character are vital, it is better to begin with plot. [4] Novice writers often get held up by the notion that creative writing is somehow an abstract form of art, in which characters are appreciated just for existing, however moodily, brilliant, or emotionally sensitive they may be. [5] While such characters can certainly be interesting, they are nothing without a story—nothing without some set of problems, dilemmas, and events in response to which they behave in certain compelling ways. [6] _____, plot is the natural place to begin.

Question Type: Fact vs. Opinion

16. Sentences 3–6 are examples of which of the following?

    A. facts
    B. poor writing
    C. description
    D. opinion
    E. explanation

This writer, who could be a creative writing teacher or student, is clearly giving his or her opinion of how best to begin to conceive a short story. There are no *facts* (choice A) in these sentences (unlike sentence 1, which, if accurate about the contents of how-to books, could be said to be a fact). Granted, the writer may be basing the advice on experience; however, the question of whether to begin with character or plot is an open one, as the variation of advice given by how-to books demonstrates. The passage is in no way poorly written (choice B), and sentences 4–6 are not *description* (choice C), since they don't all convey the characteristics of a particular object or phenomenon. We could view sentences 4–6 as an *explanation* (choice E) of the assertion made in sentence 3, but the question asks about all four sentences, and sentence 3 is not an explanation. The correct answer is **D**.

Question Type: Assess the Strengths and Weaknesses of an Argument

17. Which of the following numbered sentences provides the strongest evidence that a primary focus on character can lead to poor writing?

    A. 2
    B. 3
    C. 4
    D. 5
    E. 6

Sentence 4 allows us to infer that the writer has had enough experience as a creative writing teacher to know that inexperienced writers are often overly focused on creating artsy characters who do little more than exist. This is the best answer choice. While sentence 5 goes on to make the point that a story is *nothing* without plot, it does little more than assert this idea. Sentences 2 and 3 set up the dichotomy between plot and character, and sentence 6 offers a conclusion that reiterates the second part of sentence 3. The correct answer is **C.**

Question Type: Inserts and Transitions

18. Which of the following word pairs, when used to fill in the two blanks in the passage, would clarify the relationship between the first part of the passage and the latter part?

    A. However; But
    B. Yet; Also
    C. Furthermore; However
    D. Furthermore; Also
    E. Although; Thus

In sentence 3, the writer is about to disagree with how-to books that recommend character as a primary emphasis; however, the writer does agree that character is also an essential element of a good story. The conjunction *although* (which, when used, is typically found at the start of a dependent clause) says, *despite the fact that X is true, or may be the case, it is also or more true that Y is the case.* This is precisely what the writer does here. Sentence 6 is the writer's re-statement of what is proposed in the latter half of sentence 3. Thus, the word *thus,* which means therefore, is fitting. The correct answer is **E.**

Question Type: Summaries in Outline Form

19. Which of the following brief outlines best characterizes the passage's contents?

   A. I.   creative writing books
      II. sensitive characters

   B. I.   exciting characters
      II. the necessity of dilemma

   C. I.   character vs. plot
      II. the primacy of plot

   D. I.   plot over character
      II. abstract forms of art

   E. I.   first steps
      II. character behavior

The first part of the passage focuses on whether character or plot is the most vital initial consideration for a short story writer, and the second part of the passage proposes that plot is primary. Choice A.I. is too general, and A.II. cites a small fragment of a larger point the writer is making (as do both elements of choice B, as well as choice D.II.). Although D.I. is not incorrect, the writer hasn't quite made this case yet. Both elements of choice E are far too general. The correct answer is **C.**

Section 2: Long Passages – Intermediate Difficulty

Now that you have a comprehensive overview of brief passage question types that appear on the SAT, PSAT/NMSQT, PPST, GRE, and CBEST, let's look at longer passages of intermediate difficulty. A few longer passages of intermediate difficulty do appear on the CBEST, but those below are more typical of passages found on the SAT, PSAT/NMSQT, GRE, and similar exams.

Strategies for Long Passages

Long passages can be time-consuming and can leave the unsuspecting reader overwhelmed. But if you can become skilled at reading long passages, all passages will become easier to tackle. To approach long passages:

- First, look at the title and the short italicized abstract (if provided) at the beginning of the passage to get a sense of the author's topic, tone, and main purpose. You may be able to determine the passage's *tone* by paying attention to the diction used in the sentences. Determine whether the writer has a positive or negative attitude. Understanding the author's attitude will help you eliminate improbable answer choices.

- Then, look for *specific* information within the questions and passage before you look for *general* information. Do this by skimming the questions for literal information related to specific references, facts, and details to circle (or write down on scratch paper) before you read the passage. Long passages can contain up to fifteen questions, and if you are rushed for time, chances are you will at least be able to complete the direct, specific questions before reading every word in the passage. If this applies to your test-taking experience, answer the specific questions first, but be careful about where you fill in the correct answer for the corresponding question on your answer sheet.

- Some tests may include *line number references* to help direct you to relevant information within the passage. After you circle or write down the reference line number(s) in the question, circle or write down the sentence(s) in the passage and make any necessary notes in the passage's margins. For example, if the question says, "In line 27, the quotation marks around the word *abnormal* refer to . . . ," you should circle *abnormal* within the passage and quickly write down *line 27* and the words *refers to* in the margins. This will help keep your mind focused on what to look for in line 27.

The following passage is lengthy, yet not as challenging as the chemistry passage that we will come to later.

Questions 20 through 24 are based on the following passage.

Source: http://en.wikipedia.org/wiki/History_of_the_internet

Passage

The history of the Internet began with the development of computers in the 1950s. This began with point-to-point communication between mainframe computers and terminals, expanded to point-to-point connections between computers and then early research into
(5) packet switching. Packet switched networks such as ARPANET, Mark I at NPL in the UK, CYCLADES, Merit Network, Tymnet, and Telenet, were developed in the late 1960s and early 1970s using a variety of protocols. The ARPANET in particular led to the development of protocols for Internetworking, where multiple
(10) separate networks could be joined together into a network of networks.

In 1982, the Internet Protocol Suite (TCP/IP) was standardized and the concept of a worldwide network of fully interconnected TCP/IP networks called the Internet was introduced. Access to the ARPANET was expanded in 1981 when the National Science
(15) Foundation (NSF) developed the Computer Science Network (CSNET) and again in 1986 when NSFNET provided access to supercomputer sites in the United States from research and education organizations. Commercial Internet service providers (ISPs) began to emerge in the late 1980s and 1990s. The ARPANET was
(20) decommissioned in 1990. The Internet was commercialized in 1995 when NSFNET was decommissioned, removing the last restrictions on the use of the Internet to carry commercial traffic.

Since the mid-1990s the Internet has had a drastic impact on culture and commerce, including the rise of near-instant communication by
(25) electronic mail, instant messaging, Voice over Internet Protocol (VoIP) "phone calls," two-way interactive video calls, and the World Wide Web with its discussion forums, blogs, social networking, and online shopping sites. The research and education community continues to develop and use advanced networks such as NSF's very high speed
(30) Backbone Network Service (vBNS), Internet2, and National LambdaRail. Increasing amounts of data are transmitted at higher and higher speeds over fiber optic networks operating at 1-Gbit/s, 10-Gbit/s, or more. The Internet continues to grow, driven by ever-greater amounts of online information and knowledge, commerce,
(35) entertainment, and social networking.

It is estimated that in 1993 the Internet carried only 1 percent of the information flowing through two-way telecommunication. By 2000 this figure had grown to 51 percent, and by 2007 more than 97 percent of all telecommunicated information was carried over the Internet.

(40)   The Internet has precursors that date back to the 19th century, especially the telegraph system, more than a century before the digital Internet became widely used in the second half of the 1990s. The concept of data communication—transmitting data between two different places, connected via some kind of electromagnetic medium, (45)   such as radio or an electrical wire—predates the introduction of the first computers. Such communication systems were typically limited to point-to-point communication between two end devices. Telegraph systems and telex machines can be considered early precursors of this kind of communication.

(50)   Early computers used the technology available at the time to allow communication between the central processing unit and remote terminals. As the technology evolved, new systems were devised to allow communication over longer distances (for terminals) or with higher speed (for interconnection of local devices) that were necessary (55)   for the mainframe computer model. Using these technologies it was possible to exchange data (such as files) between remote computers. However, the point-to-point communication model was limited, as it did not allow for direct communication between any two arbitrary systems; a physical link was necessary. The technology was also (60)   deemed as inherently unsafe for strategic and military use because there were no alternative paths for the communication in case of an enemy attack.

Question Type: Identify the Writer's Tone

20. The writer's tone throughout this passage is generally

    A.   critical.

    B.   reactionary.

    C.   somber.

    D.   objective.

    E.   encouraging.

The writer is presenting a history of the Internet, without any argument for or against its value. He or she is, therefore, attempting to be objective. The correct answer is **D.**

Question Type: Draw Inferences Based on the Passage's Contents

21. The writer implies which of the following about the Internet?

    A. Its use will continue to grow.

    B. It has reached the limits of its growth.

    C. It has not advanced significantly beyond its precursors.

    D. It is basically the same as the ARPANET.

    E. It is better understood now than it was in the 1990s.

By presenting figures that indicate the increasing growth of Internet use, reaching more than 97 percent by 2007 (line 38), the writer is establishing a pattern that implies continued growth. The correct answer is **A.**

Question Type: Envision the Intended Audience

22. The writer assumes which of the following about the audience for this passage?

    A. They understand the meaning of the acronym ISP.

    B. They understand the meaning of packet switching.

    C. They are not regular users of the Internet.

    D. They do not know how to use a telegraph.

    E. They were not using the Internet in 1993.

The writer does not define "packet switching" (line 5), even though it is not a commonly understood term. The writer does define ISP (lines 18–19), and does not provide any content that would point to choices C, D, or E. The correct answer is **B.**

Question Type: Draw a Conclusion

23. The writer concludes which of the following?

    A.   Communication is a basic human need.

    B.   The Internet would never have evolved without the support of the U.S. government.

    C.   The Internet is not a reliable means of communication during an enemy attack.

    D.   The high point of worldwide Internet use was 2007.

    E.   Data was being transmitted from point to point more than one hundred years before the Internet was in general use.

The writer makes this point explicitly in the passage. Choice A is too general of a conclusion to be associated with this particular passage. With respect to choice B, although the passage indicates that there was government activity associated with the Internet's development, there is no suggestion that the Internet *never* would have evolved without it. Content in the passage does not support choice C, and choice D implies that Internet growth stopped in 2007 without any supporting evidence in the passage. The correct answer is **E.**

Question Type: Direct Comprehension

24. When the writer says, "The Internet continues to grow, driven by ever greater amounts of online information and knowledge, commerce, entertainment, and social networking" (lines 33–35), he or she is including which of the following elements as an aspect of the Internet?

    A.   the telegraph

    B.   the ARPANET

    C.   VoIP

    D.   telex machines

    E.   television

VoIP is the only choice that the writer includes in his discussion of the Internet's impact (lines 25–28). The correct answer is **C.**

Section 3: Paired (Comparative) Reading Passages

Description

The SAT's reading comprehension section, referred to as "critical reading," contains not only passages from a single source, but also questions on pairs of passages (Passage 1 and Passage 2) that address a similar topic, but in different ways.

The LSAT's reading comprehension section contains four sets of passages followed by questions. The fourth set, however, is made up of two passages (Passage A and Passage B) that are followed by several questions that ask the test-takers to compare the two.

Strategy

Paired and comparative passages can agree or disagree with one another, as well as complement one another. As you read the passages, use active reading skills to note in the margins, or on scratch paper, important points about how the passages are alike and different.

Questions 25 through 28 are based on the following pair of passages.

Passage 1

Today's consumers have begun to take more control over their health, partly as a result of the Internet age. Numerous websites offer information on health-related issues and problems. One can research and compare physicians to be sure that a given doctor has the
(5)   credentials to treat a particular illness. One can also find patient reviews that discuss a given doctor's practices and bedside manner. One can also learn about one's condition and prescribed medications online, both from official sources and through chats with fellow sufferers. Better-informed patients are able to evaluate their medical
(10) care more intently and to have a hand in their own treatment protocols. Also, communication with fellow sufferers works against the feelings and experiences of isolation associated with illness, particularly with stigmatized diseases such as cancer and HIV infection.

Passage 2

(15)   One effect of today's easy access to medical information is that it plays into the hands of those who would profit from health care as a consumer-oriented business. Direct-to-consumer (DTC) advertising of pharmaceuticals is a part of this phenomenon. Patients who once had little awareness of the types and names of prescription medications are now exposed to media ads that make them far more aware of what

(20)   they see as possible solutions to their pains and disorders. There's Nexium for heartburn, Imitrex for migraine, Zocor for cholesterol, Paxil for social anxiety disorder, and so on. DTC advertising of pharmaceutical products has been legal in the United States since 1985. However, the practice became much more common in 1997,

(25)   when pharmaceutical ads were no longer required to include a full list of known side effects. Health consumers are often encouraged through such ads to self-diagnose and to request particular drugs from their physicians.

25. Which of the following most accurately describes the relationship between the two passages?

A.   Passage 2 is a pessimistic spin on passage 1.

B.   Passage 1 sheds a skeptical light on passage 2.

C.   Passage 2 invalidates passage 1.

D.   Passage 1 holds a positive view of DTC, while passage 2 does not.

E.   Passage 1 holds a positive view of the cultural context in which today's health-care consumer finds himself or herself, while passage 2 holds a negative view of that context.

The writer of passage 1 makes wholly positive statements about the contemporary health consumer's access to medical information, while passage 2 points out the problems that can result from this phenomenon. Choice A may seem correct, but the writer of passage 2 shows no familiarity with the kinds of points made by the passage 1 writer. Choice B is incorrect for the same reason: The writer of passage 1 makes no points that bespeak awareness of the points made in passage 2. Choice C is incorrect not only for the same reason that choice A is incorrect, but also because what is said in passage 2 does not falsify what is said in passage 1. Choice D is incorrect because the writer of passage 1 does not discuss DTC. The correct answer is **E.**

26. Which of the following best represents the main difference in focus between the two passages?

   A. Passage 1 focuses on Internet benefits for the health consumer, while passage 2 finds the Internet potentially harmful.

   B. Passage 1 focuses on Internet benefits for the health consumer, while passage 2 focuses on the potentially harmful effects of DTC marketing.

   C. Passage 2 is concerned with the potentially harmful effects of DTC marketing, while passage 1 argues that DTC is of benefit to the consumer.

   D. Passage 2 emphasizes the names of certain drugs, while passage 1 emphasizes the names of certain diseases.

   E. Passage 1 characterizes an active health care consumer, while passage 2 characterizes a passive one.

Choice A is incorrect because passage 2 says nothing about the Internet. Choice C is incorrect because passage 1 says nothing about DTC. Choice D is incorrect because, while the statements may be true, neither is the focus of the passage as a whole. Choice E is incorrect because passage 2 also features an active health care consumer. Each writer's focus is correctly stated in answer choice **B.**

27. It can be inferred from passage 1 that the writer

   A. believes that there are no abuses of health care consumers in an Internet age.

   B. is not necessarily opposed to DTC pharmaceutical marketing.

   C. has suffered from a serious illness.

   D. has spoken to people who use Internet health care chat rooms.

   E. is aware of DTC pharmaceutical marketing.

Answer choice **B** is correct because, even though passage 1 says nothing directly about DTC, the writer is making a case for the positive benefits of a well-informed and self-reliant medical consumer. Praise for consumers who have a hand in their own treatment protocols is suggestive of a writer who could possibly find some benefit in DTC marketing. We cannot, however, feel as comfortable with choice A since the writer could very well acknowledge that abuses can occur if consumers are not careful. There is nothing in the passage to support choices C, D, and E.

28. How can one tell that the writer of Passage 2 is against DTC pharmaceutical marketing?

A. There passage has an angry tone.

B. The writer cites the names of misused drugs.

C. The statement that *it plays into the hands of those who would profit from healthcare as a consumer-oriented business* (lines 14–15) suggests an indictment.

D. The writer knows which dates are significant in the history of DTC.

E. The writer mentions that people are encouraged to request certain drugs from their doctors (lines 26–28).

The words and phrases *plays into the hands of, profit,* and *health care as a consumer-oriented business* are strongly indicative of a writer that disapproves of DTC marketing. The remainder of the paragraph is to be read in that context. There is no evidence of anger in the passage, so choice A is incorrect. Though the writer does cite the names of potentially over-prescribed drugs, this in itself does not indicate a negative attitude toward DTC marketing. Choice D is wrong for the same reason. Choice E is incorrect because the statement that *health care consumers are often encouraged . . . to request particular drugs from their physicians* is not, by itself, indicative of an attitude toward the phenomenon on the writer's part (though alongside the passage's first sentence, it does resonate as negative). The correct answer is **C**.

Note: Since the "paired" or "comparative" passage question type may be either of intermediate or challenging difficulty, both levels will be included in the practice test that follows the next section on challenging passages, but not in the next section itself.

Section 4: Long Passages – Challenging

Following is one of the longer, more difficult passages of the sort that may show up on the GRE, LSAT, GMAT, and other exams.

Questions 29 through 34 are based on the following passage.

Passage

A chemical formula consists of a single symbol or a group of symbols with number subscripts representing the composition of a substance whether it is a free element or a compound. The formula may represent 1 molecule of the substance if it exists in the molecular

(5) form. For ionic compounds—which exist in the form of charged ions rather than neutral molecules—the formula represents the atomic composition in terms of the simplest ratio of atoms.

A subscript is a small whole number in a formula, following a symbol and below it, indicating the relative number of atoms of a

(10) given element. We omit using the subscript when only 1 atom is present. A coefficient is a number placed before a formula, which multiplies every constituent in the formula. For example, the formula I_2 represents 1 molecule of the element iodine, consisting of 2 iodine atoms chemically combined. The expression 2 I indicates 2 separate

(15) atoms of iodine not in combination. The formula HNO_3 represents 1 molecule of nitric acid, containing 1 atom of hydrogen, 1 atom of nitrogen, and 3 atoms of oxygen. The expression 3 HNO_3 represents 3 molecules of nitric acid. The total number of atoms represented by 3 HNO_3 would be 3 atoms of hydrogen, 3 atoms of nitrogen, and 9

(20) atoms of oxygen. The formula KNO_3 represents 1 potassium ion (K+) and 1 nitrate ion (NO_3-), which is the simplest ratio of these ions forming a neutral entity. Only knowledge of the chemistry of the various elements would allow us to know whether a certain compound exists in ionic or molecular form.

(25) If we would perform a chemical analysis of a sample of the element sulfur, we would, of course, find that it was 100% sulfur. The symbol for sulfur is S and we may be tempted to write the formula for sulfur as S, which would indicate that elemental sulfur—that occurring in nature—consisted of sulfur atoms. However, various experiments

(30) show that sulfur at room temperature consists of molecules, each containing 8 sulfur atoms in a puckered-ring structure. The formula for sulfur is S_8. Twenty-five sulfur molecules would be represented by the expression 25 S_8.

According to the Law of Definite Proportions, pure compounds

(35) contain the same elements in the same proportion by weight, regardless of when and where the compound is found. A pure sample of aluminum sulfate (formula $Al_2(SO_4)_3$), an ionic compound containing 2 A 1 +3 ions for every 3(SO_4)$_3$-2 ions, the simplest ratio of ions forming a neutral entity) contains by weight 15.8% A1, 28.1% S, and

(40) 56.1% O. That is, whenever or wherever a 100-gram sample of aluminum sulfate is decomposed to the elements, the products would be 15.8 g of Al, 28.1 g of S, and 56.1 g of O. From percent composition by weight data, we can readily determine the "simplest" or "empirical" formulas of compounds.

Question Type: Identify the Writer's Primary Purpose

29. The primary purpose of the passage is to

    A.   combine elements to produce new chemical compounds.

    B.   compare the weights of several chemical substances.

    C.   eliminate misconceptions concerning chemical notation.

    D.   invent representations of natural elements.

    E.   explain methods of chemical notation.

The first word of each answer choice is a clue to eliminating incorrect choices. *Combine* (choice A), *compare* (choice B), *eliminate* (choice C), and *invent* (choice D) are not relevant to the obvious, overall purpose of the passage, which is to explain. The correct answer is **E.**

Question Type: Direct Comprehension

30. According to the passage, the Law of Definite Proportions can lead a chemist to

    A.   estimate weights that apply only to 100-gram samples.

    B.   decompose chemicals into free ions.

    C.   apply other chemical laws that simplify complex compounds.

    D.   determine the relative weight of the elements in a compound.

    E.   discover formulas for performing "simple" chemical experiments.

Using the extended example of aluminum sulfate in the final paragraph, the passage illustrates determination of the relative weight of the elements, using the Law of Definite Proportions. Choice A is contradictory. Choices B, C, and E are irrelevant to the information given in the passage. The correct answer is **D.**

Question Type: Understand the Meaning of Words

31. The writer of the passage assumes that the reader knows the meaning of which of the following terms?

   A.   molecule
   B.   chemical formula
   C.   subscript
   D.   coefficient
   E.   Law of Definite Proportions

Molecule is the only term that is not explicitly defined or explained in the passage. The correct answer is **A.**

Question Type: Draw a Conclusion

32. Which of the following conclusions does the passage support?

   A.   Elemental sulfur is the most unusual of all chemical compounds.
   B.   The chemical formula for a pure element may contain a subscript.
   C.   The ratio of atoms in a compound is disregarded by a chemical formula.
   D.   The 3 in the expression *3H* indicates the number of combined atoms.
   E.   The total number of atoms in a chemical compound is not represented by a chemical formula.

Only choice **B** is explicitly supported in the passage (in the second to last paragraph). Each of the other choices contradicts information in the passage.

Question Type: Make an Inference

33. We may infer which of the following about the atomic composition of any molecule?

    A.   It yields a configuration that resembles a type of ring.

    B.   It most likely exists in ionic form.

    C.   It can be represented by a chemical formula if it consists of known elements.

    D.   It is unknown to scientists until molecules are studied at room temperature.

    E.   It is the same as a pure sample of an element.

As we've seen, a question that asks for information that is implied or inferred is asking you to derive conclusions or information that is suggested rather than explicitly stated. The correct choice here is **C,** a choice you may arrive at through the process of elimination. Choices A and D are true about sulfur but irrelevant to molecular composition in general; choices B and E contradict the passage, which explains that a molecule is not the same as an ion or a pure element.

Question Type: Direct Comprehension

34. The passage provides answers to which of the following questions?

    A.   Why do the elements in aluminum sulfate occur in a particular proportion?

    B.   Can any chemicals besides sulfur be represented by a puckered-ring structure?

    C.   Are ions charged differently than molecules?

    D.   Does potassium occur in compounds other than potassium nitrate?

    E.   Do changes in temperature alter all chemicals in a particular way?

This type of question is time consuming because you must locate the section of the passage relevant to each answer choice/question as you survey the answer choices. Choice C's question is answered in the third sentence of the first paragraph (lines 5–7). The correct answer is **C.**

How to Mark Passages

Sampling the questions first, you see that for question 29 you must pay special attention to the passage's primary purpose; for question 30, to the discussion of the Law of Definite Proportions; for question 31, to the meaning of scientific terms; and for question 33, to the discussion of atomic composition. Note that question 32 gives you no particular clue as to what to look for in the passage.

Keeping in mind the questions you must answer, and paying attention to any sections of the passage that stand out as important or interesting, you should read and mark the passage. A marked version of the chemistry passage follows.

Note: If you are taking a computer-based test, use the scratch paper or note-board provided to take important notes about the passage and questions.

When you mark passages, be sure to identify the following important aspects of the material:

1. the passage's main idea
2. details that support the main idea
3. the writer's purpose
4. particular words that are highly significant to the points being made
5. style and tone of the language

Underline the main point of the passage, the writer's conclusion, and the main point of each paragraph. **Circle** important terms and phrases, especially those that are mentioned in the questions. **Use margin brackets** to indicate the definitions of important terms, exceptions to a point being made (look for signaling words and phrases such as "however" or "on the other hand"), and definitions or explanations (look for signaling words or phrases such as "for instance"). When you sense that a word or phrase is important, but don't know how to categorize it, put an **asterisk** in the margin of the line in which it appears.

A chemical formula consists of a single symbol or a group of symbols with number subscripts representing the composition of a substance whether it is a free element or a compound. The formula may represent 1 molecule of the substance if it exists in the molecular form. For ionic compounds—which exist
5   in the form of charged ions rather than neutral molecules—the formula represents the atomic composition in terms of the simplest ratio of atoms.
    A subscript is a small whole number in a formula, following a symbol and below it, indicating the relative number of atoms of a given element. We omit using the subscript when only 1 atom is present. A coefficient is a
10   number placed before a formula, which multiplies every constituent in the formula. For example the formula I_2 represents 1 molecule of the element iodine, consisting of 2 iodine atoms chemically combined. The expression 2 I indicates 2 separate atoms of iodine not in combination. The formula HNO_3 represents 1 molecule of nitric acid, containing 1 atom of hydrogen,
15   1 atom of nitrogen, and 3 atoms of oxygen. The expression $3\ HNO_3$ represents 3 molecules of nitric acid. The total number of atoms represented by $3\ HNO_3$ would be 3 atoms of hydrogen, 3 atoms of nitrogen, and 9 atoms of oxygen. The formula KNO_3 represents 1 potassium ion (K^+) and
20   1 nitrate ion (NO_3^-), which is the simplest ratio of these ions forming a neutral entity. Only knowledge of the chemistry of the various elements would allow us to know whether a certain compound exists in ionic or molecular form.
    If we would perform a chemical analysis of a pure sample of the element sulfur, we would, of course, find that it was 100% sulfur. The symbol for
25   sulfur is S and we may be tempted to write the formula for sulfur as S, which would indicate that elemental sulfur—that occurring in nature—consisted of sulfur atoms. However, various experiments show that sulfur at room temperature consists of molecules, each containing 8 sulfur atoms in a puckered-ring structure. The formula for sulfur is S_8. Twenty-five sulfur
30   molecules would be represented by the expression $25\ S_8$.
    According to the Law of Definite Proportions, pure compounds contain   *
the same elements in the same proportion by weight, regardless of when and where the compound is found. A pure sample of aluminum sulfate
35   (formula $Al2(SO_4)_3$, an ionic compound containing 2 Al^{+3} ions for every $3(SO_4)_3{}^{-2}$ ions, the simplest ratio of ions forming a neutral entity) contains by weight 15.8% Al, 28.1% S, and 56.1% O. That is, whenever or wherever a 100-gram sample of aluminum sulfate is decomposed to the elements, the
40   products would be 15.8 g of Al, 28.1 g of S, and 56.1 g of O. From percent composition by weight data, we can readily determine the "simplest" or "empirical" formulas of compounds.

Answer Sheet for Reading Comprehension Practice Test

(Remove this sheet and use it to mark your answers.

Section 1: Brief Passages

Set 1

1 (A) (B) (C) (D) (E)
2 (A) (B) (C) (D) (E)
3 (A) (B) (C) (D) (E)
4 (A) (B) (C) (D) (E)
5 (A) (B) (C) (D) (E)
6 (A) (B) (C) (D) (E)
7 (A) (B) (C) (D) (E)
8 (A) (B) (C) (D) (E)

Set 2

9   (A) (B) (C) (D) (E)
10 (A) (B) (C) (D) (E)
11 (A) (B) (C) (D) (E)
12 (A) (B) (C) (D) (E)
13 (A) (B) (C) (D) (E)
14 (A) (B) (C) (D) (E)
15 (A) (B) (C) (D) (E)
16 (A) (B) (C) (D) (E)

Set 3

17 (A) (B) (C) (D) (E)
18 (A) (B) (C) (D) (E)
19 (A) (B) (C) (D) (E)
20 (A) (B) (C) (D) (E)
21 (A) (B) (C) (D) (E)
22 (A) (B) (C) (D) (E)
23 (A) (B) (C) (D) (E)
24 (A) (B) (C) (D) (E)
25 (A) (B) (C) (D) (E)
26 (A) (B) (C) (D) (E)

Section 2: Long Passages – Intermediate Difficulty

Set 1

27 (A) (B) (C) (D) (E)
28 (A) (B) (C) (D) (E)
29 (A) (B) (C) (D) (E)
30 (A) (B) (C) (D) (E)
31 (A) (B) (C) (D) (E)
32 (A) (B) (C) (D) (E)
33 (A) (B) (C) (D) (E)
34 (A) (B) (C) (D) (E)
35 (A) (B) (C) (D) (E)

Set 2

36 (A) (B) (C) (D) (E)
37 (A) (B) (C) (D) (E)
38 (A) (B) (C) (D) (E)
39 (A) (B) (C) (D) (E)
40 (A) (B) (C) (D) (E)
41 (A) (B) (C) (D) (E)
42 (A) (B) (C) (D) (E)
43 (A) (B) (C) (D) (E)

Set 3

44 (A) (B) (C) (D) (E)
45 (A) (B) (C) (D) (E)
46 (A) (B) (C) (D) (E)
47 (A) (B) (C) (D) (E)
48 (A) (B) (C) (D) (E)
49 (A) (B) (C) (D) (E)
50 (A) (B) (C) (D) (E)
51 (A) (B) (C) (D) (E)

Set 4 | Set 5

52 Ⓐ Ⓑ Ⓒ Ⓓ Ⓔ	61 Ⓐ Ⓑ Ⓒ Ⓓ Ⓔ
53 Ⓐ Ⓑ Ⓒ Ⓓ Ⓔ	62 Ⓐ Ⓑ Ⓒ Ⓓ Ⓔ
54 Ⓐ Ⓑ Ⓒ Ⓓ Ⓔ	63 Ⓐ Ⓑ Ⓒ Ⓓ Ⓔ
55 Ⓐ Ⓑ Ⓒ Ⓓ Ⓔ	64 Ⓐ Ⓑ Ⓒ Ⓓ Ⓔ
56 Ⓐ Ⓑ Ⓒ Ⓓ Ⓔ	65 Ⓐ Ⓑ Ⓒ Ⓓ Ⓔ
57 Ⓐ Ⓑ Ⓒ Ⓓ Ⓔ	66 Ⓐ Ⓑ Ⓒ Ⓓ Ⓔ
58 Ⓐ Ⓑ Ⓒ Ⓓ Ⓔ	67 Ⓐ Ⓑ Ⓒ Ⓓ Ⓔ
59 Ⓐ Ⓑ Ⓒ Ⓓ Ⓔ	68 Ⓐ Ⓑ Ⓒ Ⓓ Ⓔ
60 Ⓐ Ⓑ Ⓒ Ⓓ Ⓔ	69 Ⓐ Ⓑ Ⓒ Ⓓ Ⓔ
	70 Ⓐ Ⓑ Ⓒ Ⓓ Ⓔ

Section 3: Long Passages – Challenging Difficulty

Set 1 | Set 2

71 Ⓐ Ⓑ Ⓒ Ⓓ Ⓔ	89 Ⓐ Ⓑ Ⓒ Ⓓ Ⓔ
72 Ⓐ Ⓑ Ⓒ Ⓓ Ⓔ	90 Ⓐ Ⓑ Ⓒ Ⓓ Ⓔ
73 Ⓐ Ⓑ Ⓒ Ⓓ Ⓔ	91 Ⓐ Ⓑ Ⓒ Ⓓ Ⓔ
74 Ⓐ Ⓑ Ⓒ Ⓓ Ⓔ	92 Ⓐ Ⓑ Ⓒ Ⓓ Ⓔ
75 Ⓐ Ⓑ Ⓒ Ⓓ Ⓔ	93 Ⓐ Ⓑ Ⓒ Ⓓ Ⓔ
76 Ⓐ Ⓑ Ⓒ Ⓓ Ⓔ	94 Ⓐ Ⓑ Ⓒ Ⓓ Ⓔ
77 Ⓐ Ⓑ Ⓒ Ⓓ Ⓔ	95 Ⓐ Ⓑ Ⓒ Ⓓ Ⓔ
78 Ⓐ Ⓑ Ⓒ Ⓓ Ⓔ	96 Ⓐ Ⓑ Ⓒ Ⓓ Ⓔ
79 Ⓐ Ⓑ Ⓒ Ⓓ Ⓔ	97 Ⓐ Ⓑ Ⓒ Ⓓ Ⓔ
80 Ⓐ Ⓑ Ⓒ Ⓓ Ⓔ	98 Ⓐ Ⓑ Ⓒ Ⓓ Ⓔ
81 Ⓐ Ⓑ Ⓒ Ⓓ Ⓔ	99 Ⓐ Ⓑ Ⓒ Ⓓ Ⓔ
82 Ⓐ Ⓑ Ⓒ Ⓓ Ⓔ	100 Ⓐ Ⓑ Ⓒ Ⓓ Ⓔ
83 Ⓐ Ⓑ Ⓒ Ⓓ Ⓔ	
84 Ⓐ Ⓑ Ⓒ Ⓓ Ⓔ	
85 Ⓐ Ⓑ Ⓒ Ⓓ Ⓔ	
86 Ⓐ Ⓑ Ⓒ Ⓓ Ⓔ	
87 Ⓐ Ⓑ Ⓒ Ⓓ Ⓔ	
88 Ⓐ Ⓑ Ⓒ Ⓓ Ⓔ	

Reading Comprehension Practice Test

Following are sets of reading comprehension questions based on passages that are brief, passages of intermediate difficulty, and passages that are challenging. While you should concentrate on those sections that approximate your test in length and difficulty level, answering the questions from *all* difficulty levels is excellent practice for developing basic reading comprehension skills. The Answer Key for these practice units begins on page 383, and the complete explanatory answers begin on page 385.

Directions

Each statement or passage in this test is followed by a question or questions based on its content. After reading a statement or passage, choose the best answer to each question from among the five choices given. Answer all questions following a statement or passage on the basis of what is *stated* or *implied* in that statement or passage.

Section 1: Brief Passages
Practice Set 1: Brief Passages I, II, III, IV

Questions 1 and 2 are based on Passage I.

Passage I

Religious groups across the globe have, at one time or another, been involved in conflict. In Northern Ireland, for example, Protestant and Catholic factions have clashed with one another. And in India, there has been tension between Muslims and Hindus. In the twenty-first century, however, we can see that conflict between religious groups has considerably decreased over time.

1. Which of the following best expresses the passage's main point?

    A. Although religious persecution is less widespread now than it had been, it is no less repulsive.

    B. Catholics and Protestants have not been in conflict for some time.

    C. Only those groups that have been persecuted can call themselves religious.

    D. Becoming a member of any religious group entails the risk of persecution.

    E. Although religious conflict has affected a number of religious groups, it is not so widespread now as it has been.

333

2. We may infer which of the following conclusions from this passage?

    A.   Only Catholics and Protestants have been in conflict.

    B.   Religious conflict was more widespread in the sixteenth century than it is today.

    C.   Northern Ireland and India are very similar regions.

    D.   Religious persecution in the United States is more of a problem than elsewhere in the world.

    E.   Hindus hold beliefs similar to those of Protestants, and Muslims hold beliefs similar to those of Catholics.

Questions 3 and 4 are based on Passage II.

Passage II

The size of the American family has gradually grown smaller. One reason for diminished family size has been growth in urbanization: whereas a large family may be practical on the farm, since it means more hands to help in the work, child-labor laws and relatively high living expenses make more than a few children prohibitive in the city.

As we consider today's world, we see that there are many other factors that contribute to the U.S. birth rate. Historical patterns across the twentieth and twenty-first centuries consistently show that birth rates decline during a depression or recession. For instance, the birth rate began to drop in 2007 as a result of adverse economic conditions during a major recession.

3. The passage supports all of the following statements *except* which of the following?

    A.   The American family's size is related to the growth of cities.

    B.   The nature of farm work favors a large family.

    C.   The size of families in other countries has also increased.

    D.   The percentage of families with several children was once higher than it is now.

    E.   The cost of living in the city affects the size of families.

4. Which of the following brief outlines best characterizes the contents of the passage?

A.   I.   American population
     II.   recession

B.   I.   American farms
     II.   twenty-first century recession

C.   I.   decreasing family size
     II.   reasons

D.   I.   American population and urbanization
     II.   American population and economic conditions

E.   I.   larger families
     II.   smaller families

Questions 5 and 6 are based on Passage III.

Passage III

A number of special psychotherapeutic techniques have been developed. In psychodrama, people are placed in a staged situation involving one of their real-life conflicts, and they work through their problems there. In group therapy, a number of persons meet (in the presence of a therapist) to talk together about their problems. Play therapy, usually done with children, uses dolls, playhouses, and other toys to permit children to release, on these inanimate objects, the reactions they are otherwise forbidden to show.

5. The writer would probably agree that psychodrama, group therapy, and play therapy all encourage which of the following?

A.   strange behavior
B.   contact with the unconscious
C.   theatrical techniques
D.   introversion
E.   self-expression

6. In the last sentence, the writer assumes which of the following?

   A. Some children hide their true reactions.

   B. Dolls are most useful to the therapist when they are set in a playhouse.

   C. Children love to do violence to inanimate objects.

   D. Play therapy is the only type of therapy appropriate for children.

   E. Most children do not have dolls and playhouses in their own homes.

Questions 7 and 8 are based on Passage IV.

Passage IV

Brainwashing refers to techniques used during the Korean War to extract war crimes confessions from captured American soldiers. The goal of these appalling techniques was to reeducate the prisoners to think in ways acceptable to their captors. This involved "unfreezing" old beliefs by an intensive propaganda campaign under conditions of social isolation, changing beliefs by forcing prisoners to develop "confessions" acceptable to their captors and themselves, and reinforcing ("refreezing") new beliefs by requiring active participation in the brainwashing of other prisoners.

7. According to the passage, each of the following is true about brainwashing *except* that

   A. it was employed during the Korean War.

   B. it was practiced on all those captured during the Korean War.

   C. it attempted to destroy old beliefs.

   D. it forced prisoners to confess to war crimes.

   E. the victims of brainwashing were socially isolated.

8. The writer's attitude toward his or her subject is one of

   A. outrage.

   B. neutrality.

   C. distaste.

   D. approval.

   E. wonderment.

Practice Set 2: Brief Passages V, VI, VII, and VIII

Questions 9 and 10 are based on the following chart in Passage V.

Passage V

sophomore grade distribution in percentages

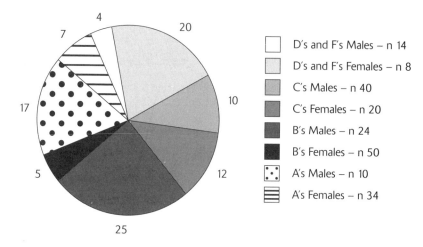

In the pie chart above, *n* represents the number of students in each category, and the pie chart slices represent the percentage of students in each category.

9. How would the pie chart slices' size change if they represented the number of students in each category, rather than the percentage?

   A. The slice size would not change.

   B. The slices representing females would be twice as large.

   C. The slices representing males would be twice as large.

   D. There would be double the number of slices, each proportionally smaller.

   E. There would be two pie charts, with identically sized slices in each.

10. What general conclusion can we draw about the female students' academic performance?

   A. The female students will graduate with higher grades than the male students.

   B. The female students take different classes than do the male students.

   C. The female students have higher grades overall than the male students.

   D. The female students have a higher proportion of lower grades than the male students.

   E. The female students study harder than the male students.

Questions 11 and 12 are based on Passage VI.

Passage VI

In successive IQ tests on the same person, the score may vary. Even if given under very similar conditions, identical tests given to the same test-taker will often yield score variations. This is likely due to differences from day-to-day in the test-taker's mood, alertness, physical condition, and other personal factors.

Select *all* correct answers to question 11. Be sure to select *only* correct answers, because credit is given only if all selected answers are correct.

11. Maria is taking an IQ test today. Which of the following factors can influence her score, according to this passage?

   A. She woke up with a headache.

   B. She has not taken an IQ test before.

   C. Her landlady warned her that she's behind on her rent.

12. This passage supports which of the following conclusions?

   A. Other tests are more reliable than IQ tests.

   B. Many educators no longer consider IQ test scores to be important.

   C. People usually take the same IQ test a number of times.

   D. A person who takes the same IQ test three times may get three different scores.

   E. IQ test scores are infallible indicators of intelligence.

Questions 13 through 15 are based on Passage VII.

Passage VII

There are three major sources of frustration. The physical environment provides many instances in which people are blocked from goals. For example, there are fences around swimming pools and washed-out bridges across roads. The social environment is also frustrating. A person may be blackballed by a fraternity or turned down by a highly desirable dating partner. Finally, personal limitations can lead to frustration. For instance, most adolescents desire but cannot achieve some radical change in their bodily attributes to meet a social norm.

13. The writer of the passage above would probably agree that

    A. dating partners are not often highly desirable.
    B. situations that occur in everyday life can cause frustration.
    C. the frustration of personal limitations is the worst frustration of all.
    D. frustration is a problem that can be eliminated.
    E. adolescents are usually less frustrated than are adults.

14. By *blackballed,* the writer means

    A. debarred.
    B. punished.
    C. converted.
    D. arraigned.
    E. commended.

15. Which of the following is one implication of the passage's last sentence?

    A. Personal limitations are no longer frustrating once one has passed adolescence.
    B. A number of social norms are simply not fair.
    C. Some adolescents desire a more socially acceptable appearance.
    D. Personal limitations are not related to the social environment.
    E. Adolescence is the most frustrating period of one's life.

Question 16 is based on Passage VIII.

Passage VIII

To reduce teacher workload, Pacific University is considering going from Monday/Wednesday/Friday classes that are taught for fifty minutes to Monday/Wednesday classes that last seventy-five minutes.

16. Which of the following, if true, would justify this change on the part of Pacific University?

   A.   Students prefer a Monday/Wednesday class schedule.
   B.   It is quicker to prepare two class sessions per week than three.
   C.   Departments hold faculty meetings every Friday.
   D.   There is no shortage of classroom space at Pacific University.
   E.   There are more student absences on Fridays than on any other day of the week.

Practice Set 3: Passages IX, X, XI, XII, and XIII

Questions 17 and 18 are based on Passage IX.

Passage IX

"Vote! Vote! Regardless of how you vote, get out and vote!" All mature Americans are accustomed to being besieged by such pleas. And convincing statistics are advanced that indicate a smaller proportion of Americans vote than citizens of most European countries. _____, making voting accessible remains a bigger chore in most states than it does in most European countries.

17. According to the passage, the response of most Americans to the *get out and vote* message is

   A.   loud complaining about the real difficulty of getting to the polls.
   B.   not as strong as it used to be.
   C.   attention to statistics, which keeps them away from the polls.
   D.   not as strong as the response of many Europeans.
   E.   looked upon with the suspicion that their votes are being "bought."

18. Which of the following best summarizes the passage?

    A.   Americans have become too accustomed to hearing pleas that they vote.

    B.   As voting participation grows, democracy in America will rival that in Europe.

    C.   Although Americans are urged to vote, a large proportion of them do not.

    D.   It is much easier to get out and vote in European countries.

    E.   Voters in Europe rarely need encouragement.

Questions 19 and 20 are based on Passage X.

Passage X

Neurotransmitters are necessary for the functioning of the brain and body. They are chemicals in the brain that activate and regulate a wide range of bodily functions, ranging from breathing to digestion. Some neurotransmitters, such as epinephrine, are excitatory, and can cause stress and sleeplessness when they are elevated. Others, such as serotonin, are inhibitory, and can reduce anxiety and insomnia. Neurotransmitters can also affect emotion: some scientists think that adrenaline, dopamine, and serotonin are all heightened in someone who is falling in love.

19. The author of this passage implies which of the following:

    A.   Bodily functions are not influenced by neurotransmitters.

    B.   Serotonin is a neurotransmitter, but adrenalin and dopamine may not be.

    C.   The body contains neurotransmitters in addition to those in the brain.

    D.   Neurotransmitters have a role in how fast the human heart beats.

    E.   Excitatory neurotransmitters are preferable to inhibitory neurotransmitters.

20. The main point of the passage may be restated as follows:

    A.   Neurotransmitters are the building blocks of life.

    B.   The brain and body cannot function without neurotransmitters.

    C.   Falling in love is a kind of chemical dependence.

    D.   Neurotransmitters can be either excitatory or inhibitory.

    E.   Scientists now know how all neurotransmitters work.

Questions 21 and 22 are based on Passage XI.

Passage XI

Working behind closed doors during the hot summer of 1787, a group of distinguished representatives from twelve of the American states debated, contended, espoused, and compromised until they had produced a proposed new Constitution of the United States of America. When the doors were thrown open and the results of their handiwork revealed to the world, a mixed response followed.

21. Which of the following best describes this passage's content?

    A.   hints of why the new Constitution was not immediately welcomed by all

    B.   account of the problems that challenged the writers of the Constitution

    C.   explanation of the reason that the writers of the Constitution met behind closed doors

    D.   list of reasons that the Constitution received a mixed response

    E.   brief summary of the writing of the U.S. Constitution

Select *all* correct answers to question 22. Be sure to select *only* correct answers, because credit is given only if all selected answers are correct.

22. Which of the following is/are true, according to this passage?

    A.   The representatives did not come to the meeting with all of the same ideas.

    B.   At times, the representatives openly disagreed with one another.

    C.   Representatives championed their own beliefs.

Questions 23 and 24 are based on Passage XI.

Passage XII

There is an expression, "Let the facts speak for themselves." But facts do not speak; people do. Facts are meaningless without interpretation. When people ask the questions "Why?" or "What does it mean?" they want an interpretation or evaluation. Thus, it seems inevitable that people will require philosophies.

23. The writer of this passage implies which of the following?

    A. Most people are full of questions.
    B. Facts are not meaningful if they are independent of people.
    C. Some facts *do* speak for themselves.
    D. Some expressions are more correct than others.
    E. Philosophies are more numerous than facts.

24. The writer suggests that *philosophies* consist of

    A. interpretation or evaluation.
    B. facts speaking for themselves.
    C. persons asking constant questions.
    D. belief in common expressions.
    E. feelings.

Use the excerpted index below from Passage XIII to answer questions 25 and 26.

Passage XIII

25. On what page(s) should one look to find information on a domestic cat's digestive tract?

    A. 10
    B. 20–25
    C. 34–37
    D. 15–17
    E. 11–12

26. Which subject is not covered in the "domestic cats" section of this book?

    A.   fears about black cats

    B.   allergic reactions to cats

    C.   what type of food to feed your cat

    D.   where the English word *cat* originated

    E.   when in history cats first appeared

Section 2: Long Passages – Intermediate Difficulty

Practice Set 1: Long Intermediate Passages I and II

Questions 27 through 30 are based on Passage I.

Passage I

It is characteristic of human beings to make moral judgments with reference to conduct. Some actions are called right or good, and others are said to be bad or wrong. These judgments are made concerning one's own conduct as well as that of other people. They

(5)   may apply to individuals, to groups of people, or even to society as a whole. Moral philosophy is an attempt to understand this phenomenon. It is not an easy task, for it involves many questions that are highly controversial, and these cannot be settled by using the same type of procedure that is employed in the natural sciences.

(10)   Some of the questions that must be given careful consideration include the following: What is the basis for making any distinction between right and wrong? Is morality merely a matter of custom? Is right identical with what people think is right, or is it possible for people to be mistaken in their judgments? What is the role of

(15)   conscience in matters of right and wrong? From what source or sources can knowledge about morals be obtained? Is it the function of ethics to describe how people act, or should it attempt to indicate how they ought to act? If it is the latter, what constitutes the standard by which their conduct can be judged to be right or wrong? Should

(20)   morality be based on motive, consequences, intelligence, or a combination of these? To what extent is morality based on one's feelings?

These and questions of a similar nature are bound to arise in any serious discussion of morality and its problems. The fact that they (25) cannot be answered by means of observation and experiment does not mean we can know nothing about them or that no other method is available for making an intelligent decision with reference to them. One can discover the implications involved in alternative answers and in the light of these, select that answer that makes the most reasonable (30) interpretation of one's experiences.

Intuition is a way of knowing through personal feelings. In the field of ethics, it means that one is made aware of what is right and good by direct and immediate experience, rather than by means of thinking or sense perception. Sometimes it has been identified with the voice of (35) conscience, which is interpreted to mean that God's will is revealed directly to the human soul. Some intuitionists have maintained that we have a special sense for knowing right and wrong, just as we have a sense of sight that reveals colors or a sense of hearing that reveals sounds. Others have recognized that only certain elements of one's (40) moral consciousness are known intuitively. For example, some have taught that, while the general principles of morality are known this way, their application to particular situations is the work of reason. All intuitionists agree that there are at least some elements included in anyone's consciousness of morals that can be known only in this way.

27. The writer of this passage states that questions about morals

    A.   are too numerous to be answered.

    B.   cannot be answered by scientific experiments.

    C.   can only be answered through feelings.

    D.   do not usually provoke arguments between moral philosophers.

    E.   are more relevant to individuals than to society.

28. According to the passage, moral action in a particular situation

    A.   does not usually consider general principles of morality.

    B.   is never detached from our intuitive sense of scientific principles.

    C.   is a concern addressed by ethics rather than by moral philosophy.

    D.   involves neither our sense of sight nor sense of learning.

    E.   may involve both intuition and reason.

29. With reference to the passage, moral philosophy may be summarized in which of the following ways?

    A. a body of knowledge primarily concerned with intuition
    B. the production of a series of questions about moral decisions
    C. the study of moral judgments that influence human conduct
    D. the study of the role of conscience in human behavior
    E. the explanation of human ways of knowing

30. As defined in the passage, intuition is distinguished from

    A. feelings
    B. reason
    C. knowledge
    D. conscience
    E. morality

Questions 31 through 35 are based on Passage II.

Passage II

Probably no concept is more difficult to define or describe in sociology than that of social change. This is true for many reasons. Its causes are often attributable to a variety of social variables, all interacting with one another in a complex pattern. Change can be
(5) analytically distinguished in two separate spheres: social and cultural. Social change focuses primarily on the alterations taking place in the society (such as social relationships, forms of interaction, etc.), while cultural change emphasizes the ongoing transition within the social heritage as various traits and patterns are added or disappear. Change
(10) in one of these areas is likely to bring about change in the other. In reality, it is often impossible to separate the overlap between the two.

Until relatively recently, most sociological research was conducted at a single point in time. The result was a "snapshot" of social phenomena. When the intervention of time is controlled for or
(15) excluded, however, it has been impossible to delineate subtle shifts occurring in the subject under study. In the past, a concentration on discovering the social structure or social order has led to an unconscious bias against the importance of change. The relative lack of knowledge sociologists have had concerning change is being
(20) rectified today, though.

One cause of social change is individuals' behavior. Social deviants have often been in the vanguard of social change. There must, however, also be receptivity of the society toward a particular change for it to take hold. Change that is too threatening for a majority to accept will (25) likely not occur. In this sense, individual behavior is not a sufficient cause, since it alone cannot produce change.

Relative conformists can contribute to change as well. Studies of leaders suggest that those who closely adhere to the group norms will occupy such positions where they can initiate action and most (30) effectively "get things done." It is then possible for those who "play the game by the rules" to be as, or possibly be more, effective than the "rebel" who chooses to accomplish it by a disapproved of means.

But whether the person attempting to introduce change is deviant or conformist, to be most successful that person must:

(35) 1. Cloak the change so that it appears innocent and harmless.

2. Attain a position of relative prestige so that he or she will not be regarded as a "crack-pot."

3. Be aware of the culture into which the change is to be introduced, so that the person will neither offend anyone who can prevent the (40) change, nor cause unintended but disastrous changes in other areas.

It remains true, however, that change is an inescapable, ever-present fact of life. All societies and cultures are continuously changing, although the rate and direction will be different (it is often claimed that the United States has a very high rate of change). The uniqueness (45) of the individual personality, the "imperfections" of all societies and cultures, and human desires to be creative, have new experiences, escape boredom, and realize unmet needs all combine to guarantee modifications in the pattern of social life.

No society is an "island unto itself." Outside forces occasionally act (50) upon a country in such a way as to produce big changes. Many countries have changed radically under the influence of Westernization, sometimes for the better and sometimes not. The use and exchange of technology has lead to a promising globalization of world culture. In other cases, certain outside forces can be so overwhelming that they (55) virtually destroy a given society. For instance, the North American Indians were once in danger of complete eradication because of the wars, disease, and alcoholism that were introduced to them by European colonists.

31. The writer's primary purpose in this passage is to

    A.   survey familiar examples of social change.
    B.   argue that the elimination of change is impossible.
    C.   define and describe social change.
    D.   criticize sociological research.
    E.   compare the value of rebels and conformists.

32. Which of the following does the passage mention as evidence that a society cannot insulate itself from the forces of change?

    A.   the near-elimination of the Indians
    B.   the number of wars that have occurred in the twentieth century
    C.   the threat of interference by social deviants
    D.   the efforts of researchers to influence the cultures they study
    E.   the high rate of change in the United States

33. The criticism of *most sociological research* (line 12) may be stated in which of the following ways?

    A.   By studying a society at a particular moment in time, researchers do not detect social changes that occur over time.
    B.   Sociologists tend to be unaware of the histories of societies.
    C.   Most sociologists prefer slow rather than rapid social change.
    D.   Sociologists' knowledge of change is very weak at present.
    E.   Sociologists would like to pretend that time stands still.

34. The passage allows us to conclude that change will not occur if

    A.   it is perceived to be dangerous.
    B.   it is introduced by a social deviant.
    C.   it includes a respect of group norms.
    D.   a majority does not agree that change is necessary.
    E.   it requires the approval of conformists.

35. We may characterize the writer's attitude toward social change as

    A.   occasional suspicion.
    B.   stiff resistance.
    C.   informed acceptance.
    D.   lack of interest.
    E.   unbridled anger.

348

Practice Set 2: Long Intermediate Passages III and IV

Questions 37 through 39 are based on Passage III.

Passage III

The term *Industrial Revolution* describes the process of economic change from a stable agricultural and commercial society to a modern industrial society dependent on the use of machinery rather than hand tools. While the process was historically a gradual one and not the
(5) sudden change that the word *revolution* suggests, the economic, social, and political results were indeed revolutionary.

The shift from hand tools to machinery was possible in 1769 when James Watt improved on Thomas Newcomen's steam engine of 1708, making it practical for industrial use. At this time, a domestic system
(10) of production (goods produced in many homes and gathered for sale by a middleman) was replaced by a factory system. Coupled with this, technological advances—that first affected the cotton textile industry and the iron and coal industries in England—were equally significant technological improvements in agriculture.

(15) Historically, then, the first stage of the Industrial Revolution began around 1750, gathered momentum after 1815, and extended into the 1870s. During this period, the main source of power continued to be the steam engine, and profits for "capitalists" came from the manufacturing process itself. Soon, however, profits began to come
(20) from the transportation of goods. At this time, coal replaced wood as fuel, and iron machines replaced wooden machines.

The second stage of the Industrial Revolution, which began during the 1870s and extended to 1914, was defined by a new source of power: electricity! The adoption of mass production techniques and the
(25) development of finance capitalism were characteristic of this stage. Now profits were derived from the investment of finance capital rather than from the manufacturing process alone. It was in this second stage that the swift industrialization and urbanization of Western Europe and the United States took place.

36. We may infer which of the following from the writer's discussion of economic change?

   A. Previous to 1760 no significant economic changes had occurred in England.

   B. It is difficult to name the type of change associated with the Industrial Revolution.

   C. Economic change in the twentieth century constituted the third stage of the Industrial Revolution.

   D. The term *revolution* may refer to the results rather than the suddenness of change.

   E. Social and political change is a separate phenomenon from economic change.

37. The writer would probably agree that a *revolutionary* economic change

   A. replaces one dominant system of production with another.

   B. is not recognizable until long after it has occurred.

   C. is not likely to occur in the near future.

   D. is presently threatened.

   E. must now include regions besides Western Europe and the United States.

38. According to the passage, which cause and effect sequence below is correct?

   A. Hand tools led to machinery.

   B. Machinery led to the steam engine.

   C. The transportation of goods led to manufacturing.

   D. Electricity led to mass production.

   E. Urbanization led to electricity.

39. Which of the following is a generalization supported by information in the passage?

   A.   Since the eighteenth century, economic change has been characterized by the development of new sources of profit.

   B.   The Industrial Revolution did not significantly affect social life until the twentieth century.

   C.   At the end of the first stage of the Industrial Revolution, the American standard of living was remarkably high.

   D.   Unlike steam power and electric power, atomic power has not had economic effects.

   E.   The Industrial Revolution contributed to wretched conditions for working people.

Questions 40 through 43 are based on Passage IV.

Passage IV

No one individual influenced the course of public education in the United States during the first half of the twentieth century more than John Dewey. The founder of what has become known as "progressive education," Dewey has been widely acclaimed as one of the greatest

(5)   educators of modern times. To be sure, his ideas have never been universally accepted, and there have been critics who were bitterly opposed to his position. Nevertheless, his influence has been tremendous. For many years, two of the best known institutions for teacher training in this country were dominated by his philosophy. His

(10)   high standing as an educator has been recognized throughout the world, and many countries have sought his counsel and advice. His views were illustrated in the Experimental School at Chicago, which was under his direction, and they have been stated in his book *Democracy and Education,* one of his most popular publications.

(15)   Philosophy and education have been so closely related in Dewey's thought that it is scarcely possible to consider one apart from the other. The spirit of instrumentalism is the guiding factor in both, and the betterment of human society is the goal for each. Both repudiate the idea of authoritarian control, and provide encouragement for

(20)   creative thinking on the part of each individual. Both are democratic in the sense that they advocate equal opportunity for all people to develop the talents and capacities particular to them.

Dewey was critical of many of the ideas and practices that were recurrent in the schools of his day. One of these in particular was the

(25)   "transmissive" concept of education, which conceived of education as
       a process of transmitting to the new generation of students the ideas
       and customs of the older generation. This approach emphasized the
       memorization of content in textbooks, to the extent that the substance
       of the materials could be repeated in an examination. In Dewey's
(30)   opinion, the transmissive method was more of a hindrance than a
       help to real learning, which, for Dewey, meant enabling students to
       think creatively for themselves.

       Recognizing that typical American students were not predominantly
       interested in dry intellectual pursuits, Dewey recommended that
(35)   teachers begin with the interests students did have. He believed that
       people learn primarily by doing things and therefore thought students
       should be given projects on which to work. He thought this would
       stimulate a desire on the parts of students to extend their knowledge
       further, and that it would lead them into new fields related to their
(40)   original subject. Because of the organic relationship fields of
       knowledge have to one another, Dewey thought the scope of students'
       inquiries would be practically boundless. Essentially, information
       gained in response to one's own sense of inquiry, rather than forced on
       them from without, would be more powerful in changing them for the
(45)   better.

40. Which of the following is the most appropriate title for this passage?

    A. Theories of Progressive Education in the Twentieth Century

    B. John Dewey and the Experimental School at Chicago

    C. Creative Thinking and Transmissive Teaching

    D. Dewey's Philosophy of Education

    E. Twentieth-century Progress in Intellectual History

41. According to the passage, John Dewey would probably agree with
which of the following statements?

    A. Learning is not a result of obedient listening.

    B. Students must memorize facts before they can put them to use.

    C. Students should be writing textbooks rather than reading them.

    D. Authoritarian control and creative thinking both have as their
goal the betterment of human society.

    E. The real purpose of education is difficult to determine.

42. We may conclude which of the following about the educational theories and practice that prevailed before Dewey's views became popular?

    A.   They accounted for the weaknesses in Dewey's own education.

    B.   They accounted for the large number of teachers at the time.

    C.   They were especially well known in Chicago.

    D.   They were consistent with the transmissive concept of education.

    E.   They helped to undermine American democracy.

43. The passage implies that a human characteristic that Dewey found absolutely essential to learning was

    A.   love.

    B.   curiosity.

    C.   humor.

    D.   memory.

    E.   obedience.

Practice Set 3: Long Intermediate Passages V and VI

Questions 44 through 47 are based on Passage V.

Passage V

    In the life and works of Plato, Greek philosophy reached one of its highest points of achievement. Plato was one of the greatest minds of all ages, and the influence of his thinking can be seen throughout the entire history of the Western world. Philosophers of every succeeding
(5) generation have studied and interpreted his teachings. People from many different nations and races have written accounts and evaluations of his works, and they will undoubtedly continue to do so for generations yet to come. Plato was not only a great thinker but also a prolific writer, and for this reason it is impossible within a brief
(10) amount of space to give more than a bare outline of a few major events in his life and writings.

    He was born in 427 BCE. He came from an aristocratic family that had for a long time been identified with leadership in the city of Athens. He was named Aristocles, but because of his broad shoulders,

(15)   high forehead, and success as an athlete, he was given the nickname "Plato," and it is by this name that he has become known to posterity.

His early education began under the supervision of well-chosen tutors who guided his instruction in the elementary disciplines, including gymnastics, music, reading, writing, and the study of
(20)   numbers. After reaching the age of eighteen, he spent two years in military training, during which time he gave special emphasis to the development and proper care of the body. This was followed by a more advanced period of study in which he gained familiarity with the earlier schools of Greek philosophy. He received instruction also from
(25)   several of the more prominent Sophists, the early rhetoricians who were especially active at that time. Finally, Plato spent several years as a pupil of Socrates, whose influence on his own thinking outweighed that attained from any other source.

Plato was ill at the time of Socrates' death, and this prevented him
(30)   from being present when a group of close friends made their last visit to the prison where Socrates was incarcerated (for supposedly "corrupting" the youth in his teaching academy), and where he spent his last hours. Because Socrates had been put to death under the auspices of the Athenian government and Plato was known as one of
(35)   his most devoted disciples, Plato felt that it was expedient to leave Athens for a time. He went at first to Megara, where he carried on conversations with Euclid (the "Father of Geometry"). He then made extensive journeys to Egypt, Cyrene, Crete, and southern Italy, thus obtaining direct contact with Pythagorean, Heraclitian, and Eleatic
(40)   philosophies.

About 390 BCE, when Plato was about forty years old, he undertook an experiment in government. He had been interested in political affairs from the time of his early youth, and his observations had convinced him that only persons who are well-educated should be
(45)   entrusted with the power to rule over others. At the coast of the island of Sicily, a friend and pupil by the name of Dion urged him to undertake the education of Dionysius, known as the tyrant of Syracuse. Dionysius appeared willing to take instruction from Plato, and this made it possible for Plato's theory of government to be tried
(50)   out under actual conditions. The experiment was unsuccessful. Dionysius was not an apt pupil, and when Plato rebuked him for his stupidity, the tyrant retaliated by having Plato put in chains and sentenced to death. Dion used his influence to get the sentence changed, and Plato was made a slave. Soon afterward, a fellow
(55)   philosopher purchased his freedom, and Plato was allowed to return to Athens.

44. The writer of the passage would probably agree that Plato's *experiment in government* (final paragraph) in Syracuse was

   A. an unwise project from the start.
   B. more appropriate to the exploits of a youth than to a forty-year-old.
   C. an act of great courage but not great wisdom.
   D. unsuccessful only because Plato was a tactless teacher.
   E. a major event in the life of the Greek philosopher.

45. By *expedient* (line 35), the writer of the passage means

   A. considerate.
   B. obtuse.
   C. politic.
   D. adventurous.
   E. shameful.

46. The passage creates which of the following impressions of Plato's education and intellectual interests?

   A. His instruction as a youth was limited, but the interests he developed later were broad and varied.
   B. His education provided a rich and comprehensive background, and his later intellectual pursuits were extensive.
   C. Deficiencies in his early education were counterbalanced by his extensive travel to intellectual centers of the ancient world.
   D. He was too heavily influenced by Socrates in his youth, and he became a mature philosopher only because of Socrates' death.
   E. Despite his lack of traditional education, he was able to create a philosophy that stands as one of the greatest of all time

47. Which of the following statements strengthens the conclusion that Plato was a unique individual?

   A. He was a philosopher in the ancient world.
   B. He was born before the birth of Christ.
   C. During his life, he was both an aristocrat and a slave.
   D. He traveled widely.
   E. He had a great interest in politics.

Questions 48 through 51 are based on Passage VI.

Passage VI

No event in modern history so completely shocked the world as did the French Revolution, in which the radical cry of "Liberty! Equality! Fraternity!" for the masses challenged the protected interests of the privileged few. The effects were profound, for Europe and the world
(5) would never be the same. The French Revolution began as an attempt by the leaders of the industrial and commercial classes to sweep aside the injustices and abuses of the Old Regime. It soon swept away the French monarchy, yet it also allied all of Europe against the rising tide of French republicanism.

(10) Newly formed citizen armies in France became the first in modern history. The new warfare was a rapid movement of large armies carrying small supplies and living off the land. These citizen armies gave the common man—formerly a "nobody" among the lowly masses—the opportunity to take to the battlefield on the side of
(15) justice, and the youth of France poured into the republican armies, spurred on by the stirring "La Marseillaise," an anthem celebrating revolution. Columns of professional French and foreign infantrymen, supported by massive artillery, were rolled back, and the revolutionaries were able to penetrate far beyond the farthest advance of Louis XIV's
(20) troops. At this time, a great wave of enthusiasm for France and the idea of a republic swept the French people. There was to be no compromising of republican principles at home or abroad. At home, the hated royalists were to be stamped out, and abroad, France would become the protector and backer of all revolutionaries.

(25) However, due to the excesses of the Reign of Terror at home (which involved mass executions of those against revolution), and a lack of capable and responsible leadership, French national morale began to falter. The monarchical powers formed new coalitions to suppress the upstart republic, and the revolutionaries' momentum dissolved when
(30) they were placed on the defensive. The cause of republicanism seemed lost. It was at this crucial period that Napoleon Bonaparte— acknowledged by both critics and admirers as the world's greatest military genius—appeared on the scene. Calling himself the "Son of the Revolution," he relentlessly sought fame on the battlefield and through
(35) the formation of the "First French Empire." Though he was accused of betraying the republic, many believe that he actually saved France from the forces of monarchical reaction for decades, allowing the progressive theme of the French Revolution to be carried to all corners of Europe.

48. We may infer which of the following statements from the passage?

    A. Military strategy in the twentieth century was modeled on Napoleonic principles.

    B. Before the Revolution, the citizen armies of Europe were less powerful.

    C. The modern world was influenced by the French Revolution.

    D. Professional armies are never a match for citizen armies.

    E. Kindness was a virtue much practiced during the French Revolution.

49. The passage suggests that if Napoleon had not taken over the leadership of France,

    A. the Reign of Terror would not have occurred.

    B. the concept of "military genius" might still be foreign to us.

    C. a leader would have arisen out of the citizen armies of France.

    D. the causes of the Revolution, in their weakened state, would have failed.

    E. liberty and equality would never have become strong national virtues in countries outside of France.

50. According to the passage, which of the following is true about French republicanism during the Revolution?

    A. It began as the nobility's effort to strengthen the Old Regime's forces.

    B. Napoleon introduced it at a time when the Revolution's causes were faltering badly.

    C. It stood in opposition not only to monarchical forces inside of France but also to armies from other European countries.

    D. It provided the foundation for beliefs associated today with the Republican Party of the United States.

    E. It depended on the services of professional armies because citizens were occupied with political demonstrations rather than military activities.

51. Which of the following can be said about Napoleon, according to the passage?

    A.   There have been mixed reactions to his role in French history.

    B.   Napoleon was responsible for the Reign of Terror.

    C.   He clearly betrayed the republic.

    D.   He restored the Old Regime.

    E.   He replaced the First French Empire with a citizen government.

Practice Set 4: Long Intermediate Passages VII and VIII

Questions 52 through 55 are based on Passage VII.

Passage VII

     What is history? Is it a record of what has actually happened, or is it merely what a majority thinks has happened? Can history be rewritten, or is it something that remains fixed for all time to come? What are historical facts? Do they exist in historians' minds when they are writing, or do
(5) historical facts belong to past events? Philosophy of history is a serious attempt to provide adequate answers to these and other related questions. And yet proffered answers to such questions vary depending on the philosopher. This is because no one is in possession of the final or absolute truth about history, and it is impossible for anyone to do more than
(10) formulate the view that seems to him or her to be most nearly satisfactory at the time. While there seems to be general agreement about what is meant when one speaks of the historical process as a whole, there is a great deal of disagreement about most historical phenomena.

     Skepticism concerning any meaningful interpretation of historical
(15) events has appeared at various times and places in the history of Western thought. It has not always taken the same form, for there are several different ways in which the essential idea may be expressed. One of these forms, known as historical nihilism, is an outright denial of any meaningful pattern or purpose in the historical process. Another form,
(20) frequently referred to as historical skepticism, neither affirms nor denies that historical events have particular meanings, but insists that it is impossible for anyone to fully know or understand these meanings. A third form, called historical subjectivism, asserts that any meaningful interpretation of historical events is something that exists only in the
(25) mind of the historian, and does not refer to anything external to this human mind. All of these forms are opposed to the idea that there is a cosmic force or power that directs the course of human events.

52. The writer introduces which of the following possibilities in the passage?

   A.   Facts may exist only in the mind of the historian conveying them as such.

   B.   Although historians and philosophers may not be able to agree on which particular facts are true, they find it relatively easy to agree on the meaning of a particular series of events.

   C.   Responsible history is never influenced by the historian's point of view.

   D.   Those who know the absolute truth about history find that it is a meaningless subject.

   E.   Meaningful events in an individual's everyday life are unlikely to ever be regarded as "historical."

53. Which statement below might have come from a historical nihilist, as defined in the passage (lines 18–19)?

   A.   We cannot claim that the events that preceded the Civil War caused it or even might have caused it.

   B.   The victory of the Northern armies in 1865 really began with events that occurred as early as 1863.

   C.   As a Confederate sympathizer, I view the conclusion of the Civil War as a victory for the South rather than a defeat.

   D.   There are three clear reasons that General Lee's forces were eventually overcome.

   E.   The defect of the South is analogous in some ways to the defeat of the British during the American Revolution.

54. One of the characteristics that historical nihilism, historical skepticism, and historical subjectivism share in common is

   A.   their concern for the importance of meaningful historical interpretation.

   B.   their respect for the power of the human mind to make experience meaningful.

   C.   their proposal that although facts may be controversial, we must accept the most reasonable ones.

   D.   their claim that all historical reporting must be scrutinized carefully for truth value.

   E.   their disbelief in the power of some superhuman force or "fate" to influence history.

55. Which of the following is one purpose the passage fulfills?

    A.   to argue for historical skepticism as the most reasonable view of historical events

    B.   to raise more questions than it answers

    C.   to repeat the same question in many different ways

    D.   to introduce some famous historical skeptics

    E.   to propose that a general agreement about the historical process is in order

Questions 56 through 60 are based on Passage VIII.

Passage VIII

The railroads played a key role in the settlement of the West. They provided relatively easy access to the region for the first time, and caused many farmers to settle there. Even though most recognize that the railroads played an essential role in extending the American

(5)   frontier and helping to achieve national unity, the railroads have actually been criticized for their part in settling the West so rapidly that economic unrest was the result.

The real tragedy, however, of the rapid settlement of the Great Plains in particular was the shameful way Native Americans were

(10) treated.

Threatened with the destruction of their entire way of life, the "Indians" (as they were then called) fought back savagely against the "white man's" incursion. Justice was almost entirely on the Indians' side. The land was clearly theirs, and in many cases a treaty negotiated

(15) with the federal government legally certified their entitlement to it. The Indians, however, lacked the military force and political power to protect their rights. Not only did settlers encroach on the Indians' hunting grounds, they also rapidly destroyed the Indians' principal means of subsistence: the buffalo. It has been estimated that some 15

(20) million buffalo roamed the plains in the 1860s, but by 1869, the herd had been cut in half, and by the 1880s, all but eliminated. Sadly, buffalo were often killed merely for sport.

The plains Indians were considered to be different from the Indians the English colonists encountered on the Atlantic coast. Mounted on

(25) horses descended from those brought by the Spanish to Mexico many years before, typical plains Indians were fierce warriors who could shoot arrows with surprising accuracy while galloping at top speed. Although they quickly adapted themselves to the use of the rifle, the

(30) Indians were not equal to the firepower of the United States army and thus were doomed to defeat.

(35) In theory at least, the government tried to be fair to the Indians, but all too often the federal agents were either too indifferent or corrupt to carry out the government's promises conscientiously. The army frequently ignored the Indian Bureau and failed to coordinate its policies with the civilians who were nominally in charge of Indian affairs. The settlers hated and feared the Indians and wanted them exterminated.

56. Which of the following characteristics of the passage suggests that abuse of Indians is a more significant topic for the writer than the beneficial role of the railroads?

A. the statement that *the railroads have actually been criticized for their part in . . . [causing] economic unrest* (lines 5–7)

B. the amount of discussion devoted to the abuse of the Indians

C. the reliance on statistical details in the second paragraph

D. discussion of the power of the Plains Indians

E. the perception that achievement of national unity was one of the services the railroad performed

57. The writer's attitude toward the treatment of American Indians by settlers is one of

A. qualified regret.

B. violent anger.

C. strong disapproval.

D. objective indifference.

E. unfair bias.

58. The writer implies which of the following about the forces at work during the settlement of the Great Plains?

A. The federal government represented the moral use of law.

B. Justice was overcome by military firepower.

C. Attempts by the government to be fair were rejected by the Indians.

D. The settlers' hatred and fear was offset by the Indians' attempts at kindness.

E. The Indians and the settlers shared a sporting interest in the hunting of buffalo.

59. What is meant by the word *incursion* at line 13?

    A.   injustice

    B.   ineptness

    C.   intrusion

    D.   inaction

    E.   infirmity

60. What is the point of the comparison between plains Indians and the Atlantic coast Indians (paragraph 3)?

    A.   The Atlantic coast Indians were not as abused by white settlers.

    B.   Because they were considerably better warriors than the Atlantic coast Indians, the plains Indians were more of a match for the United States military.

    C.   If Indians such as those on the Atlantic coast had populated the plains, the bloodshed of the white settlement would have been lessened.

    D.   The Indians encountered by English colonists posed no violent threat to the colonists.

    E.   The Atlantic coast Indians were unfamiliar with horses.

Practice Set 5: Paired Passages IX and X

Questions 61 through 65 are based on two passages for IX (1 and 2).

Two Passages for IX

Passage 1

Social networking has become an umbrella term for the many ways that we stay in touch with one another through technology. It includes the use of email, texting, and "tweeting" through Twitter, as well as networking sites and tools such as Facebook and LinkedIn. Through

(5)   social networking, we can communicate with people we've never met in person, but who share our interests, ideologies, and values. In 2009, 2.5 billion text messages were sent per day in the United States. This already astounding number continues to increase, indicating that social networking is becoming a way of life. We can find old friends

(10) and reconnect with distant relatives. We can feature our credentials and career aspirations to potential employers. We can get answers to our health problems, and learn about virtually any subject we wish. Political candidates also now rely on Internet campaigning to increase their chances of winning public office. Many speak of Barack Obama's

(15) presidential campaign as the first to make full and successful use of online campaigning. This entire way of life has given new meaning to the word *community,* which is now much more than just a geographic location. In fact, a community can be any collection of individuals who regularly communicate with one another, whether they live across

(20) the street, across the country, or across the world. Through social networking, we have truly become a global village.

Passage 2

At the beginning of the twenty-first century, Robert Putnam argued in *Bowling Alone* that in-person social intercourse was declining in the United States. His perspective has reinforced the view that our

(25) increasing use of technology is drawing us away from one another, causing a decline in membership in civic and social organizations, and reducing our participation in the discussions and debates that are crucial to a healthy democracy. Putnam reinforces the concerns of many of us who think that more time spent writing emails and surfing

(30) the Internet means less time on genuine human contact. An email, text message, or tweet is a "disembodied" representation of a living, breathing human being, and can never substitute for real conversation, and real face-to-face communication with the people who matter to our lives. While a phone call was once the standard to acknowledge

(35) our relationships with others, say, to send birthday wishes to a relative or friend, a Facebook or text message wish is fast becoming the new norm. Online education is also a poor substitute for the face-to-face classroom, where the give and take of real people's class discussion in real time makes learning exciting.

61. One example in Passage 2 that does not appear in Passage 1 is

   A.   email.

   B.   the Internet.

   C.   text messaging.

   D.   online education.

   E.   tweeting.

62. The writers of Passage 1 and Passage 2 disagree on the value of

   A. democracy.
   B. debate.
   C. community.
   D. time.
   E. social intercourse via technology.

63. The position of each writer is revealed through the use of

   A. *we* and *us*
   B. *way of life* and *genuine human contact*
   C. *one another* and *in-person*
   D. *community* and *democracy*
   E. *interests, ideologies, and values* and *living, breathing human being*

64. Each writer deals in different ways with

   A. the connotation of social networking.
   B. the denotation of social networking.
   C. human nature.
   D. media theory.
   E. the transition from the twentieth to the twenty-first century.

65. Understanding each of these passages would require

   A. a Twitter account.
   B. general familiarity with common forms of social networking.
   C. experience with both civic organizations and Facebook friends.
   D. a well-developed opinion on the value of social networking.
   E. background in social psychology or sociology.

Questions 66 through 70 are based on Passage X.

Passage X

The study of human population is known as demography. Demography as a branch of sociology concerns itself with three variables: fertility, mortality, and migration. Demography is also focused on the composition and distribution of population and its

(5)   allied characteristics. At a larger level, it encompasses the relationships of nations with regard to important population variables; for instance, a nation may be concerned with the rapid increase of population in another country if this increase is perceived to bring about military superiority of that country.

(10)   The study of population must above all involve social and cultural factors as an integral part of its analysis. Many population experts prior to World War II learned from bitter experience that it was not sufficient to construct future population estimates from antecedent trends. A host of very low estimates (some of which actually predicted

(15)   a decline in population by 1970) were proffered in the late 1930s that proved to be very far from the mark. The subsequent "baby boom" in the years after the war proved long lasting and pervasive, such that it was not until 1957 that fertility began to decline again.

Fertility is generally measured by crude birth rates, which consist

(20)   of the number of births occurring in a given year per thousand people. As an overall figure and a quick synopsis of the general fertility in a population, the crude birth rate is an acceptable measure to use. It can be misleading, however, when comparisons are made from one country to another. For example, it is entirely possible for country A to have a

(25)   higher crude birth rate compared to country B, but at the same time have a lower rate of actual births than country B. In essence, country A could have a larger proportion of its population in the childbearing ages, while country B does not; yet, the women of country A in the childbearing ages may have a *lower* rate of childbirth in comparison to

(30)   the women of childbearing ages in country B, who make up a smaller proportion of the country's population.

Mortality is also measured by a crude rate, termed the *death rate*. As with crude birth rates, there is room for error in the meaning of such statistics. One country can be healthier than another but have a

(35)   higher crude death rate, since a greater proportion of its population is at an advanced age. To rectify such ambiguities, age-specific birth and death rates have been introduced, especially when comparisons between countries are being made. For example, a comparative age-specific birth rate would be the number of births per thousand women

(40)   aged fifteen to forty-four (childbearing ages). Such considerations control for the effect of differential age distributions from one society to the next.

66. The passage implies which of the following general conclusions about demography?

    A.   Although demographers are concerned with the variables of fertility, mortality, and migration, other variables are irrelevant.

    B.   For a demographer, the terms *birth rate* and *death rate* require further definition that specifies the methods of measurement and analysis.

    C.   Population estimates being prepared now are likely to be absolutely reliable predictors of population change.

    D.   Demography was a crude science prior to World War II.

    E.   Sociologists are not, as a rule, interested in demography.

67. A demographer who wishes to correct for possible inaccuracies that result when measuring crude birth rates may do which of the following?

    A.   compare the birth rate with the death rate

    B.   check the estimates of population prepared by earlier analysts

    C.   use a sample larger than a thousand people

    D.   specify a particular age group in the population being measured

    E.   first perform a quick synopsis of the general fertility in the population

68. Which of the following is the most appropriate substitute for the use of the word *rectify* at line 36?

    A.   correct

    B.   revise

    C.   help

    D.   advance

    E.   question

69. We may infer from the passage that a nation wishing to create a perception of military superiority might do which of the following?

    A.   commission a demographic study of enemy nations

    B.   calculate the age-specific death rate that occurs in its armed forces

    C.   encourage an increase in its population

    D.   look skeptically on demographic predictions of population growth

    E.   offer greater financial benefits to those who join the armed forces

70. According to the passage, which factor should not even be taken into account when it comes to predicting the future rate of population growth?

    A. the crude birth rate
    B. a country's military interests
    C. the past
    D. patterns of migration
    E. a present decline in fertility

Section 3: Longer Passages – Challenging

Practice Set 1: Passages I, II, and III

Questions 71 through 76 are based on Passage I.

Passage I

Gnosticism was both a religious and a philosophical movement. It did not, however, have its origin in Christian times, nor were its teachings confined to Christian circles. In many respects it resembled the mystery religions, given that its main concern was salvation from (5) the present (essentially "evil") world. Salvation could not be accomplished through human beings' efforts alone, but relied also on the aid of supernatural powers. Because the Pauline interpretation of Christianity resembled the mystery cults in so many ways, some of the Gnostics found it congenial to their way of thinking and came to (10) regard themselves as Christians. Two of the more prominent members of this group were Valentinus and Marcion, both of whom lived in the city of Rome. Among the beliefs the Gnostics generally accepted are:

(1) The universe was conceived as a thoroughgoing dualistic affair in which matter and spirit, good and evil, light and darkness were not (15) only opposite in nature, but also forever at war with one another. The dualism went somewhat beyond that of Plato and was more like that characterized in Persian Zoroastrianism.

(2) The Gnostics were pessimistic with reference to the present world. There was no hope for its becoming any better, and salvation (20) meant an escape from it. Salvation was not for the flesh, but only the spirit.

(3) Like the Neo-Platonists, the Gnostics could not accept the idea of a supreme God coming into direct contact with degraded matter. They therefore developed the idea of a series of emanations, which they called

(25)   *aeons,* that were said to have originated with God but decreased in potentiality as they moved further away from God. At some point in the past, one *aeon* was far enough away from God to have contact with matter, and it was this *aeon* that brought the world into existence.

(30)   (4) In this world (considered to be a combination of matter and spirit), some souls are touched by sparks of divinity that make them long to return to the spiritual realm. These souls do not feel at home on the earthly plane. They are pilgrims and strangers waiting for a better kind of existence.

(35)   (5) *Gnosis,* the Greek word for *knowledge* from which the term *Gnosticism* is derived, stands for a special kind of knowledge essential for salvation. This knowledge is not obtained through the process of thinking, nor is it derived directly from the senses. It is a kind of intuitive knowledge imparted to the believer from a supernatural source.

(40)   (6) The Gnostics were not in complete agreement among themselves concerning the proper methods to be followed in preparation for salvation. Some of them advocated a strict type of asceticism to overcome the demands of the flesh. Others advocated an opposite course: yielding completely to the demands of the flesh on the grounds that the flesh was unimportant and the only thing that mattered was
(45)   the life of the spirit.

71. According to the passage, the Gnostics' concept of the universe in terms of dualisms is represented by each of the following pairs of terms *except*

   A.   matter/spirit.
   B.   good/evil.
   C.   faith/reason.
   D.   light/darkness.
   E.   earthly life/after life.

72. The writer implies which of the following about the relationship of Gnosticism to other philosophies and religions?

   A.   Gnosticism stands apart as a unique system of beliefs.
   B.   Christianity and Gnosticism are not easily compared.
   C.   Gnosticism is comparable in some respects to both Greek philosophy and Persian Zoroastrianism.
   D.   Roman mythology was the basis of beliefs of some of the early Gnostics, especially Valentinus and Marcion.
   E.   Modern religions have ignored Gnosticism completely.

73. Which of the following examples from the passage best illustrates the tendency of some Gnostics to prepare for salvation in a different manner from others?

    A.   different attitudes toward the demands of the flesh

    B.   adaptation of the Pauline interpretation of Christianity

    C.   disagreements between Valentinus and Marcion

    D.   disagreements among the Gnostics about the definition of knowledge

    E.   the tendency of some Gnostics to prefer earthly existence to spiritual salvation

74. The Gnostic version of the creation of the world may be summarized as follows:

    A.   God created matter immediately and directly, but this was his only direct contact with matter.

    B.   Because enduring contact with matter was impossible for the deity, his representative created the world.

    C.   An emanation from God rather than God himself created the matter of our earthly abode.

    D.   In a duel between matter and spirit, matter was victorious and the earth was thus created.

    E.   The world was created by the forces of evil and remains completely separate from the supreme deity.

75. The passage supplies information that would answer which of the following questions?

    A.   What was the attitude of the Gnostics toward the earthly world?

    B.   What were the practices of the mystery cults?

    C.   To what extent were Gnostic beliefs approved by early Christians?

    D.   Are there any traces of Gnosticism in the modern world?

    E.   Why did Christianity become a more popular religion than Gnosticism?

76. Which of the following characteristics of Gnosticism is most emphasized in the passage?

    A.   the Gnostics' adaptation of Neo-Platonism

    B.   the concern of the Gnostics with salvation

    C.   the definition and origin of *gnosis*

    D.   the Gnostic distinction between three types of knowledge

    E.   the influence of the more prominent members of the Gnostic religion

Questions 77 through 82 are based on two Passages for II (A and B).

Two Comparative Passages for II

Passage A

A manager's function in a large corporation is to handle unanticipated problems. The manager must define the problem, generate possible solutions, come to a decision, and take appropriate action. Some of these steps may be delegated to other executive
(5) personnel, but the manager always remains in a position of final authority within the organizational structure. Manager training often begins with job rotation through the key departments of the company, providing an overview of company functions and an assessment of where the management trainee might best fit. In some cases,
(10) managerial skills are developed through "problem-centered group training," which stresses the "casework method." In this approach, senior management may hold problem-solving interviews with personnel psychologists, who involve employees in role-playing and group discussion. Such activities are designed to make managers more
(15) sensitive to the problems and feelings of the company's workers.

For both managers and their subordinates, fatigue effects show up in decreased output, increased errors, or both. Decreased output occurs when employees doing jobs that require physical effort or sustained accuracy begin to take longer to do as much work as they
(20) did at some earlier point in time. Increased errors occur when workers, who have no control over the rate at which they work, are pushed to the point of fatigue. This decrease in work performance can best be overcome by offering employees sufficient breaks and, in some cases, a shortened workday.

Passage B

(25)　　Managers are becoming obsolete. This is because the workplace has shifted in recent years to a team-based organizational structure with a minimal emphasis on "the boss." This shift has resulted from Asian, largely Japanese, influence on the efficiency, accuracy, and cost-effectiveness of production, distribution, and innovation.
(30)　American approaches to leadership have become more focused on how people work together than on a "command and control" approach that typically results in greater employee dissatisfaction, employees' desire to avoid work, a decrease in productivity, greater fatigue, and a higher incidence of injuries and accidents.

(35)　　The team-based workplace is not perfect but can be more effective because it unites employees in a common goal and doles out rewards and promotions to those who work most effectively as members of a group, rather than those who are best at ordering others around. In this model, there is a hierarchy of managers and subordinates, but the
(40)　most effective, well-regarded, and well-rewarded managers are those who roll up their sleeves and are visible contributors to the team, rather than invisible inhabitants of the corner office. Of course, this model requires a company owner who sees that such an organizational structure has a positive impact on the bottom line, realizing that the
(45)　company that is happier is also more productive and profitable.

77. Which of the following titles best describes both passages considered together as a whole?

    A.   Varieties of Fatigue in the Corporate Workplace

    B.   The Manager's Overview of Company Functions

    C.   The Corporate Functions of People and Managers

    D.   Managerial Control Over Human Dynamics

    E.   Contrasting Approaches to Management and Productivity

78. The writers of both passages would agree about which of the following statements?

    A.   Fatigue in the workplace is a problem.

    B.   Managers exist to solve problems.

    C.   The whole is greater than the sum of its parts.

    D.   American workplaces are in the midst of a radical transition.

    E.   Good work should be rewarded.

79. The likely purpose for each passage is

    A.   a critique of capitalism.

    B.   company evaluation.

    C.   employee orientation.

    D.   leadership training.

    E.   the appreciation of managers.

80. The writer of Passage B would tell the writer of Passage A that a shortened workday will not be necessary for employees if

    A.   the team makes the products quickly enough so that a shortened workweek is possible.

    B.   they are energized throughout the day through teamwork and recognized productivity.

    C.   the company psychologist is able to effectively treat those who are most fatigued.

    D.   the manager is sensitive to employees' needs.

    E.   the need for output is adjusted to match the team's capacity.

81. The primary purpose of Passage A's writer is to

    A.   present information that any manager with experience would be expected to know.

    B.   suggest that workers are treated with less respect than managers.

    C.   survey a number of aspects relevant to working in a company.

    D.   point out similarities and differences between managers and workers.

    E.   argue that all managers must be good psychologists.

82. According to the information given, each writer's personal experience as a manager is

    A.   more likely than unlikely.

    B.   unlikely but possible.

    C.   implied but not explicit.

    D.   an obvious element of both passages.

    E.   unknown.

Questions 83 through 88 are based on Passage III.

Passage III

In most societies, culture is transmitted through kin groups, the network of social relationships that play a central role in the lives of human beings. While membership in family groups is pre-determined (even if not always welcome), membership in others is voluntary. In (5) stratified societies—in which there is a vast range of persons belonging to differing socio-economic, ideological, cultural, and religious groups—voluntary associations are key. Voluntary associations are prevalent in the United States, for instance.

In Samoa, on the other hand, many associations are pre-determined. (10) For instance, young males who are both unmarried and untitled automatically belong to an association called *Amauga* that virtually constitutes a communal labor force. And young girls, as well as wives of untitled males, belong to the *Aualuma*. Titled males belong to the *Fono,* an association with ritualistic and political functions. Here, (15) members of an age-set share mutual rights and obligations throughout their lives. They support and help each other. For example, a group of adolescent boys will form an age-set of "warriors." After the boys marry and establish a family, thus becoming responsible members of the community, their specific age-set will function as a political unit, (20) and they become a council of elders who serve political ends. Age-sets are also prevalent in East African pastoral societies.

In such societies, marriage tends to be endogamous, meaning that it is confined to the tribe or social class, with membership in a class being inherited. Membership in a particular social class must, however, (25) also be validated for it to be in effect. (It should be noted that upward social mobility may be rewarded in some societies, while downward mobility never is.) Among the general characteristics of a social class, in addition to the fact that status is ranked and that each class has its own subculture, are the possession of a dialect, as well as distinctive (30) clothing, housing, and etiquette. A social class thus molds an individual's behavior patterns and serves as a reference for judging other people's conduct.

Some societies have a system of outcasts whose low-ranked members are forced into endogamy and have a limited choice of (35) occupations. An example is the Japanese *Eta* group, whose members are required to live in segregated areas, slums, or suburbs, and to perform undesirable menial jobs. Like the pariahs of India, *Etas,* because excluded from the recognized castes within society, are not even considered worthy of human company.

(40) The Indian caste system is complicated by the vagueness of the caste structures and the simultaneous specificity of the local sub-castes, or *jatis*. Because a totality of all Indian castes does not exist in any concrete form, castes are thought of as loose reference groups, almost in the way that social class is a loose classification in U.S.
(45) culture.

In some totemic cultures (whose members are believed to be linked to the supernatural spirit of an animal or plant), affiliation in a totemic group may be inherited unilineally. In some parts of Australia, for instance, one is a member of a specific totem on the basis of where
(50) one's mother was walking at the time she believes conception occurred. Totemic groups are often exogamous (taking on associations from *outside* the tribe or caste).

83. The passage supports which of the following statements?

A. Members of the same class are unlikely to share similar tastes in clothes.

B. No society admires upper-class members who join the lower class.

C. Group membership cannot be based on kinship.

D. Behavior patterns provide little evidence of an individual's social class.

E. Individuals who claim membership in a particular class tend to be believed.

84. The passage's content is best summarized in which of the following ways?

A. An individual who belongs to one social group is prohibited from joining another.

B. From Polynesia to India and Australia, kin groups are the sources of culture.

C. Different systems of association prevail across different societies.

D. The laws of association that define any society are present in many regions.

E. Social groups in every culture are similar to the Indian caste system.

85. The writer implies that the members of the same age-set in an East African pastoral society

    A. tend to model their behavior after the elders in their society.

    B. are not representative of the behavior of age-sets in other parts of the world.

    C. may either accept or reject the social responsibilities for which they are eligible.

    D. are more likely to quarrel with each other than to cooperate.

    E. will serve a series of social and communal functions as they grow older.

86. Which of the following does the passage mention as evidence that the members of a pseudo-caste are forced into living only with members of their own kind?

    A. Samoan Amaugas

    B. Japanese Etas

    C. Totemic Australians

    D. East African elders

    E. American fraternities

87. The discussion of associations that operate in Samoa best supports which of the following statements?

    A. Every life task in Samoa is connected with a particular association.

    B. Unmarried males are always untitled as well.

    C. Unmarried males are prohibited from expressing political opinions.

    D. One of the functions an association may serve is sexual segregation.

    E. There is no association for the daughters and wives of titled males.

88. Which of the following is true of the Indian caste system, according to the passage?

    A. The sub-castes are difficult to define.

    B. India is the most famous example of a caste society.

    C. The structure of the castes is neither simple nor clear.

    D. Upward mobility is impossible.

    E. Individuals who belong to a sub-caste are often outcastes as well.

Practice Set 2: Passages IV and V

Questions 89 through 94 are based on Passage IV.

Passage IV

"Money" is anything that can be used to purchase goods and services, and to discharge debts. The money supply in today's United States consists of currency (paper money), coins, and demand deposits (checking accounts). Currency and coins are government-created
(5)   money, whereas demand deposits are bank-created money. Of these three constituents of our money supply, demand deposits are by far the most important. Thus, most of our money supply is invisible, intangible, and abstract. At the same time, the two most important attributes that money must possess in a modern, credit-based economy
(10)   are acceptability and stability. Members of a given population must not only agree on a particular form of money, but must also recognize a particular form of money as having a particular value.

The four functions that money often serves are (1) standard of value, (2) medium of exchange, (3) store of value, and (4) standard of
(15)   deferred payment. In a modern, specialized economy such as that in the U.S., the standard of value and the medium of exchange are most important. Although it is agreed that the value of money has fallen in the United States over time, there is not a single explanation for this phenomenon. Most economists today believe that rising prices, called
(20)   inflation, is best explained by the matter of supply and demand.

Most of our presently circulating coins are credit money or token money, since the market value of metal in the coin is usually worth less than the face (or mint) value of the coins. Gresham's Law—that bad money tends to drive out good money—explains why coins with a
(25)   greater market value than mint value stop circulating. Most of the paper money in the United States consists of Federal Reserve notes; the remaining minor types of paper money are called treasury currency. Demand deposits are bank-created money, the supply of which is limited for any single bank to the amount of its total legal
(30)   reserves. If a bank lends more than the amount of its excess reserves, it will have an adverse clearing balance. Modern fractional reserve

banking grew out of the experiences of early goldsmiths who found that 100 percent reserves were not needed. With a reserve requirement ratio of, say, 20 percent, the banking system as a whole could expand (35) its demand deposits in a 5:1 ratio to its reserves. If some money leaks out of the banking system, its coefficient of credit expansion is reduced from the 5:1 ratio indicated above.

The Federal Reserve, or Fed, is a central bank whose prime function is to monitor and control the nation's money supply and credit through (40) monetary policy; in the attempt to stifle inflation, promote economic growth with high employment; and help with the sale of government bonds. It is not clear that the Fed has always understood its powers and purposes. It has had much more success in helping with the sale of government bonds and in performing its service functions than in (45) promoting growth and maintaining stability.

89. From the writer's discussion of the importance of acceptability and stability (lines 8–12), we may infer which of the following?

A. Over time, the relative importance of certain attributes of money changes.

B. The phrase *legal tender* on currency may be disregarded.

C. The evolution of money and monetary institutions is drawing to a close.

D. Acceptability and stability are important in a modern credit economy.

E. The modern money supply is in danger of becoming unstable.

90. One of the writer's purposes in this passage is to

A. explain the misuse of money that results from misunderstanding the economy.

B. argue that Gresham's Law needs to be revised.

C. question whether the national money supply is really related to the Fed's actions.

D. explain important aspects of the U.S. money system.

E. survey the definitions of money that were popular with the early goldsmiths.

91. In saying that *most of our money supply is invisible, intangible, and abstract* (lines 7–8), the writer is referring to the fact that

    A.   banks are often reluctant to supply currency and coin in exchange for a check.

    B.   checking accounts are not in general use in the purchase of goods and services.

    C.   information about the balances in checking accounts is not publicly available.

    D.   the balance in a checking account is not an actual stack of currency or pile of coins sitting inside a bank.

    E.   the balance in an individual's checking account is in a constant state of fluctuation

92. By *constituents* (line 6), the writer means

    A.   basics.

    B.   possibilities.

    C.   capacities.

    D.   elements.

    E.   submissions.

93. According to the passage, fractional reserve banking is a practice in which

    A.   a coin's metal value is a fraction of its mint value.

    B.   100 percent reserves are required only in certain federally defined cases.

    C.   a fraction of a bank's reserves leaks out of the system.

    D.   credit expansion reduces tangible reserves to an unacceptable fraction.

    E.   the currency and coin a bank has on hand is less than the total of its demand deposits.

94. The writer of this passage might be characterized as a(n)

    A.   disgruntled banker.

    B.   argumentative spectator.

    C.   interested lay person.

    D.   informed analyst.

    E.   curious investor.

Questions 95 through 100 are based on two Passages for V (A and B).

Two Comparative Passages for V

Passage A

The history of philosophy began with the Sophists, many of whom pre-dated both Plato and Aristotle. All of the major Sophists addressed the relationship between reality and language, arguing that the latter shapes the former: how we express what we see determines and limits our understanding. Because many of the Sophists were themselves adept at manipulating language to make a persuasive argument, we today associate sophistry with speciousness. Plato wrote against the Sophists in several dialogues, most notably in *Gorgias* and *Phaedrus*. In the earlier dialogue, Plato's Socrates proposes to Gorgias that a sophistic argument requires only a knack for flattery, rather than an interest in seeking the truth. In *Phaedrus,* Socrates shows that a sophistic argument about the nature of love can never get to the divine essence of love, which is spiritual. Plato's arguments about the value of ideal truth did not suit Aristotle, who was more interested in what we would see as a scientific approach to finding truth, based on logic, reason, and evidence. In this way, Aristotle more closely approaches the epistemology of the Enlightenment science, which is framed by Descartes' central statement, "I think, therefore I am." For many of the Enlightenment philosophers, writing centuries after Aristotle, the human mind's capacity to use reason for discovering truth is what separates human beings from lower animals. The systematic application of reason to evidence constitutes scientific method, which has not varied significantly since the seventeenth century, and which has always involved the rigorous testing of hypotheses. However, as Kuhn shows in *The Structure of Scientific Revolutions* (a study that turned philosophy and science on their heads in the twentieth century), all scientifically derived truths are and must be contestable, and can be revolutionized through the paradigm shifts that characterize, for instance, the great shift from a Ptolemaic to a Copernican universe. These days, we cannot imagine a universe without the sun at its center, but would do well to remember—as Kuhn would remind us—that even the Copernican universe is based on a paradigm that can be challenged. It is over-simple to conclude from this brief history that the Sophists were right in their belief that truth is relative, and that Plato was also right that the human mind cannot apprehend absolute truth, which requires Divine understanding. Indeed, without the rigorous and complex apparatus of scientific method to keep us grounded in actual evidence, we would begin to move backwards in intellectual history, to a time when assertion was mistaken as fact.

Passage B

(40) The New Age movement, characterized by the pseudo-sciences of astrology, palmistry, and the like in the later twentieth century, has given way to a rich rebirth of spirituality, and the subordination of Western philosophy and science to possibilities more in tune with nature and the divine. Nowhere has this been more apparent than in the work of Eckhart Tolle, whose twenty-first-century adaptation of Eastern

(45) thought and practice addresses the pain we often cause ourselves when we rely on Descartes' infamous dictum, "I think, therefore I am." The history of science and philosophy in the West has, unfortunately, prioritized the mind as the agency of truth and understanding. However, as is evident in much Eastern thought, and even in a non-ideological

(50) reading of Jesus' teachings, the mind primarily functions as an obstacle to happiness and understanding, and it is, rather, in the space between thoughts, in the realm beyond language—in silence—that we leave the world of "forms" (physical and linguistic), and experience oneness with the present moment. Tolle was himself a student of Western philosophy

(55) at the University of London, but found himself suffering from depression and anxiety, and getting no remedy from his studies. Experiencing an unexplained inner transformation in 1977, he embarked on a career of spiritual teaching that stresses the ego's destructive nature, and the power of experiencing the present moment, unburdened

(60) by the problems of the past or anxiety about the future. In *The Power of Now* (published in 1999), Tolle teaches that we cannot get beyond the ego and into the "now" through the use of Western reason. Reason has practical value, of course, and helps us make certain decisions, but it should not be confused with the essence of human existence, which is

(65) oneness with the present moment. This conclusion makes the history of Western philosophy and science seem rather trivial, with its ego-driven debates among the Sophists and Plato and Aristotle over the nature of the good and the true, its elaboration of Cartesian philosophy into a scientific method that rules out the spiritual and the divine, and its

(70) nearly incomprehensible treatises of the late twentieth and early twenty-first centuries, by figures such as Derrida and Lacan. To all of them, Eckhart Tolle might say, "All the things that truly matter—beauty, love, creativity, joy and inner peace—arise from beyond the mind."

95. The two writers of these passages fundamentally disagree about which of the following?

    A. the value of the scientific method
    B. the origin of the universe
    C. the history of Buddhism
    D. the interpretation of Plato
    E. the source of human anxiety

96. The structure of Passage A is chronological, while the structure of Passage B is

    A. loose and free flowing.
    B. a series of counterpoints to the points made in Passage A.
    C. primarily focused on a single figure's biography and thought.
    D. a movement from the New Age to previous ages.
    E. cause and effect.

97. Both writers assume which of the following about their readers?

    A. familiarity with Eckhart Tolle
    B. religious beliefs that include Buddhism
    C. scientific training
    D. knowledge of the history of philosophy and science
    E. philosophical training

98. The writers have very different interpretations of which of the following?

    A. the influence of ancient philosophy on modern science
    B. approaches to depression and anxiety
    C. the everyday value of practical thinking
    D. Plato's prominence in the history of science and philosophy
    E. Descartes' "I think, therefore I am."

99. Neither writer addresses

    A. Eckhart Tolle's transformation.
    B. major contributors to the history of philosophy and science.
    C. the value of Enlightenment philosophy.
    D. the origins of New Age thinking.
    E. the value of the present moment.

100. Which of the following does only the writer of Passage A assume?

A. Earlier periods in intellectual history were characterized by less accurate thinking than in later periods.

B. There have been few revolutionary moments in the history of philosophy and science.

C. The sun may not actually be at the center of the universe.

D. Plato and Aristotle agreed more than they disagreed.

E. Eastern philosophy gets us nowhere.

Answer Key for Reading Comprehension Practice Test

Section 1: Brief Passages

Practice Set 1

1. E
2. B
3. C
4. D
5. E
6. A
7. B
8. C

Practice Set 2

9. A
10. C
11. A, C
12. D
13. B
14. A
15. C
16. B

Practice Set 3

17. D
18. C
19. D
20. B
21. E
22. A, B, C
23. B
24. A
25. E
26. D

Section 2: Long Passages – Intermediate Difficulty

Practice Set 1

27. B
28. E
29. C
30. B
31. C
32. A
33. A
34. A
35. C

Practice Set 2

36. D
37. A
38. D
39. A
40. D
41. A
42. D
43. B

Practice Set 3

44. E
45. C
46. B
47. C
48. C
49. D
50. C
51. A

Practice Set 4

52. A
53. A
54. E
55. B
56. B
57. C
58. B
59. C
60. D

Practice Set 5

61. D
62. E
63. A
64. A
65. B
66. B
67. D
68. A
69. C
70. C

Section 3: Long Passages – Challenging

Practice Set 1

71. C
72. C
73. A
74. C
75. A
76. B
77. E
78. A
79. D
80. B
81. D
82. E
83. B
84. C
85. E
86. B
87. D
88. C

Practice Set 2

89. A
90. D
91. D
92. D
93. E
94. D
95. A
96. C
97. D
98. E
99. D
100. A

Answers and Explanations for Reading Comprehension Practice Test

Section 1: Brief Passages

Practice Set I, Passages I, II, III, and IV

1. **E.** Although other choices may be *suggested* by the information in the passage, only choice E summarizes the writer's overall point.

2. **B.** The passage states that *conflict between religious groups has considerably decreased over time,* implying that persecution was more widespread in the sixteenth century than today.

3. **C.** This choice is completely irrelevant to the information in the passage, which discusses *American* families only.

4. **D.** The first part of the passage discusses the effects on population of urbanization, and the second part discusses the effects on population of economic conditions. Choices A.I. and C.I. do not represent the lion's share of the passage's content, which focuses on urbanization. Choices A.II., B.I., and B.II. all leave out the matter of population. Choices C.II., E.I., and E.II. are all too general.

5. **E.** Each therapy is associated with some form of self-expression. Choice C may be relevant to psychodrama only.

6. **A.** By mentioning *reactions they are otherwise forbidden to show,* the writer assumes that some children hide their true reactions.

7. **B.** All other choices were stated by the passage. The word *all* in choice B makes the statement untrue. We cannot assume that brainwashing was practiced on *every* captured soldier.

8. **C.** The writer evinces *distaste* when s/he uses the word *appalling,* which means dreadful or atrocious. There is really not enough in the passage to indicate *outrage* (choice A), however.

Practice Set 2, Passages V, VI, VII, and VIII

9. **A.** The percentage of students in each category would not change, whether the pie chart represented the number or the percentage. Because the proportional relationship between the slices would not change, the slices' size would also not change.

10. **C.** It is apparent that a higher number and a higher percentage of females get passing grades than do males. Choice D contradicts the information on the chart, and the other choices require information the chart does not contain.

11. **A, C.** The passage clearly states that personal factors such as physical condition and mood can influence a test-taker's results. A headache indicates that Maria is not in top form physically and, presumably, Maria would not feel good about being behind on her rent. Although studies of standardized testing do indicate that test-takers tend to improve their scores on successive tests, the passage does not address this issue.

12. **D.** This choice is supported directly by the passage's first sentence.

13. **B.** The passage uses examples from everyday life to illustrate the different sources of frustration. Choices C and D are not addressed in the passage. Choices A and E are conclusions the passage does not support.

14. **A.** *Debarred* means excluded or prohibited. This nicely complements being *turned down* by a potential date; *punished* (choice B) does not complement this part of the sentence as well.

15. **C.** *Some radical change . . . to meet a social norm* implies a more socially acceptable appearance. Choice D is contradictory, and the other choices are unsupported conclusions.

16. **B.** Since the number of minutes spent teaching is identical, and the number of students in class is also the same, the only workload savings would come from the time it takes to prepare a class session. Choices A, D, and E are irrelevant to the stated goal to reduce teacher workload. Choice C could actually undermine the action plan, if travel time to and from the university were to be considered as a workload factor.

Practice Set 3, Passages IX, X, XI, XII, and XIII

17. **D.** The passage compares the relatively small proportion of Americans voting to *citizens of most European countries.*

18. **C.** Each of the other choices generalizes beyond the information actually given in the passage.

19. **D.** The association of neurotransmitters with stress and anxiety, along with the general statement that they affect a wide range of bodily functions, supports choice D. No evidence in the passage supports choices A and C; choice E can be eliminated because

non-preferable conditions are associated with both excitatory and inhibitory neurotransmitters; and B may be eliminated because the sentence implies that adrenalin and dopamine *are* neurotransmitters.

20. **B.** The main point is stated in the first sentence, and choice B is an accurate reworking of that sentence. Choice A is too broad to be the passage's main point, and choices C and D are too narrow. Choice E is a conclusion the passage doesn't support.

21. **E.** *Summary* is the key word here. It refers clearly to the essential characteristic of the passage: it surveys, or summarizes, the writing of the Constitution.

22. **A, B, C.** All answer choices to this question are correct. That they *contended* with one another tells us not only that they did not all arrive at the meeting with the same ideas, but also that they openly disagreed with or opposed one another. That they espoused tells us that they championed or argued for their own points of view and plans for the Constitution.

23. **B.** The writer emphasizes that people make facts meaningful: *Facts do not speak; people do.*

24. **A.** Because people *want . . . interpretation or evaluation,* they *will require philosophies.* Each of the other choices is clearly irrelevant or contradictory.

25. **E.** Information on a cat's digestive tract would be found in the anatomy and physiology section.

26. **D.** The matter of the English word *cat* would be found in a discussion of English etymology (word origins), which this part of the book does not cover. Fears about cats (choice A) are likely to be found on page 19. Allergic reactions to cats (choice B) is likely covered within pages 43–45. Feeding suggestions are likely to be found within pages 13–14, and the first appearance of cats is likely to be found within pages 34–37.

Section 2: Longer Passages – Intermediate Difficulty

Practice Set 1: Passages I and II

27. **B.** The writer states that moral questions *cannot be settled by using the same type of procedure that is employed in the natural sciences* (lines 8–9).

28. **E.** The passage states that some teach that the application of morality to particular situations is the work of reason (lines 40–42). Choices A and C contradict information in the passage, and choices B and D are statements irrelevant to the question.

29. **C.** Choices A and D are too specific, choice E is too general, and choice B contradicts lines 6–7 in that moral philosophy involves an attempt to understand rather than simply to formulate questions.

30. **B.** Intuition is a way of knowing through the feelings (line 31), a type of direct and immediate experience that is different from thinking, sense, perception, or the work of reason (lines 33–34).

31. **C.** Each of the other choices describes a secondary or subordinate purpose of the writer, but only choice C is comprehensive enough to cover the *primary* purpose.

32. **A.** To support the statement that *no society is an island unto itself,* the writer mentions the plight of the North American Indians. None of the other choices is relevant to the focus of the question.

33. **A.** Choices B, C, and E reach conclusions beyond the scope of the passage, and choice D contradicts the final sentence of the second paragraph.

34. **A.** A successful change must appear to be *innocent and harmless* (line 35). The passage contradicts choice B, and the other choices are not addressed by the passage.

35. **C.** The writer states that *change is an inescapable, ever-present fact of life* (lines 41–42) and supports this opinion/attitude repeatedly throughout the passage.

Practice Set 2: Passages III and IV

36. **D.** This choice is supported by the passage's first paragraph. Choices A and C are irrelevant to information in the passage; choices B and E are contradictory.

37. **A.** Each of the other choices requires information beyond the scope of the passage. Choice A summarizes the types of revolutionary changes the writer describes.

38. **D.** If you trace the sequence of events described in the passage, you will see that this is the only correct answer.

39. A. Both the third and fourth paragraphs discuss changes in sources of profit, changes that coincided with the effects of the Industrial Revolution. Each of the other choices is irrelevant to the passage.

40. D. Each of the other choices is either too broad and general or too specific and limited to adequately cover the information in the passage.

41. A. Dewey believed that *people learn primarily by doing things* (lines 35–37), so he would probably agree with this choice that rejects a type of *passive* learning.

42. D. The passage associates the *transmissive concept of education* with *many of the ideas and practices that were recurrent in the schools* (lines 23–27) of Dewey's day.

43. B. The passage stresses *desire on the parts of students to extend their knowledge further* (lines 38–39) as fundamental to Dewey's concept of education.

Practice Set 3: Passages V and VI

44. E. By devoting a full paragraph to Plato's exploits in Syracuse, the writer identifies it as one of the *few major events* (lines 10–11) to be treated in the passage. None of the other choices is supported by information in the passage. Choice D is a weaker choice than E because it singles out Plato's tactlessness as the *only* factor in the failure of his experiment, when we are also told that Dionysius was not a receptive pupil.

45. C. The passage emphasizes Plato's connection with Socrates, saying *Plato was known as one of his most devoted disciples* (lines 34–35), as a reason for his departure from Athens, while also mentioning that *Socrates had been put to death* (line 33). Plato undoubtedly feared that the government might seek to imprison him as well. Both *expedient* and *politic* mean wise or judicious.

46. B. Each of the other choices proposes that Plato's education or interests were, in one way or another, weak or deficient. The passage does not support a conclusion of this kind, since Plato's education is presented in an entirely positive light.

47. C. Each of the other choices might apply to a great number of individuals, but choice C is quite rare and therefore strengthens our sense of Plato's uniqueness.

48. C. We are told that because of the French Revolution, *the world would never be the same* (lines 4–5).

49. D. Napoleon appeared at a *crucial period* and *saved France* (lines 31 and 36) from forces that would have checked the Revolution. The Reign of Terror, which occurred before Napoleon's rise, is irrelevant to the question. Outcomes described in B, C, and E could potentially have occurred if Napoleon had not risen to power; however, there is no evidence of any of these "non-Napoleon" outcomes in the passage.

50. C. Choices A, B, and E contradict explicit information in the passage, and choice D is irrelevant. The passage states that *all of Europe* (line 8) was allied against the forces of French republicanism.

51. A. Each of the other choices contradicts explicit information in the passage. Choice A is supported by the passage's last sentence.

Practice Set 4: Passages VII and VIII

52. A. Only choice A can be supported by the contents of the passage.

53. A. Only choice A completely denies that any meaningful conclusions can be drawn about historical events. Choice C might come from someone practicing historical subjectivism.

54. E. This choice is supported by the final sentence of the passage.

55. B. The series of questions that comprise nearly half of the passage suggests that this is the obvious choice. Choice C is not the best choice because the writer raises a series of distinct, substantially different questions rather than reiterating the same one.

56. B. Three of the passage's four paragraphs are devoted to discussing the abuse of the plains Indians. The weight that the writer gives to this topic suggests its significance.

57. C. Although the writer does not express violent anger, the characterization of the treatment of the Indians as a *tragedy* (line 8), as well as the discussion of the settlers' killing of buffalo for sport and wishing extermination on the Indians, are strong indications of the writer's strong disapproval. Incidentally, the writer is sensitive enough to his or her subject to know that the term *Indian* has sometimes been criticized as offensive, and offers the more politically correct term, *Native Americans* at line 9.

58. **B.** We are told that, although *justice was almost entirely on the Indians' side* (lines 13–14), *the Indians were not equal to the firepower of the United States army* (lines 28–29). Each of the other choices contradicts information in the passage.

59. **C.** *Incursion* means *intrusion* or evasion. Though *injustice* (choice A) certainly fits the passage's theme, it is not the right synonym for *incursion*.

60. **D.** The point of comparison is that the Atlantic coast Indians were not fierce warriors like the plains Indians, and thus posed less of a threat of violence (paragraph 3).

Practice Set 5: Passages IX and X

61. **D.** The writer of Passage 2 refers to email, the Internet, texting, and tweeting, and adds an observation about online education, something Passage 1 does not address.

62. **E.** The writer of Passage 1 writes positively about the value of technology to create a *global village* (line 21), while the writer of Passage 2 values *genuine human contact* (line 30).

63. **A.** Each of the other choices includes at least one term that does not convey the writer's position on the topic. However, both writers' use of *we* and *us* tells us that they identify with the position statements they are making.

64. **A.** The connotation of a term is an interpretation of its significance, usually either negative or positive. In this case the two writers interpret the significance of social networking differently: the writer of Passage 1 interprets it as a positive activity, and the writer of Passage 2 interprets it as a negative activity. The *denotation* (choice B) of a term, on the other hand, is its literal meaning.

65. **B.** Both passages are written for a general contemporary audience that has some knowledge of social networking elements such as email and the Internet.

66. **B.** Choices A, C, and D are irrelevant to the information provided in the passage, while choice E contradicts the identification of demography with sociology in the second sentence.

67. **D.** The passage discusses *age-specific* birth rates as a measurement that rectifies the *ambiguities* (line 36) of crude birth rates.

68. **A.** To *rectify* is to set right or correct. *Revise* (choice B) is close in meaning to *rectify;* however, we don't generally say that we *revise* ambiguities.

69. **C.** The passage discusses the relationship between population increase and perceptions of military superiority in the first paragraph. Although choice E is a reasonable choice for the nation in question, it is irrelevant to the passage's focus.

70. **C.** The passage concludes that *it was not sufficient to construct future population estimates from antecedent trends* (lines 12–14).

Section 3: Long Passages – Challenging

Practice Set 1: Passages I, II, and III

71. **C.** Only this choice is not mentioned in the passage as a Gnostic dualism. Choice E is close; however, the distinction between *earthly life* and an *after life* is not made in these terms in the passage. It is true, however, that an afterlife is only suggested by the phrase, *a better kind of existence,* at lines 33–34.

72. **C.** Greek philosophy is mentioned in connection with Gnosticism (note the references to Plato and Neo-Platonism at lines 16 and 22), as is Persian Zoroastrianism (line 17). Choices A, B, and D contradict information in the passage, and choice E is irrelevant.

73. **A.** This example is explicitly connected to disagreement among Gnostics about preparing for salvation (see belief #6).

74. **C.** The creation is explained in terms of emanations, or *aeons* (lines 24–25). Each of the other choices is contradicted by the passage.

75. **A.** This question is answered explicitly and directly in belief #2.

76. **B.** Each of the other choices receives limited discussion in the passage; however, the concern with salvation is mentioned and discussed repeatedly and highlighted by the writer at line 4 as the Gnostics' *main concern.*

77. **E.** Each passage's first sentence expresses the essential contrast that the passages go on to develop. Each of the other choices is either focused on one passage rather than both, too general, or irrelevant.

78. **A.** Both writers mention fatigue as a problem, though Passage A treats it more extensively than Passage B. Though the writer of Passage A might agree with choice E, it is not implicit or explicit in the passage.

79. **D.** Both passages deal with how best to structure and manage a workplace, so the most likely purpose is guidance for workplace leaders.

80. **B.** This is the only choice that refers to teamwork, the value and effects of which are emphasized throughout Passage B.

81. **D.** The passage's first paragraph deals primarily with manager training, and the second paragraph makes points relevant to *both managers and their subordinates* (line 16).

82. **E.** There is no content in either passage that expresses or implies the writer's personal experience. All of the other choices would involve an inference unsupported by the passages.

83. **B.** Lines 25–27 state that no society rewards downward mobility. Choices C and E are irrelevant to the information in the passage, and each of the other choices is contradictory.

84. **C.** In general, the passage addresses systems of association in different cultures.

85. **E.** The passage describes the progress of an age-set from warriors to family heads to political elders (lines 16–20). Choices A, B, and D contradict information in the passage, and choice C is not addressed, and is therefore irrelevant to the passage.

86. **B.** Although Indian pariahs are mentioned along with Etas as outcastes (lines 37–39), this is not one of the choices. Only choice B is correct.

87. **D.** The distinction between the Amauga and the Aualuma supports this choice. Choosing any of the other answers would require generalizing beyond available information in the passage. Choice B may look correct, but the phrase young males who are both unmarried and untitled (line 10), does not preclude a male being, married and untitled, or vice versa.

88. **C.** *The Indian caste system is complicated* and characterized by *vagueness* (line 40). However, the sub-castes are characterized by *specificity* (line 41), so choice A cannot be correct.

Practice Set 2: Passages IV and V

89. **A.** By discussing the forms money takes *in today's United States* (lines 2–3), as well as the importance of *members of a given population [needing to] agree on a particular form of money* (lines 10–11), the writer implies choice A. Choice D is consistent with the passage, but it is explicit rather than implied information.

90. **D.** This purpose is evident throughout the passage. Choices A and E are irrelevant, and choices B and C contradict information in the passage.

91. **D.** The writer states that currency and coin are *government-created* (line 4), or minted, money, distinguishing their tangible existence from that of a demand deposit, or checking account.

92. **D.** *Constituents* are elements or components of a whole.

93. **E.** Lines 33–35 explain fractional reserve banking in terms of a 5:1 ratio of demand deposits to reserves.

94. **D.** The writer seems, for the most part, both objective and learned in matters of money, credit, and banking. Therefore, choice D is the best.

95. **A.** Each writer refers to scientific method. The writer of Passage A regards it as a positive that keeps us from moving *backward* (line 37), while the writer of passage B regards it as one of the *trivial* (line 66) elements of the history of Western philosophy and science. Choice D is only addressed in Passage A, and other choices reflect content not given in either passage.

96. **C.** Passage B is structured around Eckhart Tolle's life and thought. Although it starts with a reference to the New Age, it does not then move to a discussion of previous ages, so choice D is incorrect. Although Passage B includes some explicit or implied counterpoints to Passage A, it is not structured as a series of counterpoints, so choice B is incorrect.

97. **D.** Among these choices, the only subject that both writers address is the history of philosophy of science, often at a level of sophistication that presumes readers are already familiar with figures such as Plato and Descartes.

98. **E.** This statement is quoted in both passages, as a *central statement* (a positive connotation) at line 17, and as an *infamous dictum* (a negative connotation) at line 46.

99. **D.** Though New Age thinking is mentioned in Passage B, its origins are not. Each of the other choices is addressed in one of the passages.

100. **A.** The writer asserts that moving *backward* in intellectual history takes us to a *mistaken* (line 38) period.

PART III

WRITING TIMED ESSAYS

Chapter 6: Approaches to Writing Timed Essays

Chapter 6
Approaches to Writing Timed Essays

Most standardized tests include a writing sample (an exception is the PSAT/NMSQT). You are asked to respond to an essay question or questions under time constraints. In this section, you will find scoring guidelines and criteria, and typical questions and topic prompts, along with techniques for generating ideas, organizing material, writing, and proofreading. Here is a quick reference guide that shows what you can expect to encounter on each test.

Quick Reference Guide								
Section	**Page No.**	**GRE**	**GMAT**	**LSAT**	**SAT**	**ACT**	**PPST**	**CBEST**
Scoring Guidelines	pp. 398–402	✓			✓			✓
Scoring Criteria	pp. 402–403	✓	✓	✓	✓	✓	✓	✓
General Strategies	pp. 403–404	✓	✓	✓	✓	✓	✓	✓
Practice Topics	--------	pp. 430–434	pp. 435–436	pp. 437–440	pp. 440–441	pp. 442–444	pp. 444–445	pp. 445–447
Types of Essays								
Narrative/ Descriptive	pp. 404–414				✓			✓
Analytical/ Expository: Analysis of an Issue	pp. 414–418	✓			✓			✓
Analytical/ Expository: Analysis of an Argument	pp. 419–421	✓	✓					
Argumentative or Decision Prompt	pp. 422–427		✓	✓		✓	✓	

Scoring

To better appreciate the techniques presented, you should first understand the customary criteria and scoring procedures used to evaluate timed writing on standardized tests. The most common method for evaluating national and state writing tests is "holistic" scoring. This means that *all* aspects of a well-written essay count toward your final score: well-developed ideas, good organization, supporting evidence, and the effective use of grammar and language. Faced with hundreds of essays and the need to produce reliable scores, professional readers evaluate each essay with a "general impression" number that reflects the reader's overall conclusion.

Most scoring scales assign numbers in a range from 1 to 4, 0 to 6, or 1 to 6. A successful essay is one that receives an "upper-half" score from each reader. On the 1 to 4 scale, an upper-half score is a 3 or 4. On the 0 to 6 or 1 to 6 scale, an upper-half score is a 4, 5, or 6. An exception is the LSAT, which does not score the essay at all, but uses it as an auxiliary or supplemental part of the overall qualifications that a law school may incorporate in making final decisions.

Each essay is read and scored by two readers who are not aware of each other's scores. The total score is determined by averaging the two scores. For example, if the first reader assigns a score of 4 and the second reader assigns a score of 5, the two scores will be combined and averaged to give you a score of 4.5. Note that some exam administrators assign one score from a human reader, and another from a computer program (an "electronic reader") that rates your essay.

If there is more than a 1-point discrepancy between the scores—let's say one essay is a 3 and the other essay is a 6—the essay will be reviewed by a third reader who makes the decision to settle the discrepancy. Note, however, that the incidence of divergent scores is generally quite low because readers employ similar criteria, as you can tell from the three sample models on the following pages.

Scoring Guidelines

Here is a scoring guide used for each test:

Test	Score Range
GRE	0–6
GMAT	0–6
SAT	1–6
ACT	0–6
LSAT	unscored
PPST	0–6
CBEST	1–4

Though scoring criteria can vary a bit from test to test, the following three models (GRE, SAT, and CBEST) should give you a general sense of the elements your readers will consider in evaluating your essay.

GRE (Analysis of an Issue) Scoring Guidelines	
6	**Score of 6: Convincing and Persuasive** The highest scoring essays present a convincing and articulate analysis. These essays: ❑ present a clear and insightful position that responds directly to the task ❑ provide well-developed and persuasive reasons and/or examples ❑ present an organized, focused analysis that uses transitions to connect ideas ❑ use well-chosen vocabulary and varied sentence types to skillfully convey meaning ❑ demonstrate ease with correct usage of the conventions of standard written English
5	**Score of 5: Thoughtful and Well-Developed** These essays present a thoughtful and well-developed analysis. These essays: ❑ present a clear, considered position that responds directly to the task ❑ provide reasonable and logical reasons and/or examples ❑ present an organized, focused analysis that connects ideas ❑ use appropriate vocabulary and varied sentences to convey meaning ❑ demonstrate ease with correct usage of the conventions of standard written English
4	**Score of 4: Competent** These essays present a complete and reasonably clear analysis: These essays: ❑ present a clear position that responds to the task ❑ provide appropriate reasons and/or examples ❑ present an organized, focused analysis ❑ use language to convey meaning with adequate clarity ❑ demonstrate general control of the conventions of standard written English, but with some minor errors in grammar, spelling, and sentence structure
3	**Score of 3: Flawed** These essays show limited competence in responding to the prompt. These essays: ❑ may be vague or limited in responding to the specific prompt ❑ may use weak or irrelevant reasons and/or examples for support ❑ may lack focus or be poorly organized ❑ may have language problems that interfere with communication ❑ may demonstrate major errors or frequent minor errors with the conventions of standard written English
2	**Score of 2: Weak** These essays show serious weakness in responding to the specific directions for the task. These essays: ❑ may be unclear or very limited in responding to the specific prompt ❑ may not develop a clear position ❑ may provide few reasons and/or examples for support ❑ are lacking focus and are poorly organized ❑ have serious language problems that impede communication ❑ have major errors with the conventions of standard written English

continued

1	**Score of 1: Deficient** These essays show major deficiencies in analytical writing. These essays: ❏ present little understanding of the task or issue ❏ provide little or no evidence or support ❏ have severe language problems that prevent communication ❏ have serious errors with the conventions of standard written English
0	**Score of 0** These essays are often off-topic, do not respond to the writing task, are written in a foreign language, simply copy the issue statement, consist of random keystrokes, or are left blank.

SAT Scoring Guidelines

6	**Score of 6: Convincing and Persuasive** These clear and consistently competent essays have only minor errors and are characterized by: ❏ effective and insightful coverage of the tasks the exam question requires ❏ good organization and development, with relevant supporting details ❏ command of standard written English, with a range of vocabulary and sentence variety
5	**Score of 5: Thoughtful and Well-Developed** These reasonably thoughtful and well-developed essays have occasional errors or lapses in quality and are characterized by: ❏ effective coverage of the tasks the exam question requires ❏ generally good organization and development, with some supporting details ❏ good handling of standard written English, with some range of vocabulary and sentence variety
4	**Score of 4: Competent** These competent essays have occasional errors or lapses in quality and are characterized by: ❏ coverage of the tasks the exam question requires ❏ adequate organization and development, with some supporting details ❏ handling of standard written English, but with minimal variety and some grammar or word choice errors
3	**Score of 3: Marginally Adequate** These marginal papers are characterized by: ❏ failure to fully cover required tasks ❏ weak organization and/or development ❏ failure to use relevant supporting details ❏ several errors of grammar, diction, and sentence structure

2	**Score of 2: Inadequate**
	These inadequate papers are characterized by:
	❏ failure to cover the assignment
	❏ poor organization and development
	❏ lack of supporting details
	❏ frequent errors of grammar, diction, and sentence structure
1	**Score of 1: Severely Flawed**
	These severely flawed papers are characterized by:
	❏ failure to cover the assignment
	❏ very poor organization and development
	❏ errors of grammar, diction, and sentence structure so frequent as to interfere with meaning
	❏ extreme brevity or shortness

As you practice writing essays for some exams like the CBEST, use the following Analysis Checklist Questionnaire as a guide to evaluate your progress. Although this analysis checklist was designed with the CBEST in mind, it is also helpful for other exams.

Analysis Checklist Questionnaire				
Questions	**Score 4**	**Score 3**	**Score 2**	**Score 1**
1. How well does the writer **present the central idea or point of view**?	clearly presents	adequately presents	poorly presents	poorly presents
2. Is the **focus** of the topic **maintained**?	yes, well focused	generally clear focus	sometimes loses focus	no, unfocused
3. How is the **reasoning** in the response?	well reasoned	adequately reasoned	simplistically reasoned	lacks reason
4. How are the **ideas or points organized**?	logically arranged	generally clear	some order evident	disorganized
5. How well is the **response supported**?	well supported with specific examples	adequately supported with some examples	partially supported, lacking detail	unsupported, no details
6. How good is the **word choice** in the essay?	precise, careful, accurate word choice	adequate word choice	generally imprecise word choice	poor word choice
7. How well is the **topic addressed**?	completely addressed	adequately, but not fully addressed	incompletely addressed	not addressed
8. Does the essay use **language and style appropriate** to the given audience?	yes, appropriate language and style	fairly appropriate language and style	inadequately appropriate language and style	inappropriate language and style

continued

9. To what extent is the writing **free from grammatical and mechanical errors?**	only a few minor flaws	some errors, but not serious	distracting errors	numerous errors
10. How is the **writing sample formed?**	well formed	adequately formed	partially formed	inadequately formed
11. How well is the **message communicated?**	effectively communicated	adequately communicated	effort made to communicate	not communicated

Each test varies with respect to scores assigned to particular criteria. You should consult the official website for *your* test to get familiar with its specific rating scale and how it weights the writing portion in relation to other test sections as a whole. For example, on the CBEST you must receive a score that equates to about 70 percent of the total possible score to achieve passing standards.

CBEST Scoring
4 = pass
3 = marginal pass
2 = marginal fail
1 = fail

Scoring Criteria

If you understand scoring procedures and criteria, you can adjust your writing to your readers' expectations. Remember that they will likely read carefully yet quickly, perhaps spending no more than a few minutes on your essay or essays. Therefore, the most effective and successful writing will be clear and direct so your readers can proceed efficiently. Also, realize that no reader will expect a perfect, polished essay. Under time constraints, even the best writer's essay is viewed as a first draft.

It is fair to say, in general, that the criteria for scoring timed essays are as follows:

1. **Fullness of response:** Credit is given to an essay that responds fully to all parts of the question. The essay's main idea and generalizations should be supported by evidence, specific details, reasons, and examples. Plan to accomplish this in an essay of about 250-400 words.

2. **Appropriateness of response:** Write in answer to the prompt(s) you have been given. Credit is not given to essays that avoid the prompt and wander off into other topics.

3. **Organized flow of ideas:** Even though essays written under timed conditions are not expected to be perfect, credit is given to those whose paragraphs have a logical sequence of ideas that a reader can easily follow. Smooth transitions—a word, phrase, sentence, or sentences—help readers understand the relationship one idea has to another.

4. **Adequate development of ideas:** Each paragraph of your essay, especially in its body, should develop a main idea. Don't write an essay sprinkled with an array of ideas that you don't fully flesh out. Instead, focus each paragraph on a single main idea.

5. **Coherence:** Support your thesis, or primary proposition, throughout the essay.

6. **Freedom from faulty arguments:** Your readers will downgrade your essay if it contains internal inconsistencies, failures to distinguish between fact and opinion, or unjustified conclusions.

7. **Correct grammar, usage, and spelling:** Although occasional errors are allowed, credit is *not* given to essays that display frequent mistakes. Your writing should obey the rules of standard written English, so that your ideas are clearly and correctly expressed.

8. **Awareness of audience:** Your tone and word choice should be appropriate to an audience of well-educated adults who are experienced evaluators of student writing. Use the proper tone of voice, and express your ideas in a sophisticated and mature way. Tip: Vary the length and complexity of your sentences, not only to demonstrate mastery over the English language, but also to make your writing more appealing.

General Strategies for Essay Writing

Before we proceed to discuss, exemplify, and offer more detailed advice about various types of essay questions, consider the following general strategies for ensuring your success.

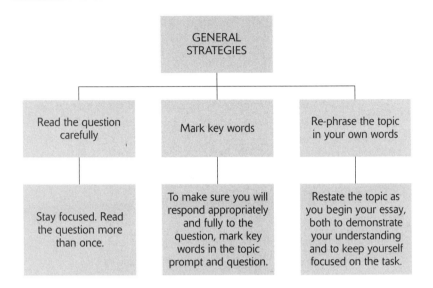

Strategies for Specific Types of Essays

The section will provide you with strategies associated with specific types of essays and procedures for writing an effective essay. Essays described in this section are:

- The Narrative/Descriptive Essay (CBEST and SAT)
- The Analytical/Expository Essay: Analyze an Issue (GRE, SAT, CBEST)
- The Analytical/Expository Essay: Analyze an Argument (GRE and GMAT)
- The Argumentation or Decision Prompt Essay (LSAT, ACT, and PPST)

The Narrative/Descriptive Essay

The narrative/descriptive essay (sometimes called "expressive") asks you to draw directly from personal experience—to show (describe) and tell about (narrate) a significant event in your life. You are, in a sense, telling a story about yourself in the narrative portion. To make your personal story descriptive, appeal to your reader's senses by including details pertaining to sight, sound, touch, taste, and smell.

You will find this kind of essay prompt on the CBEST (which asks you to write not only a narrative/descriptive essay, but also an analytical/expository piece, as you will see in the next section). Also, those taking the SAT may choose to write a narrative/descriptive essay for the writing portion of the test, whose general question prompts do not specify a particular essay genre. (Sample topics specific to each exam appear later in this chapter.) While the subject will differ from question to question and from test to test, your response's form will be similar in each case.

Sample Task 1 – Narrative/Descriptive Essay

Here is a relevant sample topic:

> We all face significant challenges in our lives. Write an essay about a recent, difficult challenge you have faced, either willingly or unexpectedly. Discuss why the challenge was difficult, describe the way in which you responded to or prepared for it, and tell whether you were successful or unsuccessful in meeting this challenge.

Overview of Sample Task 1

A careful consideration of the question reveals that you must first select a *recent, difficult challenge* from your experience (you should have marked these words). Quickly choose the challenge about which to write. Don't waste time worrying about whether the experience you choose is "important" or "interesting" enough. Just get started, since you are writing under strict timed constraints.

Notice too that the question asks for a three-part response in which you *discuss* the *difficulty* of the challenge, *describe* your *response* or *preparation,* and *tell* the *results* (again, you should mark the words in the question that specifically indicate what you are being asked to do). Of course, you must respond to all three parts if you want full credit for answering the prompt. If you respond insufficiently to any one of the parts, you very likely will receive a lower-half score.

Stages of the Writing Process

For any timed writing task, work through these three stages for a competent finished product:

1. Preparing to write
2. Writing
3. Proofreading

Preparing to Write

It can be difficult and perhaps impossible to invent and organize information at short notice unless you are equipped with an effective prewriting technique. If you are allowed notepaper, or have space in your test booklet or on your test screen, generate some prewriting content that can help you develop your essay. (If you do not have a space for prewriting available, mentally develop your prewriting content, and hold it in mind.)

A well-suited technique to the timed essay is the "cluster outline":

Step 1: Write down the experience you will discuss, and circle it. In this case, the topic is "Running a 10K." Then, surround this experience by writing down the three aspects of the experience that the question has asked you to consider, draw circles around each one, and connect each to the experience by drawing a line from it to the center, like this:

Step 2: Consider each of the three sub-areas of "Running a 10K," and continue to cluster outward from these elements, writing whatever comes to mind (see the illustration with Step 3).

Step 3: Add more information to what you have so far. Additional information can answer questions such as, "Why?" "How?" or "So what?" or it might give a concrete example or "for instance."

Here is a completed cluster outline for "Running a 10K":

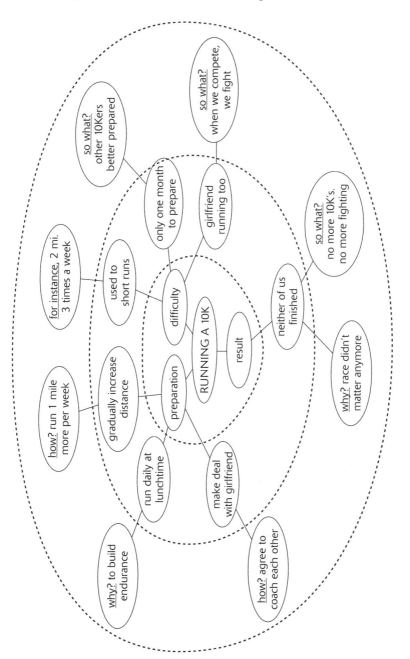

You'll need to practice the cluster outline to master it, but as you become more familiar with this technique, you should be able to generate a wealth of information in just a few minutes. (Note that you can use fragment sentences and abbreviations to save time.) Once your cluster outline is complete, you will have more than enough information, grouped into categories for easy organization, and you will be ready to write your opening paragraph.

Now, let's take a look at how a cluster outline can be used to full advantage in a piece of writing.

Writing

Opening Paragraph

A strong opening paragraph is essential. One type of introduction (easy to master and very effective) is a *Generalize-Focus-Survey* structure. This is a three- or four-sentence paragraph in which the first sentence generalizes about the given topic (this is a good place to re-phrase the topic in your own words), the second sentence focuses on what you have chosen to discuss, and the last part—made up of a sentence or two—surveys the particulars you intend to present. Referring to the essay question and, in this case, to your cluster outline, jot down the following: 1) the central idea from the given topic, 2) the specific content that responds to your subject, and 3) the several aspects of your subject that you plan to discuss. Here is an example:

1. General topic: difficult challenge
2. Focused content: running a 10K
3. Aspects to survey: increasing distance, building endurance, maintaining relationship

Step 1: In your first sentence, use the general topic.

Difficult challenges can be physical and emotional.

Step 2: In your second sentence, focus on the subject you have chosen to discuss.

> When I decided to *run a 10K*, I knew it would be a tough physical challenge. Ten kilometers is equal to more than six miles, and running such distances is not only hard on the feet and knees, but can also cause hyperthermia and glucose shortages. These hardships I expected. But I did not expect running in a marathon to be emotional as well.

Step 3: Finally, survey the aspects you will discuss.

> While *increasing my running distance* and *building endurance* taxed me physically, I also faced the emotional challenge of *maintaining a relationship* with my chief competitor: my girlfriend.

An effective first paragraph tells your reader what to expect in the body of the essay. The *Generalize-Focus-Survey* paragraph points toward the specifics you will discuss and suggests the order in which you will discuss them. Notice the variation in the length and complexity of the writer's sentences here. The two brief sentences *these hardships I expected* and *but I did not expect running in a marathon to be emotional as well* function as a nice pause for emphasis in between the longer, more complex sentences that surround them.

Body

Writing the body of the essay involves presenting specific details and examples related to the elements you have introduced, some of which should appeal to the senses of sight, sound, touch, taste, and smell. The body may consist of one longer paragraph or a few shorter ones. If you choose to break your longer discussion into multiple paragraphs, make sure each contains at least three sentences. Very short paragraphs suggest that you haven't fully developed your ideas, and they make your essay appear insubstantial.

Be realistic about how much you will be able to write. Your readers will not give you more credit for writing a longer essay. Although they want you to support your points adequately, they understand that you must write concisely to finish in time.

It is sufficient to provide one substantial example or "for instance" for each element you discuss in the body of your essay. Here is an example of a two-paragraph body:

About a year ago, I was a "jogger" but not yet a "runner." I jogged two miles three times per week, but wondered whether I had the ability to endure the 10K's run of more than six miles. My legs would ache as if being pounded by mallets on many of my shorter runs. When the Independence Day 10K was only one month away, I began a very difficult training program. I laced up my feather-light running shoes and began running three miles daily for a week. I then extended my run to four miles, then five, and, finally, with a mere week until the race, I was running six miles per day, my feet drumming in measured beats against the solid concrete. My friends warned me that I was driving myself too hard, and my constant exhaustion told me that as well. But pushing myself this hard seemed like the best way to build endurance and increase distance in time for the race.

The physical challenge was matched by the emotional challenge I faced while working on my relationship with my girlfriend. She had decided to train for the race as well, and I was afraid that, because we were both so competitive, we would end up constantly speaking in angry and aggressive tones. So early on, I made a deal with Jane. She would help me and I would help her. We'd support each other. We began running together, but there were moments every day during training when cooperation seemed almost impossible. Tired and soaked with sweat, we began to grumble at each other, our voices sounding like rusty, old bike chains that rubbed against each other. But we would quickly remember the deal and stop a potential argument from arising; however, it was hard work at times to restrain myself from arguing with her.

Notice that so far this essay deals with two of the question's three parts. It discusses the challenge's difficulty and describes the writer's preparation for it. Notice also that not all details in the cluster outline also appear in the essay. Don't expect to use every detail from your outline. And realize that new ideas and details will come up as you write, so use them to your advantage. Also, notice the many places in which the writer includes details that appeal to one of the five senses.

Conclusion

As you prepare to write the conclusion, pay special attention to the time that remains. You must allow enough time to write the conclusion *and* to proofread the entire essay.

The conclusion may function in one or more of the following ways: 1) to *complete* your response to the essay question, 2) to *add* information that was not introduced earlier, and/or 3) to *point toward the future*.

The conclusion below serves all three functions:

> The day of the race arrived, but neither of us was really ready. We both felt we had trained too hard and too often, and we were right. After running just three miles, we simply could not continue and dropped out. Laughing at our common weakness, we threw our arms around each another and basked in the warmth of our affection. However, we agreed that learning to cooperate with one another turned out to be more important than finishing the race! It was then that we stopped competing and fighting with each other for good.

Proofreading

Always allow about five minutes to proofread your essay for errors in grammar, usage, and spelling. Common problems in these areas are discussed at length in Chapter 3. Also, watch for omitted words and typographical errors. To make sure you do not proofread hastily, try covering all but your essay's first line with a sheet of paper if you have one available, and then read that line carefully. Reveal and read the second line, then the third, and the fourth, and so on. This method will ensure a focused and careful proofreading of your work.

If you detect an error on a paper-based test, cross it out by carefully drawing a line through it, and then insert the correction neatly. Keep in mind that your handwriting must be legible. You may write in cursive if your handwriting is easy to read. If your handwriting is not clear, print your essay; but since you are given only so much writing space, be careful not to make your letters too large, skip lines, leave wide margins, or write outside the lined space you have been provided. Or, you might elect to take a computer-based version of your test, if available.

Essay Writing Checklist

Check to make sure your essay meets the following criteria:

✓ Your opening paragraph is relevant to the body of your essay.

✓ Your ideas are clearly expressed.

✓ You have used transitional words to provide unity and coherence.

✓ Your conclusion reiterates your essay's main points and adds a novel element, such as a question, suggestion for further thought, or comment about the future.

Note: When proofreading, never make an effort to radically change your entire essay. You do not have time. At this point, the best you can do is to add a few minor elements to strengthen your work.

Sample Task 2 – Narrative/Descriptive Essay

Below is another sample narrative/descriptive prompt and essay, along with prewriting material:

One common theme in science fiction and fantasy literature is "time travel," the power to go forward or back in time and actually alter past or future. If you had the power to travel backward through your educational process, what single event from this aspect of your life would you change? Describe the event, explain why you would change it, and tell how the change would have affected your present life and your future.

Overview of Sample Task 2

This question requires a three-part response: 1) describe the past educational event you would change, 2) give reasons for your change, and 3) tell the effects your change would have.

Begin by spending a few minutes sketching a cluster outline and constructing an opening paragraph in which you *Generalize-Focus-Survey*, as in the following example:

1. Generalized topic: time travel backward through education

2. Focused content: finishing my master's thesis

3. Aspects to survey: the day I stopped writing, pressure from family to give it up, resulting career limitations

Sample Essay Response - Task 2

Some may wish to travel back in time to alter some great historical event, but I have a much more modest and more personal wish. I would like to travel back fifteen years and pull out my unfinished master's thesis, "Educational Reform in the Eighteenth Century." I imagine the dust blossoming out into the air as I throw the thesis down on the table with a thud! If only I had written the entire thesis and earned my degree, my opportunities for career advancement would be much broader today. But my family convinced me to quit back then, and I now regret the limitations I have imposed on my career by making that decision.

Two weeks before my twenty-third birthday, I had still been engrossed in research about eighteenth-century educators and was delighted to discover that even then people were concerned about the growth of young minds. In particular, I admired Descartes and planned to write a chapter about the application of Cartesian philosophy to modern educational problems. As I began to write, enjoying the active scrawling sound of the pen on blank paper, I got a phone call from the school district with the offer of a full-time job (teaching third grade) that left me confused about what to do.

If I were to take a full-time job, I knew I would have no time to write. I was raising a family at the time, and this along with teaching would certainly occupy all my time. I discussed the matter with both my husband and my parents, and they all advised me to set aside the thesis. "You can write some other time," my husband said in a dismissive tone of voice. "Jobs are scarce," my father said sternly. Weak-willed and easily persuaded, I agreed, and quit my master's program. That night, I felt like a ragdoll as I collapsed onto my bed and sobbed until my chin was wet with tears.

The *first paragraph* introduces the points the writer intends to discuss and addresses the question fully. The writer also appeals to the reader's senses: the sight of blossoming dust, the sound of the thesis coming down with a thud.

Concrete details contribute to the paragraph's clarity, along with transitions such as *in particular*.

A *concise* survey of the factors influencing the decision rather than an unnecessarily wordy, rambling one strengthens this paragraph. And yet the writer takes time to include sensory detail.

Because the lack of a master's degree has limited my pay raises and excluded me from several administrative and teaching opportunities, I now deeply regret this decision. I also now realize that my decision should have been my own, in any case, and not based on the attitudes of others. I should have recognized that both my husband's and my father's opinions were just that: their opinions. But because I gave into their influence, rather than follow my own interests, I now walk with slouched shoulders, and feel I am less self-determined than I might have been.

> Here the writer addresses the question's second part, and she explains the reasons for the change directly and extensively.

Had I finished that thesis, I would now be qualified to apply for the several professors' positions that recently opened up at Wicker Community College. A position such as this would allow me to look forward to a more intellectually stimulating career, and to greater independence than I now enjoy. But most of all, a completed thesis would have boosted my self-esteem, which I still find wanting. Some day, I'd like to walk tall, my shoulders back, my chest out, and my head held high. But since time travel is just a fantasy, I suppose the only way to realize this dream is to go back to school and earn a higher degree.

> Here the writer addresses the question's third part and includes new information about her self-esteem that makes the conclusion stronger and fresher.

The Analytical/Expository Essay

In general, an analytical/expository essay topic asks you to explain or analyze an issue, argument, situation, statement, decision, policy, or quotation. For this type of essay, you are to take a position on the matter presented; you thus want to state your position, and offer the information or reasons that support your position. You will find this essay type on the GRE and GMAT, and CBEST.* The GRE asks you to write two essays, one in which you analyze an *issue* and another in which you analyze an *argument*, while the GMAT requires only one essay that invites you to analyze an *argument*. Those taking the SAT may also choose to write an analytical/expository essay for the writing portion of the test, whose general question prompts do not specify a particular essay genre. (Sample topics specific to each exam appear later in this chapter.)

*Many universities require students to take an English placement test to determine what level of first-year writing class they are qualified to take. These placement tests often include one or two essay questions, some narrative/descriptive, others analytical/expository. The instruction in this book for the effective pre-writing and writing of these essay types applies to many English placement tests as well.

Sample Task 1 – Analytical/Expository Essay: "Analyze an Issue"

Here is a sample topic relevant to the more common "analyze an issue" type:

> Consider the following, written by Lewis Thomas:
>
> We learn, as we say, by "trial and error." Why do we always say that? Why not "trial and rightness" or "trial and triumph"? The old phrase puts it that way because that is, in real life, the way it is done.

Overview of Sample Task 1

Thomas suggests that learning occurs when mistakes are made, rather than when things are done correctly. Decide whether he is right or not, and support your decision by discussing trial and error with reference to a particular modern problem.

You may approach this question just as you would a narrative/descriptive question. First, *mark the key words* in the question. You will see that you're asked to both *decide* about Thomas and to *support* that decision by discussing a *particular modern problem.*

The writer represented below prepared to write by making this cluster outline:

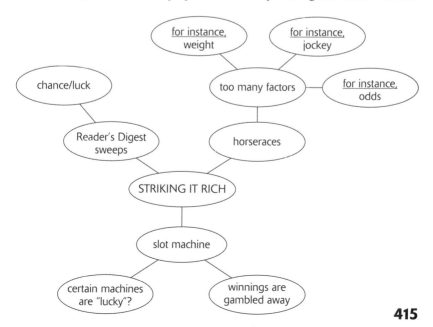

You may notice that this outline is less extensive than the "Running a 10K" outline we saw earlier. This writer spent just a few minutes jotting down ideas and examples, but could not think of more information than what appears here. Knowing that he or she must not spend excessive time on the outline—and trusting that more ideas would emerge while writing the essay—this writer simply began to compose the first paragraph.

The *Generalize-Focus-Survey* introduction might proceed as follows:

1. Generalized topic: trial and error
2. Focused content: striking it rich
3. Aspects to survey: horseraces/racetrack, *Reader's Digest* sweepstakes, slot machines

Sample Essay Response – Task 1

Key words have been italicized for your benefit:

Lewis Thomas claims that we learn through *trial and error*. We make a mistake, consider what went wrong, make a change, and then try again. The problem is that people with addictions often don't realize or consciously deny that they are making a mistake. One addiction with which thousands of people struggle every day is that of beating the odds and *striking it rich*. People place their bets at the *racetrack*, mail their entries to the *Reader's Digest sweepstakes*, and fill casino *slot machines* with coins—learning nothing new from losing again and again.

For every gambler's "trial," there is more "error" than "triumph," so I would agree with Thomas that trial and error go together. Whether we actually learn from gambling losses is another matter, however. Conducting "research" at the Santa Anita racetrack this summer, I found that although every gambler aims to pick a winner in accordance with relevant factors such as the horse's condition, jockey, and odds, most groaned at their losses after the finish and then groaned again after each race. I didn't experience gamblers winning any more bets in the ninth race than in the first. As far as I could tell, nobody learned a thing. As Santa Anita's horseracing season ends, some of these same gamblers migrate to Las Vegas, where they pour money into slot machines, and inevitably go home busted all over again. Once home, they dejectedly fill out entries to the *Reader's Digest*

> Note that this writer has taken a novel approach to the question. Rather than worry about whether the *modern problem* chosen is serious or dignified enough, the writer chooses a topic that feels comfortable (meaning he or she has substantial things to say about it), and causes it to fit the question.

> This is an example of a one-paragraph body.

sweepstakes, and any other sweepstakes game that comes in the mail, only to receive nothing in response for their time.

Gamblers should learn something from their errors: that gambling is fundamentally a matter of chance and luck, even for professionals. It is questionable whether they ever do learn this, though. After years of errors and wasted money, many continue to gamble. It's sad to think of the impact their addiction must have on the family members who love them. I take a special interest in this subject because my uncle has lost thousands of dollars to his gambling problem, and his family has been and continues to be adversely affected by his inability to learn.

> In the conclusion, the writer adds new information, as well as a new perspective that follows from what he or she has written, but that was not included in the earlier material.

Sample Task 2 – Analytical/Expository Essay: "Analyze an Issue"

Below is another sample analytical/expository essay, along with prewriting material:

> "The typical human response to the unknown is fear and aggression." Write an essay in which you agree or disagree with this statement, and support your position with relevant examples.

Overview of Sample Task 2

This question requires two main elements: a position statement and supporting details. The cluster outline and the *Generalize-Focus-Survey* first paragraph are productive for this writing assignment.

The "fight or flight" response, in which a perceived threat causes the sympathetic nervous system to becomes hyper-aroused, may be thought by some to occur only in lower animals. If an animal sees that it is about to be attacked by another creature, it will either run away or prepare for battle. Its heart rate increases, pumping more blood to its muscles, and it experiences a rush of adrenaline that supercharges the body for action. Supposedly, humans are rational beings, and do not mindlessly attack or run and hide when threatened. Or do they?

> The writer adapts the *Generalize-Focus-Survey* structure to the topic, announcing in the third sentence the details to be discussed.

Forty years ago, the families in my parents' neighborhood behaved like animals when they mistreated an immigrant family that tried to join the community. Faced with the "unknown" (in the form of a family with Eastern European customs and clothes), they responded with fear and aggression. Both of my parents were raised in a small Midwestern town "defined by middle-American values," as my dad puts it. "Mom, the flag, and apple pie" were the ideals my neighbors worshiped. When the Luzinskis moved to town, hopeful that they could share the "American dream" of opportunity and prosperity, they were met by smiling, courteous citizens—until the sun set. Certain angry neighbors claimed that the Luzinskis "didn't fit in" and organized groups to hide in the darkness, shout insults at this new family, and hurl rocks through their windows. After only two weeks, the Luzinskis' hopes were so bruised that they quietly left town.

> The writer supplies supporting details in a brief narrative. Note especially the vivid adjectives and active verbs that are used.

My community could not cope with the unknown; they were afraid of strangers who, in their minds, disrupted established values, and so they attacked. Like the little boys in Golding's *Lord of the Flies*, who are so frightened by the ominous jungle darkness that they blindly strike out at each other, these "lovers of liberty" savaged their fellow beings. I cannot help but conclude that these ordinary citizens had a wrong-headed response to the unfamiliar. Thank goodness things have changed considerably since those days, and thank goodness for my parents, who never participated in hazing the Luzinskis and taught me to see my common bond with people of all ethnicities.

> The writer ties the conclusion to the essay topic, and strengthens the conclusion by adding new information about Golding's novel, an analogous situation, and reflections about himself and his parents.

Five-Paragraph Essay

Another way to approach the analytical/expository essay is to map it out in a conventional five-paragraph form. In this case, you would begin by writing out your position statement, and then listing three reasons that your position is sound. Label this material as *Paragraph 1*. Then list a relevant example for reason one. Label this *Paragraph 2*. Do the same for reasons two and three (using *Paragraph 3* and *Paragraph 4*). Finally, jot down ideas for a conclusion; you might summarize what you've said and then point beyond this by adding new information. Label this material *Paragraph 5*. Now, you are ready to develop this content into a fully elaborated five-paragraph essay.

Analyze an Argument Essay

Now that you've seen two examples of the "analyze an issue" type of analytical/expository essay, let's look at the "analyze an argument" variety, found on the GMAT and GRE. Here is a sample topic, followed by prewriting material that uses the five-paragraph essay form, and the essay itself:

Sample Task 3 – Analytical/Expository Essay: "Analyze an Argument"

Here is a sample topic relevant to the GRE and GMAT:

> The following appeared in the "Letters to the Editor" section of a daily newspaper:
>
> > "The County Board of Supervisors should switch to a new employee health plan provider that charges the County a lower premium. Basic health care coverage is a necessity, but economic conditions—which have caused a 5 percent salary reduction for all county employees—must be accompanied by lower costs. Although all the lower-cost providers under consideration feature little coverage for preventive care, this feature will not impact the health of County employees: County statistics for the last five years indicate a low incidence in the category of 'preventable deaths.' Most important, if the new provider is contracted, that there will be no rise in health care premiums in the next annual budget."
>
> Discuss how well reasoned you find this argument. Be sure to refer to specific evidence in the argument, and to consider whether the evidence is or is not used well. For instance, you may wish to focus on unanswered questions in the argument, unstated assumptions, evidence that would be needed to strengthen the argument, the structure of the argument, or the points that an effective counter-argument might make.*

Note: This sort of prompt, which refers to a number of elements or features of the argument that might be considered, is typical of the GMAT. The "Analysis of an Argument" section on the GRE will normally specify just one feature of the argument that you should address. For instance, one GRE prompt may ask you to focus on what questions are left unanswered in the argument; another prompt may ask you to develop alternative explanations for the evidence presented. In other words, the GRE prompt may be more focused than the GMAT prompt. However, the task is the same on both tests: focus on the problems with the evidence given, or on what evidence is needed with respect to the argument's soundness, plausibility, and logic. Sample topics specific to the GRE appear later in this chapter.

Don't overthink what you are asked to do here. The task is to *focus* on the argument's reasoning. To do this, carefully select the points that structure and support the argument, and consider their flaws. *Do not* attempt to write an essay that tries to address every kind of evidence that the prompt includes or excludes: questionable assumptions, alternative explanations, counterexamples, evidence that would strengthen the argument, the logical structure of the argument, and so forth. You don't have enough time to write a brief essay that comprehensive.

Instead, focus on three to four pieces of evidence or lines of reasoning that are weak or incomplete, and structure your response with these three to four pieces in view.

With this advice in mind, you might structure your response to this prompt in line with the five-paragraph essay format described on p. 418. In fact, computer-based GMAT writers are likely to get their best scores by writing a five-paragraph essay in response to the analytical prompt, in part because the non-human rater that produces one of your two essay scores will focus strongly on structure, and will expect an easily identifiable essay form. You should also take care to provide—both at the beginning of and within paragraphs—clear and definitive transition words or phrases such as *for example*, *therefore*, *in addition*, *first*, *second*, *specifically*, *to illustrate*, *clearly*, *as a result*, *one reason is that*, *in summary*, etc., so the computerized rater can easily follow your train of thought.

In this case, your response could be organized as follows:

> Paragraph 1: important questions about costs, impact of coverage, future premiums
>
> Paragraph 2: Question #1: lower costs for whom?
>
> Paragraph 3: Question #2: relationship between preventive care and "preventable death"?
>
> Paragraph 4: Question #3: long-term outlook for premium increases?
>
> Paragraph 5: conclusion, restate reasons, point to future

Here is the way one writer used the five-paragraph structure to respond to this prompt:

Important questions about the effects of a change are not addressed in the argument for a lower-cost health care provider. Whose costs will be lowered? What is the relationship between preventive care and preventable death? What is the outlook for premium increases beyond the next year? These questions must be addressed before we can determine whether the argument is reasonable.

> In paragraph 2, the writer begins to focus the response on the kinds of questions employees would ask, and this approach gives the writing a good focus. The writer wisely notes the relationship between one section of the essay and another (in this case, the second sentence and the last sentence).

Although the argument cites the economic necessity for lower costs, and says that employees have had their salaries reduced, it does not tell whether the employees themselves will have their costs lowered. This is an important consideration. The argument states in its last sentence that employee premiums will stay the same, but not whether they will change after one year. Since employees are those affected by this provider change, fuller explanations that address their welfare are necessary.

Also, an employee might want to know more about the "preventable death" statement in the argument. What is a preventable death? If a person doesn't look both ways before she crosses the street, and is therefore run over by a speeding car, we could say that it was a preventable death. But this kind of death has no relationship to preventive medical care, in which annual physical exams, inoculations, and weight loss programs play a vital role in people's health. With this statement, the argument assumes a relationship between medical care and death that raises important questions.

> This paragraph begins with a good transition from paragraph 2 to paragraph 3, and then supplies a brief, clever alternative example to a medically preventable death. At the end, it also restates, in general terms, the questions the argument raises.

> As the writer continues, he maintains the essay's focus on the questions it raises. He also strengthens the coherence of the response when he ties paragraph 4 back to an earlier statement.

In addition, the last sentence of the argument does not supply key information. As I mentioned above, the argument does not make clear that employee costs will go down. With this last sentence, one could easily conclude that costs will go down for the County, but not for the employee. That leads to the important additional question whether, after one year, employee costs will start to rise again. In recent years, employees across the nation have seen their benefits costs rise while their salaries have remained virtually stagnant.

The questions this argument raises can be summarized in a single question: "Are you saying I'm going to get reduced care *and* higher costs?" Such an outcome would clearly be undesirable. Without offering answers to questions that any reader would ask—about the relationship between the quality of health coverage and its costs—the argument is likely to be regarded by most as unreasonable and ineffective.

> The writer concludes the essay by briefly capsulizing the points made in paragraphs 2, 3, and 4, and then tying the response back to the prompt's terms.

The Argumentative or Decision Prompt Essay

You will find this essay question type on the LSAT, ACT, and PPST. (Many, but not all, colleges and universities either require or recommend that ACT takers complete the writing portion of the test. You can check the ACT standards of colleges throughout the U.S. at: https://actapps.act. org/writPrefRM/.) Those taking the SAT may also choose to write an argumentative essay for the writing portion of the test, whose general question prompts do not specify a particular essay genre. (Sample topics specific to each exam appear later in this chapter.)

Exam	Description
LSAT	The LSAT gives you a "decision prompt" that asks you to write an argument for taking a particular action, such as hiring or promoting a particular candidate, choosing a certain object for a particular purpose, or taking a certain plan of action. You will be presented with both choices, and asked to argue for one choice over the other; this implies that it is a good idea to include some arguments against the rejected choice.
ACT	The ACT presents you with an issue of interest to high school students, and two points of view on this issue. You are asked to either support one of the two perspectives given or to offer your own perspective on the matter.
PPST	The PPST presents you with a general topic statement, and asks you to agree or disagree with it. Realize that your readers do not evaluate your essay based on the particular choice you make or perspective you hold. They are interested only in the quality of your argument and the technical aspects of your essay.

Sample Task 4 – Decision Prompt Essay, "LSAT"

Here is a sample topic relevant to the LSAT:

> Read the following description of Considine and Burdett, possible hosts for a late-night talk show on network television. Then write an argument that *either* Considine *or* Burdett should be hired.
>
> Use the information in this description, along with these criteria:
>
> 1. The host must be popular with viewers thirty to fifty years old.
> 2. The host must have been a success on network television as a sketch comedian and a talk show interviewer.

Considine started as a nightclub comedian twenty years ago when he was only nineteen years old. Although his humor at that time seemed shocking to all but the most radical members of his own generation, he is now regarded as not all that controversial. In 2000, he hosted a network comedy-variety program that featured sketches satirizing political issues, and although the show received top ratings, especially from young-adult viewers, it was cancelled because network executives objected to some of the more biting satire.

Since 1998, Considine has appeared in nightclubs around the world and has been a frequent guest and guest-host on late-night television. His recent TV special, "Remember the 1990s," was the year's most highly rated program.

Burdett was an amateur comedienne and homemaker until, at age forty, friends encouraged her to take on comedy full time. Five years into work in small, east-coast nightclubs, her popularity began to rise rapidly. In 2006, she was asked to star in a situation comedy called *Anything Can Happen*, for which she received rave reviews from critics, one of whom referred to her as a comedic genius with "hilarious perceptions of everyday life." Since the series ended last year, Burdett has been busy as the writer and director of her first feature film; however, she occasionally drops in on a late-night talk show and upstages the host.

Overview of Sample Task 4

In response to this prompt, you should do the following:

1. Choose the person whose qualifications appeal most to you;
2. emphasize the *strengths* of your choice;
3. minimize the *weaknesses* of your choice;
4. acknowledge the rejected candidate's strengths; and
5. stress what is lacking in the rejected candidate.

Let's see how this writer handled the writing task.

Famous late-night talk show hosts, such as David Letterman, Jay Leno, Jimmy Fallon, and Jon Stewart, are known in part for their ability to satirize current events, politicians, and celebrities. Clearly we must hire Considine, who has had a great deal of experience in this area. He is a host who appeals to a broad and mature adult population, and his past success speaks for itself. He remains popular with the viewers who loved him in the 1990s, and brings seasoned talent to late-night television.

Those teenagers and young adults who accounted for Considine's high ratings years ago are precisely the viewers who comprise our target audience today. The twenty-year-old rebel of 1998 is now the older viewer who loves late-night television, and may prefer network shows to the edgier and often raunchier cable shows. Although these viewers no longer fight for controversial issues, they recall with happy nostalgia those days of groundbreaking comedy and identify with the heroes of their youth. Considine is one of those heroes, as the popularity of his "Remember the 1990s" special demonstrates. Surely, Considine has lost none of the comedic talent that brought him tremendous early popularity. He continues to be in demand internationally, and he is invited back again and again for late-night appearances. His talent as a sketch comedian was remarkable in his first series and has matured since then.

I should add that Burdett too has talent to offer as host of a late-night talk show. A rapid rise in popularity led to a hit situation comedy and praise from critics. Though she is also no stranger to the late-night comedy scene, Burdett's interests seem, however, to have moved elsewhere. Busy writing and directing her first feature film, Burdett not only does not have the time needed to devote to a late-night talk show that airs five nights per week, but her shift to film demonstrates that she is currently less interested in television. She may upstage late-night TV hosts with her comic sensibility; but, having begun her career little more than ten years ago, she has significantly less entertainment experience than Considine.

Although the network rejected Considine before, times have changed. Jokes that would have been considered too vulgar or lewd for network TV in the 1990s now seem tame, even docile. In other words, network tolerance has broadened such that Considine's brand of comedy is now perfect for prime-time television. If we hire Considine, we will bring our viewers a legend of the past whose talent nonetheless remains a hit.

> In the second paragraph, the writer deduces general conclusions that fit the argumentative purpose from the description's facts, and makes common-sense assumptions based on those facts. He "invents" material, but only says what is plausibly based on details given in the prompt.

> The writer acknowledges Burdett's abilities, yet strategically points out weaknesses in her candidacy. The writer also ends the paragraph by creating a transition back to Considine.

> The writer deflects the potential criticism that Considine's talent is not what it used to be, and actually turns this possible weakness into a strength.

Sample Task 5 – Argumentative Essay, "ACT"

Here is a sample topic relevant to the ACT:

> Most states have formally adopted the standards for mathematics and English language arts set out in 2010 by the "Common Core Standards Initiative." The CCSI seeks to standardize state teaching curricula so that students across the United States are exposed to a shared body of knowledge that every American needs to achieve success. This measure's proponents argue that a common core curriculum will dependably provide students with a high quality education, and will better prepare students for college, the workplace, and global competition. The measure's critics maintain that we should not reduce teaching to a formulaic, uniform standard, and observe that, despite all the fears about global competition, the United States remains a powerful economic force in the world.
>
> Should all school districts adopt the Common Core Curriculum Standards? Support your position with solid reasons and specific examples.

Overview of Sample Task 5

If you are prepared to adopt one of the two views of the CCSI given in the prompt (you can also write a differing view, if you wish), you might invent a five-paragraph structure.

> Paragraph 1: In favor of the CCSI, No Child Left Behind = too many standards initiatives?
>
> Paragraph 2: Reason #1, E.D. Hirsch, shared culture strengthens us
>
> Paragraph 3: Reason #2, core only, some uniformity necessary
>
> Paragraph 4: Reason #3, global ranking may slip
>
> Paragraph 5: Conclusion, restate reasons, point to future

You can see from this sketch that the writer intends to support the CCSI. You can also see that, although the prompt does not directly ask the writer to discuss features of the opposing viewpoint, this writer intends to do so. You should add some material, however brief, to your ACT essay that acknowledges the other side to make your essay more substantial and complete.

Let's see how the writer elaborates the material she has sketched.

I, like many education leaders across the U.S., am in favor of the "Common Core Standards Initiative," or CCSI. While some may believe that standards initiatives, such as the CCSI or "No Child Left Behind," force teaching into an overly-regulated box, I find that certain shared features of education across schools can only strengthen America as a whole. Many intelligent commentators share my position, and thus I feel sure it is the right one to hold.

> In the opening paragraph, the writer restates the question prompt contents in her own words, and makes clear where she stands on the issue.

For example, my tenth grade English teacher told our class about E.D. Hirsch, who wrote a number of books that address the importance of shared knowledge. In *Cultural Literacy*, Hirsch says that schools teach students how to think critically, but don't focus enough on teaching them content. Hirsch believes that people need a basic understanding of certain things—a core knowledge relevant to being an American. We should know about American and world history, literature, civics, math, music, and technology, among other things. This shared knowledge allows us to communicate in a coherent way, and forms a foundation for all new knowledge that comes into being. I believe that those who created the CCSI had Hirsch in mind.

> In paragraph 2, the writer relates the question prompt to a book a teacher used in class. Hirsch's book is an excellent example of her position that the CCSI is a good idea, something she reinforces before she ends this paragraph.

Those who object to too much uniformity in teaching forget that the CCSI has the word "core" in it. Core means "an essential or important <u>part</u>" of something. I underlined the word "part" to suggest that, even though all students will be taught a certain amount of shared information, this is <u>not all</u> that students will learn. The CCSI must allow some space for teachers to introduce additional knowledge and activity into the classroom. So, even though some uniformity is necessary, teachers can also pursue some variation.

> In paragraph 3, the writer qualifies her position, arguing in a fresh way that the CCSI need not be all-determining with respect to school curricula. Though the writer does not know the details of the CCSI, she plausibly remarks that it need not necessarily be a narrow initiative.

In paragraph 4, the writer takes up the concern of CCSI detractors who say there is no reason to worry about America's ranking in international terms. She cites news reports she's heard that indicate the opposite may be true. She also intelligently demonstrates a complex view of the matter when she mentions the importance of *honor[ing] our unique heritages.*

Although the U.S. still has a very high ranking in the global marketplace, it is possible that, without shared knowledge and better standards, our country could slip in the rankings in the future. I have heard many discussions on the news about other countries beginning to pass us by on a number of fronts, public education being one of them. Countries such as Finland, Japan, and Canada are said to have surpassed us already. But if we Americans can all learn to speak a common language (even as we honor our unique heritages), we will likely remain a world leader.

In conclusion, I support the CCSI because it is an answer to the lack of shared knowledge that concerns E. D. Hirsch, because it applies to only part of a larger American education, and because it may allow the U.S. to remain a role model for other nations. We have long served as a positive example to other nations, and the CCSI could be one initiative that allows us to continue to be an example where public education is concerned.

As she closes the paragraph, the writer sums up her reasons for supporting the CCSI, and points toward a positive future.

Sample Task 6 – Argumentative Essay, "PPST"

Here is a sample topic relevant to the PPST:

Rather than work constructively on current social problems, too many people look back with nostalgia on a non-existent, supposedly better past.

In the space provided, write an essay in which you discuss your agreement or disagreement with the opinion stated, and support your position with distinctive reasons and examples from your own experience, observations, education, or reading.

Overview of Sample Task 6

Though the instructions for writing the PPST essay vary slightly from those for the ACT, the sample essay for the ACT (above) can serve as a viable model for a PPST essay. You would simply agree or disagree with the statement, rather than choosing from among two contrary viewpoints.

Additional Question Types and Techniques

Compare and Contrast Essays

Analytical/expository and argumentative prompts can come in the form of either "pro and con" style questions (that require you to assess whether something is good or bad) or "compare and contrast" style questions (that require you to find both overlapping and differentiating qualities in two objects, points of view, or other phenomena). Though the cluster outline can be used for any type of essay, another technique that can be used as preparation for writing both the analytical/expository and the "choose between options" essay is to make lists. For example, the following lists might be inspired by the question in the analytical/expository section that asks whether Lewis Thomas' quote about "learning through trial and error" is true or not:

Pro	Con
right in most cases	chronic gamblers
learning is a process	gamblers don't learn
mistakes show us what not to do	losses don't deter them
won't repeat my own errors	racetrack—unhappy faces
	sweepstakes
	casinos
	chance/luck

We can easily see from these pro and con lists why the writer chose to pitch gambling as an exception to Lewis Thomas' rule about trial and error. The writer clearly had much more to say about gambling than about the correctness of Thomas' statement, and the content in the con column is far more interesting and promising of originality than that in the pro column.

For a "compare and contrast" style essay, prewriting might include sketching a four-paragraph essay. For example, the question in the argumentative section, about whether to hire Considine or Burdett, might inspire the following sketch, similar to the one we saw for a five-paragraph essay:

Paragraph 1: Considine is the best choice: broad appeal, past success, experience

Paragraph 2: Support Considine: audience following for twenty years, suited to network TV, international demand, maturity

Paragraph 3: Acknowledge and dismiss Burdett: popularity, critical praise, late-night experience undercut by move away from TV into film, less experience

Paragraph 4: Conclude: Considine now suitable for network TV, legendary status

Steps to Writing a Successful Essay

No matter which essay question type you address, the steps to writing a successful timed essay are as follows:

1. Read the question or prompt two or three times, and mark the question/topic carefully, underlining key words and phrases. You should *never write on a topic of your own invention.* Directions given in the essay portions of standardized tests typically sound a loud warning, such as the following: ESSAYS THAT DO NOT ADDRESS THE GIVEN TOPIC ARE NOT ACCEPTABLE.

2. Prepare to write by noting ideas and examples, perhaps in the form of a cluster outline, list(s), or multi-paragraph outline.

3. Write an introductory paragraph using the *Generalize-Focus-Survey* structure.

4. Write a body of one or more paragraphs, adding relevant examples and "for instances."

5. Write a concluding paragraph that adds new information, completes a full response, or points toward the future.

6. Proofread carefully, line by line, and make neat corrections if necessary.

Essay Writing Practice

Following are examples of topics relevant to several types of essay exam sections. Multiple topics are listed under specific exams; however, even if your exam is not specifically mentioned, it is likely that the essay questions will be similar to the representative topics that follow. Note, for example, that many teacher competency and credentialing exams are very similar to CBEST and English placement essay types.

To actively practice essay writing, use the following steps:

1. Determine the type of essay you will be required to write both from the quick reference guide that begins this chapter and from the information listed in the official bulletin for your exam.

2. From the following sample topics, choose one listed among those for your test, or choose one closest in type to the essay you will be required to write.

3. Write an essay under the time limit specified in your particular exam's directions. Do not exceed this time limit in your practice. (You may find it helpful to actually reduce the time by a few minutes in your practice sessions to train yourself to work quickly.) Remember to make use of all strategies discussed in the early part of this chapter. If you are taking a computer-based version of your test, practice writing a timed essay on a computer.

4. Give your completed essay to a qualified friend or teacher to evaluate. Have the evaluator complete one of the removable Essay Checklists (at the end of this section).

5. Review your essay with the evaluator, and concentrate on any difficulties you have had.

6. Repeat this process until you feel comfortable that you can produce essays of consistently high quality in the time allowed.

GRE

The GRE asks you to write two analytical/expository essays: one that analyzes an issue, and another that analyzes an argument. You have thirty minutes to write each essay. The GRE uses the 1-6 scoring method.

If you take the computer-based GRE, you will be able to insert and delete text, as well as cut and paste and undo a previous action. You will not, however, have access to a grammar or spell checker.

Sample Topics

Analyze an Issue

Each set of specific instructions below tells you how to respond to the prompt.

1. Given the many marriages that now take place across racial and ethnic lines in the U.S., interest in one's particular racial/ethnic heritage is bound to decline.

Discuss the extent to which you either agree or disagree with this statement, and give reasons for your perspective. As you make your arguments, take into account specific considerations about the truth or falsity of the statement and explain how these considerations influence your view.

2. People should not be allowed to have driver's licenses until they reach the age of eighteen.

Discuss the extent to which you agree or disagree with this recommendation, and give reasons for your perspective. As you make your arguments, consider the advantages and disadvantages of the recommendation, and explain how these considerations influence your view.

3. Students who do not receive grades will not do their best work.

Discuss the extent to which you either agree or disagree with this claim, and give reasons for your perspective. In addition to making arguments that support your position, acknowledge arguments and examples that oppose your position, and address them.

4. Claim: The President of the United States should serve only one six-year term.

Reason: As it is now, U.S. presidents spend the greater part of their first terms in office running for re-election.

Discuss the extent to which you either agree or disagree with this claim, and be sure to comment on the reliability of the reason given for the claim.

5. Some people believe that government should regulate the airlines, since air travel has become a necessity in modern life. Others believe that it is better to let market forces prevail, so that only the best airlines will survive.

In an essay, tell which perspective is closest to the one you hold and give reasons for your choice. Be sure to discuss both of the positions put forward.

6. There should be a community-service learning component in all college degree programs.

Discuss your assessment of this policy, and give reasons for your perspective. As you make your arguments, consider the possible outcomes should the policy be put into action, and explain how these considerations influence your view.

Note: The specific instructions that accompany each of these six prompts closely represent instructions given on the actual GRE.

Analyze an Argument

Realize that the "Analyze an Argument" essay does not ask you to share your personal opinions on the subject with your reader. Instead, you are to evaluate the stated argument. Each set of specific instructions below tells you how to respond to the prompt.

1. The following appeared in a speech given by the president of Camptown State University.

   Camptown State University was built in the 1960s, and prided itself at that time on small classes and a low student-to-faculty ratio. As state funding for colleges and universities has been steadily reduced over the decades, many universities have built larger classrooms—some of which accommodate several hundred students—to teach each class more cost-effectively. Now many decades old, Camptown State has not renovated the size of any of its classrooms, and the largest classroom seats forty students. The only way for Camptown State to stay in step with its sister institutions is to immediately begin a fundraising campaign for the construction of larger classrooms.

   In an essay, determine what actual evidence you would need to assess the truth of this argument. Explain how the argument would be either verified or proved false based on this evidence.

2. The following was part of a consultant's report to a high school task force.

   Poor nutrition can have a significant negative effect on body weight and size, and can influence the size of the brain itself. Therefore, when students score poorly on tests, bad nutrition or malnutrition may be the culprit. This problem can be rectified if all test scores are adjusted upward in a way that is proportionate to how much a student's body weight falls below the average for that age group, and if all students who weigh more than 10 percent below average are entitled to free breakfasts and lunches on the school site.

   In an essay, describe this argument's implicit or and/or explicit assumptions. How are these assumptions necessary to the argument? What would happen to the argument if the assumptions were flawed?

3. The following was taken from an auto assembly workers union newsletter.

   Over the last ten years, the proportion of employees in managerial positions has grown faster than the proportion of employees in assembly line positions. In other words, those on the assembly line do more work for less pay. In addition, the assembly line process has changed significantly to accommodate new technology, which has speeded up the auto assembly process, but which has also required additional training for most employees. Assembly line workers are asked to do more with less. To correct this problem, all new hires should be assembly line workers, and the management positions should be reduced.

In an essay, tell what additional information you would need to accept the recommendation and arguments in favor of it. Why is this information necessary to your assessment of the issue?

4. The following was taken from the advice column in a newspaper:

Relationships usually break down when one person seeks control over another. Though the initial impulses that form a relationship may be related to attraction and affection, as time passes the dynamic changes to competition. This is especially true when the partners in a relationship age, and begin to suffer the depression that sometimes accompanies the loss of youth and beauty, along with the increased aches and pains that go along with aging. As compensation for the lack of control they have over their own physical changes, they seek greater control over their partner, and therefore become more critical and demanding. My first piece of advice to anyone seeking a lasting, rewarding relationship is to resist the impulse to change or control your partner.

In an essay, tell what additional information you would need to accept the advice and arguments in its favor. Why is this information necessary to your assessment of the advice?

5. The following was taken from a speech given by a state legislator:

I am recommending to the governor three measures that will lead to an employment increase of at least 4 percent and the elimination of the current budget deficit. The first measure is free job training and placement services for all workers over forty who lose a job for reasons unrelated to performance. The second measure is a 10 percent increase in the state surcharge on tobacco products. The third measure is an increase of staff in the state's External Relations office, so that experts can bring in new companies from out of state.

In an essay, tell what additional information you would need to trust that the recommendation would in fact bring about the specified outcome. Why is this information necessary to your assessment of the recommendation?

6. Since the carpool lanes have been in operation on all expressways in Fairstone County, travel time has decreased by 10 percent, and traffic accidents have decreased by 5 percent. These figures do not meet the goal set when the carpool lanes were proposed, however. That goal

was a 20 percent decrease in travel time and a 10 percent decrease in traffic accidents. We recommend that the carpool lane requirement be modified, to increase from two to three the number of inhabitants required for an automobile to qualify for carpool lane access. This will result in even fewer cars on the road, and therefore further reduce travel time and decrease accidents.

In an essay, tell what additional information you would need to accept as plausible both the recommendation's outcome and the arguments in its favor. Why is this information necessary to your assessment of the prediction?

7. The graduation rates of students at Stateside University have increased by double digits over the last four years. Stateside University's library dean explains that this increase in graduating students is largely the result of greater use of the new state-of-the-art library building, which opened its doors exactly four years ago. Since that opening, the number of students who enter the library has increased by 200 percent, the number of students who check out books has increased significantly, the library's coffee shop has become the busiest coffee shop in the city, the new and more comfortable group-study areas are almost always full, and all of the new, wireless laptops available at the circulation desk are checked out by noon each day. The dean concludes, "Because the library is a popular destination, more students involved in learning do better in their classes, and graduate."

In an essay, invent your own explanation for this phenomenon, and explain why your explanation better accounts for the facts of the case.

8. According to a recent study by Mall Walkers of America, holiday shopping can be hazardous to your health. This group has determined that during the last holiday season a 15 percent increase in shoppers who buy online, rather than in stores, signals a significant reduction in those for whom shopping provides beneficial aerobic exercise. A sedentary lifestyle is associated with the risk of ailments that range from obesity to depression to anxiety. On the other hand, a brisk walk through the mall contributes to cardiovascular health, burns calories, and provides the benefits of a controlled climate free of air pollution and extreme weather. The Mall Walkers conclude, "When shopping is your goal, get out and get moving!"

In an essay, tell what additional information you would need to accept the conclusion and the arguments in its favor.

Note: The specific instructions that accompany each of these eight prompts closely resemble instructions given on the actual GRE.

GMAT

The GMAT asks you to write one analytical/expository essay that analyzes an argument. You have thirty minutes to write your essay. The GMAT uses the 0-6 scoring method.

Realize that the GMAT's "Analysis of an Argument" essay does not ask you to share your personal opinions on the subject with your reader. Instead, you are to evaluate the stated argument.

As discussed on page 420, recall that a computerized rater will easily recognize a five-paragraph essay from those who take the GMAT in its computer-based form. Be sure to use strong transitions to introduce new paragraphs.

If you take the computer-based GMAT, you will be able to insert and delete text, as well as cut and paste and undo a previous action. You will not, however, have access to a grammar or spell checker.

Apply the instructions given in topic #1 to all subsequent topics.

Sample Topics

1. The following appeared in a letter from the Community Library's board of directors:

   Over the next year, the Community Library will gradually eliminate its collection of hard-copy books to shift all library resources online. As state budget reductions continue to limit our capacity to purchase and store books and other paper materials, and to force significant reductions in personnel, our only viable option is to move to online holdings. In voluntary responses to a recent survey, more than half of our adult customers who use the library regularly said they read online books. To serve customers who do not have access to the Internet, we will install additional computer workstations when the shelved books are removed. The sale of currently shelved books to the general public, at significantly reduced prices, will help offset the first year's cost of online subscriptions and purchases.

   Discuss how well reasoned you find this argument to be. Be sure to refer to specific evidence in the argument, and to consider whether the evidence is used well, or not. For instance, you may wish to focus on unanswered questions in the argument, unstated assumptions, evidence that would be needed to strengthen the argument, the argument's structure, or the points that an effective counter-argument might make.

2. The following was taken from a leaflet distributed by citizens gathering signatures for a proposed ballot measure:

   Closing the Central City $300,000 budget gap is best achieved through the imposition of a special tax on junk food. Our state has a higher number of obese citizens than do forty other states, which indicates that good nutrition must become a higher priority. Central City should take the lead on this by imposing a 5 percent tax on all low-nutrition foods, which will generate approximately $300,000 per year, according to the city's independent budget analyst. The higher cost of junk food will reduce demand and promote weight loss. Without this tax, both our city's fiscal health and our citizens' physical health are in jeopardy.

3. The following was part of a proposal to Valley City Council members:

   Air pollution reduces life expectancy by many months or many years, depending on the level of pollution and the extent of an individual's exposure. One thing is clear: cleaner air has significant health benefits. To reduce the severe pollution that plagues Valley residents, we must pass a proposal to ban drive-through businesses. On an average day at the busiest drive-through in town, 310 cars and 150 trucks use the drive-through lane; they spend a daily average of 1,215 total minutes idling, and this releases 10,704 grams of unhealthy emissions. In addition, over the last five years, the use of drive-throughs has increased by 50 percent in the Valley; this corresponds with a 64 percent increase in hospital admission rates. If we ban drive-throughs, we will improve health and quality of life for us, for our children, and for generations to come.

4. Since the mayor and city council were re-elected nearly four years ago, the unemployment rate has hit an all-time high. Jobless residents now number nearly 12 percent of the total population. The mayor and city council have voted together on job-creation initiatives, brought two new companies into the city, and provided free training and placement services for mid-career workers who have been laid off. But the unemployment rate has not improved. For this reason, we must not vote to re-elect either the mayor or the city council in November.

5. The following appeared in an article about television in a magazine for new parents:

   On average, children spend 20 percent of the day watching television. Over a lifetime, this equates to thousands of hours of observing crime and violence, and causes increasingly violent behavior among the viewers themselves. Given that violent television programs have traditionally been the most popular, the only solution for parents is to keep the television unplugged while children are awake, and to involve them in homework, reading, and play. If you keep television *out* of your children's lives, you will bring good behavior *into* their lives.

LSAT

The LSAT asks you to write one argumentative essay in response to a "decision prompt." You have thirty-five minutes to write your essay. Recall that the LSAT essay is *unscored*, and used only as a supplement to your candidacy for law school admission. Even though you do not receive a precise score on the essay for the LSAT, do your best work, since a poorly written essay could be the difference between acceptance and rejection.

Typically, the writer must make a choice between two candidates for a particular position, two objects for a particular purpose, or two plans of action. The topic is not controversial, and it is not important to the reader which choice is made. What is important is how the writer supports that choice given the criteria and qualifications listed in the essay topic. In addition to writing in support of your choice, you are also expected to argue against the other option.

Sample Topics

1. Read the following descriptions of Arbola and Wolfe, two candidates for the position of park ranger for a national park. Then write an argument that supports either Arbola or Wolfe as the best hire. Use the information in the descriptions, along with these criteria:

   - A National Park Service Ranger must faithfully preserve and protect the wildlife of our parks.

   - Not only must a National Park Service Ranger work well with the public, but he or she must also be able to impart extensive knowledge about plant and animal life in the national parks.

   Arbola was born in the High Sierras thirty-five years ago and has lived there ever since. As an expert in the region's flora, she often leads expeditions of naturalists into the wilderness, where they live in a survival situation for several weeks and consume only what the forest provides. Indeed, her commitment to the area's plant life has earned her the honor of having had a previously unknown type of fern named after her, a fern that she discovered some twelve years ago. Though she is somewhat shy and reclusive, her love for the park's flora often causes her to become animated as she relates interesting and notable facts about plant life to those who accompany her in her travels throughout the park.

Wolfe received his Ph.D. in animal wildlife and has been a noted author on wildlife for the past twenty years. A one-time high school science teacher, he initiated and developed the Wildlife Retreats that now send more than 100,000 high school students into the national parks for a week each year to study and appreciate our country's natural beauty. Born and raised in New York City, he is an advisor at the Bronx Zoo and a trustee of the Museum of Natural History–Animal Division. He often laments, however, that his writing and advising chores keep him too far from his first love, the forest, which, due to present commitments, he is able to visit only two weeks each year.

2. Mideast State University faces a 20 percent budget reduction, which means that some academic programs must be reduced or eliminated. An advisory committee has presented two plans that implement the reduction to the university's president. As the president's chief of staff, you are to write a recommendation to the president that favors either Plan A or Plan B. Write your recommendation in the space below. Two principles must guide your recommendation:

- There should be minimal impact on the progress of currently enrolled students toward graduation.

- Any increase in tuition or fees should affect all currently enrolled students equally.

Plan A calls for a two-pronged approach to the budget reduction: 1) Make up half the reduction through the elimination of all elective classes that do not fulfill a specific graduation requirement for one or more majors. Most faculty members who teach the classes that are to be eliminated will be laid off, but those who also teach classes that fulfill graduation requirements will not be laid off. The reduction in faculty and the need to accommodate both currently enrolled and newly admitted students will mean that class sizes must be increased. 2) Make up the other half of the reduction through an increase in tuition by 5 percent for all students, and by 7 percent for all students who take two or more classes that are not required for graduation in their chosen major.

Plan B relies exclusively on an increase in tuition. It calls for an 8 percent increase in the tuition paid by currently enrolled students, and a 10 percent increase in the tuition paid by newly admitted students. This will assure that the number of classes currently in place will not be reduced. Class sizes will not be increased, and all faculty members—including some of the most talented who would otherwise be laid off—will be retained.

3. Read the following descriptions of the Comet and the Antelope, two automobiles Acme Taxicab Company is considering for purchase. The company must buy thirty of one type of automobile. Then write an argument in favor of the purchase of either a fleet of Comets or a fleet of Antelopes. Use the information in the descriptions, along with these criteria:

- The automobile chosen must be not only comfortable but also extremely reliable because time spent in the maintenance bay lowers profits.

- The automobile chosen must get excellent gas mileage because most driving is done in the city.

The Antelope is a relatively new automobile, having been on the market for only one year. However, in that time it has impressed auto experts both with the way it handles and with its gas mileage. In an independent study, the Antelope was found to get fifty-five miles per gallon on the highway and forty-eight miles per gallon in the city. No other automobile comes close to this achievement. The Antelope also has large trunk space as well as ample foot room in the front and back seats. The ride is smooth and easy, even over potholes and rough city streets. In a survey of fifty taxicab drivers in a neighboring city, forty-eight ranked the Antelope as "excellent."

The Comet is the classic taxicab. First manufactured in 1981, it has been the choice of cab companies for more than thirty years for its excellent ride and long-term dependability. Designed and co-built by the owner of a New England cab company, the Comet typifies what a cab is often envisioned to be. Leather seats and extensive legroom for passengers (enough, in fact, for extra baggage) are two of the Comet's hallmarks. Its heavy frame yields a smooth, comfortable ride, though its weight significantly decreases its mileage (35 highway/28 city). But its most impressive feature is its longevity. Comets built in the 1980s are still driven on city streets today. In fact, a recent study revealed that of all cars on the road, Comets are the most problem free. They require fewer repairs than any other currently manufactured car.

4. Read the following descriptions of Block and Blitzer, two candidates for the position of chief referee for this year's Super Bowl football game. Then write an argument that either Block or Blitzer be hired. Use the information in the descriptions, along with these criteria:

- The chief referee must have a thorough working knowledge of professional football.

- Because the Super Bowl is the year's most important game, and is viewed by a national television audience of more than 100 million fans, the chief referee must be able to work effectively under intense pressure.

The Pro Football Hall of Fame recently honored Block, who authored the now widely used *New Official Rule Book of Football*. Prior to his work, the two conferences used different rules. Now both conferences use his regulations. He is also a consultant for the national football commissioner when questions about rulings, procedures, or protests occur during the season. Though Block has refereed at the college level only, his name is synonymous with the rules of professional football.

Blitzer has been a professional football referee for the past twenty years. Though occasionally his judgment has been questioned on certain calls, he has refereed the season's biggest games as well as the playoffs. Most players in the game today respect his clarity and quickness of thought as well as his fairness in assessing personal fouls. Blitzer is a former Marine captain decorated for excellence under fire. Indeed, he has been known to calm rookie referees when teamed with them for big games.

SAT

The SAT asks you to write one essay on a topic that is of general interest to high school students. You have twenty-five minutes to write the essay. The SAT uses the 1-6 scoring method. SAT essay prompts are general enough so that you can write in any of the three genres covered previously: narrative, analytical, or argumentative.

However, you may also write an essay that belongs to the persuasive genre. Though an argumentative essay is meant to be persuasive, an essay considered to fall into the persuasive category is one in which the writer does not argue between two options (as the argumentative essay does), but instead tries to get the reader to see things from his or her point of view. Recall that a narrative/descriptive essay would require you to draw from personal experience to answer the prompt, and that an analytical essay involves your agreement or disagreement with the prompt. Some elements may overlap these three genres, so don't worry too much about whether your essay perfectly fits one or another category. SAT readers will not be concerned with that.

Though the following prompts do not set out two distinct points of view on an issue, you may nonetheless write an argumentative essay by entertaining what someone who disagrees with your view might say. In other words, you can create both sides of an argument in your essay if you wish.

SAT essay prompts begin with a brief statement (some are quotes or excerpts from a book) that introduces a theme in broad terms; you are then asked to express your own view of the matter.

Apply the instructions given in topic #1 to all subsequent topics.

Sample Topics

1. If we believe we have certain limitations, we will not be able to press beyond them. As Henry Ford said, "Whether you think that you can, or that you can't, you are usually right."

   Is achievement primarily a matter of the thoughts we have? Plan a response to this question, and write an essay in which you express your point of view on this issue. Support your position with a sound line of reasoning and examples. You may cite personal experience and observations, as well as ideas taken from your reading or education.

2. When prize money climbs to very large amounts in U.S. multi-state lotteries, ticket sales soar even though the chances of winning are practically non-existent. Despite being founded on principles of hard work and the notion of the "self-made man," our country has become a place of easy money worship. From lotteries to instant celebrity on reality TV shows and competitions, chances to try your luck at hitting it big have mushroomed.

   Do you think there is too much emphasis placed on lucky wins in America?

3. The U.S. Department of Health and Human Services has taken an interest in measuring happiness in America. This is not surprising since "the pursuit of happiness" has long been a primary American value. But happiness may be an overrated feeling or sensation.

   Do you think Americans overrate happiness?

4. Some cities now hold parents responsible when their minor children engage in "tagging," or graffiti damage. Parents may have to pay fines and/or participate in community service when their underage kids vandalize property with spray paint. This allows cities to recoup the costs of repair and encourages parents to intervene more strongly should their children break the law.

Do you think parents should be responsible for their minor children's wrongdoing?

5. Goals are overrated as essential to success in today's world. While it's fine to have a general sense of the kind of life we'd like to lead in the future, and to take steps toward that life, we shouldn't lock ourselves into an overly determined plan.

Can goals be too limiting?

ACT

Recall that not all colleges and universities require the writing portion of the ACT. You can check the ACT standards of colleges throughout the U.S. at: https://actapps.act.org/writPrefRM/. Those who do need to take the ACT's writing portion are asked to write one argumentative essay on a topic of general interest to high school students. You have thirty minutes to write the essay. The ACT uses the 0-6 scoring method.

You are presented with two points of view on this issue, and asked to either support one of the two perspectives given, or to offer your own perspective on the matter.

Sample Topics

1. Some schools have adopted a curriculum that includes "character education," in which certain values are taught to students in an effort to encourage them to become good citizens. In such programs, an array of attributes such as honesty, kindness, generosity, respect, fairness, leadership, charity, and bravery, are—it is said—universally recognized as good. Critics argue that such programs may simply engender conformity in young people because they do not include such values as independence, innovation, critical thinking, and individuality.

   What is your view of character education? Do you agree with one of the two perspectives given, or do you see things in yet another way? Support your position with solid reasons and specific examples.

2. Education leaders have long promoted reduction in class size as a way to improve student-learning outcomes. Fewer students per teacher means more individual attention and, presumably, better teaching results. But some suggest that smaller classrooms don't yield better results if teaching methods do not change or improve. These people argue that teachers can offer more individualized attention even in larger classrooms if they cut back on lecture-style approaches to teaching to free up time for more personalized interaction with students.

What do you think of the class size issue? Are smaller classes a must, or can teachers do more to facilitate learning even in larger classrooms? Or do you see things in yet another way? Support your position with solid reasons and specific examples.

3. Self-esteem has long been regarded as necessary to happiness, so much so that in the recent past, teachers and parents have been encouraged to praise young people for relatively small accomplishments. Those who take this approach believe that young people who feel good about themselves will earn higher grades, have better social relationships, and grow up to be more successful. Others say that this approach does more harm than good because young people can become easily self-satisfied and are thus not motivated to work as hard to improve themselves or to take on challenging endeavors.

   What is your outlook on giving ample praise to build self-esteem in young people? Support your position with solid reasons and specific examples.

4. A significant debate persists between those who recommend grade retention for those failing in school and those who advocate social promotion. Grade retention occurs when a failing student is held back from advancing to the next grade level, and must repeat the grade level in which the failure has occurred. Social promotion occurs when a failing student is allowed to advance to the next grade level despite his or her failure. Those who recommend grade retention argue that social promotion sets students up to fail again, that it rewards them for poor work, and that it gives parents a false sense of their child's ability. Those who recommend social promotion argue that grade retention causes low self-esteem, makes students vulnerable to bullying, and increases dropout rates.

   What is your view on this subject? Do you lean toward grade retention or social promotion for failing students, or can you think of yet another approach to take? Support your position with solid reasons and specific examples.

5. Tracking in schools, a long-standing practice, occurs when students are separated into groups according to their academic abilities. Three categories are typically employed: above average, normal, and below average. Tracking allows teachers to deliver material appropriate to the group he or she is teaching, and strongly benefits above-average students who are challenged to grow to their fullest potential. Tracking opponents argue that below-average students often come

largely from minority households, that their self-esteem may suffer from being categorized in this way, and that they may fail to be challenged to grow academically.

Do you support or reject tracking? Or can you think of a different approach that might be taken? Support your position with solid reasons and specific examples.

PPST

The PPST asks you to write one argumentative/expository essay on a topic of general interest to educated people. You have thirty minutes to write the essay. The PPST uses the 0-6 scoring method.

On the computer-based PPST, the screen is split horizontally with the top part displaying the topic; you type your essay onto the lower part of the screen. If you take the computer-based PPST, you will be able to insert and delete text, as well as cut and paste and undo a previous action. You will not, however, have access to a grammar or spell checker.

Apply the instructions given in topic #1 to all subsequent topics.

Sample Topics

1. Films have the power to change our lives. Only through them can we access certain feelings and situations that otherwise would remain unavailable to us.

   In the space provided, write an essay in which you discuss your agreement or disagreement with the opinion stated, and support your position with distinctive reasons and examples from your own experience, observations, education, or reading.

2. The quality of a public education can be improved by considerably raising teacher salaries. Teachers need more incentive to do their best work.

3. Today's popular music is largely of poor quality. Quality lasts, (think of Mozart, Beethoven, and Verdi, as well as Ellington, Gershwin, and the jazz greats), and most of what is produced today disappears very quickly.

4. Albert Einstein once said, "Genius is 1 percent inspiration and 99 percent perspiration."

5. Cigarette smokers should pay a substantial tax for their addiction.

6. Reality television gives us a completely false picture of what life is actually like for most people.

7. The quality of communication has been greatly diminished due to text messaging and email.

8. We've all heard the expression, "Where there's smoke, there's fire."

9. There should be no such thing as a for-profit college.

10. Employers should have the right to access a potential employee's social networking profile.

CBEST

On the written essay portion of the CBEST, you will have sixty minutes to write on two assigned topics, one that calls for a narrative/descriptive essay about a personal experience (also called "expressive"), and another that calls for an analytical/expository essay that allows you to demonstrate your critical thinking skills. You must divide the sixty minutes between the two essays. The CBEST uses the 1-4 scoring method.

The computer-based CBEST allows you to print out the question topics so you can refer to them during your prewriting and writing processes. Each printout includes not only the question topic, but also directions and lined space for your work. Also, you will be given a "Writing Score Scale" that articulates the criteria for each of its designations on a 1-4 scale; this will remind you of a successful essay's features. If you take the computer-based CBEST, you will be able to insert and delete text, as well as cut and paste and undo a previous action. You will not, however, have access to a grammar or spell checker.

Sample Topics

Narrative/Descriptive

1. Few individuals are completely satisfied with themselves. If you could change one thing about yourself, what would it be and how would that change make you better?

2. Describe a teacher who has had a major positive influence on your life. How did this teacher inspire you to be your best self and to pursue your goals and dreams? Give specific details and examples in your essay.

3. Recollect a family problem you once had to resolve. Describe how it affected you or your family, how you or your family intended to solve it, and how you were or were not able to solve it.

4. Throughout our formal education, each of us has taken an array of different courses that focus on various subject matters. Think back on your classes and choose one particular course that was particularly valuable to you and one that was not. Compare and contrast these two classes by focusing strictly on the subject matter, without reference to the teachers or to your classmates.

5. Think of one machine in your life that you could never do without. Using specific examples, explain why that particular machine is so necessary for daily life.

Analytical/Expository

6. Two opposite philosophies of life can be expressed in adages. One is, "You are your brother's keeper." The other is, "Live and let live." Choose the philosophy that you feel is most prevalent in America today and give reasons that demonstrate why this philosophy is prominent.

7. New common core standards for K-12 education have been adopted throughout the country. One goal of these standards is to provide students with real-world skills that are directly applicable to jobs and careers. Therefore, the standards de-emphasize the study of literature and include more practice in reading non-fiction such as newspapers and scientific and technical writing. Opponents of this feature argue that less exposure to literature means less opportunity for students to experience and develop a creative imagination. Do you feel that the development of a creative imagination is as important or more important than the development of real world reading skills? State your position and support it with appropriate examples from your experience or observations.

8. Grades are important motivators for most students. The prospect of earning an "A" drives students to focus on what is required, to learn the material that will be tested, and to move on to the next lesson. However, this focus on grades can work against real learning, because the student is extrinsically motivated—by the grade—and not intrinsically motivated by the desire to learn. Do you think grades are good motivators or not? State your position and support it with appropriate examples from your experience or observations.

9. Some educators argue that "problem-based classes" (in which students actively work together to solve problems related to the course material) are more effective than lecture-based classes (in which the teacher talks about the course material while students listen and take notes). Others insist that students learn a great deal and are often inspired by good

lectures delivered by a talented teacher. Do you feel that the method through which course material is delivered influences how well students learn? State your position and support it with appropriate examples from your experience or observations.

10. Television is no doubt a powerful medium in American society. Some believe that television is a positive force that both enlightens people with news and entertains them with comedies and dramas. Critics of television claim it plays a more negative role, that its news is shallow, and that its entertainment is of low quality. Do you feel that, on the whole, television is a positive or negative force in our society? State your position—either positive or negative—and support it with appropriate examples from your experience or observations.

Note that a number of CBEST prompts focus on matters of interest to those preparing to be teachers.

Essay Response Checklist

As we've seen, a well-written exam essay will always be successful in a number of ways. It will:

- ✓ Give a full and pertinent answer to the question or prompt
- ✓ Provide adequate detail
- ✓ Contain a logical sequence of ideas organized into substantial paragraphs
- ✓ Use transitional words and phrases to connect the paragraphs
- ✓ Support the main idea throughout
- ✓ Contain well-made arguments
- ✓ Be free of grammar, usage, and spelling errors
- ✓ Demonstrate tone and vocabulary appropriate to the audience
- ✓ Be legible (neatly and clearly written so it can be read and understood)

Critical evaluation and practice can help you improve your ability to write essays. Use the Essay Response Checklists on the following pages to evaluate your written work.

How Effectively Does Your Essay...

Address the Topic?	Evaluation		
	Excellent	Average	Poor
1. Does the essay focus on the assigned topic?			
2. Does the essay complete all the tasks the assignment sets?			
3. Are such topic words as either, or, and, etc., correctly addressed?			

Organize Thoughts?	Evaluation		
	Excellent	Average	Poor
4. Is there an effective introduction?			
5. Are the paragraphs logically arranged?			
6. Are the paragraphs connected by transitional words and phrases?			
7. Does each paragraph focus on one main idea?			
8. Does every major point and paragraph support your thesis?			

Support Its Points?	Evaluation		
	Excellent	Average	Poor
9. Are there sufficient specific details for each point?			
10. Are the examples given relevant to the issue?			
11. Are specific examples fully developed?			
12. Are paragraphs full rather than skimpy?			

CUT HERE

449

Use Language Correctly?	Evaluation		
	Excellent	Average	Poor
13. Is the language mature and varied?			
14. Is punctuation correct?			
15. Is spelling correct?			
16. Are grammar and usage correct?			

Present Itself?	Evaluation		
	Excellent	Average	Poor
17. Is the handwriting legible?			
18. Is the paper neat?			

CUT HERE

How Effectively Does Your Essay...

Address the Topic?	Evaluation		
	Excellent	Average	Poor
1. Does the essay focus on the assigned topic?			
2. Does the essay complete all the tasks the assignment sets?			
3. Are such topic words as either, or, and, etc., correctly addressed?			

Organize Thoughts?	Evaluation		
	Excellent	Average	Poor
4. Is there an effective introduction?			
5. Are the paragraphs logically arranged?			
6. Are the paragraphs connected by transitional words and phrases?			
7. Does each paragraph focus on one main idea?			
8. Does every major point and paragraph support your thesis?			

Support Its Points?	Evaluation		
	Excellent	Average	Poor
9. Are there sufficient specific details for each point?			
10. Are the examples given relevant to the issue?			
11. Are specific examples fully developed?			
12. Are paragraphs full rather than skimpy?			

CUT HERE

451

Use Language Correctly?	Evaluation		
	Excellent	Average	Poor
13. Is the language mature and varied?			
14. Is punctuation correct?			
15. Is spelling correct?			
16. Are grammar and usage correct?			

Present Itself?	Evaluation		
	Excellent	Average	Poor
17. Is the handwriting legible?			
18. Is the paper neat?			

CUT HERE

How Effectively Does Your Essay...

Address the Topic?	Evaluation		
	Excellent	Average	Poor
1. Does the essay focus on the assigned topic?			
2. Does the essay complete all the tasks the assignment sets?			
3. Are such topic words as either, or, and, etc., correctly addressed?			

Organize Thoughts?	Evaluation		
	Excellent	Average	Poor
4. Is there an effective introduction?			
5. Are the paragraphs logically arranged?			
6. Are the paragraphs connected by transitional words and phrases?			
7. Does each paragraph focus on one main idea?			
8. Does every major point and paragraph support your thesis?			

Support Its Points?	Evaluation		
	Excellent	Average	Poor
9. Are there sufficient specific details for each point?			
10. Are the examples given relevant to the issue?			
11. Are specific examples fully developed?			
12. Are paragraphs full rather than skimpy?			

CUT HERE

Use Language Correctly?	Evaluation		
	Excellent	**Average**	**Poor**
13. Is the language mature and varied?			
14. Is punctuation correct?			
15. Is spelling correct?			
16. Are grammar and usage correct?			

Present Itself?	Evaluation		
	Excellent	**Average**	**Poor**
17. Is the handwriting legible?			
18. Is the paper neat?			

CUT HERE

How Effectively Does Your Essay...

Address the Topic?	Evaluation		
	Excellent	Average	Poor
1. Does the essay focus on the assigned topic?			
2. Does the essay complete all the tasks the assignment sets?			
3. Are such topic words as either, or, and, etc., correctly addressed?			

Organize Thoughts?	Evaluation		
	Excellent	Average	Poor
4. Is there an effective introduction?			
5. Are the paragraphs logically arranged?			
6. Are the paragraphs connected by transitional words and phrases?			
7. Does each paragraph focus on one main idea?			
8. Does every major point and paragraph support your thesis?			

Support Its Points?	Evaluation		
	Excellent	Average	Poor
9. Are there sufficient specific details for each point?			
10. Are the examples given relevant to the issue?			
11. Are specific examples fully developed?			
12. Are paragraphs full rather than skimpy?			

CUT HERE

Use Language Correctly?	Evaluation		
	Excellent	Average	Poor
13. Is the language mature and varied?			
14. Is punctuation correct?			
15. Is spelling correct?			
16. Are grammar and usage correct?			

Present Itself?	Evaluation		
	Excellent	Average	Poor
17. Is the handwriting legible?			
18. Is the paper neat?			

CUT HERE